Lidka Lesnik

An Introduction to the
Old Testament Pentateuch

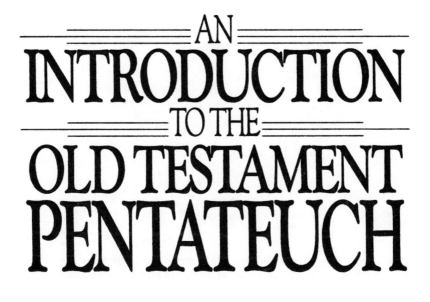

AN INTRODUCTION TO THE OLD TESTAMENT PENTATEUCH

Herbert Wolf

MOODY PRESS
CHICAGO

All Scripture quotations, unless noted otherwise, are from the *Holy Bible: New International Version*. Copyright © 1973, 1978, 1984, International Bible Society. Used by permission of Zondervan Bible Publishers.

The use of selected references from various versions of the Bible in this publication does not necessarily imply publisher endorsement of the versions in their entirety.

Library of Congress Cataloguing in Publication Data

Wolf, Herbert M.
  An introduction to the Old Testament Pentateuch / by Herbert M. Wolf.
      p.   cm.
  Includes bibliographical references and index.
  ISBN: 0-8024-4129-7
  1. Bible. O.T. Pentateuch—Introductions.   I. Title.
BS1225.2.W655   1991
222'.1061—dc20   91-22824
                                                                   CIP

5 7 9 10 8 6

Printed in the United States of America

To my father and mother
Gottfried Hermann and Melanie Seyfert Wolf

CONTENTS

PREFACE

Anyone who attempts to do justice to the words of Moses is facing a challenging assignment indeed. How can one adequately explain the wonders of creation or God's miraculous dealings with the Israelites? From Genesis to Deuteronomy we are introduced to the person and work of the God of Abraham, Isaac, and Jacob and to the marvelous potential of man created in His image but all too quickly expelled from Eden and overwhelmed by sin. The Pentateuch is the story of how God restored mankind, lovingly and graciously redeeming them out of sin's slavery and raising up a people through whom He would touch the whole world. Although this book does deal with these tremendous themes, I realize that I have only begun to understand Moses' teachings and their implications for our day and age.

During the years this manuscript was in preparation I have received help and encouragement from many quarters. The editorial staff of Moody Press has patiently worked with me and has seen this project through to the end, and I am particularly grateful for the strong support of Garry Knussman and Joe O'Day. I wish to thank the administration of Wheaton College and Graduate School for a sabbatical leave that enabled me to concentrate solely upon this book.

As the individual chapters were finished, the secretaries of the Department of Biblical, Theological, and Archaeological Studies faithfully typed them into the computer, and I am indeed grateful to Janet Seaberg, Jayne Christianson, and Mary Lou McCurdy for all their help. Graduate assistants Peter Malvicini and Bill Pitkin have also contributed many hours of research and typing, without which the book could not have been completed. Similarly, I owe a great debt of gratitude to the students who over the years have taught me so much about these books through their perceptive comments in class and the papers that delved into many of the problem areas of the Pentateuch.

Finally I would like to thank my wife, Clara, for allowing me to spend several summers working on this manuscript when I could have been painting or otherwise contributing to the upkeep of house and home. Her understanding and love continue to be an inspiration to all of my work, and she has taught me to appreciate why the Lord said, "It is not good for the man to be alone." But before I was united to my wife the Lord gave me two wonderful parents, who not only took me to church in infancy and put me under the teaching of God's Word but also gave me an example of what a godly life was all about. To Gottfried Hermann and Melanie Seyfert Wolf I dedicate this book, thankful for their consistent walk with the Lord and for the way they impressed on me the commandments of the law about which I have tried to write (Deut. 6:7).

ABBREVIATIONS

The abbreviations in this volume conform to those adopted by the *Journal of Biblical Literature*, with the following additions and exceptions.

AnJapB	*Annual of the Japanese Biblical Institute*
AltORAT	*Alter Orient und Altes Testament*
BangTFor	*Bangalore Theological Forum*
BethM	*Beth Mikra*
BETS	*Bulletin of the Evangelical Theological Society*
BibBh	*Biblehashyam*
BibIll	*Biblical Illustrator*
BibOrPont	*Biblia et Orientalia, Pontifico Instituto Biblio*
BibTB	*Biblical Theology Bulletin*
BibRes	*Biblical Research* (Chicago Society of Biblical Research)
BiTod	*The Bible Today*
BiTrans	*The Bible Translator*
BRev	*Bible Review*
CalvTJ	*Calvin Theological Journal*
ConcordJ	*Concordia Journal*
DD	*Dor le Dor*
EBC	*Expositor's Bible Commentary*
EDT	*Evangelical Dictionary of Theology*
GTJ	*Grace Theological Journal*
ISBEns	New Series of ISBE
ILR	*Israel Law Review*
IndJT	*The Indian Journal of Theology*
ITS	*Innsbrucker Theologische Studien*
JASA	*Journal of the American Scientific Affiliation*
JJurPapyr	*Journal of Juristic Papyrology*
LexTQ	*Lexington Theological Quarterly*
MasST	*Masoretic Studies*

NASB	*New American Standard Bible*
NBD	*New Bible Dictionary*
NIV	*New International Version*
OTWerkSuidA	*Die Ou Testamentiese Werkgemeenskap, Suid-Africa*
PrWcJesSt	*Proceedings of the World Congress of Jewish Studies*
REX	*Review and Expositor*
RIDA	*Revue Internationale des Droits de l'Antiquité*
RSV	*Revised Standard Version*
RTR	*Reform Theological Review*
ScrB	*Scripture Bulletin*
ScotJT	*Scottish Journal of Theology*
SwJT	*Southwestern Journal of Theology*
TB	*Tyndale Bulletin*
Them	*Themalios*
TJ	*Trinity Journal*
TOTC	Tyndale Old Testament Commentaries
TWOT	*Theological Wordbook of the Old Testament*
VE	*Vox Evangelica*
VoxR	*Vox Reformata*
WEC	The Wycliffe Exegetical Commentary

1

INTRODUCTION

The five books of the Pentateuch are foundational to all of Scripture and rank as one of the most important sections in God's Word. Just as a knowledge of the four gospels is essential for understanding the New Testament, so the content of the Pentateuch is crucial to the rest of the Old Testament and for that matter the whole Bible.[1] The four gospels tell us about the incarnation as the Son of God came to dwell among men. In Exodus 40:34-38 the glory of God fills the Tabernacle as the Lord dwelled among Israel to speak to them and to guide them in their travels. Even though we usually think of the wrath and power of God in connection with the Old Testament, Moses told Israel that God was near them whenever the people prayed to Him (Deut. 4:7). The Lord marvelously protected them from danger and revealed to them His laws and decrees, and even the pagan prophet Balaam had to admit that

> The Lord their God is with them;
> the shout of the King is among them.
> (Num. 23:21)

God worked in a wonderful way in the family of Abraham, not only to make of that people "a kingdom of priests and a holy nation" (Ex. 19:6) but also so that "all peoples on earth will be blessed through you" (Gen. 12:3). Ultimately that blessing came in the Person of Jesus Christ, who was the mediator of a better covenant than the one established by Moses, so that salvation might come to the whole world.

The Fivefold Division of the Pentateuch

The first five books of the Bible are commonly referred to as the "Pentateuch," a word derived from the Greek *penta* ("five") and *teuchos* (a case for carrying papyrus rolls but in later usage the scroll itself). The five-volume book

---

1. Samuel J. Schultz, *The Gospel of Moses* (Chicago: Moody, 1979), p. 1.

corresponds to the Jewish description of the "five fifths of the Law" found in the Talmud.[2] This division of Moses' writings into five separate books may owe its origin to a practical consideration. No scroll could hold all of the words, whereas the five leather scrolls could be handled quite easily. Such an explanation also fits the division of the book of Psalms into five sections, since the 150 separate hymns likewise took up too much space.

The fivefold division of the law is also attested in the Samaritan Pentateuch and the Septuagint, both of which have five names for Moses' writings. The Jewish historian Josephus also spoke of the five books of the law in the first century A.D. Origen was the first to use the word *Pentateuch* in his commentary on John, and he was followed by Tertullian in his disputes with the Marcionites.[3]

Scripture itself refers to Moses' writings as "the Book of the Law" (Josh. 1:8; 8:34), "the Book of the Law of Moses" (Josh. 8:31; 23:6; 2 Kings 14:6), "the Law of Moses" (1 Kings 2:3), "the Book of Moses" (Ezra 6:18; Neh. 13:1; Mark 2:26), "the Law of God" (Neh. 10:28, 29), "the Law of the Lord" (Luke 2:23, 24), "the Law" (Ezra 10:3; Luke 10:26), or simply "Moses" in the phrase "Moses and the Prophets" (Luke 16:29; 24:27).[4]

To the Jews the single word *Torah* best described this part of Scripture. Torah means not only "law" but also "teaching" or "instruction." These five books contain God's teaching about the origin of the world and of Israel and explain how a sinful people can meet with a holy God. For the Jew the Pentateuch contained an authority that the rest of the Old Testament—the prophets and the writings—did not seem to match, just as the importance of Moses exceeded that of any other Old Testament figure. When the Jews were driven from their homeland to take up residence in exile, it was the books of Moses that were read most frequently in the synagogues. It was common to read through the Pentateuch every three years, whereas other books were covered less systematically.

THE UNITY OF THE PENTATEUCH

The books of Genesis through Deuteronomy present a coherent picture of the origins of mankind and the birth and development of Israel as a nation. Except for the book of Genesis, these volumes focus upon the life and ministry of Moses, a man called by God to lead the Israelites out of Egypt to the Promised Land. Shortly after their release from slavery—a release predicted in Genesis 15:14—the people stopped at Mount Sinai, where God revealed to them His law and the principles of holy living. This important encounter lasted almost a year and is described in Exodus 19-40, the whole book of Leviticus, and Numbers 1-

---

2. R. K. Harrison, *Introduction to the Old Testament* (Grand Rapids: Eerdmans, 1969), p. 495.
3. Ibid., citing *Patrologia Latina*, ed. Migne, II, col. 282.
4. E. J. Young, *Introduction to the Old Testament*, rev. ed. (Grand Rapids: Eerdmans, 1958), p.39; W. LaSor, F. Bush, D. Hubbard, *Old Testament Survey* (Grand Rapids: Eerdmans, 1982), p. 62.

10. From Mount Sinai the Israelites journeyed to Kadesh-Barnea, where they wavered in unbelief and refused to trust God to bring them safely into Canaan. The rest of Numbers quickly covers the forty years of wandering in the desert prior to the arrival of the Israelites at the plains of Moab in Numbers 22:1. There they barely survive the machinations of Balaam and Balak and were given instructions by Moses about life in the Promised Land. While situated there on the eastern banks of the Jordan River Moses delivered his final addresses to the people, summarizing God's work on their behalf and encouraging them to be faithful to the Lord in the coming years. These final messages given by the great leader constitute the book of Deuteronomy, which ends with the account of Moses' death.

John Sailhamer has noted that the main narrative sections of the Pentateuch are concluded by poetic material sometimes followed by an epilogue. For example, at the close of the patriarchal narratives stands the poetic blessing of Jacob in Genesis 49 and an epilogue in chapter 50. The Exodus narratives are concluded by the song of Moses in Exodus 15, whereas the wilderness wanderings are followed by Balaam's oracles in Numbers 23-24. At the end of the Pentateuch we find the double poetic section containing Moses' song of witness and blessing on the twelve tribes in Deuteronomy 32-33 and then the epilogue in chapter 34.[5]

Along with the overall continuity in the narrative, we can also point to the grammatical features that underscore the unity of the Pentateuch. For some reason these five books fail to distinguish between the third person pronouns, "he" and "she." Instead of using *hû* and *hî* like the rest of the Old Testament, the Pentateuch uses only the masculine form. The same is true of the words for "boy" and "girl." "Girl is normally written *na'arâ*, but the Pentateuch uses *na'ar* without the feminine ending."[6]

In spite of strong arguments in favor of the unity of the Pentateuch, a number of scholars support the idea of a hexateuch or a tetrateuch. Julius Wellhausen thought that Joshua should be combined with the first five books to form a "hexateuch."[7] Going in the opposite direction, Martin Noth spoke of a "tetrateuch" ending with Numbers, and he placed Deuteronomy at the head of a history that included the historical books through 2 Kings. The "deuteronomic work," as he called it, was composed during the Exile, and Deuteronomy 1-3 functioned as an introduction to the entire corpus.[8] Although it is true that Deuteronomy is closely connected with Joshua, even the first chapter of Joshua distinguishes between the "Book of the Law" and other materials (v. 8). The law

5. John Sailhamer, "Genesis," in *EBC* (Grand Rapids: Zondervan, 1990), 1:7.
6. Gesenius, Kautzsch, and Cowley, *Hebrew Grammar* (Oxford: Clarendon, 1910), p. 107.
7. Julius Wellhausen, *Die Composition des Hexateuchs* (1876-77).
8. Martin Noth, *Uberlieferungsgeschichtliche Studien* (1943 reprint; Tubingen: Max Niemeyer Verlag, 1957), p. 9.

was given by Moses, and the unity of the five books is strongly supported by Jewish tradition and by internal considerations.

THE IMPACT OF THE PENTATEUCH ON THE OLD TESTAMENT

Rather than disturbing the unity of the Pentateuch by detaching Deuteronomy from the other four books, we should recognize that Deuteronomy and the rest of the Pentateuch greatly influenced the entire Old Testament. The law of Moses was intended as a guide both to the nation and to individuals within the nation, so it is little wonder that subsequent writers wrote under the shadow of the Pentateuch. The impact of the Pentateuch was greatest upon the prophetic writers, but as we shall see, it influenced the poets and historians as well.

ON THE HISTORICAL BOOKS

Joshua served many years as Moses' chief aide and commanding general, and the book that bears his name reflects their close association. Three chapters in particular emphasize the Book of the Law given by Moses (Josh. 1, 8, 23), for Joshua was to urge the people to obey the teachings of his great predecessor. If they responded, God would bless the nation abundantly, but if they rebelled, the curses of the law would afflict them (Josh. 8:34; 23:6-13). Judges and part of Samuel recount how these curses did in fact fall upon the nation, but the rule of King David brought a return to godliness and blessing. The promise that David's son would build a house for God's Name (2 Sam. 7:13) ties in with the words of Deuteronomy 12:5 that God would choose a place to put His name.

David's final words to Solomon stressed the commands and requirements written in the law of Moses (1 Kings 2:3). In subsequent centuries the godly kings Hezekiah and Josiah followed the Lord with all their hearts and all their strength, according to the commands given through Moses (2 Kings 18:6; 23:25). References to the Mosaic requirements and especially "the Book of Moses" are more frequent in 1 and 2 Chronicles (see 1 Chron. 5:15; 22:13; 2 Chron. 8:13; 25:4; 35:12). Ezra and Nehemiah also refer several times to Moses and his writings, probably because Ezra was a scribe by occupation.

ON THE PROPHETIC BOOKS

Both the major and minor prophets contain important links with the books of Moses. Isaiah begins his majestic prophecy by calling on heaven and earth as witnesses, an allusion to the solemn call of Moses in Deuteronomy 30:19 and 32:1. Moses warned that disobedience would bring judgment, and Isaiah is about to announce the disaster soon to come. The God who will judge is called "the Mighty One of Israel" (or "Jacob") in Isaiah 1:24; 49:26; and 60:16—a title drawn from Genesis 49:24. Isaiah also calls God the "Rock" and "Savior"

(17:10), names found together in Deuteronomy 32:15. God is the Creator as well as the Redeemer. Just as Israel had been rescued from Egypt, so will the remnant be delivered from Babylon. Isaiah 12:2 quotes those great lines celebrating the victory won over Egypt at the Red Sea (cf. Ex. 15:2).

Jeremiah is heavily indebted to the book of Deuteronomy for some of its concepts. The stubbornness of the people's hearts—mentioned in 9:14; 13:10; 23:17; and elsewhere—confirms the evaluation of their condition in Deuteronomy 9:27. Moses had said that an idolater was like a root that produced "bitterness" and "poison" (Deut. 29:18 [HB 29:17]). These two words—*rō'š* and *la'anâ*—occur together in Jeremiah 9:14; 23:15 and in Amos 6:12. The fruit had been borne, and judgment was soon to follow. Repeatedly Jeremiah, who derives his wording from Deuteronomy 28:37, notes that Judah will be devastated and become an object of scorn and ridicule (25:9, 11; 29:18; etc.).

A sizable number of the curses found in Leviticus 26 and Deuteronomy 28-29 are cited in the prophetic books, an indication that these chapters were among the best-known in the Old Testament. For example, the blight and mildew threatened in Deuteronomy 28:22 do ruin the crops in Amos 4:9 and Haggai 2:17. Droughts and insects also ravage fields and vineyards (Hag. 1:10-11; Joel 1:4), in accord with the predictions of Deuteronomy 28:23, 38-39.

ON THE POETIC BOOKS

The influence of the Pentateuch is not as pervasive in the poetic books, where even the word *torah* can mean "teaching" or "instruction" rather than the "Law" of Moses (cf. Prov. 1:8). Much of the poetic materials deal with either reflective or practical wisdom, concentrating on the meaning of life (as Job or Ecclesiastes) or on the importance of hard work and controlling the tongue (as Proverbs). Nevertheless, the book of Psalms begins where Joshua did, encouraging meditation upon "the law of the Lord . . . day and night" (cf. Ps. 1:2; cf. Josh. 1:8). Psalms 19 and 119 also extol the law with its precepts and statutes. Since the priests did much of the teaching in Israel it is likely that "the strands of reflective and practical wisdom and the Temple and priests were closely associated."[9]

THE IMPACT OF THE PENTATEUCH ON THE NEW TESTAMENT

The ministry of Jesus and the apostles took place in a century when the Jews were keenly interested in the law of Moses, so it is not surprising that there are numerous references to the Pentateuch in the New Testament.

9. C. Hassell Bullock, *An Introduction to the Old Testament Poetic Books* (Chicago: Moody, 1979), p. 26.

QUOTATIONS

Except for Psalms and Isaiah, the books of the Pentateuch are the most frequently quoted in the New Testament. Deuteronomy is a close third over all, followed by Exodus, Genesis, and Leviticus.[10] Only Numbers with its three quotations lags behind. The chapters most frequently cited are Genesis 2, 12, and 15, Exodus 3 and 20, Leviticus 19, and Deuteronomy 5, 6, and 32. Leviticus 19:18 is quoted some nine times in the synoptic gospels (Matt. 5:43; 19:19; 22:39; Mark 12:31, 33; Luke 10:27) as well as Romans 13:9, Galatians 5:14, and James 2:8. The whole law could be summed up in the one rule: "Love your neighbor as yourself." Likewise the crucial doctrine of justification by faith is firmly rooted in Genesis 15:6 (cf. Rom. 4:3, 9, 22; Gal. 3:6). When Jesus was tempted by Satan in the desert, He quoted three verses from Deuteronomy (8:3; 6:13, 16; cf. Matt. 4:4, 7, 10).

TYPOLOGY

The experiences of the patriarchs and of the children of Israel are often used as "examples" or "types" (1 Cor. 10:6, 11) to illustrate spiritual truths.[11] Abraham's encounter with Melchizedek, king of Salem and priest of God Most High, enabled the writer of Hebrews to speak of Christ as a priest "in the order of Melchizedek" (Heb. 7:1-17). The rivalry between Hagar and Sarah and their offspring in Genesis 16-21 was used by Paul to illustrate slavery and freedom, bondage to the law versus freedom in Christ (Gal. 4:24-31).

Israel's wandering in the wilderness formed the background to Paul's reference to drinking "from the spiritual rock that accompanied them, and that rock was Christ" (1 Cor. 10:3). The episode at Mount Horeb where Moses struck the rock emphasized the satisfaction of physical thirst (Ex. 17:6). Similarly the manna God sent to sustain Israel during those forty years led Jesus to refer to Himself as the "bread from heaven" and the "bread of Life" (John 6:32, 35). The bread was Jesus' flesh, which He would "give for the life of the world" (John 6:51). Finally those who looked in faith at Moses' bronze snake and recovered from the bites of poisonous snakes (Num. 21:9) were like those who look to Jesus for deliverance from eternal death (John 3:14-15).

Christ's death is also compared in some detail to the ministry of the high priest in Moses' Tabernacle. On the day of atonement the high priest had to enter the most holy place to sprinkle blood on the cover of the Ark of the Covenant (Lev. 16:15-17). Hebrews 9:12 says that Christ "entered the Most Holy Place

---

10. This comparison uses the index in the 3d edition of *The Greek New Testament*, ed. Kurt Aland, Matthew Black, Carlo Martini et al. (New York: United Bible Societies, 1975), pp. 897-900.
11. Because of the fanciful interpretation of some commentators, typology was largely ignored for many years. In recent times it is making a comeback, however, partly due to the influence of Gerhard von Rad in his *Old Testament Theology* (New York: Harper & Row, 1965), 2:363-87.

once for all by his own blood, having obtained eternal redemption." The "man-made sanctuary . . . was only a copy of the true one"; Jesus "entered heaven itself" (Heb. 9:24-25).

Through His death, Christ became the mediator of the New Covenant, a covenant far superior to the old one made at Mount Sinai. The New Covenant "is founded on better promises" (Heb. 8:6) and associated with joy, not the darkness and terror of Mount Sinai (Heb. 12:18-22).

THE THEOLOGY OF THE PENTATEUCH

Almost from start to finish the Pentateuch contains a rich store of theological truth, touching virtually every major area of theology. We learn about God's power and transcendence, but at the same time we see Him walking in the Garden of Eden or fellowshiping with Moses on Mount Sinai. God is the sovereign Creator unlike any other god, but He reveals Himself by word and deed to individuals and to His covenant people Israel. Even the Egyptians learned that Yahweh was God.

Although man was made in the image of God, Genesis quickly tells us of man's sin and graphically describes the judgment of God. Yet in the midst of a fallen world, God graciously reached down to bring people back to Himself. Sacrifices can be offered to make atonement for sin, and Leviticus in particular describes how a sinful people can approach a holy God. The slaying of the Passover lamb in Exodus 12 and the sacrifices of the Day of Atonement in Leviticus 16 wonderfully portray the ultimate sacrifice of Christ on Calvary. In His loving dealing with mankind, God forgives sin and calls for the wholehearted obedience of His people. In spite of His righteous anger that repeatedly brought down judgment on sinners, the Lord is the "compassionate and gracious God . . . abounding in love and faithfulness" (Ex. 34:6). Nowhere are these qualities seen more clearly than in the Pentateuch.

GOD

God as Creator. The Pentateuch begins with a description of God as Creator of heaven and earth (Gen. 1:1), and it ends with a reference to God as the Father and Creator of Israel (Deut. 32:6, 15). The verb "create" (*bārā'*) occurs five times in Genesis 1 (vv. 21, 27) and another five times between Genesis 2:4 and 6:7. God is always the subject of the verb, and there is never a reference to any material used in creating. The verb translated "Creator" in Deuteronomy 32:6 is *qānâ*, which can also mean "to possess," "to buy," or "to bring forth" (Gen. 4:1; but see Ps. 139:13). This verb also appears in Genesis 14:19, 22, where Melchizedek calls on "God Most High, Creator of heaven and earth." In Genesis 1 the climax of God's creative activity is the creation of man—both male and female—in verse 27. A more detailed account of the making of Adam in 2:7 states that God "formed man from the dust of the ground." "Formed" (*yāṣar*) is the verb used of a potter as he fashions the clay (cf. Isa. 45:9, 11).

God as Creator is separate from and prior to the material world, whereas according to a Babylonian creation epic, the universe was made from the body of the slain Tiamat, and man was created from the blood of another god named Kingu.[12] God's separateness from nature is also evident in that the sun and the moon, commonly worshiped as gods throughout the ancient Near East, are mentioned only as "the greater light" and "the lesser light" (Gen. 1:16). The same verse includes the creation of the stars almost as an afterthought. The great creatures of the sea, likewise feared by the ancients, are fully under God's control (v. 21). God alone is the sovereign one, the God whom all must worship.

God as Redeemer. A second major portrait of God is His work as Redeemer. This is directly linked to the rescue of the nation of Israel from the land of Egypt, the greatest example of salvation in the Old Testament. The word *redeem* (*gā'al*) is explained most fully in Leviticus 25, a chapter that describes how property and personal freedom may be recovered. Land that was sold could be repurchased by the original owner or by a relative of his (vv. 25-27). If a man became poor and had to sell himself into slavery, he or a relative had the right to purchase his freedom. This, too, is referred to as being "redeemed" (vv. 47-49). Another important use of redeem occurs in Numbers 35, a passage dealing with murder and accidental homicide. When a man was killed, it was up to a relative to put the murderer to death. This relative was called "a redeemer of blood" (*gō'ēl dam*), translated as "a blood avenger," or "avenger of blood" (v. 19). If the killing was accidental, the individual was protected from the avenger of blood as long as he stayed in one of the cities of refuge (vv. 25-27).

God's work as Redeemer blends together the concepts of purchasing freedom and also avenging mistreatment. During the four hundred years in Egypt, the Israelites were oppressed and badly beaten as the slave drivers "worked them ruthlessly" (Ex. 1:12-13; 5:14). When the Pentateuch mentions the redemption of Israel, it usually links it with freedom from slavery (Ex. 6:6). Deuteronomy states repeatedly that God "redeemed you from the land of slavery" (7:8; 13:5). In the song of victory commemorating the triumph over Pharaoh at the Red Sea, Israel is referred to as "the people you [God] have redeemed" (Ex. 15:13). Moses connects the redemption from Egypt with the fulfillment of God's promises to the patriarchs (Deut. 7:8). Since God is faithful to His word, the people are urged to love Him and to follow His commands and decrees.

As a title for God, "Redeemer" is developed most fully by the prophet Isaiah. Between 41:14 and 63:16 the word occurs thirteen times, and other forms of the verb are also used. Isaiah argues that the God who redeemed Israel from Egypt will be able to rescue them from Babylon: a new "exodus" is in the off-

12. Alexander Heidel, *The Babylonian Genesis* (Chicago: U. of Chicago, 1951), p. 118.

ing. Because of His great love for Israel, God will ransom His people as He takes vengeance on the Babylonians. Israel's release is called "the year of my redemption" in Isaiah 63:4, and in 52:9 the prophet speaks of the songs of joy that will accompany freedom from Babylon.[13] Just as a kinsman-redeemer bought back the land of a relative, so Israel's Redeemer will restore the nation to her homeland and even enlarge her borders (54:1-8).

The attributes of God. Although the work of God as Creator and Redeemer is emphasized in the Pentateuch, other aspects of His character and work are also given due attention. For example, the holiness of God is especially seen in Leviticus, where the nation of Israel is commanded to "be holy because I, the Lord your God, am holy" (19:2). A holy God could only be worshiped in a sanctuary set apart from the community at large and under the supervision of a priesthood consecrated to Him. Yet the entire nation was to be "a kingdom of priests and a holy nation" to demonstrate to the whole world the difference between their God and lifeless idols (Ex. 19:5). As God revealed Himself to the people at Mount Sinai, the whole mountain became holy ground, just as it had been for Moses a year earlier (Ex. 3:5; 19:11-13).

The holy and awe-inspiring God was clearly sovereign over His creation, fully able to take a Noah and an Abraham and through them to bring blessing to a cursed earth. When it appeared that God's purposes were being thwarted with the sale of Joseph to Egypt, God turned the intended harm into blessing for his brothers and for many surrounding nations as well (cf. Gen. 45:7; 50:20). When the Egyptians conveniently forgot all about Joseph and subjected the Israelites to cruel punishment, God taught Pharaoh through the plagues and the destruction at the Red Sea that He alone was Lord (cf. Ex. 15:11). As if to prove His sovereignty Yahweh "made the Egyptians favorably disposed toward the people," (Ex. 11:3) so that as they left the country they in effect "plundered" the people who had oppressed them (Ex. 12:36).

Throughout the Pentateuch we also learn that this powerful God is a God of love. He is "the compassionate and gracious God, slow to anger, abounding in love and faithfulness" (Ex. 34:6)—a description repeated in part in Numbers 14:18; Psalm 103:8; Joel 2:13; and Jonah 4:2. In spite of the stubbornness of the Israelites and their apostasy in the golden calf incident, Yahweh had mercy on them in response to Moses' intercession. Israel was indeed punished for their sins, but Yahweh would keep His "covenant of love to a thousand generations" (Deut. 7:9; cf. Ex. 20:6). When the people were groaning because of their slavery, God "remembered his covenant with Abraham" (Ex. 2:24), just as He had "remembered Noah" in the midst of the Flood (Gen. 8:1). Even during the predicted Exile, God would take delight in His people and bring them back to the Promised Land (Deut. 30:9).

13. See Herbert M. Wolf, *Interpreting Isaiah* (Grand Rapids: Zondervan, 1985), p. 214.

Although we prefer to emphasize God's love and compassion, it is equally clear that His holiness and justice demand that sinners be punished. In Genesis God's wrath was poured out on a corrupt world through the waters of the Flood, and Noah's descendants were themselves punished for trying to build the tower of Babel. In Canaan the cities of Sodom and Gomorrah were destroyed for their sexual immorality, even though Abraham begged "the Judge of all the earth" to do right and spare the righteous who lived there (Gen. 18:25). The awesome power of God was displayed in the plagues that ravaged Egypt and humiliated Pharaoh and his army at the Red Sea.

After the Exodus it was Israel's turn to feel the wrath of God as thousands died at Mount Sinai and on the plains of Moab for their idolatry (Ex. 32:28; Num. 25:9). Aaron's two oldest sons perished for offering "unauthorized fire before the Lord" (Lev. 10:1-2), and the earth swallowed up Korah and his followers for rebelling against Moses and Aaron (Num. 16:31-33). Those who complained about conditions in the wilderness were struck down by fire or fiery snakes (Num. 11:1; 21:6). Finally Yahweh warned the Israelites that, even after they entered the Promised Land, if they disobeyed His commands He would be angry with them and drive them into exile in humiliation and disgrace (Lev. 26:27-32; Deut. 28:58-64). The diseases and plagues of Egypt would be sent to ruin them as they had destroyed Pharaoh.

The names of God. The Pentateuch contains almost all the major names for God. God reveals Himself to the patriarchs and to Moses through His actions and also through His names. Since a person's name expresses his nature and his very essence, great importance must be attached to the various designations for deity.

God. The Hebrew for "God" is *'elōhîm*, the generic word for "God" equivalent to Ugaritic *el* or Akkadian *ilu*. "Elohim" is the word used throughout Genesis 1, where it stresses God's work as Creator (see above). The Hebrew form is a plural, but it is consistently used with a singular verb. Scholars have explained this as a plural of majesty or of respect,[14] although W. F. Albright points also to the use of "Ashtoroth" (the Ashtoreths) and suggests that this connotes a deity's "totality of manifestations."[15] It is wrong to argue that the plural proves the doctrine of the Trinity, but it does allow for its later development.[16]

Elohim is often used in conjunction with the personal name "Yahweh," which precedes Elohim. The compound name, usually translated "Lord God," first occurs in Genesis 2:4. In Genesis 24 Elohim is "the God of heaven and the God of earth" (v. 3) and the "God of my master Abraham" (vv. 12, 26, 43).

---

14. R. J. Williams, *Hebrew Syntax: An Outline* (Toronto: U. of Toronto, 1976), p. 6.
15. W. F. Albright, *From the Stone Age to Christianity*, 2d ed. (Baltimore: Johns Hopkins U., 1957), p. 213.
16. Jack Scott, *TWOT*, ed. Laird Harris et al. (Chicago: Moody, 1980), 1:44.

He is called the God of Abraham and Isaac (28:13) and "the God of Abraham, the God of Isaac and the God of Jacob" (Ex. 3:6).

LORD (Yahweh). The personal name for God, whose meaning was explained most fully to Moses, was "Yahweh," better known as "Jehovah." The exact pronunciation of this name is not clear; only the four consonants—YHWH—are given in the Hebrew Bible. In scholarly discussion the intriguing name is sometimes called the tetragrammaton, the Greek word for "four letters." The vowels are not indicated because the Jews eventually refused to pronounce the name, not wanting to take the name of Yahweh in vain (Ex. 20:7) and perhaps to prevent pagan people from misusing it. When this sacred name appeared in a verse the Jews pronounced it "Adonay," the other word for "Lord" (see below). The vowels of "Adonay" were merged with YHWH to produce "Yehowah" (=Jehovah). The correct pronunciation was probably closer to "Yahweh," whose first syllable is preserved in "Hallelujah"—that is, "Praise Yah"—"Yah" being a shortened form of "Yahweh." Most modern translations avoid the problem by using "LORD" to render this name.

When Moses asked God what name he should use when the Israelites inquired as to who sent him to lead the nation from Egypt, God said to tell them that "I AM has sent me to you" (Ex. 3:14). Since "I AM" is a word spelled almost like "YHWH," we are quite sure that it holds the key to the meaning of this most intimate name for God. In verse 12 God says, "I will be with you," and this is likely the way "I AM" is also to be understood: "I am he who is there (for you)—really and truly present, ready to help and to act," especially in a time of crisis.[17] Just as Immanuel means "God with us" (Isa. 7:14), so "Yahweh" indicated that the God of Abraham had not forgotten His promises. The patriarchs were familiar with this name, but they did not know the full dimensions of its meaning (cf. Ex. 6:3). When Israel experienced God's redemption from Egypt (6:6-7), the people would understand Yahweh's gracious provision more fully.

Because the words "I AM" are ambiguous, some interpreters connect them with God's role as Creator, the One who exists eternally or who brings into being. Although these meanings make excellent sense in the light of Genesis 1 and similar passages about creation, the contexts in which the name is used indicate otherwise. Yahweh first appears in Genesis 2 in connection with the Garden of Eden and God's instructions to Adam. The name is often used in a covenant context since it indicates God's desire to fellowship with man. This is especially evident in the passages that describe the establishment of the Abrahamic Covenant (Gen. 12:1-9; 15:1-19). Similarly, when God entered into a covenant with Israel at Mount Sinai, the name "Yahweh" appeared frequently (Ex. 19:7-10;

---

17. LaSor et al., *Survey*, p. 136. Cf. Victor P. Hamilton, *Handbook on the Pentateuch* (Grand Rapids: Baker, 1982), pp. 150-51; Gleason Archer, Jr., *A Survey of Old Testament Introduction* (Chicago: Moody, 1974), p. 128; J. B. Payne, in *TWOT*, 1:210-12.

20:2; 24:1-18). Moses warns the people that if they disregard the covenant, Yahweh will send plagues and disasters against them. Therefore, they must "revere this glorious and awesome name—the LORD your God" (Deut. 28:58-59). When Jesus claimed the name "I AM" in John 8:58, He clearly identified Himself with the God of the Old Testament and in doing so was nearly stoned for blasphemy. The Israelite who "blasphemed the Name" and was stoned to death at Moses' command probably was guilty of cursing the sacred name of Yahweh (Lev. 24:11, 16).

Lord (Adonay). The other word for Lord, *'adōnay*, has the basic idea of "Lord" or "master." Pharaoh is referred to as "their master, the king of Egypt" (Gen. 40:1), and Sarah refers to Abraham as "my master" (Gen. 18:12; cf. 1 Pet. 3:6). Abraham uses the same word to address his heavenly visitors in Genesis 18:3, although it is not clear that he was aware of their supernatural character (cf. 19:2). When applied to God Himself, "Adonay" is usually combined with "Yahweh" and is rendered "Sovereign LORD" in the NIV (Gen. 15:2, 8). Both verses in Genesis 15 and the two in Deuteronomy (3:24; 9:26) employ "Sovereign LORD" in a context of prayer. Abraham pleads with the Lord for an heir, whereas Moses begs the Lord not to destroy His people and later prays that he might be allowed to see the Promised Land. In Deuteronomy 10:17 Yahweh is called "God of gods and Lord of lords."

God Most High. The name *El Elyon* (*'ēl 'elyôn*) is composed of the shorter equivalent of Elohim, plus the adjective/substantive *'elyôn*, which means "high, most high." It occurs four times in Genesis 14:18-22 and once in Numbers 24:16 and Deuteronomy 32:8. In Genesis, Melchizedek is introduced as "priest of God Most High." Twice the name is coupled with "Creator of heaven and earth" (vv. 19, 22). Both names are associated with Canaanite deities also, although this does not mean Melchizedek worshiped false gods. The Ugaritic equivalent of Elyon, *'ly*, is an epithet of the god Baal in the Keret epic.[18]

In Numbers 24:16 "Most High" is used by another non-Israelite, Balaam, as he uttered an oracle about Israel. Both this verse and Deuteronomy 32:8 occur in poetic passages that talk about God's sovereignty over the nations.

God Almighty. Shaddai (*šadday*) is one of the most common names for God in the book of Job (thirty-one times), and it occurs eight times in the Pentateuch. Six of those times it is preceded by the word "El," (God). *El Shaddai* may mean "God of the mountain" if the connection with Akkadian *šadû* is correct.[19] The power and strength of the age-old mountains belongs to God.

El Shaddai is used in passages in which God appears to Abraham and Jacob to confirm the covenant with them and to assure them of increasing numbers (Gen. 17:1; 35:11). In three other passages Isaac (Gen. 28:3) and then Jacob

18. See *Ugaritic Textbook* 19, no. 1855, 3:6-9; G. Lloyd Carr, *TWOT*, 2:668-70.
19. See W. F. Albright, "The Names Shaddai and Abram," *JBL* 54 (1935), pp. 173-93; Victor P. Hamilton, *TWOT*, 2:907.

(Gen. 43:14; 48:3) speak to their sons with the prayer that God Almighty will bless them and show them mercy. In Exodus 6:3 God reminds Moses that He appeared to all three patriarchs as "God Almighty" rather than "the LORD." In Numbers 24:4 and 16 Balaam speaks as "one who hears the words of God" and "who sees a vision from the Almighty." Each verse is followed by an announcement of blessing upon the tribes of Israel, even though Balaam had been hired by the king of Moab specifically to curse them.

Eternal God. After Abraham made a treaty at Beersheba with Abimelech king of Gerar, he planted a tamarisk tree and "called upon the name of the Lord, the Eternal God" (*'ēl 'ôlām*, Gen. 21:33). Although this name per se does not occur elsewhere in the Pentateuch, the concept of God's eternality appears at least twice more. Exodus 15:18 states that "the Lord will reign for ever and ever," and Deuteronomy 32:27 contains these beautiful lines: "The eternal God ['*elôhê qedem*] is your refuge, and underneath are the everlasting arms." Israel had undergone terrible suffering and was faced with many enemies, but the God who had maintained her in Egypt and in the barren wilderness would never cease to help her.

The Fear of Isaac. Genesis 31:42 contains a reference to "the Fear of Isaac" (*paḥad yiṣḥāq*), which may very well be a name for God corresponding to "the Mighty One of Jacob" (see below). In Genesis 31 Jacob meets for the last time with Laban and speaks about the assistance of God, "the God of Abraham and the Fear of Isaac." As the two made a covenant not to harm one another, "Jacob took an oath in the name of the Fear of his father Isaac" (v. 53). Speiser has suggested "the Awesome One of Isaac" as a preferable translation of the name,[20] whereas Albright adopts the less likely alternative of "the kinsman of Isaac."[21]

The Mighty One of Jacob. Another significant title is "the Mighty One of Jacob" (*'abîr ya'aqōb*) found in Genesis 49:24 and five other verses (Ps. 132:2, 5; Isa. 1:24; 49:26; 60:16). The word *'abîr* is probably related to the adjective *'abbîr*, which also means "strong" or "powerful" and is used to describe warriors (Jer. 46:15), bulls (Ps. 22:12; Isa. 34:7), and horses (Judg. 5:22).[22] In Genesis 49:24 the "Mighty One of Jacob" is linked with several other names for God in a context that emphasizes God's provision for Joseph. In spite of the great adversity Joseph suffered, he did not weaken and fail, because the God of Jacob helped him and blessed him. God's ability to save and redeem His people is also mentioned twice in Isaiah where "the Mighty One of Jacob" occurs (49:26; 60:16).

20. E. A. Speiser, ed., *Genesis*, AB (Garden City, N.Y.: Doubleday, 1964), p. 243.
21. Albright, *From the Stone Age*, p. 248. D. R. Hillers argues against Albright in "Pahad YI-SHAQ," *JBL* 91, pp. 90-92. "Kinsman" comes from the meaning of "thigh" for a different root, *paḥad* (cf. Job 40:17).
22. The Ugaritic *'br* ("bull") may also be related. See *TWOT*, 1:8-9; *TDOT*, 1:42-43.

The Rock. Deuteronomy 32 contains the words of a song Moses recited before the whole assembly of Israel, and in this song the name "Rock" (ṣûr) is used for God several times (vv. 4, 15, 18, 30, 31). "Rock" is parallel to "fortress" in Isaiah 17:10, for God is like an inaccessible fortress where men can flee for safety. This sort of rock is a place of refuge (Deut. 32:37; Ps. 18:2), a secure stronghold that cannot be breached. Since God is Israel's Rock, their armies cannot be defeated unless God abandons them (Deut. 32:30). There is no god with greater power than the Rock of Israel (v. 31).

Another possible connotation of God as the Rock has to do with the time Moses struck the rock and water flowed out for the thirsty people (Ex. 17:6). Although this connection is not made in Deuteronomy 32, Psalm 78:20 refers to water gushing from the rock, and verse 35 mentions "God their Rock." A more precise identification is found in 1 Corinthians 10:3-4, where Paul speaks of Israel in the wilderness drinking from the spiritual rock, "and that rock was Christ."

In Jacob's final blessing he uses a closely related title for God, "the Stone of Israel" ('eben, Gen. 49:24). This name is parallel to "the Mighty One of Jacob" (see above) and may not be noticeably distinguishable from "Rock." Yet the prophet Isaiah refers to "a stone in Zion" parallel to "a precious cornerstone for a sure foundation" (28:16). Those who build their lives upon the God of Israel will not be disappointed.

Father. Only once in the Pentateuch is the name "Father" applied to God (Deut. 32:6), but it is nonetheless an important concept. God was Israel's Father because He was their Creator, the one who made them and formed them. The verb qānâ, which follows "Father," can also mean "to bring forth" (see "God as Creator" above) and fits in with the picture given in verse 18, where God is the One "who gave you birth."

God was the Father of Israel in that He chose that one nation to be His special people. The Exodus was a demonstration of God's love for them (cf. Ex. 6:6-7), and at Mount Sinai a covenant relationship between God and Israel was formalized (Ex. 19:5-6). All the years that the nation wandered in the desert God carried them "as a father carries his son" (Deut. 1:31), an act of compassion referred to by Isaiah centuries later (Isa. 63:9, 16). God's love was so great that Moses was amazed at the rebellion of the nation. The people "acted corruptly toward him" (Deut. 32:5) and generally abandoned God's laws and commandments. Moses warned them that unless they responded to God in obedience and trusted Him as an honored father they would face His judgment.

MAN

The books of Moses present a portrait of man that reaches extremes found nowhere else in Scripture. We see a sinless Adam and Eve in the Garden of

Eden, and we see a totally corrupt society in Sodom. Enoch and Noah walked with God, but the rest of mankind excelled only in wickedness, so God destroyed them in a Flood. Exodus describes Moses on Mount Sinai fellowshipping with God face to face, while at the same time the nation of Israel was at the foot of the mount engrossed in sin. Genesis introduces us to an unselfish Abraham and to a Jacob who burned with undying love for Rachel, but it also tells us how Cain murdered Abel and how Joseph's brothers callously sold him to Egypt. Joseph was a source of great blessing for Egypt, and yet after Joseph was gone the Egyptians oppressed the Israelites and worked them mercilessly. God marvelously rescued Israel from that house of slavery, but the people soon complained bitterly about life in the desert.

Made in God's image. Since man is like God, he was given authority over the rest of creation as God's representative on earth. Man was made ruler over the fish and the birds and the animals (1:26) and was told to subdue the earth (1:28). "Rule" and "subdue" are strong terms and imply a measure of opposition against man's authority, but as the writer of Hebrews notes, man has by no means achieved full dominion over creation (Heb. 2:8). Through Christ's death and exaltation, redeemed mankind will someday be able to exercise the dominion that was crippled by the Fall (cf. Heb. 2:9).

The early church Father Irenaeus argued that there was a difference between the "image" and "likeness" of God in man, the former consisting of rationality and free will, whereas the latter was the gift of God's righteousness. The reformers rightly rejected this distinction, asserting that after the Fall man's whole moral fiber was damaged and he was no longer free to obey God.[23]

Although the word *image (ṣelem)* is sometimes used for the idols worshiped by the pagans (cf. 2 Kings 11:18), the Old Testament makes very clear that God was never to be represented by any idols (Ex. 20:4-5). God is incomparable, and no image can be placed alongside Him (Isa. 40:18). At the same time we are warned not "to project God in man's image" and make man divine.[24] When Herod Agrippa I was praised for having "the voice of a god, not of a man" (Acts 12:22), "an angel of the Lord struck him down" because he failed to give God the glory (v. 23).

The climax of Genesis was the creation of man in the image of God on the sixth day. Both male and female were made in God's image and likeness and this distinguished them from all other creatures. Man is like God primarily in his moral and spiritual capacity and was created with the ability to be righteous and holy (cf. Eph. 4:24). He was given a glory and honor above all the other creatures and possessed a mind that also reflected the Person of the Creator. Karl

23. H. D. McDonald, "Man, Doctrine of" in *EDT*, ed. Walter A. Elwell (Grand Rapids: Baker, 1984), pp. 678-79.
24. Carl F. H. Henry, "Image of God," in *EDT*, pp. 545-46.

Barth has argued that the plural pronouns "us" and "our" in Genesis 1:26 anticipate the human plurality of male and female and indicate something about the nature of the divine existence also. This "conjunction of man and man" reflects the fellowship and interaction within the divine being, a relationship the New Testament portrays as the Trinity.[25]

Adam and Eve were placed in the Garden of Eden and given a perfect environment. There they fellowshiped with God and enjoyed all the provisions of paradise. When sin entered the picture our first parents were banished from the Garden, but they did not lose the image of God. That image was marred and distorted, but Genesis 9:6 states that even after the Flood man retains the image of God and for that reason murder is wrong. Ironically, Satan's assertion that Adam and Eve "will be like God" (Gen. 3:5) proved to be a call to rebellion rather than an enhancement of their relationship with God.[26] In the New Testament, James denounces those who curse men because all "have been made in God's likeness" (3:9). Those who receive Christ as Savior have become "a new creation" (2 Cor. 5:17) and are in the process of being "conformed to the likeness" of God the Son (Rom. 8:2). Whether man believes or disbelieves, he possesses a spirit that will live forever. This immortality is another aspect of the image of God.

The Fall. Before Genesis can get very far in unveiling the beautiful relationship between God and man and between man and woman, the perfection is shattered by the entrance of sin. Adam and Eve had been created "a little lower than the heavenly beings" (Ps. 8:5) with a freedom for worshiping God that apparently exceeded that of the angels. But they were free both to sin and not to sin, and, urged by the tempter, they exercised the freedom to sin. The seemingly insignificant act of eating fruit from the tree of the knowledge of good and evil had the drastic repercussions of plunging the whole human race into sin. According to Romans 5:12, sin and death came into the world through one man, "and in this way death came to all men, because all sinned." From that time on anyone born into the world would possess a fallen, sinful nature and would be in need of salvation to restore fellowship with God.

The New Testament places the responsibility for the Fall squarely on Adam's shoulders, even though Eve was the first to partake of the forbidden fruit. "Eve was deceived by the serpent's cunning" (2 Cor. 11:3), whereas Adam was not deceived (1 Tim. 2:14). He ate at the invitation of his wife and may have understood the consequences of his action more completely. In any event, it is in Adam that all die, and it was Adam whom God addressed in the Garden of Eden (Gen. 3:9; 1 Cor. 15:22). Paul balances the awful truth of death through Adam with the joyful news of life through Christ, the second Adam, for "in Christ all

---

25. Karl Barth, *Church Dogmatics* (New York: Scribner's Sons, 1958), 3 (part 1):195; cf. Sailhamer, "Genesis," in *EBC*, 2:38.
26. G. C. Berkouwer, *Man: The Image of God* (Grand Rapids: Eerdmans, 1962), p. 104.

will be made alive" (1 Cor. 15:22). The death of Christ paid for the sin of Adam and all his descendants, and the resurrection demonstrated that Christ was indeed the Son of God (Rom. 1:4). The obedience of Christ overcame the disobedience of Adam and opened the way to eternal life. All who exercise saving faith in Christ are given a new nature, a "new self" that can be pleasing to God and obedient to His will (Col. 3:10).

The sinfulness of man. One might think that the Fall of man would be followed by a series of "minor" sins that would gradually become worse as the generations became more distant from the perfect Adam and Eve. Nothing could be further from the truth, for sin reaches a peak in Genesis 6 and the rest of the Pentateuch is a sad recital of human degradation. We begin with the murder of Abel in Genesis 4. Cain's anger over God's disapproval of his offering led him to take his brother's life. The descendants of Cain evidently developed a civilization diametrically opposed to the ways of God, because by Genesis 6:5 the wickedness of mankind was so great that God decided to send a flood to wipe them out. Even after the Flood, however, judgment came when man in his pride rebelled against God and built the Tower of Babel.

The coming of the patriarchal age did not bring much improvement. God told Abraham that the sin of the Amorites had not yet reached its peak (Gen. 15:16), but the homosexual behavior of the men of Sodom (Gen. 18-19) brought to several cities a rain of burning sulphur. Abraham's family was not without guilt, for his nephew Lot committed incest with his daughters (Gen. 19:32-38). Abraham himself told lies about Sarah, and his grandsons Jacob and Esau schemed and hated one another. Joseph's brothers sold him into slavery, and his boss's wife tried to seduce him and then had him thrown into prison (Gen. 39:11-20).

The later suffering of the Israelites in Egypt demonstrated man's inhumanity to man. God eventually freed His people from slavery, but they grumbled and complained about conditions in the desert. At Mount Sinai the people worshiped the golden calf in defiance of God (Ex. 32). Aaron's sons Nadab and Abihu "offered unauthorized fire before the Lord" and were struck dead for their folly (Lev. 10:1-2). When the nation left Mount Sinai, they refused to believe that God could give them victory over the Canaanites, and their unbelief meant forty years of wandering in the desert (Num. 14:34). Yet when the forty years were finally over the people engaged in sexual immorality and in the worship of Baal of Peor, and 24,000 died in the plague that followed there on the plains of Moab (Num. 25:1-9).

In Moses' final addresses to the nation, he reviews some of the unsavory episodes of Israel's history. He also warns them of the terrible curses that will come upon them if they refuse to follow Yahweh wholeheartedly. Before his death, Moses is told that Israel will indeed abandon the Lord and will face many disasters and difficulties (Deut. 31:14-18). Sin always brings judgment, and even the chosen nation will feel the wrath of God.

SALVATION

The rapid development of sin both on the personal and national levels exposes the desperate condition of the human race. What could be done to reverse the effects of the Fall? How could mankind have fellowship with God restored? The Pentateuch describes how atonement can be made through blood sacrifices so that sin might be forgiven. The importance of faith is underscored in the life of Abraham, "who believed the Lord, and he credited it to him as righteousness" (Gen. 15:6). A few passages talk about an individual—a descendant of Abraham and Judah who will be a prophet like Moses—through whom the world will have hope.

THE MESSIAH

When sin made its tragic entrance into the world, God cursed the serpent who had deceived Eve. But He also announced that there would be enmity between Eve and the serpent "and between your offspring and hers" (Gen. 3:15). This verse has been called the *protoevangelium* (the "first gospel"), because many believe that the "offspring" or "seed" refers to Christ and His triumph over Satan. Justin Martyr and Irenaeus suggested this as early as the second century A.D.[27] When Christ did come He was "born of a woman, born under law" (Gal. 4:4). Paul alludes to Genesis 3:15 quite clearly in Romans 16:20: "The God of peace will soon crush Satan under your feet." This implies that believers will play a part in the crushing of Satan.[28]

The word "offspring" or "seed" (*zera'*) has additional messianic implications later in Genesis. In 12:3 Abraham is given the promise that "all peoples on earth will be blessed through you." This is expanded slightly in Genesis 22:18 and 26:4 to indicate that all nations will be blessed "through your offspring." According to Acts 3:25 this blessing is connected with the coming of Christ, who died and rose again so that sin could be forgiven. The apostle Paul argues in Galatians 3:16 that "the promises were spoken to Abraham and to his seed" and he identifies the "seed" with Christ. Abraham and his descendants were promised the land of Canaan as their inheritance, but the whole world benefits from the promise fulfilled through Christ.

Another important but difficult passage that is often interpreted in a messianic sense is Genesis 49:10, a verse found in Jacob's final blessing or "testament" to his sons. Verses 8-12 are directed to Judah, and verse 10 indicates that

27. H. P. Ruger, "On Some Versions of Gen. 3:15, Ancient and Modern," *BiTrans* 27, no. 1 (January 1976), p. 106.
28. Ronald Youngblood, *How It All Began* (Ventura, Calif.: Regal, 1980), p. 66.

the ruler of the twelve tribes will come from Judah. The scepter will remain in Judah's possession "until Shiloh [*šay lōh*] comes" (NASB) or "until he comes to whom it belongs" (RSV, NIV). The latter rendition of this obscure Hebrew expression is supported by Ezekiel 21:25-27, which talks about removing the crown of the king of Israel "until he comes to whom it rightfully belongs." Jesus was the descendant of Judah and David, and He will rule on David's throne forever (Isa. 9:7).

A third interpretation of this line reads "until tribute comes to him." The bringing of gifts indicates that "the obedience of the nations is his," a splendid parallel to the final line.[29] All three interpretations have their advocates, but the last two seem to have stronger exegetical support.

"Scepter" is also a crucial term in another significant passage—Numbers 24:17. The verse is found in the fourth oracle of Balaam, a prophet of sorts hired to curse Israel. Instead, he blessed them repeatedly, and in this particular oracle he saw a star or scepter rising out of Israel that would crush Moab—the very nation whose king had hired Balaam. Both the star and scepter probably refer to the messianic king who will rule Israel and the nations (cf. v. 19). Although Numbers 24:17 is not quoted in the New Testament, there are several references to it in the Dead Sea Scrolls. The Qumran community apparently understood the "star" and "scepter" as two different individuals, one a priest and the other a king.[30]

The office of "prophet" is also brought into discussions about the Messiah because of Deuteronomy 18:15, 18. There, Yahweh revealed to Moses that He would someday "raise up for them a prophet like you." Whatever that prophet says must be heeded, for God will put His words in his mouth (v. 19). In Peter's sermon at Solomon's Colonnade at the Temple, he links the "offspring" of Genesis 22:18 (see above) with the "prophet" of Deuteronomy 18:18 (Acts 3:22-23). Christ was the prophet of whom Moses spoke, and His words are God's words. Stephen quoted the same verse in his scathing denunciation of the religious leaders, who, like their countrymen, persecuted the prophets from Moses to Jesus (Acts 7:37).

FAITH

The "second Adam," who would be the author of salvation for all people, is only faintly seen in the Pentateuch. Similarly, the method of individual appropriation of that salvation is not clearly outlined. Since the "Torah" is the

---

29. Cf. Speiser, *Genesis*, pp. 365-66; Ronald Youngblood, *Faith of Our Fathers* (Glendale, Calif.: Regal, 1976), p. 140.
30. See the Damascus Document and G. Vermes, *The Dead Sea Scrolls* (Philadelphia: Fortress, 1981), pp. 49, 96. Scholars disagree as to whether or not the Qumran community anticipated the coming of one or two Messiahs (or "messiahs"). The "Messiah of Aaron and Israel" is referred to several times.

"Law," we expect and see an emphasis upon obeying the commands and requirements of Yahweh (cf. Gen. 26:5; Deut. 6:2). Yet in the case of Abraham we are given enough information to know that he was justified by faith and that this was the means of salvation in the Old Testament as well as in the New. The faith of Abraham, Moses, and others receives due attention in the verses of Hebrews 11.

The verse in Genesis that summarizes Abraham's faith is a brief one: "Abram believed the Lord, and he credited it to him as righteousness" (15:6). Paul quotes this verse several times to prove that we are justified by faith, not by works (Rom. 4:3, 20-22; Gal. 3:6), and James quotes it even while writing a book that stresses the importance of demonstrating faith through works (2:23). Abraham put his faith in the Person of God and in the word of God, the promise that Abraham's offspring would be as numerous as the stars (Gen. 15:5). He continued to trust or "fear God" even when asked to offer his son Isaac on the altar (Gen. 22:12).

The association between believing and fearing God is also seen in Exodus 14:31, where "the people feared the Lord and put their trust in him and in Moses" after the mighty miracle of crossing the Red Sea.[31] The performing of miraculous signs had earlier convinced the nation that God had indeed appeared to Moses (Ex. 4:1, 5, 31). The faith of the nation proved fickle, however, for they did not trust in Yahweh when the spies reported that Canaan was a land of fortified cities and powerful warriors (Deut. 1:32; cf. Num. 14:11). The difference between the faith of the people and the faith of Abraham was that the people tended to trust when they saw a great sign whereas Abraham believed God when all he had to go on was a promise. Exodus emphasizes that faith in God involved believing in Moses (cf. 19:9). For Abraham no mediator is in the picture.

The simplicity and effectiveness of faith is illustrated in the episode of the poisonous snakes. When the people complained about their miserable life in the desert, they were bitten by snakes. To save their lives, God told Moses to make a bronze snake and put it on a pole. Anyone who simply looked at that snake would not die from the snake bite (Num. 21:4-9). What a beautiful illustration of the one who looks in faith at the Savior hanging on the cross (John 3:14-15).

ATONEMENT

The writer of Hebrews states that "without the shedding of blood there is no forgiveness" (9:22). The objective basis on which all who believe are forgiven is the death of Christ. In anticipation of that sacrifice the Pentateuch is filled with references to the sacrifice of animals and the sprinkling of blood to purify from sin. Indeed, there is greater emphasis on the various sacrifices and offer-

31. Walter C. Kaiser, Jr., *Toward an Old Testament Theology* (Grand Rapids: Zondervan, 1978), p. 67.

ings than there is upon the Person of the Messiah or the faith that is necessary to obtain eternal life.

The importance of sacrifices is seen early in Genesis. After Adam and Eve sinned, God clothed them in garments of skin taken from slain animals and probably instructed them about the need for sacrifice (Gen. 3:21). This would explain why Abel brought an offering to Yahweh from his flock (Gen. 4:4) and why Noah sacrificed burnt offerings after the Flood (Gen. 8:20). In the patriarchal period Abraham, Isaac, and Jacob built altars to Yahweh as they worshiped him (Gen. 12:6; 13:18; 26:25; 35:7). Abraham's near sacrifice of Isaac graphically illustrated the substitutionary nature of sacrifice, for the ram caught in a thicket was finally slain upon the altar in place of Isaac (Gen. 22:13). The offering of the Passover lamb demonstrated the same point, since the firstborn son was spared in every home that had blood sprinkled on the doorframe (Ex. 12:23).

The last section of Exodus describes the construction and significance of the Tabernacle (chaps. 25-40). This divinely designed building provided the setting for the presentation of offerings to make atonement for the people. A list of the different offerings and the meaning and procedures for each are outlined in Leviticus 1-7. If a flawless animal is brought and if it is presented in the prescribed way, Yahweh will accept the offering to make atonement for sin (Lev. 1:4; 4:26, 31). The Hebrew verb "to make atonement" (*kippēr*) is related to the noun *kōper*, which means "ransom." This symbolizes how the innocent life of the animal is given in exchange for the guilt of the offerer.[32] Another cognate, *kappōret* ("atonement cover"), is applied exclusively to the golden cover of the Ark of the Covenant, the most sacred article in the entire Tabernacle. On the Day of Atonement, the high priest took the blood of a bull and a goat and sprinkled it on the atonement cover (Lev. 16:11-15). This was the only time anyone could enter the Most Holy Place, and it was this ritual that the writer of Hebrews compares most closely to the work of Christ. By His death "he entered the Most Holy Place once for all by his own blood, having obtained eternal redemption" (Heb. 9:12).

The individual Israelite who brought his burnt offerings and sin offerings to Yahweh was not thereby automatically assured of salvation. Implicit in the offering was a genuine repentance for sin and a commitment to the God of Israel. This is partially illustrated by Jacob's actions when he prepared to meet Esau, the brother he had so deeply offended twenty years earlier. Genesis 32:20 (HB 32:21) uses the verb *kippēr* when Jacob says that he hopes to *pacify* Esau with gifts in the hope that Esau will forgive him and spare his life. Jacob had experienced a change of heart since he fled from the revenge-seeking Esau years earlier.

32. Laird Harris, *TWOT*, pp. 452-53.

THE COVENANTS

A covenant is a sworn agreement between two parties, where no blood relation exists. The Pentateuch contains examples of covenants between individuals, nations, and God and man. On the national level a number of scholars have noted similarities between biblical covenants and international treaties, especially the Hittite suzerainty treaties of the second millennium B.C. The basic structure of these treaties has been compared at length with Exodus 20 and the entire book of Deuteronomy.[33] There is a strong possibility that God relates to Israel as a suzerain did to a vassal and that He expected the same allegiance demanded by the Hittite king.

The two major covenants are the Abrahamic Covenant in Genesis and the Sinai (or Mosaic) Covenant in Exodus, later renewed in Deuteronomy. The covenant with Noah follows the Flood (Gen. 9), and there is also a "covenant of peace" guaranteeing the priesthood to Phinehas (Num. 25:12, 13). On a more secular level, Abraham made a treaty at Beersheba with Abimelech, a Philistine king. The treaty followed a dispute over ownership of a well (Gen. 26:26-33). Jacob was another who concluded a treaty rather than engage in violence. When Laban caught up with the fleeing Jacob, the two rivals agreed to separate peaceably and stay in their respective homelands (Gen. 31:43-55). The last two treaties mention both an oath and a meal as the agreement was concluded.

The Noahic Covenant was an everlasting covenant made with Noah and his descendants. God promised that never again would He destroy the world with a flood (Gen. 9:8-11). As a sign of the covenant, God designated the rainbow as a reminder of His binding promise. Since the word for "rainbow" also means a "war bow" (*qešet*), it has been suggested that a bow pointed toward the heavens constitutes a self-maledictory oath. Von Rad argues that the rainbow was a sign that God had laid aside His war bow; the judgment was over.[34]

God's covenant with Abraham marks the theological high point of Genesis and perhaps of the entire Pentateuch. First introduced in chapter 12, the covenant is officially instituted in chapter 15, and the sign of the covenant is specified in chapter 17. Isaac and Jacob receive confirmation of the covenant in 26:2-5 and 35:11-12. In summary, God promises Abraham that his descendants will become a great nation, will inherit the land of Canaan, and will bring blessing to the whole earth (see "The Messiah" above). Like the Noahic Covenant, the Abrahamic Covenant will be everlasting (17:7, 13, 19), and it is unconditional. The only stipulation was that Abraham leave home and travel to an unknown land (12:1). In the covenant ceremony, God alone took an oath by

33. George Mendenhall was the first to explore these relationships. Also cf. Meredith Kline, *The Treaty of the Great King* (Grand Rapids: Eerdmans, 1963); Kenneth Kitchen, *Ancient Orient and Old Testament* (Chicago: InterVarsity, 1966), pp. 91-98.
34. Gerhard von Rad, *Genesis*, trans. John H. Marks (Philadelphia: Westminster, 1961), p. 130.

passing between the pieces of the slain animals (15:17). Abraham and his male descendants were required to be circumcised as a sign of the covenant (cf. 17:10-11). Galatians 3 emphasizes the promissory nature of the Abrahamic Covenant and affirms that the giving of the law did not set aside that covenant (vv. 17-18). After the passing of several centuries, God proved His faithfulness by remembering the covenant with Abraham when the Israelites were suffering in Egypt (Ex. 2:24; 6:5). He therefore effected their freedom in order to take them to the Promised Land (Ex. 6:8).

Shortly after the Exodus, Israel was challenged to make a covenant with God at Mount Sinai, and the people responded that they would do everything Yahweh had said (Ex. 19:8). Moses "told the people all the Lord's words and laws," and again they responded positively (Ex. 24:3). To confirm their vows Moses sprinkled blood on an altar and on the people, and the covenant was official (Ex. 24:8).

The heart of the Sinai Covenant was the two tablets of stone containing the Ten Commandments. These commandments are variously called "the words of the covenant" (Ex. 34:28), "the two tablets of the Testimony" (Ex. 34:29), "the tablets of the covenant" (Deut. 9:11, 15), and even "his covenant" (Deut. 4:13). To insure their significance, Moses placed the tablets in the Ark of the Covenant at Yahweh's command (Deut. 10:1-2, 5). The first commandment stated that "you shall have no other gods before me" (Ex. 20:3), so Israel was forbidden to make a covenant with either the people or the gods of Canaan (Ex. 23:32). If the nation made a treaty with the people of Canaan, they would soon be tempted to worship their gods (Ex. 34:12-16). In Deuteronomy seven Canaanite "nations" are mentioned in connection with the prohibition against making a treaty or intermarrying with them. Pagan spouses will advocate giving allegiance to other gods (7:1-4).

The Sinai Covenant differs from the Abrahamic Covenant in that it is not called an everlasting covenant. Yet certain aspects of the covenant are referred to as "lasting" or "permanent." For example, the Israelites were to observe the Sabbath "as a lasting covenant" (*berît 'ôlām*). The Sabbath was the sign of the Sinai Covenant, corresponding to circumcision for the Abrahamic Covenant. Every Sabbath day the priests set out the twelve loaves of bread—the bread of the Presence—before Yahweh "as a lasting covenant" (Lev. 24:8). Similar terminology is applied to Aaron and his sons, who received the priesthood "by a lasting ordinance" (Ex. 29:9). When Aaron's grandson Phinehas took courageous action to stop a terrible plague, the priesthood was confirmed to him and his descendants. They were to have "a covenant of a lasting priesthood" because of Phinehas's zeal for Yahweh (Num. 25:12-13). As priests for the entire nation, the descendants of Aaron were allowed to eat certain portions of the animals brought by the people as sacrifices. This right is referred to as "an everlasting covenant of salt before the Lord" (Num. 18:19). Salt was added to all the offerings, and the phrase "the salt of the covenant" (Lev. 2:13; cf. 2 Chron. 13:5) points to the permanency of the agreement.

After the forty years of wandering in the wilderness, God renewed the covenant with the generation about to enter the Promised Land. Such treaty renewal was common among the Hittites when one of their vassal kingdoms had had a new ruler.[35] The stipulations were brought up to date in light of changing conditions over the years. According to Deuteronomy 29:1, the covenant made with the new generation on the plains of Moab contained some additional terms, but it was essentially the same covenant. This is best seen in the repetition of the Ten Commandments in Deuteronomy 5. The people were to commit themselves to keeping the covenant just as their fathers had done at Mount Sinai. There was no doubt that God would be faithful to His Word; He will keep "his covenant of love to a thousand generations" (Deut. 7:9). The word "love" (*ḥesed*) indicates loyalty to the covenant relationship and the promises He had made. Israel was urged not to forget the covenant they were making, or God would judge them and drive them out of the Promised Land (Deut. 4:23, 27). But even in exile, if the people confess their sins and turn to Yahweh, He will have mercy on them. He will not forget the covenant He made with their forefathers (cf. Lev. 26:42-45; Deut. 4:31).

Through the study of the Pentateuch we can learn who God is and what He requires of mankind. God is concerned about the whole world, though He chooses to work mainly through Israel and enters a covenant relationship with her. Sadly, Israel and the nations often choose to rebel against God, but Yahweh will not abandon His covenant promise and seeks to restore and redeem mankind. God is patient and merciful, but He is also holy and righteous, and those who disobey Him are eventually judged. But the Pentateuch also looks forward to the Lamb of God who will pay the ultimate price for sin.

THE SAMARITAN PENTATEUCH

A strong testimony to the unity of the Pentateuch is the existence of the entire text in the old Hebrew script of the Samaritan Pentateuch. The earliest copies of the text are kept in Israel in Nablus (ancient Shechem) by the few hundred descendants of the Samaritans who still live there. Their allegiance to the Pentateuch developed because of the split between Jews and Samaritans after the Exile. In the days of Zerrubbabel (538 B.C.) the Jews refused to allow the residents of the land to assist them in rebuilding the Temple in Jerusalem (Ezra 4:1-4). Disputes continued in the time of Ezra and Nehemiah (Neh. 4:1-8), and during the Maccabean period John Hyrcanus conquered Samaria and Shechem

---

35. Cf. the treaty between Mursilis and Duppi-Teshub in James B. Pritchard, *Ancient Near Eastern Texts* (Princeton: Princeton U., 1950), pp. 203-4.

between 128 and 110 B.C. The deepening schism lasted into New Testament times, as is still evident in John 4.

The Samaritans argued that God had chosen Mount Gerizim rather than Mount Zion (Jerusalem) as His sacred abode (cf. John 4:20). Since Deuteronomy 11:29 specifies Mount Gerizim as the place to proclaim the blessings, this location has some scriptural support. The Samaritans did not accept any other books of the Old Testament because of the emphasis upon Jerusalem and because the Northern Kingdom of Samaria, with which they felt some kinship, was often viewed in an unfavorable light.

The earliest manuscripts of the Samaritan Pentateuch are no earlier than the tenth century A.D.[36] and are probably derived from a recension developed in the Hasmonean (Maccabean) era (about 165-60 B.C.). Frank Cross has noted that the Paleo-Hebrew script used by the Samaritans "is a derivative of the Paleo-Hebrew script which was revived or became resurgent in the Maccabean era of nationalistic archaism."[37] This script also contains the many vowel letters common to the texts of the Qumran community. These same Dead Sea Scrolls, however, have examples of variant readings that are strikingly similar to those in the Samaritan Pentateuch, but they do not exhibit the sectarian bias of the Samaritans. For example, 4QExa lines up nicely with the Samaritan Pentateuch, but it does not contain the addition about the unhewn altar on Mount Gerizim after Exodus 20:17.[38] This indicates that the Samaritan Pentateuch, like the Septuagint, comes from an Old Palestinian textual tradition (about 400 B.C.) that has substantial differences from the Masoretic Text.[39]

There are about six thousand differences between the Samaritan Pentateuch and the Masoretic Text, mostly involving spelling or grammar. In two thousand of these instances the Septuagint agrees with the Samaritan Pentateuch. This does not mean that in all two thousand cases the variant is the original reading, for often the variants smooth out difficult grammar or add a "helpful" term.[40] Sometimes, however, the agreement of the two texts is very likely the original reading. In Genesis 4:8 the words "Let's go out to the field" were probably left out of the Masoretic Text, and in Genesis 10:4 the change from "Dodanim" to "Rodanim" (the island of Rhodes) is acclaimed by all.

Bruce Waltke has classified the kinds of changes made in the Samaritan Pentateuch to show that it is essentially a "modernized" text to eliminate diffi-

---

36. Archer, *Survey*, p. 45.
37. Frank Cross, *The Ancient Library of Qumran and Modern Biblical Studies* (Garden City, N.Y.: Doubleday, 1961), p. 172.
38. Patrick Skehan, "Quamran and the Present State of Old Testament Text Studies: The Massoretic Text," *JBL* 78 (1959), p. 22.
39. Bruce Waltke, "The Samaritan Pentateuch and the Text of the Old Testament," in J. Barton Payne, ed., *New Perspectives on the Old Testament*, p. 229.
40. Ibid., pp. 212-25.

culties and improve readability. Archaic or rare forms have been replaced by more common expressions, and words or phrases have been added—sometimes from parallel passages—to achieve clarity or completeness. Passages deemed inappropriate or vulgar were modified to make them acceptable.[41] The net result is that the Samaritan Pentateuch must be used with great caution. Waltke agrees with the assessment of F. F. Bruce that "the chief value of the Samaritan Pentateuch is the witness which it bears to the essential purity of the Masoretic text of the first five books of the Bible."[42]

THE LITERARY CHARACTERISTICS OF THE PENTATEUCH

Through an examination of the literature of the ancient Near East we now have a good idea as to the richness of available written records. Laws, hymns, personal archives, epics, treaties, and proverbs are among the many genres of literature currently being studied, and most of these can be found in the Pentateuch. Although it is true that the most common designation for the Pentateuch is "law" (Hebrew, "torah"), the overall composition of these five books is much more complex. Even "law" is broken down into "apodictic" law or "case" law, and the relationship of "law" and "covenant" is a difficult one to define. Descriptions of "covenants" (or "treaties") are extremely important because of the centrality of the Abrahamic and Sinai Covenants.

Another basic literary distinction is that between poetry and prose. Most of the Pentateuch is prose, but poetic passages of exceptional beauty and power are found in Genesis 49, Exodus 15, and Deuteronomy 32-33. Poetic elements occur in Genesis 1, contributing to the already heated debate over the nature of that chapter. The Pentateuch also contains genealogical records, regulations for religious rituals, dramatic narratives, and credos.

Our understanding of literary form has been greatly enhanced by the development of form criticism (Formgeschichte) under the impetus of Hermann Gunkel and Hugo Gressmann. Gunkel was keenly interested in understanding the cultural setting or the "situation in life" (*Sitz im Leben*) that lay behind a particular type of literature. In his study, he was influenced by several broad trends current around 1900. One was the interest in the social sciences with its emphasis upon classes and community structures. A second trend was the study of the Bible in light of other literature from the ancient Near East. Archaeological finds in Mesopotamia, Egypt, and Anatolia allowed scholars to comprehend more fully the culture and writing patterns of the Old Testament world. Third, the analysis of the different literary genres was becoming popular. The Grimm brothers had subdivided German folklore into fairy tales, myths, sagas, and leg-

41. Ibid., p. 225. Deuteronomy 25:11 and 28:30 are two cases in point.
42. F. F. Bruce, *The Books and the Parchments* (Old Tappan, N.J.: Revell, 1950), p. 126.

ends.[43] Gunkel tended to treat Genesis in categories such as these. He talked about the "mythical legends" of Genesis 1-11, a series of "faded myths" because polytheistic elements were removed.[44] The patriarchal material was likewise filled with legends. Most were fictitious stories to explain why the Dead Sea area was so desolate or why Jacob's name means "he grasps the heel." Such tales were commonly told as people sat around a campfire or attended a religious festival.

Gunkel's assessment of Genesis has not been of much help to evangelicals, but the methodology he developed, particularly in his analysis of the Psalms, has benefited Pentateuchal studies. Scholars are much more alert to the setting in life, whether it be a business transaction, a court case, the giving of a final testament, or the establishment of a covenant. And by comparing the biblical accounts with other literature from a roughly contemporary era, students of Scripture can increase their understanding dramatically. Nowhere has this been more noticeable than in the study of biblical covenants, whose structure can be neatly divided into the historical prologue, stipulations, blessings and curses, and a list of divine witnesses. This structure is of great importance for Exodus 20 and the book of Deuteronomy.

Genesis presents the most complex literary picture of any of the five books. The first chapter has been called "elevated prose" by Alexander Heidel, so majestic is its description of the wonders of creation.[45] The seven-stanza structure plus the clear parallelism of verse 27 provide a poetic touch that adds to the beauty and mystery of the passage. Genesis emphasizes family records, and we find genealogies in chapters 5 and 11. These are introduced by the word *tôledôt* ("generations" or "account"), a term that occurs eleven times in Genesis and provides the overall framework (see chap. 3 under "Title" and "Literary Structure"). It also stands at the beginning of chapter 10, the "Table of Nations," which is arranged as a "modified genealogy."[46] Toledoth also occurs in Numbers 3:1, which introduces the family records of Moses, Aaron, and the Levite clans.

Much of Genesis could be called historical narrative, but chapter 14 is often singled out in this regard. The account of Abram's rescue of Lot is filled with names of kings, countries, and cities as it gives abundant information about the international politics of the day. The most extended narrative in Genesis is the story of Joseph in chapters 37-50. With great skill the author relates the sudden rise of Joseph to power and his dramatic encounters with his brothers. The climax is reached in chapter 45 as he finally makes his identity known. On a more

43. J. Hayes, *An Introduction to Old Testament Studies* (Nashville: Abingdon, 1979), pp. 124-25.
44. Hermann Gunkel, *The Legends of Genesis* (New York: Schocken, 1984), p. 14.
45. Heidel, *The Babylonian Genesis*, p. 93 n. 41.
46. Youngblood, *How It All Began*, p. 151.

mundane level, Genesis 21:22-34 describes Abraham's treaty with Abimelech, and Genesis 23 tells how he purchased a burial site for Sarah.

John H. Walton has made some interesting comparisons between the patriarchal narratives and Near Eastern epic literature, such as the Egyptian stories of Sinuhe and Wennamun and the Canaanite Keret epic. Like Genesis, these accounts record numerous episodes in the lives of these individuals and usually provide theological instruction. In each instance there is considerable discussion about the historical value of the epic, although real places and authentic names are used. Epic material vacillates between prose and poetry, and between third person or first person narrative.[47]

According to Leland Ryken the remaining narrative sections of the Pentateuch can be called "the Epic of the Exodus." It is contained in Exodus 1-20; 32-34; Numbers 10-14; 16-17; 20-24; and Deuteronomy 32-34.[48] An epic contains numerous historical references and usually has a strong nationalistic thrust, so with its description of the formation of the nation of Israel and its strong religious emphasis, "the Epic of the Exodus" is quite characteristic in its development. Unlike some epics, however, the hero of this biblical epic is not a man but is God Himself. Moses is a reluctant leader who is neither eloquent nor a great military leader, whereas the deliverance of the nation is attributed to the mighty acts of God. He is the One who routed Pharaoh at the Red Sea (Ex. 14:13-14, 27), and He is highly praised for bringing Israel through the desert to the edge of the Promised Land (Deut. 32:3-4).[49]

Poetry plays an important role in Genesis also. Throughout the book there are a number of "oracles of destiny," which often contain verbal subtleties.[50] Beginning with Genesis 3:15, these verses succinctly describe the future of an individual and the blessing or conflict in store for him or her (cf. 16:11-12; 24:60; 27:27-29, 39-40; 40:13, 19). Double meanings sometimes occur, as in Isaac's statement that God will give Jacob "of heaven's dew and of earth's richness," but Esau's "dwelling will be away from the earth's richness, away from the dew of heaven above" (Gen. 27:28, 39). The same preposition is translated quite differently in the two verses. Note also the chiastic order of "dew" and "richness" (a b b' a').

Additional oracles are found in Numbers 23 and 24 on the lips of Balaam son of Beor, whom Balak king of Moab had hired to curse Israel. Reluctant to accept the assignment at first, Balaam proceeds to bless Israel four times in oracles ranging from four to six verses. In the fourth oracle, Balaam predicts the

47. John H. Walton, *Ancient Israelite Literature in Its Cultural Context* (Grand Rapids: Zondervan, 1989), pp. 46, 59.
48. Leland Ryken, *The Literature of the Bible* (Grand Rapids: Zondervan, 1974), p. 81.
49. Ibid., pp. 83-85.
50. Derek Kidner, *Genesis*, TOTC (Chicago: InterVarsity, 1967), p. 71.

coming of a ruler who will crush Moab (Num. 24:17; see p. 34-35). Three final oracles briefly denounce other nations.

The most difficult chapters in the Pentateuch are the blessing of Jacob to his sons (Gen. 49), the song of victory after the Egyptians perished at the Red Sea (Ex. 15), and the blessing of Moses upon the twelve tribes (Deut. 33).[51] Couched in poetic lines, these chapters are filled with difficult words and constructions, but they contain some of the most beautiful and famous verses in all of Scripture. Exodus 15:2 is repeated in toto in Isaiah 12:2 and Psalm 118:14:

> The Lord is my strength and my song;
> he has become my salvation.

Deuteronomy 33:27 is perhaps even better known:

> The eternal God is your refuge,
> and underneath are the everlasting arms.

A second song of Moses is found in Deuteronomy 32, which, like Genesis 49, emphasizes the names of God (see "The Names of God" above). G. Ernest Wright called this poem a "covenant lawsuit," a legal proceeding conducted against Israel, and he divided it into the following sections: (1) a summons to witness (v. 1); (2) an accusation framed as a question (v. 6); (3) a description of God's benefits to the accused (vv. 7-14); (4) a breach of covenant asserted (vv. 15-18); (5) sentencing and judgment (vv. 19-42).[52]

The main section on law in the Pentateuch is Exodus 20-23, the Ten Commandments, and the Book of the Covenant (Ex. 24:7). The two tablets containing the Ten Commandments are central to the Sinai Covenant and sum up God's requirements for His people. As noted above, Exodus 20 is often compared to the treaty form common to the ancient Near East. Verse 2 represents the historical prologue as it succinctly describes God's relationship to Israel, the nation He redeemed out of slavery. Verses 3-17 correspond to the stipulations of a treaty and are expressed in apodictic (i.e., categorical) terms. Eight of the ten commandments are negative statements and use the strongest form of prohibition available in Hebrew. D. R. Hillers notes that the Ten Commandments are not "laws" with careful definitions and prescribed penalties. They are more like "legal poli-

---

51. See Frank Moore Cross, Jr., *Studies in Ancient Yahwistic Poetry* (Baltimore: Johns Hopkins U., 1950). Most of the book deals with these chapters.
52. G. Ernest Wright, "The Lawsuit of God: A Form-critical Study of Deuteronomy 32," in *Israel's Prophetic Heritage, Essays in Honor of James Muilenburg*, ed. Bernhard W. Anderson and Walter Harrelson (New York: Harper & Row, 1962), pp. 26-27.

cy" stating how the covenant community ought to live.[53] An elaboration of the penalties attached to the violation of the Ten Commandments is given in Exodus 21-23, among the many specific examples of "case law" spelled out in an "if—then" arrangement. These "civil statutes" were solidly grounded in the moral principles of the Decalogue.

The importance of the Ten Commandments to the Sinai Covenant is demonstrated by the preservation of the two tablets in the Ark of the Covenant, the most sacred article in the Tabernacle (Deut. 10:1-2, 5). Kline has noted that duplicate copies of the Hittite suzerainty treaties were kept in temples, one in the Hittite capital and the other in the main sanctuary of the vassal nation.[54]

This raises the question of whether or not the two tablets of the law each contained all of the Ten Commandments. In any event, both tablets were kept in the Tabernacle, since it was Israel's only sanctuary, while at the same time God, the "suzerain," was pleased to make it His dwelling place. The veneration with which the treaties were held underscores Israel's great responsibility to abide by the Ten Commandments.

The last section of Exodus describes the design and contents of the Tabernacle and includes information about the priests and their clothing. This material is contained in chapters 25-31 and is then repeated in chapters 35-40 as Moses carries out God's instructions. Such repetition can be illustrated elsewhere in the Near East. The Ugaritic Keret epic has a passage in which the god El explains to King Keret the military tactics needed to take his destined bride from her father's home. When Keret carries out the mission, the whole section is repeated.[55]

Leviticus is largely devoted to detailed instructions about sacrifices and other cultic matters. It contains regulations about diet and rituals for purification, cleansing from sin, and cleansing from any disease. Numbers resembles Exodus in that it combines historical narrative with legal and cultic materials. The census records of chapters 1 and 26 are similar to the genealogies of Genesis (see above).

The book of Deuteronomy is cast in the form of a series of addresses given to the nation by Moses just before the conquest of the Promised Land. At the same time the book represents a renewal of the Sinai Covenant as a new generation makes its commitment to God. As noted above (see "Covenants"), Deuteronomy can be outlined on the basis of the ancient covenant/treaty form. In the first four chapters—the "historical prologue" of treaty structure—Moses summarizes God's dealings with Israel over the years and encourages the people with a series of exhortations. Chapters 27 and 28 contain the blessings and

53. D. R. Hillers, *Covenant: The History of a Biblical Idea* (Baltimore: Johns Hopkins U., 1969), pp. 88ff.
54. Kline, *Treaty of the Great King*, p. 19.
55. LaSor et al., *Survey*, p. 147.

curses normally found in a treaty also. The lengthy curse section closely resembles Leviticus 26, which also outlines the punishment in store for Israel if the people choose to disobey Yahweh.

Von Rad has drawn attention to the "credos," the succinct creedal statements found in Deuteronomy 26:5-9 and 6:20-24 that preserve important elements in Israel's traditions. These "credos" recall the years of slavery in Egypt, the Exodus, and the settlement of Canaan.

THE SIGNIFICANCE OF MOSES

From a Jewish perspective, the dominant figure in the Pentateuch and the entire Old Testament is Moses. Abraham plays a key role in Genesis, but his stature and accomplishments do not match those of Moses. Although Abraham was the founding father of Israel, Moses was the one who organized the nation, promulgated their laws, and, under God, led them for forty years through the wilderness. He was a prophet, a priest, and almost a king as he directed every facet of national life.[56] The New Testament highly praises both Abraham and Moses, but it was Moses who appeared on the Mount of Transfiguration, along with Elijah, to talk with Jesus (Matt. 17:3-8).

Moses' life was unusual right from the start. He was brought up by Pharaoh's daughter and given an education that befit a royal prince. As a result he "was powerful in speech and action" (Acts 7:22). His upbringing could have kept him separate from his people, but he chose to identify with them "rather than to enjoy the pleasures of sin for a short time" (Heb. 11:25). Life involved more than accumulating the treasures of Egypt (Heb. 11:26).

Moses' concern for his people led directly to his exile from Egypt, when he killed an Egyptian who was beating an Israelite (Ex. 2:11-15). But after forty years in the desert of Midian, God called him to return to Egypt and lead Israel out of slavery. The call at the burning bush set Moses aside as a prophet, one who would speak the word of God to the Israelites and to Pharaoh. A prophet was God's spokesman (cf. Ex. 7:1), and with the help of Aaron, Moses communicated God's message of deliverance. Even after the Exodus, it was Moses who spoke God's words to Israel at Mount Sinai (Ex. 19:3, 7).

Before agreeing to lead Israel out of Egypt, Moses carried on a debate with Yahweh, expressing his reluctance to attempt so difficult a task. "Who am I, that I should go to Pharaoh and bring the Israelites out of Egypt?" (Ex. 3:11). From Numbers 12:3 we know that Moses was a very humble man, but perhaps lack of confidence would be a more accurate way to describe his feelings at this

---

56. According to several midrashic texts, the Jews in fact did consider Moses to be their king. Cf. Wayne A. Meeks, *The Prophet-King: Moses Traditions and the Johannine Christology* (Leiden: E. J. Brill, 1967), pp. 176-257. This view was based partially on equating the "king" of Deuteronomy 33:5 with Moses.

point. A little later he asserted that he was "slow of speech and tongue" (Ex. 4:10) and begged Yahweh to send someone else. Yet when God sent Aaron to be Moses' spokesman, the two brothers boldly confronted Pharaoh and challenged the mighty monarch to release the oppressed Israelites.

In his role as a prophet, Moses was unique. When Aaron and Miriam claimed that God spoke through them as well as through Moses, God replied that He spoke with Moses face to face, not through dreams and visions (Num. 12:6-8). Exodus 33:11 states that "the Lord would speak to Moses face to face, as a man speaks with his friend." On two occasions Moses spent forty days and forty nights on Mount Sinai, surrounded by the glory of God (Ex. 24:18; 34:28). The second time, Moses' face was radiant when he came down from the mount, "because he had spoken with the Lord" (34:29). Moses had to put a veil over his face as he spoke to the people (34:33-35; cf. 2 Cor. 3:13). Such intimate fellowship must have been a great encouragement for the often beleaguered leader. In Deuteronomy 18:15, 18, Moses predicts that God "will raise up for you a prophet like me." According to Acts 3:22 this was ultimately fulfilled through Christ.

Closely associated with Moses' prophetic role were the "miraculous signs and wonders" Yahweh performed through him (Deut. 34:10-11). Many of these miracles were designed to convince Pharaoh and his officials to release the Israelites, but not until the tenth plague was permission granted. Then, when the Israelites seemed trapped at the edge of the Red Sea, Moses raised his staff and extended his arm, and God made a path through the water (Ex. 14:15-22). This did not end Moses' activity, however, for several times in the desert the people were thirsty, and divine intervention was required. Moses struck the rock at Horeb, and water came out (Ex. 17:6). Later, he did the same at Kadesh, when he should have spoken to the rock instead (Num. 20:8-11). During a battle with the Amalekites, Israel's army was winning—as long as Moses held up his hands (Ex. 17:11-13).

A prophet was also a man of prayer (Gen. 20:7), and Moses' intercession on behalf of Israel again marked his greatness. When the people worshiped the golden calf at Mount Sinai, Moses cried out to Yahweh and prayed that He would spare them for the sake of His own reputation and because of His promises to Abraham, Isaac, and Jacob (Ex. 32:11-14; Ps. 106:23). This incident perhaps more than any other demonstrated the strength of Moses' leadership. Although the whole nation and even Aaron seemed intent on worshiping the golden calf, within minutes Moses ground the calf to powder and brought an end to this grim episode of apostasy. Another major crisis occurred at Kadesh Barnea after the negative report of the spies precipitated the unbelief of the nation (Num. 14). Again Yahweh wanted to destroy the people and make a great nation out of Moses, and again Moses begged Yahweh not to do it. God graciously relented, but Israel was sentenced to wander in the desert for forty years (vv. 12-19, 34-35).

Moses' ability to prophesy is linked with the Spirit of God in Numbers 11. In this passage the complaining of the people was beginning to overwhelm Moses, so Yahweh took "of the Spirit" that was on Moses and placed the Spirit on seventy elders who were to share the burden of leadership (vv. 16-17). When the Spirit rested on the seventy they prophesied, but only for a short time (v. 25). Joshua was also "filled with the spirit (or "Spirit") of wisdom because Moses had laid his hands on him" (Deut. 34:9). Closely associated with Moses during the entire forty years in the desert, Joshua was admirably trained to be the next leader of the nation. Serving as Moses' aide, Joshua led the armies of Israel and even accompanied Moses when he climbed Mount Sinai and met with God (Ex. 24:13). After many years at the side of his godly predecessor and strengthened by his final words of encouragement (Deut. 31:7-8), Joshua was ready to lead the nation into Canaan.

During the long years of wandering Moses heard a great deal of grumbling and complaining, and on at least one occasion he was ready to give up (Num. 11:11-15). In reality all of this complaining was directed as much against Yahweh as against Moses and Aaron (cf. Ex. 16:18; Num. 16:11), and Moses' displeasure with the people was not unlike the anger of Yahweh. But when God threatened judgment, Moses prayed earnestly and demonstrated a deep love for them. His compassion for them was so great that he urged Yahweh to spare them time and time again. Moses firmly believed that God would rescue Israel, and even when the Egyptians had trapped the Israelites at the Red Sea, Moses told the people to stand still and see the deliverance of Yahweh (Ex. 14:13-14). Through all of their difficulties Moses remained their faithful and loyal leader, a skilled shepherd tending his wayward flock.

The year that the Israelites spent at Mount Sinai was a significant one for Moses and the nation. It was then that Moses served as a lawgiver and became the mediator of the old covenant. The people were afraid to listen to the powerful voice of God, so God spoke to Moses and Moses gave them the laws and the statutes (Ex. 20:18-19). He "wrote down everything the Lord had said" and read to the people from "the Book of the Covenant" (Ex. 24:4, 7). Moses' role as lawgiver is connected with the writing of the Pentateuch, since all five books are referred to as "the Law." The education Moses received in Egypt would have prepared him admirably for this task, even though the Pentateuch is composed of narrative and poetry as well as legal material. The question of the writing of the Pentateuch is discussed in detail under "Authorship."

At Mount Sinai Moses also directed the establishment of national worship under the priests and Levites. Moses officiated at the ordination of the priests, offering the prescribed sacrifices and applying the blood where necessary (Lev.

8). Thus, before Aaron was installed as the high priest, Moses was the nation's priest. While on Mount Sinai, Moses received from Yahweh the plans for the construction of the Tabernacle and the regulations for the various offerings (Ex. 25:9; Lev. 7:37-38). Moses remained the spiritual leader of Israel even after the priests and Levites were carrying out their responsibilities.

One of the great titles in the Old Testament for a man of God is "the servant of the Lord." The "servant" of a king is a royal official (cf. Ex. 7:10; Isa. 37:5) or military leader. To be Yahweh's servant is to worship Him and to do His bidding. Moses is referred to as Yahweh's servant several times (cf. Deut. 34:5; Josh. 1:1), and when his position as leader was challenged by Miriam and Aaron, Yahweh spoke of Moses as "my servant," one who "is faithful in all my house" (Num. 12:7-8; cf. Heb. 3:5). The same chapter in Numbers contains the parenthetical statement that Moses was the most humble man on the face of the earth (v. 3). Surely his humility stemmed from his submission to the God he so faithfully worshiped.

Despite all his strengths and accomplishments, Moses was by no means perfect. He could become discouraged and even despondent at times (Num. 11:11-15), and like many of us he apparently had difficulty controlling his temper. It was his outburst at Kadesh when he angrily struck the rock that prevented him from entering the Promised Land (Num. 20:8-12). Even when Moses' anger seemed justified—as at Mount Sinai when the people were worshiping the golden calf—he lashed out quickly and broke the two tablets in something of a rage. His powerful emotions had also sprung into action decades earlier when he killed the Egyptian taskmaster who was beating a fellow Hebrew. "Not only did he have a burning sense of loyalty to his own people, but he had a burning sense of justice."[57] But by taking justice into his own hands he displayed the impulsiveness that played a key role in his life. Perhaps the few weaknesses that he had kept the Jews in subsequent years from placing on too high a pedestal this most remarkable leader, one of the godliest men who ever lived.

---

57. Dewey M. Beegle, *Moses, the Servant of Yahweh* (Grand Rapids: Eerdmans, 1972), p. 56.

2

AUTHORSHIP

Few subjects have generated more discussion and more disagreement than the question of who wrote the Pentateuch. Opinions range widely, with some arguing that every word was written by Moses. Others insist that they can prove that Moses had nothing whatever to do with the writing of the Pentateuch. Instead, certain sources labeled J, E, D, and P are proposed. The writers of these alleged documents, the "Yahwist," "Elohist," and so on, are regarded as the true authors of the Pentateuch. Archaeological discoveries and advances in literary criticism have added fuel to the debate in the twentieth century. The battle still rages and no end is in sight.[1]

In a way the Pentateuch is an anonymous work since it does not state its authorship unequivocally. This is especially true of Genesis, which deals with such a vast period of time, and none of it took place in Moses' lifetime. Other books of the Old Testament are also vague about their authorship. Judges, Samuel, Kings, and Chronicles are particularly difficult to deal with.[2] Other literature in the ancient Near East also tends to be this way. In Mesopotamian writing very few pieces identify the author, and even then it might be more accurate to think in terms of a compiler or editor. Probably the difficulty of writing cuneiform on clay tablets partially accounts for this situation. Nevertheless, a careful reading of the Old Testament gives the strong impression that the Pentateuch was written by Moses, its principal figure and the leader of Israel during most of that period.

THE CASE FOR MOSAIC AUTHORSHIP

Until fairly recent times most Jews have believed that Moses was the author of the Pentateuch. The first five books were called "the law" and were consis-

---

1. Cf. John H. Tullock, *The Old Testament Story*, 2d ed. (Englewood Cliffs, N.J.: Prentice-Hall, 1987), pp. 10-11.
2. W. LaSor, F. Bush, and D. Hubbard, *Old Testament Survey* (Grand Rapids: Eerdmans, 1982), p. 61.

tently linked with Moses. To suggest otherwise was to invite charges of heresy. Christians likewise have largely followed the Jews in accepting the view that Moses wrote the five books. Not until the seventeenth century was there any serious debate against Mosaic authorship.[3]

MOSES' QUALIFICATIONS

Judging from the account of Moses' life given in the Pentateuch, there is every reason to believe that he could have written the book so closely linked with his name. First, we need to consider his upbringing and training. Moses' life was spared when Pharaoh's daughter rescued him from his precarious ride in a papyrus basket close to the shore of the Nile River. Instead of perishing with the rest of the Hebrew baby boys, Moses grew up in the palace of the Pharaoh and was given an education "in all the wisdom of the Egyptians" (Acts 7:22). If we are correct in placing Moses' birth at approximately 1500 B.C., he was trained in the court of the Eighteenth Dynasty, one of the most powerful and advanced dynasties in Egyptian history. Egypt's international reputation was immense as her armies steadily expanded her borders. The Tell el-Amarna tablets discovered in 1887 revealed a group of texts written in Akkadian cuneiform by rulers of Palestine and Syria and sent to the Pharaoh from 1400-1370 B.C. The Egyptian court was in contact with diverse peoples and cultures, a factor that would have broadened the education of princes like Moses. In an era when uneducated Semitic slaves were writing on the walls of Egyptian turquoise mines in Serabit el-Khadim, surely Moses was well able to read and write.[4]

Moses' career in the upper echelons of Egyptian life came to an abrupt end when he got involved in the struggle of the Hebrews against their slave drivers. As a result he had to flee for his life to the land of Midian, where he stayed some forty years. Yet Midian was located in the Sinai desert, and Moses' experience there helped to prepare him for his later years as leader of Israel in that same desert. A substantial portion of the Pentateuch—from Exodus 16 to Numbers 20 —deals with events in the Sinai peninsula. Moses' familiarity with that area would have enhanced his ability to describe life in the desert. He knew the climate, geography, flora, and fauna. His knowledge of the land of Egypt would also have aided him in describing the experiences of his ancestors as they settled in the delta region (Gen. 37-50).

A third qualification ties in with Moses' role as the political and religious leader of Israel. He was the key figure at Mount Sinai in the establishment of the nation as God's special people bound in covenant to Him. If anyone was con-

---

3. Cf. G. Herbert Livingston, *The Pentateuch in Its Cultural Environment* (Grand Rapids: Baker, 1974), pp. 218-21.
4. Gleason Archer, Jr., *A Survey of Old Testament Introduction* (Chicago: Moody, 1974), pp. 122-23.

cerned that the nation not forget their roots nor their commitment to God, it was Moses. He had encouraged them, prayed for them, preached to them, and blessed them. Despite the nation's often rebellious attitude, he wanted them to follow God in the Promised Land. Hence, it makes sense to consider Moses a prime candidate for the writing of the Pentateuch.

We might well ask, however, whether anyone with Moses' responsibilities would have had the time to complete so long a work. He sometimes seemed overwhelmed with the burden he bore and the many decisions he had to make. Perhaps the solution lies in the forty years of wandering in the desert. Were there some months of relative calm when he might have turned to the task of preserving in writing the sacred history?[5] Moses did have some administrative help, for he followed the advice of his father-in-law, Jethro, and appointed a number of officials who handled more routine problems (Ex. 18:17-26). Seventy elders were also empowered by the Spirit of God to help Moses "carry the burden of the people" (Num. 11:16-17). These elders may have provided valuable assistance as their leader undertook the writing of the Pentateuch.

EXPLICIT STATEMENTS ABOUT MOSAIC AUTHORSHIP

In the Pentateuch. A number of passages assert that Moses wrote at least part of the Pentateuch. In Exodus 17:14 the Lord told Moses to write an account of the battle with the Amalekites, who had attacked the Israelites so soon after the Exodus. At Mount Sinai Moses wrote down all the words and laws spoken by the Lord and repeated to the people (Ex. 24:4). This "Book of the Covenant" (v. 7) apparently included Exodus 20-23. The Ten Commandments, however, were "inscribed by the finger of God" on two stone tablets (Ex. 31:18). After the first tablets were broken, Moses returned to the top of Sinai where he again wrote down the Lord's words pertaining to the covenant (Ex. 34:27). Deuteronomy also stresses Moses' writing of the law, especially in 31:24, where "Moses finished writing in a book the words of this law from the beginning to end." This is the most comprehensive statement of Moses' writing found in the Pentateuch.

Deuteronomy 31:30 also associates Moses with the words of the song he taught the Israelites "from beginning to end." The song, recorded in chapter 32, is one of the most powerful hymns in Scripture. Another influential hymn, the song of victory found in Exodus 15, is also linked with Moses in the opening verse.

The book of Numbers refers to Mosaic authorship only in connection with the list of campsites recorded in chapter 33. Verse 2 states that Moses recorded the stages in Israel's journeys at the Lord's command. This unadorned list of places almost takes the form of a diary.

5. Ronald B. Allen, "Numbers," in *EBC* (Grand Rapids: Zondervan, 1990), 2:668.

Most of Deuteronomy is actually cast in the form of several addresses by Moses to the new generation of Israelites. The prominence of the spoken word fits in with Moses' role as a prophet, for the prophets were spokesmen before they were writers. Moses' words could have been preserved by scribes or by some of the seventy elders who regularly assisted him. As noted above, Deuteronomy 31 mentions that Moses wrote down the law and gave it to the priests and Levites (vv. 9, 24). The oral dissemination of God's Word was greatly strengthened by the written transmission.[6]

In the rest of the Old Testament. The other books of the Old Testament refer to the Pentateuch often, and almost invariably mention Moses in the immediate contexts. After Moses' death, God instructed Joshua and, by implication, the Israelites "to obey all the law" given by Moses and to meditate upon the "Book of the Law" day and night (Josh. 1:7-8). At the covenant renewal ceremony at Mount Ebal Joshua built "an altar of uncut stones" following the instructions written in the Book of the Law of Moses (Josh. 8:31). Such an altar was specified in Exodus 20:25. Joshua 8:34-35 emphasizes that all the words of the law were read to the people. Joshua did not omit a word. The description indicates that extensive portions of the law were already written down at this early date. In Joshua's farewell address to the nation he urges the people to be faithful to God by obeying "all that is written in the Book of the Law of Moses" (Josh. 23:6).

Another challenge to keep the decrees and commands written in the law of Moses was given by David to his son Solomon just before his death (1 Kings 2:3). There are a number of references to the law in 2 Kings, and all of them are closely linked with Deuteronomy. Amaziah's merciful treatment of the sons of the men who killed his father is tied to Deuteronomy 24:16, quoted in full in 2 Kings 14:6. Likewise, the reigns of Hezekiah and Josiah were marked by obedience to the law of Moses. Josiah, especially, served the Lord with all his heart and soul "in accordance with all the law of Moses" (2 Kings 18:6; 23:2). This emphasis upon Deuteronomy in the references in Kings and, to some extent, in Joshua has led to the view that Moses' name was first associated with some laws, then with the book of Deuteronomy and, finally, with the whole Pentateuch.[7] Yet the strong implication in Scripture is that the whole law, not just Deuteronomy, was attributed to Moses from the very first. Deuteronomy's hortatory character lent itself more readily to citation, but this does not mean that Moses had no connection to the earlier books.

Scholars are agreed that by the time of Ezra and Nehemiah in the fifth century B.C. the Pentateuch was attributed to Moses. The phrase the "Book of Moses" appears in Ezra 6:18 and Nehemiah 13:1 as well as 2 Chronicles 25:4. During the sacred seventh month Ezra read the law to the men and women as-

6. Kenneth Kitchen, *Ancient Orient and Old Testament* (Chicago: InterVarsity, 1966), p. 135.
7. LaSor et al, *Survey*, p. 62.

sembled in the square before the Water Gate. The people stood from daybreak till noon and listened attentively (Neh. 8:3). Ezra also read from "the Book of the Law of God" each of the seven days of the Feast of Tabernacles later that same month (Neh. 8:17). As the people understood the law and responded to it, they were filled with great joy (Neh. 8:12, 17).

In the New Testament. The connection between Moses and the Pentateuch is even more direct in the New Testament, and nowhere is there any hint that some other author was involved. Whereas there are numerous references to the "Law of Moses" or the "Book of Moses" (cf. Mark 12:26), sometimes the one word "Moses" is equivalent to the Pentateuch. Three times in Luke the phrase "Moses and the Prophets" apparently refers to the entire Old Testament (16:29, 31; 24:27). In Acts 26:22 Luke quotes Paul's reference to predictions made by "the prophets and Moses."

The Pauline epistles use "Moses" in a similar way. In Romans 10:5 Paul says that "Moses describes . . . the righteousness that is by the law," and he goes on to quote Leviticus 18:5. Second Corinthians 3:15 refers to the veil that covers the hearts of the Jews "when Moses is read." Clearly, "Moses" denotes the "books of Moses."

Each of the gospels contains references to Moses and his writings, but the most important is probably the gospel of John. In chapter one the apostle states that "the law was given through Moses" (v. 17), and in verse 45 he reports that Philip told Nathanael that he had "found the one Moses wrote about in the Law," Jesus of Nazareth, who was the Messiah. Jesus Himself declared that Moses wrote about Him, but the Jews did not believe on Christ because they did not believe what Moses wrote (John 5:46-47). As His dispute with the Jews heated up, Jesus noted that Moses had indeed given them the law but none of them kept the law (John 7:19). Among the specific commands given by Moses and the patriarchs was the circumcision of baby boys when they were eight days old. Even if the eighth day fell on the Sabbath the child was circumcised. Jesus then goes on to ask why the Jews complained so loudly when He healed the sick on the Sabbath (John 7:21-23). In this debate, Jesus agreed with the Jews that the Pentateuch came from Moses. This was the one point on which they saw eye to eye. Significantly, the reference to Moses giving them circumcision implicitly attributes the authorship of Genesis to Moses also, since the institution of circumcision as the covenant sign is described in Genesis 17. Genesis is the most difficult of the five books to link to Moses, although it stands as a necessary prelude to Exodus-Deuteronomy.

POSSIBLE SOURCES USED BY MOSES

The claim that Moses wrote the Pentateuch does not eliminate the need to ask whether or not he used sources. "Source criticism" is sometimes equated with the Documentary Hypothesis (see below), but that represents only one possible way of looking at the issue. Since most writers do use sources, it is entirely possible that Moses had at his disposal both ancient and contemporary records to supplement divine revelation. This question is particularly important for Genesis, since the events discussed preceded Moses' lifetime by many centuries. Did Moses receive his information via oral tradition carefully passed on from generation to generation and then transmitted through the patriarchs? Were the accounts about Adam and Eve in the Garden of Eden revealed directly to Moses by God, or were they preserved in some written or oral form? The materials in Genesis 1-11 are the most difficult to account for because of their antiquity and scope.

THE TABLET (TÔLEDÔTH) THEORY

In 1936 P. J. Wiseman suggested that the key to understanding the sources of Genesis lay in the Hebrew term *tôledôt*, translated "account" or "generations," which divides Genesis into ten sections.[8] This is the word rendered *geneseōs* in the Septuagint, which has given us the title "Genesis" for the whole book. Wiseman theorized that each occurrence of *tôledôt* represented the conclusion of a tablet written or owned by the man whose name it contained. Such a record would correspond to the usual practice in the ancient Near East of ending a text with a colophon, which identified the scribe and the time when the tablet was written. If the tablet belonged to a series, the colophon included the first few words of the next tablet as a "catch-line" so that the proper sequence could be maintained.[9] Thus, the description of Terah as "the father of Abram, Nahor and Haran" in Genesis 11:26 functions as a catch-line and is repeated in the first words of the new "tablet," verse 27.[10] The first two occurrences of *tôledôt* are the most unusual. In 2:4 there is no name after the word "account," and in 5:1 the word "book" (*sēper*) is included: "This is the written account of Adam's line." According to Wiseman's theory, the material between 2:4 and 5:1 constitutes the "account" of Adam. The final occurrence of the term is found in 37:2, the account of Jacob. No additional tablets are necessary after that point, since the setting of most of Genesis 37-50 is Egypt, and Moses could have gained the necessary information verbally from the Israelites.

The foregoing theory is certainly an attractive one and has been ably defended by R. K. Harrison in his *Introduction to the Old Testament*. The discovery of written sources could solve the problem of Moses' remoteness from the events he describes and would fit in nicely with the known customs of the day.

8. P. J. Wiseman, *New Discoveries in Babylonia About Genesis* (London: Marshall, Morgan & Scott, 1936), p. 46.
9. R. K. Harrison, *Introduction to the Old Testament* (Grand Rapids: Eerdmans, 1969), p. 544.
10. Ibid., p. 549.

Yet the theory has serious shortcomings which must be addressed. First, *tôledôt* almost always goes more naturally with the following verses, not those that precede. Often it is immediately followed by a list of descendants, as in 5:1; 11:10, 27; 25:12; and 36:1. This is also true outside of Genesis, where the "account" of Aaron and Moses refers to their "generations" in Numbers 3:1-2 (cf. Ruth 4:18). Hence, "this is the account" should be understood as a title rather than a postscript.[11]

Second, the tablet theory implies that writing is as old as man himself, especially if "the book of the generations of Adam" (5:1) refers to material preserved by Adam or his immediate family. Although the Bible portrays Adam as a highly intelligent being, it does not insist that he invented writing. The "book" or "written account" could easily mean that Genesis 5 is the written record of the descendants of Adam—not that Adam himself did any writing. We would also wonder what language was spoken by Adam and all of mankind prior to the Tower of Babel. Would Moses have been able to read any of their written materials?

A third objection to taking *tôledôt* as a conclusion comes from the unlikely scenario that developed. Ishmael would be the one who preserved the story of Abraham (11:27–25:12); Isaac told the story of Ishmael (25:13-19); Esau kept the records of Jacob (25:19–36:1); and Jacob those of Esau (36:2–37:2). Because of the rivalry and jealousy that divided these two sets of brothers, it is hard to understand how any of these tablets would have been written.[12] Jacob and Esau in particular had almost no contact after Jacob fled for his life to Paddan Aram (Gen. 28:2).

OTHER POSSIBLE SOURCES

The only specific source quoted in the Pentateuch is "the Book of the Wars of the Lord" in Numbers 21:14. By way of contrast, the writers of Kings and Chronicles referred to numerous sources, such as the annals of the kings of Judah and Israel and the written records of various prophets (e.g., 2 Chron. 9:29). Scholars have suggested that although Moses does not mention sources, he probably did make use of sources. Since genealogical records were often kept (cf. 1 Chron. 4:33; 2 Chron. 12:15) it is likely that chapters delineating family relationships had some written antecedents. This could explain the use of "book" (i.e., "written account") at the beginning of Genesis 5, a list of Adam's descendants.[13] The famous "Table of Nations" in Genesis 10 might also fall under this

---

11. See Cyrus Gordon, "Higher Criticism and Forbidden Fruit," *Christianity Today* 4 (1959), p. 133; Archer, *Survey*, p. 171.
12. See the fine summary of these arguments by Derek Kidner, *Genesis*, TOTC (Chicago: InterVarsity, 1967), pp. 23-24.
13. Ibid., p. 80.

category, along with the genealogy of Shem in Genesis 11:10-26. The book of Numbers contains census lists (chaps. 1-4, 26) which may have been preserved by the Levites or the elders who assisted Moses.

Speiser has suggested that Genesis 14 is an adaptation of a foreign document owing to its unusual terminology and its international scope.[14] Only in this chapter do we find the expression "Valley of Siddim" for the Dead Sea (vv. 3, 8, 10). Another clue is the reference to "Abram the Hebrew" in verse 13, for "Hebrew" is the way non-Jews sometimes speak of them (cf. Gen. 39:14, 17). From a historical perspective the chapter contains a detailed account of two warring coalitions, including a reference to Amraphel King of Shinar (vv. 1, 9). "Shinar" is not used for "Babylonia" except in 10:10 and 11:2. The writer felt the need to explain certain terms: "Bela" is equal to "Zoar" (vv. 3, 8); "Siddim" is "the Salt Sea" (v. 3); and "the Valley of Shaveh" is identified as "the King's Valley" (v. 17). These parenthetical explanations would have been necessary if a foreign source were being adapted.

"The Book of the Wars of the Lord" is mentioned only in Numbers 21:14 introducing a short, poetic selection dealing with the march around Moab. Presumably this book commemorated God's intervention on Israel's behalf as the people struggled against numerous enemies. Harrison says that this source was "in its earlier stages of writing during the late wilderness period."[15] A comparable source was the Book of Jashar, quoted in Joshua 10:13 and 2 Samuel 1:18. Both of these excerpts are given in poetic form and may reflect the same kind of literature as the Book of Wars. Apparently Israelites other than Moses were interested in preserving accounts of the nation's experiences under the blessing and protection of God. Possibly the "poets" whose work is quoted in Numbers 21:27-30 played a role in the composition of the Book of the Wars of the Lord.

Another poet of importance in Numbers was the prophet Balaam. His oracles in chapters 23 and 24 predict a glowing future for Israel as God's people prepared to cross the Jordan River and enter the Promised Land. Most scholars believe the Balaam oracles found their way into the Pentateuch long after Moses, but it is worth noting that Balaam is mentioned again in Joshua 13:22. If Joshua knew about him, it is possible that Balaam's prophecies were passed along to Moses a short time after they were delivered.

INDICATIONS OF POST-MOSAIC ADDITIONS

Any objective treatment of the authorship of the Pentateuch must take into account those statements that call into question the likelihood that Moses wrote them. The most obvious problem of course is the description of Moses' death in Deuteronomy 34:1-12. Even the rabbis taught that these verses were added by

14. E. A. Speiser, ed., *Genesis*, AB (Garden City, N.Y.: Doubleday, 1964), p. 108.
15. Harrison, *Introduction*, pp. 616-17.

Joshua to complete the law, and conservative scholars have generally agreed with this conclusion.[16] It is not uncommon for books of the Old Testament to end with an appendix not written by the main author. For example, Jeremiah 51:64 states that "the words of Jeremiah end here," but chapter 52 presents an account of the fall of Jerusalem which is very similar to 2 Kings 25. Jeremiah 52 may very well be an appendix added by Baruch or a later editor.

Another problem passage is Numbers 12:3, a verse that describes Moses as the most humble man on earth. How could Moses praise himself so highly if he were indeed such a humble man? While Delitzsch and others defend the Mosaic origin of the statement in light of the objectivity required by the context, it is not necessary to insist that Moses wrote it. Instead, the verse could very well have been added by a later editor who inserted it as a parenthetical comment. Perhaps it was again Joshua who was directed by the Holy Spirit to add the verse. According to Joshua 24:26, Moses' successor wrote some words in the Book of the Law. If this "Book" refers to the Pentateuch, as it usually does (cf. Neh. 8:18), we may have an indication of further editorial activity on the part of Joshua.[17]

Other verses appear to come from a time far later than either Moses or Joshua. Genesis 36:31 mentions kings who ruled over Edom "before any Israelite king reigned," implying that there was now a king ruling Israel. Since Saul was Israel's first king, a date after 1000 B.C. is suggested.[18] One might argue that Moses knew that eventually Israel would have a king (cf. Gen. 17:6; Deut. 17:14-20), but this may be forcing the issue. It is more likely that a later editor added this note during the period of the monarchy.[19]

Further editorial activity is seen in the early chapters of Deuteronomy in connection with the displacement of certain peoples. Four passages in particular appear to be parenthetical comments dealing with the Rephaites (or "Rephaim") who used to live in Transjordan (Deut. 2:10-12, 20-23; 3:11, 13). The purpose of these comments was to help the Israelites understand how the Lord used their relatives—the Edomites, Moabites, and Ammonites—as well as their own armies to drive out the Rephaites. Since this region was part of the land given to the Israelites, it was important that they be aware of its history. Deuteronomy 2:12 compares the victory of the Edomites to Israel's triumph as they took possession of the Promised Land. This implies that the conquest of Canaan had already taken place. Similarly, the statement that Og's iron bed was "still in Rabbah of the Ammonites" (Deut. 3:11) indicates that many years had elapsed since the conquest of Bashan under Moses and Joshua. Military conquest and the

16. See Baba Bathra 14b; Harrison, *Introduction*, p. 661; Archer, *Survey*, p. 263.
17. See a discussion of this issue in Marten H. Woudstra, *The Book of Joshua*, NICOT (Grand Rapids: Eerdmans, 1981), p. 357.
18. LaSor et al, *Survey*, p. 60.
19. Ronald Youngblood, *Faith of Our Fathers* (Glendale, Calif.: Regal, 1976), pp. 105-6.

custom of giving new names to cities and districts probably lay behind the "up-dating" of certain biblical names. Scholars have noticed that Abram's pursuit of Lot and the people of Sodom took him as far as Dan (Gen. 14:14), yet "Dan" was a name given to the site of Laish (or "Leshem") when the tribe of Dan migrated to the north after the conquest of Canaan (cf. Josh. 19:47; Judg. 18:29).[20] Instead of insisting that the appearance of "Dan" in Genesis 14 proves that the chapter was written long after Moses, we should probably recognize that an editor changed the name from "Laish" to "Dan" at a later time. This same sort of proleptic use of a name is illustrated by Bethel. Although the city of "Luz" was not given the name "Bethel" until Jacob's dream there (Gen. 28:19), Genesis 12:8 says that Abraham pitched his tent near Bethel. The mention of "Rameses" in Genesis 47:11 may represent a similar updating (cf. Ex. 1:11).

Genesis 12:6 states that when Abram entered the Promised Land "the Canaanites were then in the land" (cf. 13:7). Some commentators interpret this to mean that by the time Genesis was written the Canaanites were no longer in the land because the Israelites had displaced them. But the point could well be that just as the Israelites were confronted by the Canaanites as they prepared to invade the land, so Abram had encountered them centuries earlier. They were there then and they are still there "now" (cf. Josh. 14:11).[21]

In conclusion we can see that the possible post-Mosaic materials in the Pentateuch are relatively minor. The bulk of the five books could indeed have been written by Moses or under his supervision. If there were in fact editors who added to or modified the work of Moses, their activity was superintended by the same Holy Spirit who inspired all Scripture. Any changes made by Joshua, Samuel, Ezra, or anyone else were prompted by the Spirit of God and conveyed exactly what He intended (2 Pet. 1:21).

ALTERNATIVE VIEWS OF THE FORMATION OF THE PENTATEUCH

Most scholars do not believe that Moses wrote much of the Pentateuch, and many would argue that he wrote none of it. They base their arguments on literary, historical, and theological grounds and have developed elaborate theories that attempt to explain just where the Pentateuch did come from. To understand these theories and the many currents that have contributed to their development, a historical survey is in order.

EARLY AND MEDIEVAL PERIODS

When the New Testament was being completed, Jewish writers such as Philo and Josephus clearly regarded Moses as the author of the Pentateuch. Ac-

20. LaSor et al, *Survey*, p. 60.
21. Kidner, *Genesis*, p. 16.

cording to the Talmud, Moses wrote everything except the last eight verses of Deuteronomy, which are attributed to Joshua. Nonetheless, a Gnostic leader from Alexandria named Valentinus denied the authenticity of portions of the law and the prophets. The Nazarites, a Jewish-Christian sect, rejected the idea that Moses wrote the Pentateuch, and one of the church Fathers named Epiphanius noted that the Ebionites did not accept parts of the Pentateuch.[22] The pseudepigraphical book of 2 Esdras stated that Ezra reproduced the law and other Jewish books (14:19-48) with the help of scribes who wrote very rapidly. This legend may have influenced Jerome to believe that at least the final form of the Pentateuch came from Ezra's time.

Ibn Hazam of Cordova, Spain (about A.D. 994), argued that Ezra was the main author of the Pentateuch. The great Spanish scholar Ibn Ezra (1092-1167) supported Mosaic authorship but did allow for post-Mosaic insertions in the Pentateuch.[23] Like others before him, Ibn Ezra did not believe that Moses wrote about his own death.

REFORMATION AND RENAISSANCE

With the end of the Middle Ages came a renewed interest in the original languages of the Bible and a growing concern about matters of authorship and authenticity. During the Reformation, however, there were only a few attempts to explore such issues. One of Martin Luther's rivals in Germany, a man named Andreas Bodenstein (1480-1541), argued that if Moses did not write the account of his death in Deuteronomy 34, he did not write any of the Pentateuch, since it reflected the same literary style. A Spanish Jesuit, B. Pereira, wrote a book on Genesis (1589) in which he argued for scribal additions and revision. In a work entitled *Leviathan* (1651), the deistic philosopher Thomas Hobbes defended the view that Moses wrote selected sections attributed to him but most of the Pentateuch was written long after Moses.[24]

Of greater importance was the work of the Jewish philosopher Benedict Spinoza, who was heavily influenced by the idealism of René Descartes. In his *Tractatus Theologico-Politicus* published in 1670, Spinoza outlined a systematic approach to the study of the Pentateuch in an attempt to discover the purpose and date of writing. He was bothered by the fact that Moses was referred to consistently in the third person, "he," so he decided that Ezra probably compiled the Pentateuch, using some materials that did come from Moses.[25] Richard Simon (1638-1712), a Roman Catholic priest and a professor of philosophy, concluded that the stylistic variety seen in the Pentateuch along with logical and chronolog-

22. Harrison, *Introduction*, pp. 4-5.
23. Ibid., p.7.
24. Thomas Hobbes, *Leviathan* (1651), III, chap. 33, cited by Harrison, *Introduction*, p. 10.
25. Archer, *Survey*, p. 83; Harrison, *Introduction*, p. 10.

ical problems proved that Moses could not have been the author. Whoever the later writer was, however, he did use older sources. On the Protestant side, an Armenian theologian named Jean Le Clerc published a book in 1685 in which he agreed with Simon that the Pentateuch came from a later date. According to Le Clerc it was written prior to the Samaritan schism in the fourth century B.C.[26]

THE DOCUMENTARY HYPOTHESIS

Influenced by the work of Spinoza, Simon, and Le Clerc and by the prevailing spirit of the times, a number of scholars began to look for sources and documents to explain the formation of the Pentateuch more adequately. During the course of the eighteenth and nineteenth centuries a theory was developed that continues to exert tremendous influence in the present day. It is called the documentary hypothesis.

The growth of source criticism. A theologian named Campegius Vitringa suggested in 1689 that Moses made use of ancient sources when he wrote about the patriarchs. Abraham himself, he surmised, may have brought written sources from Mesopotamia. The first real attempt to identify the sources of Genesis was made by the French physician, Jean Astruc, who in 1753 published a treatise on Genesis written in French entitled *Conjectures About the Original Memoirs Which It Appears Moses Used to Compose the Book of Genesis.*[27] In this work Astruc argued that the main clue to some of the sources was the two names for God, Elohim ("God") and Yahweh (Jehovah, "Lord"). Genesis 1, for example, represented a source in which the author knew only the name Elohim, whereas Genesis 2 constituted a second source whose author was familiar only with Yahweh. Astruc placed the chapters that used Elohim in one column (A) and those that used Yahweh in another column (B). He also laid out two other columns for repetitious materials and for non-Israelite sources, such as Genesis 14. When Moses wrote, he put the materials from these four columns together in order to form a connected narrative. Astruc did not deny the Mosaic authorship of the Pentateuch in his attempt to identify sources, but his views laid the groundwork for such a conclusion.

To understand the significance of Astruc, we must realize that at the time he wrote classical scholars were wrestling with the authorship of the Homeric epics. Men such as Frederick Wolf were dividing Homer's *Iliad* and *Odyssey* into many different sources.[28] This interest in source analysis stimulated intensive study of Astruc's suggestions regarding the Pentateuch.

26. Eugene Carpenter, "Pentateuch," *ISBE* 3 (1986), p. 743.
27. The French title: *Conjectures sur les memoirs dont il parait que Moyse s'est servi pour composer le livre de la Genese.*
28. Archer, *Survey,* p. 84.

About three decades after Astruc, the German rationalist Johann G. Eichhorn published an *Einleitung*, or *Introduction to the Old Testament*, in 1780-83. Eichhorn divided Genesis and the first two chapters of Exodus into the J (Jahwist or Yahwist or Jehovah) and E (Elohist) sources, and he discussed the possibility of finding sources behind Leviticus also. He attempted to show how the supposedly two accounts of the Flood corresponded to the J and E sources and how they tended to use characteristic words and phrases in addition to different divine names. Literary style thus became an important criterion for identifying sources. At first Eichhorn asserted that Moses was the one who edited these sources, but the later editions of this *Introduction* ruled out Mosaic involvement.

A somewhat different approach was taken by Alexander Geddes, a Scottish Roman Catholic theologian whose works were published between 1792 and 1800. In his fragmentary hypothesis, Geddes argued that the Pentateuch was compiled in the time of Solomon by a redactor (editor) who utilized numerous fragments. He used the divine names to identify two series of sources but other criteria were also necessary. Among the many fragments were some that were as old as Moses or even older. Geddes included the book of Joshua in his study and suggested that the same editor put together all six books. The notion of a "Hexateuch" has found support among a number of modern scholars also.

In 1798 Karl D. Ilgen divided up the book of Genesis into seventeen different sources. In his analysis Ilgen split the E document into E1 and E2, assigning Genesis 1-11 to the latter source. He agreed with Geddes that it was necessary to use criteria other than the divine names in order to identify sources.

The fragmentary hypothesis was further developed by Johann Vater in his commentary on the Pentateuch, published in 1802. Vater was the first to analyze the entire Pentateuch, and he identified about forty different fragments as source materials. Like Geddes he acknowledged that some of these fragments may have belonged to the Mosaic era, but the final writing and editing of the Pentateuch was assigned to the Babylonian Exile (586-38 B.C.).

The work of Wilhelm M. L. DeWette marks another important stage in the development of the documentary hypothesis. In his *Beitrage zur Einleitung in das Alte Testament* published in 1807, DeWette defended the fragmentary hypothesis, but he asserted that no part of the Pentateuch could be dated prior to David (1010-970 B.C.). And the book of Deuteronomy was none other than the Book of the Law found in the Temple by Hilkiah the priest at the start of Josiah's great reform in 621 B.C. (2 Kings 22:8). DeWette theorized that Deuteronomy was written at King Josiah's command in order to support the emphasis upon a central place of worship. Too many Jews were sacrificing at the high places, and Josiah needed a way to stop them so there would be greater religious and political unity in the land. Deuteronomy thus became known as document "D," a third major source along with J and E.

Before the documentary hypothesis gained general acceptance, a number of scholars set forth the supplementary theory. Heinrich Ewald took issue with DeWette's fragmentary approach in his work entitled *The Composition of Genesis Critically Examined* (1823). Ewald noted that the remarkable unity of Genesis could not be accounted for by an appeal to an assortment of fragments. A more likely explanation was that the Elohist document lay behind the composition of the Pentateuch. Later, parts of a J source were inserted into the E document. In 1840 DeWette supported Ewald's view of the Elohist document, agreeing that a supplemented E source made more sense than the fragmentary hypothesis. Additional support came from J. C. F. Tuch, who in a commentary on Genesis (1838) designated the E document as the key source and called it the *grundschrift*, the foundation document of the Pentateuch. This was supplemented by materials from the J document during the time of Solomon.[29]

In 1840 Ewald published a book entitled *History of the People of Israel* in which he changed his views somewhat. He now believed that E, J, and D could not account for all of the Pentateuch and that it was necessary to posit other sources. He spoke of a "Book of Covenants" composed in Judah during the time of the judges by someone who added to a small Mosaic core of material. This was supplemented by a "Book of Origins" written in the Solomonic era by a Levite who incorporated much of document E. Later writers added a biography of Moses, included the name "Yahweh" in the text and generally reedited the entire corpus. This formulation of Ewald is sometimes referred to as the crystallization theory because each successive writer reworks all of the previous material rather than adding his contribution and leaving the rest untouched.[30]

While DeWette and Ewald were shifting their positions in an attempt to arrive at a satisfactory hypothesis, an important volume on biblical theology was published in Berlin by Wilhelm Vatke. Vatke looked at biblical studies through the eyes of a Hegelian system of philosophy that deeply influenced his thinking. According to Hegel the development of religion was a three stage process: (1) a natural phase, in which God and nature are in some way equated; (2) a phase in which God was considered to be personal spirit; (3) a phase in which God is regarded as infinite spirit. Vatke arranged the biblical materials to fit this scheme: (1) Judges and early monarchy (thesis); (2) the prophets and later monarchy (antithesis); (3) the post-exilic period (synthesis). The Pentateuch came under stage 3, when Israel's legislation was formally institutionalized. Moses' monotheism fit the synthesis stage, and therefore the Pentateuch was the product of the state, not the basis and constitution for the state. Even the law's "foundation document" may have come from the period of the Exile. Vatke's views were consid-

29. Harrison, *Introduction*, p. 16.
30. Archer, *Survey*, p. 86.

ered radical at the time, but they had a powerful impact upon Wellhausen in the decades that followed.[31]

The last important development in the documentary hypothesis prior to the work of Graf and Wellhausen was found in the 1853 book of Hermann Hupfeld, *The Sources of Genesis* (German, *Die Quellen der Genesis*). Hupfeld examined the Elohist document in great detail and decided that E really consisted of two documents, although the same name for God was used in both. The E material beginning with Genesis 20 was very close to J in its vocabulary, style, and general content, closer, in fact, than it was to the rest of E. Hence, Hupfeld divided E into E1, which was the "foundation document" and the older, and E2, which resembled J. The document designated E1 contained considerable priestly material and was renamed "P" by later critics. Many of the early chapters of Genesis were relegated to E1.

In the course of his analysis Hupfeld stated that these documents made sense when studied individually and had thus been separate literary units at one time. Eventually these units were combined through the work of a final editor or redactor who wove the documents into a continuous whole. Wherever the wrong words or phrases appeared in a given document, the mistake was conveniently blamed on the redactor.

The Graf-Wellhausen Hypothesis. Not long after the work of Hupfeld the documentary hypothesis reached what has been called its classical form, mainly through the efforts of Karl Graf and Julius Wellhausen. Graf followed the lead of his teacher, Eduard Reuss, who believed that the Elohist document was the latest rather than the earliest of the documents. At first Graf had regarded Hupfeld's E1 as the "foundation document" that was later supplemented by J. But the presence of levitical laws in E1 that seemed later than Deuteronomy (621 B.C.) convinced Graf that the legal portions of E1 should be dated in the time of Ezra. He maintained, however, that the narrative parts of E1 were very early, until the arguments of Kuenen to the contrary won him over. The so-called "Holiness Code," Leviticus 1-26, was assigned to the time of Ezekiel, although it was part of the priestly code combined with E, J, and D by Ezra.

Graf's contemporary, Abraham Kuenen, was a Dutch scholar who was credited with proving the unity and the lateness of E1 (= P, the "priestly document") in his book *De Godsdienst van Israel* (*The Worship of God in Israel*, 1869). Kuenen also tackled the question of whether E2 (= E) or J was the older document, and his defense of the J-E order has not been reversed.

The man who did the most to refine and popularize the documentary hypothesis was the brilliant German scholar, Julius Wellhausen, an expert in Semitic languages and a theologian who had studied under Ewald. Wellhausen

31. Carpenter, "Pentateuch," pp. 744-45.

adopted the conclusions of Hupfeld, Graf, and Kuenen and, along with Vatke, was heavily influenced by Hegelian philosophy. Hegel's dialectic approach went hand in hand with Charles Darwin's evolutionary model set forth in his *The Origin of Species*. Buoyed by the popularity of Darwin, Wellhausen's view that Israel's religion developed from a naturalistic animism to an advanced monotheism met with almost immediate acceptance.

His overall thesis was outlined in *The Composition of the Hexateuch* (German, *Die Composition des Hexateuch*, 1876-77) and the *Introduction to the History of Israel* (German, *Prolegomena zur Geschichte Israels*, 1878). According to Wellhausen the early parts of the Pentateuch consisted of the J and E documents. J was written about 850 B.C. by someone from Judah who emphasized biography as well as ethical and religious concerns. E, on the other hand, came from the northern kingdom about 750 B.C. and probably displayed more objectivity in his narrative style. The emphasis upon Bethel, Shechem (Gen. 28:17; 31:13; 33:19), and Joseph, the ancestor of the tribes of Ephraim and Manasseh, helps establish the northern provenance of E. The two documents were combined by a redactor (R J-E) about 650 B.C. D was the book discovered and probably written by the high priest Hilkiah in 621 B.C., incorporating a number of exhortations and laws that may have been a reaction to the wicked reign of Manasseh. About 550 B.C. D was put together with J-E by a redactor (R D). The last document was P (equivalent to E1). Wellhausen followed Graf and Kuenen in assigning a post-exilic date to this source. Ezra (about 450 B.C.) was the main compiler and editor of the legal and ceremonial material that comprised P, but Ezekiel was the author of the "holiness code," Leviticus 17-26. Genealogies, origins, sacrifices, and a description of the Tabernacle were all part of the subject matter of P. With the assistance of a final redactor (R P), the "priestly document" was combined with the other three (J, E, D) to form a continuous narrative. Between 400 and 200 B.C. some minor changes were made, and the Pentateuch was complete.

The documentary hypothesis as explained by Wellhausen took the scholarly world by storm, receiving the enthusiastic support of many theologians. In Germany H. Cornhill and C. Steuernagel used the Graf-Wellhausen theory as they wrote introductions to the Old Testament. In England William Robertson Smith became a convinced documentarist and wrote several books in support of the theory, *The Old Testament in the Jewish Church* being his most important contribution. The English-speaking world received its finest description of Wellhausen's views from the pen of S. R. Driver, who published his monumental *Introduction to the Literature of the Old Testament* in 1891. It was Driver who made an appreciation of critical studies a necessity for British scholars from that time on. In the United States, Charles Augustus Briggs of Union Seminary was the first to espouse the documentary hypothesis in his volume on *The Higher Criticism of the Hexateuch* (1893). More than a decade later Briggs collaborated with Francis Brown and S. R. Driver to produce the renowned *Hebrew Lexicon of the Old Testament* (1906), affectionately known to many generations of Hebrew students simply as "BDB." This volume incorporated many of the conclusions of the documentary school.

Nineteenth-century opposition. As the documentary hypothesis grew in popularity and influence, conservative scholars vigorously opposed it. In Germany support for Mosaic authorship was led by E. D. Hengstenberg, whose book *The Genuineness of the Pentateuch* was translated into English in 1847. Two of Hengstenberg's students also played a significant role in the fight against source criticism. Moritz Drechsler published a work on the unity and genuineness of Genesis (1838), and C. F. Keil became the most prominent conservative during the last half of the century. A close associate of Keil, and a man with whom he collaborated in an excellent series of commentaries, was Franz Delitzsch. Delitzsch did make room for a supplementary theory of sorts, but he did argue that whatever the text attributed to Moses was indeed written by him, whereas other portions were added by priests during the conquest and settlement of Canaan.[32]

Other voices were equally firm in denouncing the findings of higher criticism. Gerhaardus Vos attacked the view that the priestly material was late and spoke out in favor of the Mosaic authorship of the Pentateuch (1886). In England, the eminent archaeologist A. H. Sayce began to point out the fallacies of the documentary hypothesis although he had subscribed to the liberal view earlier. Sayce wrote *The "Higher Criticism" and the Verdict of the Monuments* (1894) and *Monument Facts and Higher Critical Fancies* (1904). A more comprehensive treatment of the subject was undertaken by William Henry Green of Princeton Theological Seminary. His criticism of the Wellhausen hypothesis is best seen in two books published in 1895: *The Unity of the Book of Genesis* and *The Higher Criticism of the Pentateuch*. In these works Green demonstrated that Wellhausen could not explain the biblical data and that his methodology was inconsistent and contradictory.

Weaknesses of the Documentary Hypothesis. The opposition to the documentary hypothesis arose partly because of the subjective basis on which it rests. None of the alleged documents has ever been found in spite of the assurances of scholars that at one time each document had an existence of its own. This objection could perhaps be ignored if the critics agreed on the content of each document, but this is decidedly not the case. There is considerable debate about particular passages, and the same verse might be assigned to E or P by different scholars. As shown below, respected authorities have tentatively identified additional sources (K, L, or S) in their attempt to understand the origins of the Penta-

32. Harrison, *Introduction*, p. 23.

teuch. Such subjective handling of the text does little to increase one's confidence in the method.

The most important criticism leveled against the documentary hypothesis has to do with the use of divine names to determine sources, especially J and E. A number of scholars have noted that in ancient Near Eastern literature it is common for a deity to have more than one name. In Egypt the sun-god Ra was frequently identified with Amon, the ramheaded god of Thebes, and the combination of Amon-Re appears in many texts from the eighteenth dynasty on. The god Osiris is referred to as Wennofer and two other names in the Berlin stela of Ikhernofret. In the prologue to the code of Hammurapi Ishtar is also called "Inanna" and "Telitum."[33] Cyrus Gordon has drawn attention to the Ugaritic god "Koshar and Hasis," a deity whose compound name occurs regularly in the Ras Shamra texts.[34] Such multiple compound names correspond to the biblical names Elohim (God) and Yahweh (LORD), which are often found together as "LORD God" (Gen. 2:4f.). Yet no one has suggested that different names signify different documents with respect to Egyptian or Mesopotamian texts. The reason the Bible uses Elohim in some passages and Yahweh in others depends on the nature of the passages. In Genesis 1 the generic "Elohim" fits in best with God's work as Creator (see pp. 26-27). Thus, the two accounts of creation in Genesis 1-2 do not reflect two authors but provide complementary descriptions of God's activity. Chapter 2 emphasizes the creation of man and gives more details about Adam and Eve and the Garden of Eden.

Similarly, the alleged duplicate accounts of other events often have a reasonable explanation. When Noah is told to take into the ark two of every kind of bird and animal in Genesis 6:19-20 and then seven in 7:2-3, the text clearly states that the "seven" applies to clean animals only. Critics use this apparent discrepancy and other aspects of the Flood story to illustrate how J and P were merged into one.[35] Another showcase for the documentary hypothesis is Genesis 37, where Joseph's sale is parceled up between J and E. The reference to both Midianites and Ishmaelites in verse 28 is taken as telltale evidence that we have two different accounts underlying the text. But as Kenneth Kitchen has shown, the terms "Midianites" and "Ishmaelites" overlap and refer basically to the same group (cf. Judg. 8:24).[36] The other supposed contradictions in the story can also be explained satisfactorily.[37]

Since the Pentateuch is a complex entity made up of prose and poetry and many literary forms, some scholars have looked at the wide variations in style

33. Kenneth Kitchen, *Ancient Orient*, p. 121.
34. Cyrus Gordon, "Higher Criticism and Forbidden Fruit," p. 132.
35. Norman Habel, *Literary Criticism of the Old Testament* (Philadelphia: Fortress, 1971), pp. 29-42.
36. Kitchen, *Ancient Orient*, p. 119.
37. See Kidner, *Genesis*, pp. 184-86.

and concluded that at least four authors were responsible for it all. It was not uncommon, however, to find such variety in other literature from the ancient Near East. For example, in the biographical inscription of the Egyptian official Uni (about 2400 B.C.), we find a combination of narrative, summary statements, a victory hymn, and a pair of refrains all inscribed on the same rock at the request of Uni. It is impossible to attribute this variety to different sources that had a literary prehistory.[38] Other extant literary material helps us identify the component parts of various genres. The study of genres—properly the sphere of form criticism—enables the reader to ascertain when he is dealing with a literary unit. As noted earlier, biblical covenants can be studied in light of the structure regularly found in ancient treaties, and this structure makes it difficult to divide up chapters such as Genesis 31 and Exodus 19-20 into J and E. If this is done, essential parts of the outline are missing. Similarly, Greta Hort has argued that the sequence of the plagues in Exodus 7-10 fits in with natural phenomena that would accompany an unusually high flooding of the Nile.[39] A parceling of these chapters into J and E would destroy the sequence. Of similar import is the occurence of Hebrew poetic devices, which often link two or three lines in a meaningful sequence. For example, in Genesis 30:23-24 there are two statements about Rachel's son Joseph. The verbs "taken away" (*'asap*) and "add" (*yosep*) sound very similar and probably constitute a wordplay on the name "Joseph." This word play would be lost if one were to divide these verses into two sources simply because Elohim occurs in verse 23 and Yahweh in verse 24.

A final weakness of the documentary hypothesis has to do with the uncertainty of the date of the documents, particularly the P sources. Was P really the latest of the sources as Kuenen and Wellhausen had asserted? Cyrus Gordon has observed that the verses that describe the specifications of Noah's ark in Genesis 6 (P, according to the critics) find a parallel in the dimensions of the boat in the Gilgamesh epic, a Mesopotamian literary piece written before all the Pentateuch.[40] In a similar vein, Yehezkel Kaufmann has assembled considerable data arguing that P precedes both Deuteronomy and the Babylonian exile.[41] His evidence brings into question the correctness of the JEDP sequence, and one might well ask whether the whole theory is not resting on a shaky formulation.

Twentieth-century developments. The weaknesses of the Graf-Wellhausen documentary formulations have brought about some changes in the overall theory along with responses that have sharply deviated from the basic principles of the documentarists. Yet in spite of all the challenges that have been hurled its

38. Kitchen, *Ancient Orient*, p. 125; Harrison, *Introduction*, p. 526.
39. *ZAW* 69 (1957), pp. 84-103; *ZAW* 70 (1958), pp. 48-59. Cf. Kitchen, *Ancient Orient*, pp. 128-29, 157-58.
40. Gordon, "Higher Criticism and Forbidden Fruit," p. 131.
41. Yehezkel Kaufmann, *The Religion of Israel* (Chicago: U. of Chicago, 1960), pp. 157-66, 169-70, 175-200.

way, the JEDP hypothesists continue to enjoy wide acceptance in the scholarly world.

There are, however, serious reservations about the use of Hegel's dialectic philosphy and Darwin's evolutionary approach as the foundation of the documentary hypothesis. Many scholars have rejected the validity of applying such models to religious history and to the origin of the Pentateuch.[42] In agreement with Kaufmann, some scholars have also begun to question the accepted dates of the various documents or even the existence of a particular document. Oestreicher (1923) and Welch (1924) placed the date of P prior to Josiah, and E. Robertson (1950) argued that Deuteronomy was written in the time of Samuel.[43] John van Seters goes in the opposite direction by assigning J to the exilic period and P to the post-exilic era. And according to Volz and Rudolph, E never existed as an independent document.[44] While some of the critics were eliminating documents, however, others attempted to identify new ones. Otto Eissfeldt proposed the existence of a "Lay Source" (L) embedded within J which reflected the nomadic ideals of the Rechabites and may have been written about 860 B.C. About five years later (1927) Julius Morgenstern announced the discovery of document K (for "Kenites"), which he felt was instrumental in the reforms of King Asa around 890 B.C. (cf. 1 Kings 15:9-15). In 1941 Harvard professor Robert Pfeiffer introduced document S, which stood for Mount Seir in Edom and which he separated from J and E materials in Genesis 1-38. According to Pfeiffer, S stemmed from the days of Solomon although additions were made several centuries later.[45] Perhaps at this point we should also mention the influential German scholars Gerhard von Rad and Martin Noth, even though their work will be discussed more completely under "Tradition History." Von Rad divided P into P(a) and P(b), whereas Noth posited the existence of a G (German, *grundschrift*) source as the foundation document behind JEDP.

To counteract the argument that the documentary hypothesis had no basis in ancient Near Eastern literature, Jeffrey Tigay has shown that the Gilgamesh Epic was compiled from originally independent Sumerian stories. First combined in the Old Babylonian period, this epic passed through several editorial stages before receiving its final form in the neo-Assyrian period.[46] The evolution of the Gilgamesh Epic is nonetheless different from the JEDP hypothesis, which posits

42. See W. Kaiser, Jr., "The Literary Form of Genesis 1-11," in J. Barton Payne *New Perspectives on the Old Testament* (Waco, Tex.: Word, 1970), p. 48; John Bright, "Modern Study of the Old Testament Literature," in *The Bible and the Ancient Near East*, ed. G. E. Wright (Garden City, N.Y.: Doubleday, 1961), pp. 13-31.
43. Edward Robertson, *The Old Testament Problem* (Manchester, England: University Press, 1950), p. 42.
44. Harrison, *Introduction*, p. 42.
45. Archer, *Survey*, p. 83.
46. Jeffrey H. Tigay, *Empirical Models for Biblical Criticism* (Philadelphia: U. of Pennsylvania, 1985), pp. 26-27.

a conflation of parallel extended narratives as opposed to the combination of individual stories. If anything, the Gilgamesh Epic might be an analogue to the development of an individual document such as J or E into an integrated narrative.[47] But the existence of such an independent document remains as hypothetical as ever.

FORM CRITICISM

During the twentieth century a number of critical methodologies have appeared to augment and in some cases challenge literary (or source) criticism. One of these is the form criticism (*Formgeschichte*) or genre/type criticism (*Gattungsgeschichte*) developed by Gunkel and Gressmann just after the turn of the century. An understanding of the literary genre and the social context out of which it arose contributes significantly to an appreciation of the text. A knowledge of the structure of a literary unit prevents the reader from dividing up what was intended to be a literary whole. On occasion this knowledge presents a formidable obstacle to those who are inclined to assign the various parts of such a unit to two or more documents.

As originally conceived by Gunkel and Gressmann, form criticism was primarily concerned with the oral or preliterary stage of the various genres.[48]

This assumes that an oral development lay behind every written document and that a knowledge of that development helps us understand the written text. All would agree that an awareness of the "situation in life," the cultural setting out of which a particular literary unit arose, is most helpful to an understanding of the passage. The emphasis upon the oral stage does not necessarily militate against the documentary hypothesis. Indeed, some scholars retain their commitment to the overall JEDP structure and utilize form criticism to further their understanding of the preliterary stage behind the documents. For example, form criticism has shown that the "authors" of the documents could more accurately be described as collectors or editors of traditional material.[49]

Yet there is a tendency among form critics to emphasize oral tradition at the expense of the written documents. Those who view Genesis as a collection of essays generally hold that these stories existed in a fluid form and were not written down until late in Israel's history. Ivan Engnell, a member of the "Uppsala School" of Sweden, repudiated the documentary hypothesis, arguing that Wellhausen's view of four parallel documents arose from a faulty European approach that failed to understand how oral tradition functioned in the Near East. Accord-

---

47. As noted by Henry T. C. Sun in "Torah and Gilgamesh: An Ancient Near Eastern Non-Analogue for the Documentary Hypothesis," a paper read at the Society of Biblical Literature meeting in Chicago, November 1988.
48. Gene M. Tucker, *Form Criticism of the Old Testament* (Philadelphia: Fortress, 1971), p. 1.
49. Ibid., p. 18.

ing to Engnell, most of the Pentateuchal material did not reach written form until exilic or post-exilic times.[50]

The views of Engnell and other Scandinavian scholars are discussed more fully in the section "Tradition Criticism." Before moving on to that topic we should note that form criticism is indeed also interested in the literary stage of the text.[51]

For conservatives this means that an investigation of the form of both smaller and larger portions of Scripture can be of great help in the interpretive process.[52] Chapter 4 is an attempt to explain the main types of literature found in the Pentateuch.

TRADITION CRITICISM

Closely related to form criticism is the method that has come to be known either as "tradition criticism" or "tradition history" (German, *Uberlieferungsgeschichte* or *Traditionsgeschichte*), a technique of approaching the Bible that is as difficult to define as form criticism. Its practitioners are many, and they do not always operate the same way. Some tradition critics emphasize the history of the preliterary stage of a book or an individual theme; others stress the history of the literary stages, a procedure not far removed from redaction criticism.[53] Broadly conceived, form criticism emphasizes the beginning of the process whereas tradition criticism examines any development prior to the final written product. Implicit in such an approach is the assumption that one can separate different layers in the growth of a tradition.

In order to accomplish his task, the tradition critic has four basic concerns. First, he is interested in the group or community associated with a tradition. It is important to know whether priests, prophets, or wise men were involved in shaping the tradition. Gerhard von Rad, whose work *The Problem of the Pentateuch* was extremely influential, attributed the homiletical style of Deuteronomy to the preaching of the Levites.

A second basic concern is the geographical setting. Cities such as Bethel and Shechem are viewed as repositories for various traditions about the patriarchs. Later these traditions were reworked as they made their way into the literature.

Third, the tradition critic—like the form critic—pays close attention to the social, political, and religious context behind the material. But whereas the form

---

50. Harrison, *Introduction*, pp. 67-68.
51. Tucker, *Form Criticism*, p. 18.
52. Note the studies on Deuteronomy and my dissertation on 1 and 2 Samuel, "The Apology of Hattusilis Compared with Other Political Self-Justifications of the Ancient Near East" (Ph.D. diss., Brandeis U., 1967; Ann Arbor, Mich.: University Microfilms 67-16, 588). Cf. P. Kyle McCarter, "The Apology of David," *JBL* 99 (1980): 489-504.
53. Tucker, *Form Criticism*, p. 19.

critic could be satisfied with establishing the "situation in life" related to a particular story or speech, the tradition critic tries to trace the changes in the situation. For example, some scholars believe that the cultic milieu behind Deuteronomy was the covenant renewal festival at Shechem (cf. Deut. 27:12-13). However, a new situation emerged about 700 B.C. when the militia was revived along with the concept of holy war.[54]

A final concern has to do with themes and motifs, and how they are combined. When von Rad observed that the credos of Deuteronomy 6:20-24, 26:5b-9, and Joshua 24:2b-13 did not mention Israel's experience at Mount Sinai, he concluded that originally the tradition about Mount Sinai circulated independently of the tradition about the Exodus and settlement in the Promised Land. The two traditions were eventually put together by the Yahwist, who also included patriarchal traditions and then added primeval history (the J parts of Genesis 2-11) as an introduction to his work.

In another important book on the subject, Martin Noth likewise stressed key themes expressed in Israel's statements of faith.[55] Such motifs as guidance from Egypt, the promise to the patriarchs, and the covenant at Mount Sinai comprised the common tradition (called *Grundlage,* or G) that was formed during the period of the judges and served as source material for J and E. Where there are similarities between the two documents, this is explained by G. Noth is more famous for his identification of Deuteronomic editor responsible for the writing of Deuteronomy through 2 Kings. This "Deuteronomic work" utilized some earlier materials as it reviewed Israel's history from the entrance into the land to the fall of Jerusalem. According to Noth, Deuteronomy 1-3 functioned as an introduction to this entire corpus that was written during the Exile. In essence, this theory established a "tetrateuch" of Genesis—Numbers, although Noth did not link Deuteronomy 31-34 with the earlier books.[56]

In Sweden the "Uppsala School" followed some of the ideas of von Rad and Noth but eliminated any dependence upon the documentary hypothesis. H. S. Nyberg thought that the Wellhausen source theory diminished the significance of oral tradition, which he felt deserved more attention. Ivan Engnell supported Nyberg's views in his *Traditio-Historical Introduction of 1945* in which he spoke of "schools" or "circles" of tradition. Like Noth, both Nyberg and Engnell separated Genesis-Numbers from Deuteronomy-Kings. The former was a "P work" preserved and transmitted by priestly circles in the southern kingdom, whereas the "D work" reflected the traditions of the northern kingdom. Except for some legal materials, most of these traditions were not put in writing until the Exile.

---

54. Gerhard von Rad, *Studies in Deuteronomy* (London: SCM Press, 1953), pp. 60-69; cf. Walter Rast, *Tradition History and the Old Testament* (Philadelphia: Fortress, 1972), pp. 26-27.
55. Martin Noth, *Überlieferungsgeschichte des Pentateuch* (Stuttgart: W. Kohlhammer, 1948).
56. Ibid., pp. 5-6.

The excessive emphasis that tradition criticism places upon oral tradition constitutes its greatest weakness. Why would the Hebrews have chosen not to write down matters of deepest concern when the rest of the Near East contains abundant written materials contemporary with the patriarchs and Moses? Thousands of clay tablets record business transactions, laws, hymns, and epics sometimes quite similar to those found in the Pentateuch. Kenneth Kitchen has rightly distinguished between written transmission and oral dissemination. If something was considered important, it was written down and then orally disseminated to the people (cf. 2 Chron. 17:9).[57] This is not to deny that in some cases oral tradition played an important role in the preservation of materials, but that the tradition critics vastly exaggerate the role.

RHETORICAL CRITICISM

In an article entitled "Form Criticism and Beyond" published in 1969, James Muilenburg argued that the study of Hebrew literary composition and the devices used to organize the material as a unified whole should be called "rhetorical criticism."[58] Since form criticism does not pay enough attention to the unique characteristics of a particular pericope, those who engage in rhetorical criticism can take up the slack. By a careful study of the stylistic features of a given passage, the scholar can unravel the author's thinking in a more satisfying manner. Such a study takes note of the structural patterns used, the interrelationship of the various units, and any occurrences of repetition and artistic devices that may be employed. Most of Muilenburg's examples are taken from poetry, but prose can also provide fertile soil for the rhetorical critic.

In a study of narrative in the book of Genesis, J. P. Fokkelman has pointed out the remarkable symmetry found in the Tower of Babel account. The plans of men to build the tower to make a name for themselves are countered by God's intervention to stop the project and turn mankind's unity into confusion. The pun on the name "Babel" in verse 9 is the key to understanding the narrative.[59] Whereas Fokkelman placed the turning point of the story in verse 7, others point to verse 5 as the hinge of the account. The verses on either side of verse 5 contain discourse—the words of the builders in 3-4 and of God in 6-7—and these in turn are framed by a pair of narrative verses in 1-2 and 8-9. The result is an inverted, or hourglass, structure that is beautifully proportioned.[60]

The most intricate narrative in Genesis is undoubtedly the Joseph story found in chapters 37-50. Through an examination of the interrelationships and

57. Kitchen, *Ancient Orient*, pp. 135-36.
58. James Muilenburg, "Form Criticism and Beyond," *JBL* 88 (1969), 1-18.
59. J. P. Fokkelman, *Narrative Art in Genesis: Specimens of Stylistic and Structural Analysis*, trans. Puck Visser-Hagedoorn (Assen and Amsterdam: Van Gorcum, 1975), pp. 13, 20-23.
60. *NIV Study Bible*, ed. Kenneth Barker (Grand Rapids: Zondervan, 1985), pp. 3, 22.

verbal parallels contained in these chapters, Robert Alter has uncovered the remarkable literary artistry of the narrator. For example, Alter has drawn attention to the recurrence of the verb "recognize" (*hakker-nā'*) at the end of both chapters 37 and 38. In 37:32 Jacob was cruelly deceived when he was asked to recognize the robe of his beloved son Joseph, apparently torn apart by a ferocious animal. By way of contrast, in 38:25 Judah was asked to identify his seal, cord, and staff, which proved that he was the father of Tamar's child. In the latter instance Judah was unmasked, while in the former Jacob was deceived. The same verb plays an important thematic role in 42:8 when Joseph the ruler of Egypt recognizes his brothers but they fail to recognize him when they come to buy grain during the famine.[61]

A similar verbal parallel occurs in the repetition of the root *'ārab* in chapters 38 and 43. In 38:18 the seal, cord and staff of Judah were given to Tamar as a "pledge" (*'ērābôn*) or "guarantee" that he would bring to her the next day the young goat which was the customary payment for a prostitute's services. A few chapters later Judah is seen in a much different light when he guarantees (*'ārab*) the safety of Benjamin, whose presence was required in Egypt or the brothers could buy no more grain (43:9). Judah's concern for Jacob and Benjamin and his commitment to their welfare was a far cry from his selfish indulgences in chapter 38, and the change in his character helps explain why the leadership of the twelve tribes would eventually belong to the descendants of Judah (cf. 49:10 and the later discussion on the structure and significance of the Joseph narrative).

While Genesis may furnish the most fruitful material for rhetorical criticism, the other books of the Pentateuch also contain literary intricacies. A study of the plagues in Exodus reveals a structure of three sets of three plagues followed by the climactic tenth plague. The seven oracles of Balaam recorded in Numbers 23-24 not only present amazing prophecies about Israel's future but are also arranged in a four-three pattern with intervening narrative material. Each of the oracles is introduced by the words "and he lifted up his oracle and said," even though the last three are given in rapid succession in 24:20-24.

RECENT CRITICAL APPROACHES TO THE PENTATEUCH

There are several other recent approaches to the Pentateuch that deserve attention, but two in particular have exerted considerable influence upon current thinking: canonical criticism and structuralism. Neither of these is primarily concerned with how the Pentateuch was formed, but both engage in the study of the text as we now have it, in its final form. Here the similarities end, for canonical criticism emphasizes theological matters whereas structuralism is based upon linguistics and is interested in a "deeper" level of meaning.

---

61. Robert Alter, *The Art of Biblical Narrative* (New York: Basic Books, 1981), p. 10.

CANONICAL CRITICISM

Since it is the final form of the text that possesses canonical authority, Brevard Childs has led the scholarly world in a reexamination of the function of that text within the religious community. The Scriptures must be interpreted in the light of their function within the community that described them.[62] This means that each text must be understood in light of the entire Old Testament witness, and the Old Testament as a whole must be viewed in light of the individual texts. In this approach Childs makes use of the other kinds of biblical criticism discussed above, but he realizes the limitations of the methodology they employ. Literary criticism and form criticism are helpful and necessary, but it is wrong to stop with a study of the process that produced the Scriptures. We must study the Scriptures as we have them and try to understand the religious function of the texts. "Israel defined itself in terms of a book! The canon formed the decisive *Sitz im Leben* for the Jewish community's life, thus blurring the sociological evidences most sought after by the modern historian."[63] As the canon was shaped, certain elements of the tradition were highlighted and others were pushed aside.

An advantage of canonical criticism is its interest in the relationship of individual chapters and books. For instance, the so-called P and J accounts of Genesis 1-2 provide a link between creation and its offspring. Looking at the book of Genesis, we discover that its promises function as a prelude to the story of the Exodus.[64] The Pentateuch as a whole determined how the Israelites understood the Mosaic tradition, so the question of whether or not a tetrateuch or hexateuch ever existed becomes an important one.

In his work Childs does not spend much time arguing about the historicity or nonhistoricity of the biblical materials. He is primarily interested in the theological message that a given text conveys. The net result of this approach, however, is a neglect of the historical background of a passage and a general deemphasis upon the events themselves. Childs is also willing to see a substantial difference between the original message and the message found in the final form of the text.

STRUCTURALISM

If the emergence of canonical criticism in some respects assists the conservative in his study, the situation is quite the reverse for most forms of structuralism. The newest star on the horizon of biblical criticism, structuralism (also called "structural analysis"), finds its beginnings in the field of linguistics or

---

62. Brevard Childs, *Biblical Theology in Crisis* (Philadelphia: Westminster, 1970), pp. 164-83.
63. Brevard Childs, *Introduction to the Old Testament as Scripture* (Philadelphia: Fortress, 1979), p. 78.
64. Ibid., pp. 150-51.

semiology. A Swiss scholar Ferdinand de Saussure, wrote a book entitled *Course of General Linguistics* in 1916 that exerted a profound influence upon the scholarly world.[65] De Saussure emphasized a synchronic (static) as opposed to a diachronic (evolutionary) approach to linguistics. That is, an understanding of the historical development of language is far less important than a knowledge of the current situation.[66] Scholars such as Claude Levi-Strauss and Roland Barthes applied this insight to a study of human thought in mythology and biblical literature. They agreed that the structure of language somehow intertwined with reality and that meaning is found in the relationship of words and themes.[67] Wrestling to discern the intent of the author does not unlock the meaning of the text as much as a study of the writing itself. Inherent in this approach is a belief that there are deeper levels of meaning submerged below the surface of the text. As he works, the exegete seeks to discover the symbolic and universal structures hidden in the text.

Perhaps the key to finding these universal structures is the concept of binary opposites. Human expression basically follows a pattern of polarity in dealing with reality. In a work entitled *Genesis as Myth* Edmund Leach speaks of the opposition of death versus life, God versus man, and allowable sexual relations versus disallowed sexual relations.[68] Leach argues that by including a large number of stories about breaches of sexual morality (such as Lot and his daughters, the men of Sodom and the angels) Genesis makes it appear that the relationship between Abraham and Sarah was a virtuous one, even though Sarah was his half-sister. The repetition and variations in these stories "add up to a consistent message" that is not readily apparent to the modern reader.[69] Most interpreters would not notice this emphasis upon incest and sexual morality that Leach sees embedded within the deeper structure of Genesis.

A less radical sort of structuralism is found in an analysis of Genesis 32 by R. Martin-Achard. In this study the author notes the prominence of the concept of blessing, a theme that goes back to Genesis 12. Moreover, Jacob's struggle with the angel is a revelation of the struggle that Israel as a nation will face in the future.[70] The pattern will be repeated, but on a national level.

Because of its emphasis upon the synchronic approach, structuralism virtually ignores the role of history. It is not important to understand the historical process that produced a text or the sociological context (the *Sitz-im-Leben*) that

65. Ferdinand de Saussure, *Course in General Linguistics* (1915; reprint, New York: McGraw-Hill, 1966).
66. Ibid., p.81.
67. Carl Armerding, *The Old Testament and Criticism* (Grand Rapids: Eerdmans, 1983), pp. 69-71.
68. Edmund Leach, *Genesis as Myth and Other Essays* (London: Jonathan Cape, 1969), pp. 7-23.
69. Ibid., p. 422.
70. R. Barthes et al., *Structural Analysis and Biblical Exegesis: Interpretational Essays*, ed. Dikran Y. Hadidian, trans. Alfred M. Johnson, Jr., Pittsburgh Theological Monograph Series (Pittsburgh: Pickwick, 1974), pp. 53-55.

lay behind the text. Instead, we must seek "to discover how the text produces meaning" and what message lies encoded within the deep structure of the literature itself.[71] Such a search lays bare the "universals" that comprise the heart of the message. Thus, the structuralist bypasses the normal rules of exegesis as he looks for a more esoteric meaning in Scripture.

CONCLUSION

Although scholars in the twentieth century have uncovered much new information about literary records from Old Testament times, these discoveries have not ended the debate about the authorship of the Pentateuch. New approaches to the study of the Pentateuch continue to be developed, some by scholars as firmly committed to the non-Mosaic character of these books as Wellhausen was a century ago. Yet at the same time the case for the Mosaic authorship has been strengthened by our increasing knowledge about the history, culture, and religion of the ancient Near East. Even among more recent approaches to the Pentateuch, such as form criticism and rhetorical criticism, evidence has been found that supports the unity of the five books and the view that Moses was indeed the main author. Not all have been convinced by the data, but the documentary hypothesis is shaky at best and before long may have to be given up entirely by the scholarly world.

---

71. Armerding, *The Old Testament and Criticism*, p. 72.

3

GENESIS

In many ways Genesis is the most interesting and most difficult book in the Pentateuch. With its fascinating account of the creation of the world and of mankind, Genesis takes the reader back to paradise and allows him to see man's perfection and glory. Just as quickly, however, we see the collapse of mankind and the horrible consequences of sin. Both the account of creation and the Flood involve many issues that impinge upon science and are not easy to resolve. When all seemed lost, God took Abraham and made of him a nation that would be God's instrument of blessing to the entire world. Most of Genesis traces the development of Abraham's family and follows in detail the storied lives of Isaac, Jacob, and Joseph.

TITLE

In Hebrew the first words of a book are sometimes taken as the title, so Genesis is known as "In the beginning" (*berē'šît*), a most appropriate name in light of the emphasis upon origins. A number of scholars prefer to translate these opening words as "When God began to create," but such a rendering needlessly complicates the syntax of the first three verses and grammatically does not appear to be preferable. Besides, the gospel of John seems to pattern its prologue after the words of Genesis when it starts with "In the beginning was the Word," and then notes all things were made through Him (John 1:1, 3, 10).

The English title, "Genesis," comes from the Greek word *geneseōs*, "beginning" or "generations," which was used in the Septuagint. As noted earlier, this was really a translation of the Hebrew term *tôledôt*, which occurs eleven times in the book and serves as a convenient outline indicator.

PURPOSE AND SCOPE

Genesis was written as a prologue to the rest of the Bible, for it gives us an account of the origin of the universe, of the physical world, of human life and cultures, and of the nation of Israel. Many of the great questions that have puzzled mankind through the ages are dealt with deftly and succinctly in the opening chapters. Not only are we given a brief and majestic account of creation, but we also learn how sin entered the world and how it ruined God's original creation. After the judgment of the Flood, Moses described the growth of the nations and how they were scattered in the wake of the sad attempt to build the tower of Babel. Mankind wanted to build that tower to "make a name" for themselves (Gen. 11:4), but instead God chose Abram and promised to make his name great and to build him into a great nation (Gen. 12:2).

From chapter 12 onward, Moses concentrates upon Abram, Isaac, Jacob, and Joseph. He showed how this Hebrew nation grew and developed. Since Moses himself lived when Israel was liberated from its slavery in Egypt, it was important for the people to understand how they arrived in Egypt and why they had lived there for such a lengthy period. The role played by Joseph helped to explain the reason for the long sojourn in Egypt (also cf. 15:13-14).

The book of Genesis also supplied important information about the land of Canaan, which Moses and the Israelites were about to invade. In 9:25 we are told about the curse on Canaan, and chapters 18-19 describe the immorality and destruction of Sodom and Gomorrah. That same destruction now lay ahead for all of Canaan, for the sins of the Amorites had "reached its full measure" (Gen. 15:16). Not far from Canaan were located the nations of Moab, Ammon, and Edom, and early in her history Israel battled the people of Amalek and Midian. What was the origin of these troublesome neighbors who became a thorn in Israel's side? Again, Genesis provides the answers, for Lot was the father of Moab and Ammon (19:36-38), Edom and Amalek were descended from Esau (36:1, 12), and Midian was a son of Abraham through his wife Keturah (25:1-2). In spite of the close blood ties, however, these nations were often at each other's throats (cf. Ex. 17:8-16).

LITERARY STRUCTURE

Genesis is divided into two unequal sections, chapters 1-11 and 12-50. The first section deals quickly with the origin of the universe and the creation of man, tracing the fall of Adam and the rapid growth of sin. Following a detailed account of the devastation brought by the Flood, Moses shows how the descendants of Noah's three sons repopulated the world. Throughout these early chapters the emphasis geographically is upon the region of Mesopotamia, and the events cover many thousands of years.

The second section focuses on the patriarch Abraham, whom God called from his homeland to make a new beginning in the land of Canaan. This is in actuality the third "beginning" in Genesis (after Adam and Noah), and this time God promised to form a new nation through whom "all peoples on earth will be blessed" (Gen. 12:3). The contents of this Abrahamic Covenant are repeated

THE LITERARY STRUCTURE OF GENESIS

Part 1: The Origin of All Things

Introduction and Creation	1:1–2:3
The Account of the Heavens and the Earth	2:4–4:26
The Account of Adam	5:1–6:8
The Account of Noah	6:9–9:28
The Account of Shem, Ham, and Japheth	10:1–11:9
The Account of Shem (chosen)	11:10-26

Part 2: The History of God's People

The Account of Terah (Abraham)	11:27–25:11
The Account of Ishmael (not chosen)	25:12-18
The Account of Isaac (chosen)	25:19–35:29
The Account of Esau (not chosen)	36:1-43
[The Account of Esau Repeated]	[36:9]
The Account of Jacob (chosen)	37:2–50:26

and amplified in several other passages. Abraham is given further details in 17:6-8 and 22:11-18; Isaac in 26:4; and Jacob in 28:3, 14, and 35:11. As the book unfolds, Abraham and his descendants are told that the land of Canaan will be theirs as an everlasting possession. Although Canaan is the land of promise, the country of Egypt also plays a key role in Abraham's family history. He himself spent a brief time there during a famine (12:10-20), and the drama surrounding Joseph and his brothers takes place mainly in Egypt (chaps. 37-50). Even Isaac was tempted to take refuge in Egypt during a famine, but God told him to stay in Canaan (26:1-2). Mesopotamia remains important as the region where Isaac's wife, Rebekah, lived (chap. 24) and where Jacob spent twenty years in exile, marrying Rachel and Leah and raising a family (chaps. 28-31). Most of chapters 12-50, however, are centered geographically upon Canaan and Egypt. Unlike the first eleven chapters, the last thirty-eight cover only about four hundred years.

It is common among scholars to relegate Genesis 1-11 to the realm of mythology and to consider chapter 12 as the start of the historical section, but from a literary standpoint such a sharp distinction is difficult to make. In an article entitled "The Literary Form of Genesis 1-11," Walter Kaiser notes that these chapters contain "64 geographical terms, 88 personal names, 48 generic names and at least 21 identifiable cultural items" (such as wood, metals, buildings, musical instruments).[1] He concludes that Genesis 1-11 is prose and not poetry

1. Walter Kaiser, "The Literary Form of Genesis 1-11," in *New Perspectives on the Old Testament*, J. Barton Payne, ed. (Waco, Tex.: Word, 1970), p. 59.

and that historical narrative best describes the form of these chapters.[2] Hence, when the *New English Bible* translates Genesis 11:1 "Once upon a time," it is badly misleading the reader about the nature of the tower of Babel episode.

Another important factor in any analysis of Genesis 1-11 is the use of the introductory formula "This is the account of" (or "These are the generations of") in 2:4; 5:1; 6:9; 10:1; 11:10; and 11:27. This formula occurs another five times in the second half of the book (25:12; 25:19; 36:1; 36:9; and 37:2) where we are given information about the activities and families of Ishmael, Isaac, Esau, and Jacob. There is nothing to indicate that the records about Adam and Noah are to be understood any less historically than the material about Abraham and his descendants.

Also of interest is the way the writer of Genesis consistently leaves his discussion of the most important family members until the end. Cain's genealogy is presented before Seth's (cf. 4:17, 25); the families of Japheth and Ham are discussed prior to the sons of Seth (10:2, 6, 21); Ishmael precedes Isaac (25:12, 19); and the account of Esau comes before the account of Jacob (38:1, 31:2).[3]

Such systematic features argue for the unity of Genesis and for a unified interpretation of the whole book.

Another characteristic of Genesis that spans both sections is the occasional use of an "oracle of destiny." These verses occur in poetic form and contain weighty predictions about the fate of an individual or nation. Usually a wordplay of some sort is involved. The most famous example and one which has messianic import is Genesis 3:15 with its reference to the battle between the offspring of Eve and of the serpent. Other examples include the curse on Canaan (9:24-27); the blessing upon Abraham and Rebekah (12:2-7; 24:60); Isaac's blessing upon Jacob and Esau (27:21-29, 39-40); and Joseph's predictions about the fate of Pharaoh's cupbearer and baker (40:13, 19).

When considering the overall structure of Genesis 1-11 we should also mention the arrangement of the Babylonian *Atrahasis Epic.* Like Genesis, the *Atrahasis Epic* describes creation and the beginnings and failures of mankind, gives a list of individuals who lived before the Flood and then describes the Flood itself.[4] Although the specific content differs considerably from Genesis, it is interesting to find a similar literary pattern in a text about as old as Abraham.

PROBLEMS IN GENESIS 1-11

THE NATURE OF GENESIS 1:1–2:3

Standing as an introduction to the book of Genesis is one of the most magnificent and beautiful chapters in all of the Bible. In the scant space of thirty-

2. Ibid., pp. 59-60.
3. Gleason Archer, Jr., *A Survey of Old Testament Introduction* (Chicago: Moody, 1974), p. 187.
4. Kenneth Kitchen, *Ancient Orient and Old Testament* (Chicago: InterVarsity, 1966), p. 41.

four verses we are given a majestic account of the creation of heaven and earth during a six-day period. Not a word is wasted as Moses moves from the creation of light in day one to the creation of man in His own image in day six. This great work proceeds smoothly and effortlessly until at the end God declares that "it was very good" (v. 31). When all had been completed God rested on the seventh day and set it apart as a special day (2:3).

This remarkable chapter sets forth the work of creation in simplicity and beauty, but how is it to be understood? Should we interpret it literally or figuratively? Is it a literary gem or a scientific treatise—or both? Are the days named 24-hour days or periods of undetermined length? Does the language allow for evolutionary processes or are these completely ruled out? Each of these issues has received lengthy attention and continues to challenge our generation to a great degree. Even the most devout Christians differ sharply in their approach to these questions.

In the study of "Literary Structure" above I tried to show that Genesis 1-11 is essentially the same sort of literature as chapters 12-50. Yet Genesis 1 is written in a kind of "elevated prose" that borders on the poetic.[5] This needs to be considered in the interpretation process. Although the account of creation is not explicitly written as poetry—unlike Psalm 104, for example—there are poetic features that do stand out. In Genesis 1:1 the Hebrew words for "in-the-beginning" (*berē'šît*) and "created" (*bārā'*) both begin with the letter *b* and thus illustrate alliteration, a common poetic device. In verse 2 the words for "formless" (*tōhû*) and "empty" (*bōhû*) are identical except for the first letter. This kind of internal rhyme or "assonance" likewise occurs frequently in Hebrew poetry. Compare the verbs "be fruitful and increase in number and fill" (*perû ûrebû ûmil'û*) in verses 22 and 28 and note Psalm 122:6 where the consecutive words "pray," "peace," and "Jerusalem" are very similar in sound (*ša'alû šelôm yerûšālayim*). It is also noteworthy that the terms "formless" and "empty" are usually found elsewhere in poetic passages rather than prose (cf. Jer. 4:23; Isa. 34:11), and this is also true of the word for "the deep" (*tehôm*), which occurs in poetry thirty-one out of thirty-five times (but cf. Gen. 7:11 and 8:2) in the entire Old Testament.

Normally, Hebrew poetry is identified by the parallel lines which exist in succession to form a verse. In most modern translations, typography for books such as Job, Psalms, and Proverbs makes use of indentation to show how the parallelism of the lines is structured. Although Genesis 1 is by no means clearly arranged in parallel lines, we should observe that verse 27 comes closest to this pattern and consists of three parallel lines, each containing the word "created." Verses 24-25 likewise come close to poetry, and through a reversal of the terms for "wild animals" and "livestock" present a chiastic pattern of *a-b-b-a*.

5. Alexander Heidel, *The Babylonian Genesis* (Chicago: U. of Chicago, 1951), p. 93.

There is also a possibility that Genesis 1:1–2:3 is to be considered as a series of stanzas or strophes. Several psalms are composed of a number of stanzas, based either on the letters of the Hebrew alphabet, such as the eight-verse segments of Psalm 119, or divided by refrains, as in Psalms 42-43 (cf. 42:5, 11; 43:5). The account of creation is of course divided into seven days, six of which begin with "And God said," and end with "And there was evening, and there was morning." Most of the days also contain the statement, "And God saw that it was good" or "very good" as in the case of verse 31. Verses 1-2 may very well be the prologue to the creation account, and 2:1-3 form a fitting epilogue to the six days of work. Note how the phrase "The heavens and the earth" (1:1; 2:1) functions as a kind of "inclusio" signifying the beginning and end of the pericope.

If there is in fact a poetic flavor to Genesis 1:1–2:3, we should be careful not to expect too scientific a treatment of creation in these verses.[6] After all, the primary purpose of the chapter is theological, pointing to God as the Creator, existing prior to His creation and sovereign over every aspect of creation. There is no battle among the gods as in the Babylonian *Enuma Elish*, and those aspects of creation that are often worshiped—such as the sun and moon—are not even mentioned by name (cf. 1:15-16). Similarly, the stars are included in verse 16 almost as an afterthought, not as the highly significant astral bodies deified by the Babylonians. Scholars have also pointed out that the great creatures of the sea—so often identified by surrounding nations as evil deities (cf. Isa. 27:1)—are presented in 1:21 as part of God's creation and fully under His control. The only hint of the divine comes in the account of the creation of man, who was made "in the image of God" (1:27) at the climax of the entire creative week. Everything else that God had made was placed under man's rule.

THE MEANING OF "DAY" IN GENESIS 1:1–2:3

Even if we agree that the theological teaching of Genesis 1 is paramount, we must still strive to understand what this chapter tells us about the creation process and how it relates to modern science. A key factor in this study is the meaning of the word "day" and the major theories held by scholars.

The Twenty-Four-Hour Day Theory. The most straightforward interpretation of "day" is to understand it in terms of the rotation of the earth. The description of each day ends with the statement "And there was evening, and there was morning" (vv. 5, 8, 13, etc.), which ties in nicely with the separation of light from darkness in day one. Each twenty-four-hour period is thus divided into "day" and "night" (v. 5). Although it may be difficult to comprehend how God could have accomplished so much in twenty-four hours, we recognize that He is omnipotent, according to verses such as 3, 6, 9. He spoke the word "and

6. Derek Kidner, *Genesis*, TOTC (Chicago: InterVarsity, 1967), p. 54.

it was so" (vv. 7, 9, 11, 15, 24). On the seventh day God rested from His work (Gen. 2:3), and this is given as the reason the Israelites were to keep the Sabbath day in Exodus 20:11. Such a direct correspondence implies that the Sabbath was the same length as the seventh day of creation week.

Nevertheless, there are hints in Genesis 1 that twenty-four-hour days may not have been intended. First, we observe that the sun was not created until day four (v. 16), so how could days one–three have been regarded as solar days? This argument has been countered by those who say that the creation of the sun did take place in day one when God said, "Let there be light" (v. 3). Perhaps the sun was hidden behind thick vapor until the fourth day.

A second argument focuses upon the amount of activity that took place on the sixth day.[7] Not only did God create all of the animals, but He created Adam and told him to take care of the Garden of Eden. Then God instructed Adam to give names to all the animals and birds, and as he did this, Adam noticed that there was "no suitable helper" for him among them. To rectify this loneliness, God placed Adam into a deep sleep, took one of his ribs, and with it created Eve. When Adam awoke he was delighted with his partner and said, "This is now bone of my bones and flesh of my flesh" (Gen. 2:23). All of these events are virtually impossible to squeeze into one twenty-four-hour day, even if the animals were created instantly at the start of the day. It must have taken a long time to name the animals and birds, and Adam's excitement in verse 23 implies that the creation of woman ended a lengthy period of loneliness.

The Day-Age Theory. Diametrically opposed to the twenty-four-hour position is the view that each day in Genesis 1 represents an indefinite period of time roughly equivalent to a geologic age. If, as science teaches, the earth is millions or even billions of years old, why compress the work of creation into six short days? Advocates of the day-age theory point to verses such as Psalm 90:4, which states that "a thousand years in your sight are like a day that has just gone by" (cf. 2 Pet. 3:8). The "day of the Lord" apparently refers to an extended period of time associated with the judgment of the wicked (cf. Isa. 13:6, 9). Since God is eternal, He might have chosen to create the world in six stages covering millions upon millions of years. An age by age creation could be implied by the wording of Genesis 2:1: "Thus the heavens and the earth were completed in all their vast array."[8] Although the geologic ages do not correspond neatly with the six days of creation, scientists do agree with the general development of Genesis 1: The existence of vapor and a watery mass preceded the separation of land and sea prior to the appearance of life. Vegetable life came before the emer-

---

7. R. J. Snow, *Genesis One and the Origin of the Universe*, ed. R. C. Newman and H. J. Eckelmann, Jr. (Downers Grove, Ill.: InterVarsity, 1977), p. 125.
8. The RSV ends the verse "and all the host of man." The NASB and others have renderings such as "and all their hosts."

gence of animal life during the Cambrian period, and mankind represented the latest and most complex form of life.

At certain points, however, Genesis 1 seems to differ sharply with modern science. For instance, if each day represents a very long period, how did the plants of day three survive if the sun was not created until day four? And how did the process of pollination take place in plants if insects and birds were not made until day five, two ages later?[9] We might also object that although the Hebrew word for "day" is a flexible one, it is stretching the point to make it refer to periods thousands or millions of years long.

The Intermittent-Day Theory. A third theory combines some of the features of the first two views, though with important modifications. Usually held by "progressive creationists," this third theory "assumes that 'evening . . . morning' actually represents a 24-hour day that precedes each creative period that extends into the present and will be ended only in the future."[10] In effect, each twenty-four-hour day introduces a new creative era in which God carries out the work of that day. At some point in that era a new "day" begins and launches additional creative activity, but it does not terminate the work of the preceding day or days. This is particularly significant for days three and five, which cause problems for the day-age theory. According to the intermittent-day hypothesis, fruit plants did not appear earlier than the invertebrates and some of the vertebrates of day five. Similarly, pollinating insects would have been created at the same time as the land plants, once again combining the activity of days three and five.[11] This hypothesis suggests that we are now living in the creative period that comes between the sixth and seventh days of Genesis 1:1–2:3. God is still at work, though His main activity is the redemption of mankind.

Although there are definite advantages to the intermittent-day theory, it does introduce a new set of difficulties. "Day" seems to mean "day" and "era" at the same time, but there is really nothing in the text itself that points to such an era subsequent to a "day." In addition, this theory tends to ignore the division between the days, for the refrain at the end of each day's description implies the end of that day's activity. This is especially true of day six, where for the first time we are told that all that God had made was *very* good and the definite article is placed before the numeral: "*the* sixth day" (1:31). Chapter 2 begins with the summary statement that "the heavens and the earth were completed," enabling God to rest on the seventh day (2:1-3).

The Framework Theory. In view of the chronological difficulties encountered in a study of the Genesis account, scholars have also developed nonchron-

---

9. Wayne Frair and Percival Davis, *A Case for Creation*, rev. ed. (Chicago: Moody, 1983), p. 128.
10. Pattle Pun, *Evolution: Nature & Scripture in Conflict?* (Grand Rapids: Zondervan, 1982), pp. 264-5.
11. Ibid., p. 264.

ological approaches to this chapter. One such approach emphasizes the symmetry that exists between days one–three and days four–six. Day one records the creation of light, whereas day four mentions specific "lights"—the sun, moon, and stars. Day two speaks about the sky and the waters, and day five tells how God made the birds and the fish. Day three emphasizes land, and day six describes the creation of animals and mankind to inhabit the land. In each case the first three days speak of the formation of a sphere or substance and the next three days tell of the particular bodies or creatures that correspond to these broader spheres.

	Forming		*Filling*
Day 1	Light	Day 4	Sun, Moon, Stars
Day 2	Sky and Water	Day 5	Birds, Fish
Day 3	Dry land	Day 6	Animals, Man
		Day 7	God Rests[12]

The seventh day functions as a climax to the first six days and is set apart from the others by the summary statement found in 2:1. When God finished His work, He rested on the seventh day and "made it holy" (2:3) as a special day of remembrance.

If there is in fact a correspondence between the two sets of three days, such a structure would illustrate the beauty and symmetry of God's creative work. It would also solve the problem of accounting for the existence of vegetation and plants in day three when the sun was not made until the fourth day. Yet the same reference to seed-bearing plants and fruit-bearing trees in day three seems to correspond more closely to the days of "filling" that are supposed to characterize days four–six. In an attempt to refute the whole theory, E. J. Young also points out that the "seas" are not mentioned until day three, but fish are created in day five.[13] In fairness it should be noted, however, that day two—which should correspond to day five—does talk about both the waters under the expanse and the waters above it.

The Revelatory-Day Theory. A second nonchronological approach to Genesis 1 is the view that God revealed the account of creation to Moses in a vision that lasted six literal days. God told His servant how He made the world in a sequence that was not necessarily chronological but topical and logical. According to this interpretation, the six days bear no relationship to the actual time involved in creation.[14]

---

12. Kidner, *Genesis*, p. 46.
13. E. J. Young, *Studies in Genesis One* (Grand Rapids: Baker, 1964), p. 71.
14. Cf. P. J. Wiseman, *Creation Revealed in Six Days* (London: Marshall Morgan and Scott, 1948), pp. 33ff; Bernard Ramm, *The Christian View of Science and Scripture* (Grand Rapids: Eerdmans, 1954), pp. 218-27.

The revelatory-day theory would sidestep most of the difficulties involved in reconciling science and Scripture, and there is little doubt that much of Genesis 1-11 was revealed to Moses by God. Yet when one reads Genesis 1 there is no hint in any verse that these are six days of visionary experience. Instead, we are given the distinct impression that each day is describing what God accomplished on that day, and when He finished His work He rested on the seventh day. The reference to the seventh day and God's special blessing upon it is very difficult to fit in with the revelatory-day theory.

"Seven days" in ancient Near Eastern literature. Although there are no references to seven days of creation in other ancient literature, a seven-day period is used on occasion to describe significant events. As in Genesis, it is sometimes difficult to know whether one should interpret such references literally or figuratively. In the Ugaritic Baal epic for example, we are told that the god Baal built a palace in seven days. Does this mean that since he was considered to be a powerful deity Baal constructed the palace in a one-week period, or do the seven days represent a literary convention only loosely linked to the actual time involved in the building process?[15] In another Ugaritic epic, the hero Keret takes a seven-day journey to the land of Udm, but unfortunately we do not know the precise length of the trip.[16] An interesting feature of "seven-day" references is the pattern that usually appears. Normally the days are grouped in three sets of twos followed by a climactic seventh day.[17] Although such an arrangement could be used to support the symmetry of two sets of threes proposed by the framework hypothesis, there is no example where the 2-2-2 pattern fails to make chronological progression. Of special interest is the observation that the numerals modify the word "day" almost precisely as in Genesis: "one day, a second day." The definite article occurs only with the sixth and seventh days in the biblical text.

Scholars have also noted that the number seven plays a role in the Babylonian creation story, the *Enuma Elish*, which has been preserved on seven clay tablets. These tablets describe how the god Marduk was able to defeat the goddess Tiamat, the primeval salt-water ocean, and to make heaven and earth out of her dead body. Marduk later has Tiamat's husband, Kingu, killed and from his blood creates man to perform manual labor for the gods. Outside of a few similarities, the Babylonian account differs greatly from the biblical text, and the seven tablets do not correspond very closely to the seven days of Genesis. The polytheistic backdrop, the battles between the gods, and even the reason given for the creation of mankind diverge sharply from Genesis 1.[18]

15. Ronald Youngblood, "Moses and the King of Siam," *JETS* (Fall 1973), pp. 215-22.
16. Cyrus H. Gordon, *Ugaritic Textbook* (Rome: Pontifical Biblical Institute, 1915), 1:251, lines 105-8.
17. E. A. Speiser in *ANET* (Pritchard), 2d ed. (1955), p. 94.
18. Heidel, *The Babylonian Genesis*, pp. 96-97, 120-21.

CREATION AND EVOLUTION

Since the mid-1800s a battle has been raging between those who attribute the origin of life to the creative work of God and those who point to an evolutionary process. The latter approach was thrust into the limelight by the publication of Charles Darwin's *The Origin of Species* in 1859, a book that popularized the concept of natural selection developed by Thomas Malthus and Herbert Spencer. Although some of Darwin's ideas have been proved wrong, modern evolutionists continue to draw upon his theories in their work. Most Christians have rejected Darwin's conclusions as contradictory to the testimony of Genesis, but some have tried to harmonize Scripture and evolution by attributing the start of the process to God. Adherents to a mediating position speak of theistic evolution and understand Genesis as a succinct summary that can be reconciled with an evolutionary viewpoint.

During the last few decades a great deal of research has enabled scientists to understand more fully the physical and biological changes that occur in species, and this study has given rise to the term "microevolution" as opposed to "macroevolution." A growing number of Christians are willing to accept the idea of limited evolution within the species while at the same time rejecting the more theoretical and harder to demonstrate view that all life evolved from inorganic matter and progressed through stages until man finally appeared.

Macroevolution. "The general theory of evolution" teaches that living material came from nonliving through the process of spontaneous generation and that all organisms have been produced from this living substance over a long period of time. Down through the ages significant changes have given rise to new forms of life that have become very different from their ancestors. According to Darwin, the key to these changes was the impact of environmental factors. Those organisms best suited to survive environmental conditions succeeded in reproducing themselves, thus demonstrating their superiority. All of this proceeded rather accidentally, and the evolutionist sees no need of finding any intrinsic purpose or meaning in the universe.[19] Belief in a personal God is not at all necessary in an evolutionary scheme of things.

Proof for macroevolution is generally sought in historical and comparative studies. Historical arguments deal with the fossil records that purportedly show how animals descended from common ancestors. Comparative arguments study similarities of anatomy, physiology, and biochemistry with the underlying assumption that such similarities indicate a common ancestry.[20] Both sets of arguments have been severely criticized, however. The fossil record fails because there are too many gaps to prove ancestry, and in spite of decades of study, these

19. Frair and Davis, *A Case for Creation*, p. 33.
20. Ibid., p. 25.

gaps are not disappearing. Comparative arguments can run aground because even animals that are only distantly related can closely resemble one another because they "have adapted to comparable habitats."[21] In recent studies scientists are beginning to question the validity of long-accepted ways of grouping animals and are suggesting new systems of classification.

Although macroevolution is commonly accepted as the best scientific explanation of the origin of life, the fact remains that it is only a working hypothesis and is as hard to prove as creationism. Macroevolution remains intertwined with naturalistic presuppositions and is very difficult to reconcile with Genesis and its description of a transcendent, loving God.

Microevolution. "The special theory of evolution" teaches that there are changes within a species and that this diversification can sometimes lead to the formation of a new species or variety. Through the process of natural selection, because of environmental factors, mutations occur that affect subsequent generations in a significant way.

For example, scientists have observed the development of parasitic insects that are resistant to insecticides. The scale insects that infect the citrus trees of southern California no longer are easily destroyed by spraying with a cyanide poison. Industrial pollution played an important role in the dominant color of the peppered moth *Biston betularia* as observed in a British study. Since this moth rests on tree trunks by day, the light-colored variety was easy prey for birds in cities where the trees had been blackened by pollution. Over the years dark-pigmented moths predominated in the cities, whereas light-pigmented ones were more common in rural areas where they were not nearly as conspicuous.[22] Skin pigmentation among humans probably is related to the amount of exposure to the sun experienced by population groups. The people who live close to the equator tend to have a darker skin, which affords some protection against the damaging rays of the sun, whereas residents of northern Europe, where the sunlight is rarely intense, have very light skin.[23]

Microevolution is regarded with some favor by biblical interpreters who can accept development within a species without doing violence to Genesis. When God created the various kinds of life, He set limits to the developmental process, but creation itself need not exclude differentiation within each kind. The paleontologist George Gaylord Simpson observed that the fossil record probably illustrated microevolution rather than the much more controversial macroevolution. Yet the changes seen in microevolution provide evidence for those who believe that similar but more dramatic changes produced new families, orders, and phyla down through the ages.

21. Ibid., p. 26.
22. Pun, *Evolution*, pp. 181-82.
23. Ibid., pp. 188-89.

CHANGES IN EVOLUTIONARY THOUGHT SINCE DARWIN

The twentieth century has been an era of unprecedented growth in human knowledge, and the study of biological sciences has been no exception. Scientists have been able to make significant advances in their understanding of life and its transmission. As a result, a number of the theories held by Charles Darwin have been proved wrong, and evolutionary thinkers have had to modify their approach to certain issues. That does not mean that Darwinism is dead, but it does raise new questions about the validity of macroevolution.

Spontaneous generation. According to many ancient and medieval thinkers, life originally came from nonliving substance. Plants and animals could have had their beginning under special conditions without the intervention of a divine intelligence. Fueled by the discovery of microscopic organisms in nature, the theory of spontaneous generation provided a reasonable explanation of the origin of life until it was disproved by a series of scientific experiments. In 1861, only two years after the publication of *The Origin of Species*, Louis Pasteur used a set of swan-necked flasks to demonstrate the difference between contaminated and uncontaminated air and to show the unlikelihood of spontaneous generation. Through the efforts of John Tyndall, Pasteur's conclusions were confirmed, and it was proved that only life produces life.[24]

Undaunted, other scholars have argued that a different set of conditions must have existed millions of years ago to bring about spontaneous generation. Through tightly controlled experiments, scientists have been able to turn simple molecules into larger molecules, but they have not been able to produce any kind of self-reproducing organism.[25] Still other theorists have suggested that seeds were brought to earth from another world, perhaps by meteorites or cosmic dust. Panspermia, as this theory is called, has little real scientific support and is unlikely to resolve the dilemma faced by the naturalist.[26]

Embryology. A key plank in Darwin's evolutionary structure was the so-called biogenetic law that "ontogeny recapitulates phylogeny." This "law" taught that a human embryo goes through stages that resemble the way it actually evolved. At first the human embryo resembles a fish, then an amphibian, then a reptile, and finally a mammal. This theory developed from the work of Karl Ernst von Baer (1792-1876), who noticed close similarities in the embryos of birds, lizards, snakes, and mammals, especially in their early stages. Each has visceral (pharyngeal) pouches in the same area where a fish develops gills, but the human embryo never really possesses gills nor any gill-like function.[27] The resemblance is only general and quite unrelated to the gill slits of adult fish. In

24. Ibid., pp. 192-94.
25. Frair and Davis, *A Case for Creation*, p. 42.
26. Pun, *Evolution*, p. 195.
27. Frair and Davis, *A Case for Creation*, p. 42.

fact, the stages the human embryo goes through are different from the adult forms of the organisms from which they allegedly evolved. True, embryos are very similar in the early stages of development, but in each succeeding stage the differences increase as the patterns inherent in the genes are worked out.

Most modern biologists do not accept the recapitulation theory and the biogenetic law as stated therein. Instead, they continue to point out the similarities between the embryos of higher organisms and the embryos of the presumed ancestral forms. In this more moderate fashion, they maintain their evolutionary perspective but without the "proof" they once thought embryology afforded.

Heredity. Armed with his doctrine of natural selection, Darwin was nonetheless stymied by his inability to account for the origin of variations. To some extent he was influenced by Chevalier de Lamarck's theory of "the inheritance of acquired characteristics." Lamarck believed that the environment affected an organism's "life fluid" and that an organism's ability to adapt could be inherited by its offspring. According to Darwin, environmental influence caused the body to produce *gemmules*, particles that it sent into the blood and to the sex organs. These *gemmules* were supposed to play an important role in determining hereditary characteristics. All of this speculation was laid to rest by the research of Gregor Mendel, an Austrian monk, who developed the particulate theory of genetics not long after Darwin. Through careful experimentation, Mendel learned that inheritance particles (called "genes") in an organism's reproductive cells determined what the offspring would be like. Heredity was not a haphazard process but operated within closely defined limits.

Since the work of Mendel, scientists have discovered that genes can be altered by mutation, which "involves a change in the arrangement of bases in a DNA strand" and does alter heredity patterns.[28] Such changes are generally minor, however, and do not seem to yield the radical transformations needed for macroevolution. Each organism has a "basic body plan," and though this plan may be altered to a considerable degree, there are limits to the changes effected, owing to the very nature of the genetic code. Through artificial selection breeders have been able to increase the egg production of a white leghorn flock from 125.6 eggs per hen each year to 249.1 eggs a year over a period of thirty-two years, but they were not able to change the shape of the egg. There may be substantial variation, but it always operates within limits.[29]

Punctuated equilibrium. A cornerstone of Darwinism has been the concept of gradual evolution over a long period of time, but in more recent years scholars have become dissatisfied with this explanation, partially because the gaps in the fossil record have not been filled. Harvard University professor Stephen Jay

---

28. Ibid., p. 34.
29. Lane P. Lester and Raymond G. Bohlin, *The Natural Limits to Biological Change* (Grand Rapids: Zondervan, 1984), pp. 78, 152-53.

Gould, along with Niles Eldredge of the American Museum of Natural History, is advocating the view that lengthy eons of almost no change were interrupted, or "punctuated," by periods of rapid change.[30] Millions of years may go by before any progress is seen. If these times of change were relatively rapid, it is possible that more of the transitional forms survived in the fossil record.

While the theory of punctuated equilibrium can garner some support from the abrupt changes that have been observed in certain plant species, the mechanism by which such changes occurred in higher organisms remains to be explained. Lester and Bohlin argue that the processes and patterns involved in punctuated equilibrium are either poorly understood or virtually unknowable. Like the Neo-Darwinists, adherents of this theory must extrapolate from observable microevolutionary processes to unobservable macroevolution, a procedure that requires as much faith as someone who believes in creation.[31] Such a hypothesis depends on the faith of the adherent and in this respect is no different than belief in creation.

THEISTIC EVOLUTION

To a greater or lesser extent a number of Christians have tried to merge the teaching of the Bible and of evolution without denying the validity of either. Although they accept the reality of a personal God who created the world, they believe that He may have used the mechanism of evolution to bring about the vast variety of life as we now know it. Creation is not necessarily diametrically opposed to evolution, for God may have set the evolutionary process in motion.[32]

Those who hold to theistic evolution interpret the early chapters of Genesis along figurative or poetic lines. If Genesis gives only a general description of beginnings, it may be flexible enough to coexist with evolution. Because of the details given when God made man, some scholars argue that evolution ended before Adam came on the scene as a special creation of God. Others believe that the physical part of man did evolve from the higher animal orders, but at a certain point God endowed this creature with a soul and stamped His own image upon him.

A careful study of Genesis 1 and 2, however, does raise serious questions about the possibility of this latter view of man's origin. Genesis 2:7 specifically says that "the Lord God formed the man from the dust of the ground." Nowhere else does "dust" mean "animal" or "hominid." If "dust" could somehow be interpreted as a metaphor for "animal," one could argue that the clause

---

30. N. Eldredge and S. J. Gould, "Punctuated Equilibrium: An Alternative to Phyletic Gradualism," in *Models in Paleobiology*, ed. T. J. M. Schopf (San Francisco: Freeman, Cooper, 1972), pp. 82-115.

31. Lester and Bohlin, *Natural Limits*, p. 146.

32. Richard H. Bube, "Creation (B): Understanding Creation and Evolution," *JASA* 32 (1980), pp. 175-76.

"the man became a living being" might mean that a primate was given a soul representing "the image of God" (cf. 1:27) and at that point was transformed into a man. But such a view violates the usage of "living being" (*nepeš ḥayyâ*), which refers to livestock and other animals in 1:24, where it is translated "living creatures" (also cf. 1:20-21). Apparently "living being" refers to physical life rather than mental or spiritual capacity, and the same is true of the reference to putting the breath of life in one's nostrils (cf. Job 27:3; Isa. 2:22). Adam was not alive in any sense of the word before God fashioned him, and later, when sin had taken its toll, Adam would return to the dust from which he had been made (Gen. 2:19). Clearly this refers to physical death.

After God created the first man, He proceeded to fashion a woman from Adam's rib. Here again the biblical language is almost impossible to harmonize with an evolutionary hypothesis. The text states that Eve was formed quickly and that she was a separate creation from man (Gen. 2:22). In an article that wrestles with the issue of creation and evolution, Davis Young points out that the temporal priority of Adam before Eve is in itself an argument against an evolutionary approach to the origin of mankind.[33]

THE AGE OF MAN

If Adam and Eve were special creations of God, how long ago were they made and how do they relate to the human-like fossils analyzed by anthropologists? Was there a pre-Adamic race, or have some of the fossils been mistakenly identified as human? And how much time does the Bible allow since the creation of Adam? None of these issues can be handled easily, whatever one's viewpoint may be. There does seem to be a growing consensus among evangelicals that man in the biblical sense did not precede the Neanderthal man, the *Homo sapiens* of about 50,000 years ago,[34] but others argue for a more recent date of 10,000 to 30,000 years ago.[35]

The case for the Neanderthal man rests upon his use of a rather developed chipped stone, his burial practices, and his cranial capacity and erect posture, even though his skeletal structure was heavier than modern man. Cro-Magnon man who lived from ten to thirty thousand years ago was apparently highly intelligent and made use of fetishes and sympathetic magic in his religious practices.[36] The so-called Australopithecus man and *Homo erectus* (the Pithecanthropines) are more primitive hominids and are probably best considered as subhuman pri-

33. Davis Young, "An Ancient Earth Is Not a Problem; Evolutionary Man Is," *Christianity Today*, October 8, 1982, p. 44.
34. Frair and Davis, *A Case for Creation*, p. 125; J. O. Buswell III, "Genesis, the Neolithic Age, and the Antiquity of Man," *Faith and Thought* 96 (1967), p. 18; Davis Young, "An Ancient Earth Is Not a Problem," p. 45.
35. Gleason Archer, *Encyclopedia of Bible Difficulties* (Grand Rapids: Zondervan, 1982), p. 64; Ronald Youngblood, *How It All Began* (Glendale, Calif.: Gospel Light, 1982), pp. 53-54.
36. Frair and Davis, *A Case for Creation*, pp. 124-25.

mates, even though some of them did use various tools. Some Bible scholars would also relegate the Neanderthal and Cro-Magnon "men" to the category of hominids and place Adam and Eve after all of them. Part of the reason for this is the advanced state of civilization given in Genesis 4:17-22. The existence of agriculture and animal husbandry sounds much more like Neolithic than Palaeolithic times and points to a date later than 10,000 B.C.[37] On the other hand, it is possible that after the Fall man's cultural condition deteriorated along with the spiritual status, and he may not have recovered early levels of culture and civilization until millennia had passed. Spiritual degeneration was so thorough that God had to destroy mankind with a flood (Gen. 6:5-7), putting an end to any cultural achievements at the same time.

In 1987 scientists made use of the mitochondrial DNA (mtDNA) to reconstruct the family tree of modern humans and decided that we all descended from one female who lived about 200,000 years ago in Africa or Asia. Since the mitochondrial DNA is inherited only from the mother, geneticists dubbed the woman "mitochondrial Eve" and discussed the remarkable biological brotherhood to which their findings pointed. Although the mtDNA can provide valuable information about when and where a particular species originated, there are nonetheless serious problems about the interpretation of the data. One point of discussion is whether this woman belonged to the archaic sapiens species or to the later *Homo sapiens* branch.[38]

If it turns out that a number of ancient fossils are human, some scholars are prepared to argue that they belong to a pre-Adamic race that had no direct connection with Adam and his descendants. Such "men" were created by God but were destroyed in a great catastrophe that occurred between Genesis 1:1 and 1:2. According to this so-called "gap theory" the fall of Satan precipitated the crisis that may have included a great flood followed by a global ice age. Most of the fossils of plants, animals, and men may be attributed to this earlier destruction.[39]

Although such a theory can conveniently "solve" a number of problems posed by modern science, it is difficult to derive from the biblical text. Genesis 1:2 seems to describe the condition of the earth just before God began to form it and fill it during the six days of creation. Neither the word "formless" nor "empty" nor "darkness" has to connote the presence of evil.[40] God made both the day and the night, and the sun and moon were created to "govern" each period (Gen. 1:5-18). To establish a gap between verses 1 and 2, one must translate "the earth *became* formless" rather than "*was* formless." Yet this is almost

37. Ramm, *Christian View of Science*, p. 327.
38. See Roger Levin's discussion in "The Unmasking of Mitochondrial Eve," *Science* 238 (October 2, 1987), pp. 24-26.
39. For a full discussion of this theory, see Arthur C. Custance, *Without Form and Void* (Brockville, Canada: Arthur C. Custance, 1970).
40. E. J. Young, *Studies in Genesis One*, p. 35; Davis, *Paradise to Prison: Studies in Genesis* (Grand Rapids: Baker, 1975), p. 45.

impossible to do, because the Hebrew *waw consecutive* could have been used to express "became" much more clearly. In all probability verse 2 is a circumstantial clause closely linked with verse 1 to form a prologue to the chapter.

Another factor in this discussion about the age of man is the genealogies found in Genesis 5 and 11. Is it not possible to compute the ages given in these chapters and establish an approximate date for the creation of Adam and Eve? Unfortunately, the matter is much more complicated than it would appear at first glance because we probably are not given an unbroken genealogy of fathers and sons. When the Bible says that Seth "became the father of Enosh" (Gen. 5:6) it could mean that Seth became the father of a boy who had a son or grandson named Enosh. "Father" can also mean "grandfather" or "ancestor," and it is sometimes difficult to know which is intended.

In the case of Adam and Lamech one can argue that Seth and Noah are literal sons, partly because the naming of the child is mentioned (5:3, 29). The genealogy of Christ in Matthew 1 for the most part lists actual fathers and sons, but the reference to "Jehoram the father of Uzziah" overlooks the fact that Jehoram was the great-great-grandfather of Uzziah. Similarly, "the children born to Jacob by Zilpah" (Gen. 46:18) includes great-grandsons.

The phenomenon of omitting names from lists can be illustrated from extrabiblical material also. Professor Kenneth Kitchen has referred to the Abydos King List in Egypt—which leaves out three whole groups of kings in a list that is otherwise continuous—and to the Sumerian King List in Mesopotamia, which also omits entire dynasties.[41] This combination of continuous and broken genealogy could very well be applied to Genesis 5 and 11 also.

Part of the rationale for a selective genealogy is found in the symmetrical pattern seen in the two chapters. Chapter 5 lists ten names from Adam to Noah, and chapter 11 has ten generations from Shem to Abram. This structure is evident also in Matthew 1, which divides Christ's genealogy into three dual sets of names: fourteen generations "from Abraham to David, fourteen from David to the exile to Babylon, and fourteen from the exile to the Christ" (Matt. 1:17). As noted above, three names were omitted in the last line of verse 8.

If we allow for flexibility in the genealogies of Genesis 5 and 11, we can also better account for the date of the Flood, which was already ancient history for Gilgamesh of Uruk, who lived about 2800 or 2700 B.C.[42] A strict interpretation of Genesis 11 would place the Flood at about 2300 B.C., far later than even the start of the First Dynasty of Egypt about 3000 B.C.

In view of the strong probability that the genealogies in Genesis 5 and 11 are selective, do they shed any light at all on the age of man? Some interpreters would argue that there are no limits whatever, and that if human beings roamed

41. Kitchen, *Ancient Orient*, p. 38.
42. Ibid, p. 36.

the earth at 1,000,000 B.C. this would not contradict Genesis. Others protest that such a stretching of the genealogy would hopelessly distort the biblical record. Are there hundreds or even thousands of names missing from these lists?[43]

Judging from the other genealogies in the Bible, we know that omissions do occur, but not on the scale required for such a lengthy period of time. Even if Genesis 5 and 11 are treated as a special case with scores of names omitted, it would be difficult to push Adam and Eve much earlier than 50,000 B.C. Happily, such a figure coincides with the estimate of some anthropologists and geologists who are wrestling with both the biblical and scientific data.[44] Any date prior to 50,000 B.C. would seem to be stretching the genealogies to the breaking point.

THE IDENTITY OF THE "SONS OF GOD" IN GENESIS 6:2

As part of the sin and corruption that led to the Noahic Flood, Genesis 6:1-4 refers to the marriages between the sons of God and the daughters of men. It is clear that these relationships were highly displeasing to the Lord, but controversy surrounds the identification of "the sons of God." Are we to understand by this a kind of invasion of earth by angels, or is it a case of mixed marriages between believers and unbelievers or perhaps an escalation of the polygamy begun in Genesis 4:19? Each of these views has strong adherents.

The angel interpretation. One of the oldest views identifies the "sons of God" with fallen angels who lusted after beautiful women and cohabited with them. This interpretation is found in the book of Enoch, a pseudepigraphal work probably written in the centuries just before the birth of Christ.[45] Another work from the same period is "The Genesis Apocryphon," an Aramaic midrash discovered among the Dead Sea Scrolls at Qumran. In column II, Noah's father, Lamech, suspects that his wife was impregnated by an angel, a heavenly "Watcher," and has to be convinced to the contrary.[46] Philo, Josephus, and a number of the church Fathers also subscribed to this view.

Perhaps the strongest argument for the angel hypothesis is that the expression *benê 'elōhîm* ("the sons of God") refers exclusively to angels in the Old Testament, although it appears elsewhere only in Job (1:6; 2:1; 38:7). In the first two instances, however, Satan comes with "the sons of God" to present his case against Job, so the connection with fallen angels is apparent—"sons of God" means "supernatural ones," just as "sons of the prophets" means "members of the prophetic guild," not literal sons of recognized prophets (cf. 1 Sam.

---

43. Archer, *Survey*, pp. 186-87.
44. Frair and Davis, *A Case for Creation*, p. 125; Buswell, "Genesis, the Neolithic Age, and the Antiquity of Man," p. 18; Young, "An Ancient Earth Is Not a Problem," p. 45.
45. R. H. Charles et al., ed., *The Apocrypha and Pseudepigrapha of the Old Testament* (Oxford: Oxford U., n.d.), 2:191.
46. Geza Vermes, *The Dead Sea Scrolls in English* (Baltimore: Penguin, 1968), pp. 215-16.

10:5; 1 Kings 20:35). In the New Testament, the "sons of God" are individual believers (cf. 1 John 3:1-2), but this is quite different from the Old Testament meaning. Likewise, the contrast in Genesis 6:2 between "the sons of God" and "the daughters of men" points to two spheres—one heavenly and the other earthly.

Although angels are normally portrayed as spiritual beings, when they do appear on earth they are consistently called men (cf. Dan. 10:5, 16). The angels entertained by Abraham looked like men and ate a sumptuous meal hastily prepared by Sarah and the servants (Gen. 18:1-8). In the next chapter, two of the men are called "angels" (*mal'ākîm*) as they entered Sodom to warn Lot of the imminent destruction coming upon the cities of the plain (Gen. 19:1). Ironically, the two angels became targets of the sexually depraved men of Sodom. In Numbers 22:22 the angel of the Lord, holding a drawn sword, stood in Balaam's path, and Joshua bowed before a similarly armed man identified as commander of the Lord's army (Josh. 5:13-15). If this "male" orientation also applies to fallen angels, we could compare their lust for human flesh to the desire of demons for a body in the New Testament.

A final argument supporting the identification of the sons of God with angels comes from the New Testament. In 2 Peter 2:4-6 the apostle refers in successive verses to the sins of angels, the Noahic Flood, and the destruction of Sodom and Gomorrah. Since two of the three events are found in Genesis, the third may be also, and 6:1-4 is the only possible reference. The book of Jude places the sin of angels in juxtaposition to the sexual immorality of Sodom and Gomorrah (vv. 6-7), with the implication that the angels may have been guilty of a sexual offense also. If angels were indeed involved on earth with women, the grossness of this sin could provide another reason for the Flood. Something terrible must have been happening for God to take such drastic action against mankind.

In spite of the advantages of the angel hypothesis, it does face some serious objections. In the gospels, Christ states that after the resurrection people will not marry but will be like the angels in heaven (Matt. 22:30; Mark 12:25; Luke 20:34-36). This implies that angels never did and never will marry, so how could they be involved in the marriages of Genesis 6:2? In response one might argue that perhaps God did allow angels to marry at one time, but it clearly was impossible after the Flood.

A second major objection has to do with the absence of other references to angels anywhere else in Genesis 1-11. And why use the more obscure "sons of God" rather than the common *mal'āk*, the word for "angel" or "messenger" found in Genesis 19:1 and in each of the passages where "the angel of the Lord" (Gen. 16:7, 9, 11; 22:11, 15) or "the angel of God" (Gen. 21:47; 31:11) appears? Moreover, if angels were as guilty as men in adding to sin and corruption on earth, why is there no reference to the judgment of angels anywhere in the chapter? Yet Victor Hamilton has pointed out that the punishment is not directly aligned with the criminals, for the animals and birds perished even though the sin belonged to mankind (Gen. 6:5-7).[47]

The godly-line-of-Seth interpretation. The view that probably is preferred by most evangelicals today understands "the sons of God" to be a reference to descendants of the godly man Seth. Turning their backs on their godly heritage, these men intermarried with unbelieving women from the line of Cain and produced offspring renowned for their wickedness. With the spiritual collapse of the descendants of Seth, God pronounced judgment upon mankind in toto and sent a flood to wipe them off the face of the earth.

This view has in its favor its agreement with the strong polemic in Genesis against intermarriage with unbelievers. Whether we look at Abraham's instruction to his servant not to get a wife for Isaac "from the daughters of the Canaanites" (Gen. 24:3) or at Rebekah's distress over Esau's Hittite wives (26:34-35; 27:46), the message is the same: Do not intermarry with pagan neighbors. Jacob had to flee for his life after he deceived Isaac, but his stay in Paddan-Aram resulted in his marriage to Leah and Rachel, relatives of Abraham. Thus, if the sin of Genesis 6:2 was intermarriage, it would fit in nicely with the overall teaching of the book.

A second line of argument focuses on the use of "sons" to refer to human beings. Usually the context in which "sons" appears is talking about the children of Israel or God's chosen people (Deut. 14:1; 32:5; Isa. 43:6), even though their behavior often left much to be desired. But Hosea 1:10 looks forward to the day when the rebellious Israelites "will be called 'sons of the living God.'" The complete phrase "sons of God" is never applied to men, but Adam is called "the son of God" in the genealogy of Christ (Luke 3:38). Since Genesis 5 presents the genealogy of man from Adam to Noah and since it specifies that Adam was made "in the likeness of God" (v. 1), perhaps Genesis 6:2 employs the phrase "sons of God" with reference to the godly line of Seth that takes up the rest of Genesis 5. If that is true, "the daughters of men" would refer to the descendants of Cain, whose lineage was famous for its cultural achievements but not for its godliness (Gen. 4:17-24). The offspring of these marriages unfortunately behaved more like Cain than Seth and accelerated the evil inclinations of mankind. And it was man's wickedness—not the activity of fallen angels—that is singled out in Genesis 6:5.

Whereas the Seth hypothesis has some important advantages, it too encounters some major problems. Perhaps the most serious is the identification of "the daughters of men" with "the daughters of Cain." What evidence can prove that all the daughters of Cain were wicked and all the sons of Seth were godly? Were their respective lines kept completely separate and were they uni-

47. Victor P. Hamilton, *Handbook on the Pentateuch* (Grand Rapids: Baker, 1982), p. 64.

formly good or evil? Because of the Flood being prepared by God, the inference is that by this time many of the descendants of Seth were also wicked. If so, why would they be called "the sons of God," that is, "godly sons"? The main contrast in the two phrases is between "God" and "men" ('*ādām*), and this indicates that "the sons of God" did not belong to the sphere of mankind.

The dynastic-ruler interpretation. In light of the difficulties inherent in the other two views, Meredith Kline has suggested that "sons of God" refers to kings or dynastic rulers primarily descended from Cain.[48] These rulers continued the civilization described in 4:17-24 and like Lamech in 4:19 were guilty of polygamy. "The daughters of men" were the members of the harems possessed by these kings as a sign of their wealth and prestige.

Support for this theory comes first of all from the use of '*elōhîm* ("God" or "gods") in the limited sense of "judges" in Exodus 21:6; 22:8-9; and possibly Psalm 82:6. Understood in this fashion, "sons of the judges" could refer to a succession of kings and the authority they wielded. Second, one could point to examples in other Near Eastern literature where kings are referred to as the son of a particular deity. In Egypt the pharaoh was quite clearly regarded as divine, while in other nations a king could be called a god's son because he was chosen as ruler and enjoyed the god's favor. In the Old Testament, Solomon is called God's son because he would succeed David as king (2 Sam. 7:14), and there does seem to be a special father-son relationship between God and the king from this time on (cf. Ps. 2:7). God chose David's family to be the ruling dynasty in Israel, and He endowed them with the strength and wisdom to be effective kings. Yet this concept is not found in Scripture until 1000 B.C. and is difficult to read back into Genesis 6.

A third line of support for the dynastic ruler theory comes from the Sumerian King List, which tells us that, before the Flood, kingship was lowered from heaven and eight monarchs enjoyed very long reigns.[49] The tradition about these kings—though usually compared with Genesis 5[50]—might be reflected in Genesis 6:1-4 with its references to "the sons of God" and "the heroes of old, men of renown." If the antediluvian kings were descended from Cain, they would form a parallel line to the great heroes of Seth listed in Genesis 5.

Although Kline's interpretation has some attractive features, it suffers from lack of evidence. Why were not "the sons of God" called "kings" or "rulers" if that was intended, and why is the subject of polygamy mentioned so indirectly? The paragraph is admittedly an obscure one, but the first two theories supply more adequate solutions.

48. Meredith Kline, "Divine Kingship and Genesis 6:1-4," *WTJ* 24 (1962), pp. 187-204.
49. H. W. F. Saggs, *The Greatness That Was Babylon* (New York: Hawthorn, 1962) p. 35.
50. Cf. John Walton, "The Antediluvian Section of the Sumerian King Lists and Genesis," *BA* 44 (1981), pp. 207-8.

THE EXTENT OF THE FLOOD

Few issues have been as controversial as the debate between those who believe that the Bible teaches a universal Flood and those who are convinced that a local flood better fits the data. Since the publication of *The Genesis Flood* by John Whitcomb and Henry Morris in 1961, the debate has been particularly spirited.[51] Whitcomb and Morris have attempted to buttress biblical arguments with evidence from geology to demonstrate that the Flood must have covered the entire globe. Other scholars, such as Bernard Ramm and Davis Young, have defended the local flood hypothesis, arguing that both Scripture and science point to a limited rather than a worldwide flood.[52] Most Christian geologists favor a local flood, but biblical scholars are more evenly divided. As in other issues when science and Scripture need to be reconciled, the amount of data is mind-boggling and the interpretation of the evidence is anything but simple.

Evangelicals readily admit that God used the miraculous to accomplish His purposes, but the number and scope of the miracles is hotly debated. We should also point out that God has chosen to perform a large number of "water" miracles and that all of them are hard to explain. In the Old Testament are the crossing of the Red Sea and the Jordan River under Moses and Joshua and the floating of the ax-head and purification of poisoned water by Elisha. During Christ's ministry on earth He changed the water to wine and He walked on the Sea of Galilee. Throughout the Scriptures God has chosen to demonstrate His sovereignty over water in a way that defies natural explanations, and this should serve as a warning not to expect too many answers from a study of the Noahic Flood.

The case for a universal flood. Judging from the language used in Genesis 6 and 7, the Flood was a catastrophe of global dimensions. God decided "to destroy all life under the heavens" (6:17) because mankind had filled the earth with corruption and violence. To carry out this judgment God commanded "all the springs of the great deep" to burst forth, "and the floodgates of the heavens were opened" (7:11). It rained for forty days and forty nights as tremendous amounts of water were poured out upon the earth. This description seems to reverse the work of creation, when God "separated the water under the expanse from the water above it" (Gen. 1:7) and when He distinguished between the dry ground and the seas (1:9-10). As the Flood continued, everything disappeared in the water, and the earth became formless and empty as it had once been. Ironically, the word for "the deep" in Genesis 1:2 (*tehôm*) appears in 7:11, when the springs of the great deep burst forth. It looks as if the whole earth is returning to a watery chaos.

51. Published by Baker, Grand Rapids.
52. Ramm, *Christian View of Science*, pp. 238-47; Davis A. Young, *Creation and the Flood* (Grand Rapids: Baker, 1977).

As the waters rose "all the high mountains under the entire heavens were covered" to a depth of at least twenty feet (7:19-20). Since water seeks its own level, how would it be possible to cover one high mountain without covering the entire earth? Even if the Alps and Himalayas were excluded, hardly any creature could have survived such a tremendous flood. According to 7:23 "every living thing on the face of the earth was wiped out," including men, animals, and birds. The only survivors were Noah and his family and all the creatures that had taken refuge with them on the ark. If the Flood were only local, why would it have been necessary to take aboard animals and birds? Surely Mesopotamia would have soon been replenished with creatures that had safely avoided the area during the Flood. The size of the ark also indicates how extensive this Flood was, for it measured approximately "450 feet long, 75 feet wide and 45 feet high" (6:15). Such a ship could accommodate thousands of animals and birds, far more than would be necessary if a localized area were intended.

Similarly, the duration of the Flood tells us something about its extent. Noah and his family were in the ark for more than a year, and according to John J. Davis, "a flood which lasts 371 days cannot be anythng short of universal."[53] Moreover, when God made a covenant with Noah after the Flood, He promised that He would never again destroy the earth by means of a flood (Gen. 9:11). In view of the large numbers of devastating local floods that have ravaged our planet since then, it would seem that God has either broken His promise or the Noahic Flood was worldwide.

Since the main purpose of the Flood was to destroy sinful mankind, a strictly Mesopotamian flood would be ineffective, unless everyone were still living in that limited area. Yet when one looks at the longevity of antediluvian man, the population must have increased rapidly, making it unlikely that the many millions of people would all have been able to stay close to the Tigris and Euphrates rivers.[54] Did those who lived outside of Mesopotamia thereby escape judgment? If so, a number of scholars argue that Peter's warning about the future day of judgment loses its impact. In 2 Peter 3:3-7 the apostle addressed those who scoffed at the notion of a second coming and a day of reckoning. He reminded them that the world of Noah's day "was deluged and destroyed" as a sign that "the present heavens and earth are reserved for fire" in a judgment that will destroy all the ungodly (2 Pet. 3:6-7). Why would Peter compare the final judgment with the Noahic Flood unless the whole world were involved in both events?

The case for the local flood. In spite of the formidable arguments in favor of a global flood, a number of scholars have shown how the biblical data can point equally well to a much more limited flood. Geographically, the account of

---

53. Davis, *Paradise to Prison*, p. 125.
54. Whitcomb and Morris, *The Genesis Flood*, p. 27.

Noah and his family is set in Mesopotamia, and even after spending more than a year in the ark, they landed "on the mountains of Ararat" (Gen. 8:4), the ancient area of Urartu just to the north of Assyria. If Noah had been afloat for a year, why did the ark not drift much farther than the few hundred miles to Urartu? When we consider the vast size of the globe it is remarkable that Noah landed so close to his starting point, unless the Flood was restricted to Mesopotamia and the Near East.

In other words, when the Bible speaks of the waters increasing on the earth and covering "all the mountains under the entire heavens" (Gen. 7:19), it might be referring to that area of the world familiar to Noah and his countrymen. From their perspective the waters flooded the world that they knew and the mountains they had seen, without at all intending to include the vast peaks hundreds and thousands of miles away.

The Hebrew word for "earth" (*'ereṣ*) is in fact often translated "land" or "country," and its meaning has to be determined by context. It may be significant that the other common word for "world" (*tēbēl*) does not occur anywhere in the Flood narrative. Elsewhere in Genesis the word *'ereṣ* has the same ambiguous sense in connection with another catastrophe, an extensive famine. After Joseph wisely stored up grain in preparation for seven lean years, the text says that the whole world descended upon Egypt to buy grain, "because the famine was severe in all the world" (Gen. 41:57). According to most interpreters, the famine affected Egypt and several other countries around the Mediterranean Sea, but it is not necessary to think in terms of a "global" famine. It was a Near Eastern famine restricted to the Mediterranean world. Perhaps Peter's reference to the floodwaters that destroyed "the world of that time" has a similar limited sense (2 Pet. 3:6). In Colossians 1:23 Paul rejoices that the gospel "has been proclaimed to every creature under heaven," a statement very close to Genesis 7:19 but clearly understood as hyperbole.

Although the local Flood theory must wrestle with the problem of water seeking its own level, those who believe that the Flood was global have the equally difficult problem of explaining where the water came from and also where it went. A flood that covered mountains 15,000 feet high would require several times more water than the earth presently holds. Where did all of this water go? Genesis 8:1 says only that God "sent a wind over the earth, and the waters receded." Does this mean that the oceans were made deeper to contain much larger amounts of water?[55] Perhaps God did intervene in a miraculous way to remove the water, but Genesis states that within a year the waters receded enough to enable Noah and his family to disembark. This was a very short time for so vast a runoff. A mixing of fresh water and salt water would also have re-

55. As argued by Whitcomb and Morris, *The Genesis Flood*, pp. 77, 121-22.

quired a miracle to keep most of the fish from dying; yet the Bible says nothing about preserving any fish in the ark.[56]

Since the ark did contain large numbers of animals and birds, however, a local Flood theory could make the task of caring for them more manageable. Noah and his family had to feed these animals and birds (Gen. 6:21), an assignment that would have been overwhelming if thousands of species from all over the world were involved. But if the Flood was limited to the Near East, it is easier to understand how the animals of that region found the ark and how the eight people on board were able to take care of them. Such a view still requires a miracle to get the animals into the ark, but it reduces the scope of the miraculous to bring it more in line with the biblical evidence.

At the end of the Flood when Noah was trying to determine whether it was dry enough to disembark, a dove brought to him "a freshly plucked olive leaf" (Gen. 8:11). Here was proof that the waters had receded and that at least one olive tree had survived the Flood. This would seem to indicate that the Flood was not geologically active and that the earth's surface was relatively undisturbed.[57] Additional evidence comes from the reference to the Tigris and Euphrates rivers, in connection with the Garden of Eden. Apparently they remained in approximately the same riverbeds after the Flood, for Genesis 2:14 states that the Tigris ran along "the east side of Asshur," the region known as Assyria in later times (cf. Gen. 10:11).

Conclusion. Without question the problems associated with the Flood are challenging ones, and we must be careful about dogmatism. The judgment of God was unleashed upon an unsuspecting world with awesome power and to this day remains a warning of His great wrath. If the Flood was global, the number of miracles involved were greater than if it was local, but either way the miraculous is clearly evident throughout the account. The issue is not what *could* God have done, but what *did* He do in this great catastrophe. If one were to opt for something less than a universal flood in view of the scientific problems inherent in the universal flood approach, something on the order of a regional or continental flood might be the best choice. This would explain the need for a sizable ark and also account for the destruction of all mankind. It is unlikely that a strictly Mesopotamian flood could have accomplished this, unless the world's population was much smaller than most calculations.

The Babylonian flood stories. Since the discovery of the library of Ashurbanipal at Nineveh, scholars have been aware of another ancient account of a flood that is somewhat similar to the biblical record. In tablet XI of the Gilgamesh Epic, we have a description of the flood that wiped out everyone except

---

56. Youngblood, *How It All Began*, pp. 127-28.
57. Whitcomb and Morris, *The Genesis Flood*, pp. 104-6, argue that the olive leaf grew from a broken branch buried near the surface as the waters receded.

Utnapishtim and his family. Gilgamesh, king of Uruk around 2600 B.C., hears the story of the flood from his ancestor in a visit to the underworld, where he had journeyed in a vain attempt to find immortality. After an arduous trip through the underworld, Gilgamesh finally found Utnapishtim and learned about the flood. According to Utnapishtim, the god Ea warned him that Enlil was planning to send a flood to destroy the earth. Utnapishtim proceded to build a ship 120 cubits square and seven stories high to save his family and some animals. He also took aboard food, gold and silver, and some trained seamen. After a seven-day storm, the water began to recede and the boat landed on a mountaintop. Utnapishtim sent out a dove, a swallow, and a raven to determine if the earth was really drying out. The raven found something to eat and did not return to the boat, so Utnapishtim knew that it was safe to disembark. As he left the ship, he offered sacrifices to the gods, who gathered around the altar like flies in their eagerness to eat the meat. Enlil was distressed that any mortals had survived the flood, but he did reward Utnapishtim and his wife by turning them into gods.

Another version of the flood is found in the Atrahasis Epic, which H. W. F. Saggs believes lies behind the Gilgamesh Epic.[58] In this account, Atrahasis replaces Utrapishtim as the hero and the flood was sent because men were too noisy and the gods could not sleep. Again, it is Enlil and Ea (= Enki) who play the leading roles among the gods.

In some respects the Babylonian flood stories are remarkably similar to the biblical account. A key role is played by a hero who is divinely instructed to build a large boat to save his family and an assortment of birds and animals. The storm itself brings a terrible deluge that wipes out mankind. After the flood abates, the hero sends out birds to assess how quickly the earth is drying up. Noah sent out a raven and a dove, whereas Utnapishtim used a dove, a swallow, and a raven. As a token of gratitude to the deity, offerings are presented as soon as the ship is emptied of its precious cargo.

There are, of course, significant differences between Genesis and the Babylonian accounts, but nonetheless we must ask about possible relationships between them. Did the Hebrews derive the flood story from the Babylonians and modify certain elements to make it more acceptable? Or do both accounts go back to the same event that Genesis reports accurately and the Babylonians corruptly?[59] Certainly the dimensions of Noah's ark befit a seaworthy ship, unlike the cube-shaped Babylonian vessel that would have capsized quickly. The flood lasts only a few weeks in the Babylonian version, compared with the more realistic year-long ordeal of Noah and his family. Moreover, the sharp contrast between the righteous and holy God of Genesis and the quarreling gods of Babylon

58. Saggs, *The Greatness That Was Babylon*, p. 406.
59. Kidner, *Genesis*, p. 97; Alexander Heidel, *The Gilgamesh Epic and Old Testament Parallels* (Chicago: U. of Chicago, 1949), pp. 260-69.

with their human passions indicates the vast gap between the accounts. Only in Genesis are we given a clear reason for the Flood and an equally clear reason why only Noah and his family are saved. By way of summary, then, the Babylonian flood stories present a garbled and confused account of a real event and manage to preserve only a few details relatively intact.

THE CURSE OF CANAAN

After the Flood, God established a covenant with Noah and his descendants, promising that never again would He send a flood to destroy the earth (Gen. 9:1-17). Noah lived another 350 years, but little is known about them except for an incident that resulted in a curse on Canaan, the youngest son of Ham. On that occasion Noah drank too much wine and in his drunken state "lay uncovered inside his tent" (Gen. 9:21).

Later writers talk of the shame and disgrace of the drunk man who is stripped naked for all to see. Usually it is the judgment of God that lays a man low in humiliation and dishonor (cf. Lam. 4:21; Hab. 2:15, 16). In Noah's case we are given no reason for his behavior, shocking as it is for one who had been so righteous. Lying in his exposed condition, Noah was seen by his youngest son, Ham. According to verse 22, Ham "saw his father's nakedness and told his two brothers outside." Shem and Japheth then proceeded to cover Noah with a garment, being careful not to look at him in the process.

Since Ham was not responsible for Noah's drunken condition, the severity of the curse against Ham's family is puzzling. What was so evil about seeing Noah's nakedness? Scholars have suggested that Ham may have made fun of his father's condition, inviting others to look at the strange sight. Such mocking would have been diametrically opposed to the command to honor one's father and mother (cf. Ex. 10:12), which must have been known since the creation of man. As the youngest son (v. 24), Ham may have displayed his carelessness and immaturity by his derisive actions. Elsewhere in the Pentateuch, dishonoring one's father is related to sleeping with the father's wife (Lev. 18:7; 20:11; Deut. 27:20), and this has led F. W. Basset to suggest that Ham was really guilty of incest and that Canaan was the offspring of this relationship.[60] But the actions of Shem and Japheth in verse 23 and the likelihood that Canaan was already alive make this theory most unlikely.[61]

There is a possibility that sexual immorality was involved, however, because the expression "to see one's nakedness" is sometimes used of sexual intercourse. In Leviticus 20:17 the text literally speaks of a brother and sister seeing each other's nakedness as a euphemism for having sexual relations. Usu-

---

60. F. W. Basset, "Noah's Nakedness and the Curse of Canaan. A Case of Incest?" *VT* 21 (1971): 232-37.
61. See the criticisms by Victor Hamilton, *Handbook on the Pentateuch*, p. 78.

ally this is expressed through the idiom "uncover one's nakedness," which occurs throughout Leviticus 18 in connection with prohibitions against incestuous relationships. If Ham was guilty of some sort of homosexual activity his action would parallel the behavior of Lot's daughters, who got their father drunk and then slept with him to preserve their family line (Gen. 19:32-36). Ironically, the immorality of Lot's family occurred just after the destruction of Sodom and Gormorrah, which were judged primarily because of rampant homosexuality. Canaan was plagued with homosexuality, and it was Ham's son Canaan who was actually cursed by Noah. Was the behavior of Ham repeated by his descendants in the land of Canaan in the centuries that followed?

One other factor also points in the direction of sexual immorality in this incident. Often in Scripture drunkenness is linked with debauchery and sexual immorality (cf. Rom. 13:13; Gal. 5:19). Besides, if Ham was guilty of immorality, it would be easier to understand why his family was cursed. The punishment does not seem to fit the crime unless something more serious than simply "looking" is involved.

THE TOWER OF BABEL

Just before the account of God's call to Abram, Genesis gives a succinct description of yet another judgment, the confusion of languages and the scattering of the peoples. These nine verses (11:1-9) are given in an inverted, or hourglass, form that is beautifully symmetrical. Verses 1 and 2 parallel verses 8 and 9, all four being written in narrative style. Verses 3 and 4 match verses 6 and 7 with the emphasis on the words of men and God respectively. In both instances the phrase "Come, let us" is emphasized.[62]

At first glance it is difficult to identify the sin committed by the tower builders, but the problem was probably human pride. Like the "men of renown" in 6:4, the Babel builders wanted to "make a name" for themselves (11:4) and defy God. In Hebrew the word for "Babel" is normally translated "Babylon," and throughout Scripture Babylon represents a kingdom that is dramatically opposed to God. This is perhaps best seen in the description of the arrogant king of Babylon, who wants to raise his throne "above the stars of God" (Isa. 14:13).[63] Nebuchadnezzar was filled with pride over his accomplishments as the architect of the Neo-Babylonian Empire about 600 B.C. (cf. Dan. 4:30), and even in Revelation 17-18 the final form of the kingdom of Babylon will face God's judgment. Man must acknowledge God's sovereign ability to rule over His creation.

62. See I. M. Kikawada, "The Shape of Genesis 11:1-9," in *Rhetorical Criticism: Essays in Honor of James Muilenburg*, ed. J. J. Jackson and M. Kessler (Pittsburgh: Pickwick, 1974), pp. 18-32.
63. Cf. Herbert M. Wolf, *Interpreting Isaiah* (Grand Rapids: Zondervan, 1985) p. 113.

"Babel" sounds like the Hebrew word for "confuse" (*bālal*), and this wordplay has forever associated the word not with "gate of God" (its Akkadian meaning) but with the confusion of languages that stopped the building of the city. The strength of the people—their unity—was destroyed by their inability to communicate, and the resultant struggle was reminiscent of Adam's toilsome efforts at working the soil after God had cursed it. In a very real sense, the unity lost at Babel was restored on the Day of Pentecost, when Jews from many different nations heard Galileans speaking their languages (Acts 2:6-12). Only when individuals submit to the lordship of Christ can there be a genuine unity blessed by God. People from every nation can be one in Christ, who is building His church to the glory of God.

Ironically, the tower of Babel was most likely similar to the Mesopotamian temple towers known as ziggurats, which were intended to bring man into touch with God. Built with square bases and sloping sides, the ziggurat had a small shrine at the top where the gods could be worshiped. Although such a structure was often designed to be a staircase between heaven and earth (cf. Gen. 28:12), in this instance communication between God and man was broken off.

To punish the tower builders, God scattered them far and wide, a dispersion reflected in chapter 10. In all probability, the tower of Babel episode preceded the scattering of the families of the three sons of Noah and was the cause of their dispersion. Chapter 10 already refers to the different languages spoken by the nations as they spread throughout the world (vv. 5, 20, 31). To Moses' contemporaries, the association of "scattering" with "punishment" was a sobering warning because of the curses connected with covenant disobedience. If Israel chose to disobey God, God would scatter them among the nations and fill them with terror and dread (Deut. 28:64-67).

The choice of Israel as God's special people is connected with Noah's son Shem, and both chapters 10 and 11 contain genealogies of the family of Shem. Both genealogies mention Shem's descendant Eber (10:24-25; 11:14-17), from whom the name "Hebrew" is derived. In the more detailed genealogy of chapter 11, we are introduced to Terah and his son Abram and their journey from Ur of the Chaldeans to Haran. It is Abram (later called Abraham) and his family who occupy center stage for the rest of Genesis and the Pentateuch.

THE BEGINNINGS OF THE NATION OF ISRAEL

From a literary standpoint, Genesis 1-11 functions as a prologue to the rest of the book and to the Pentateuch as a whole. These chapters provide an indispensable introduction to Genesis and help the reader understand why God chose to make a new beginning with Abram. Although Abram was a sinner like all other men, his faith and obedience marked him as a prophet and God's friend and brought for him and his descendants unparalleled blessing.

THE ABRAHAMIC COVENANT

Of crucial importance for Genesis and the rest of the Bible is the institution of the Abrahamic Covenant, because from this point on God will deal with the nations through the special covenant nation descended from Abraham. God told Abraham to leave his country and his father's family and go to the land of Canaan. As a result of his obedience, God promised to make Abraham into a great nation and to bless him richly. Unlike the "men of renown" in 6:4 and the tower builders who wanted to "make a name" for themselves in 11:4, Abraham's greatness was in accord with God's will and benefited all mankind. "All people on earth will be blessed through you" (v. 3). The original blessing upon mankind given in the creation account (1:28) is to be extended through the family of Abraham. In Genesis, Abraham's family brings blessing to the nations through Joseph's wise provision of food in Egypt (cf. 41:57), but the primary emphasis is upon the spiritual blessing that would come through Jesus Christ, a descendant of Abraham (cf. Acts 3:25-26). Paul calls this promise to Abraham "the gospel in advance" (Gal. 3:8). Just as Abraham believed God (cf. 15:6), so those who have faith in Christ "are blessed along with Abraham " (Gal. 3:9).

Implicit in God's promises to Abraham was possession of a land where the nation could develop. When Abraham arrived in Canaan, God announced that this land would be given to his offspring (12:6). In chapter 15 the boundaries of the land are broadly defined as the river (or wadi) of Egypt in the south and the Euphrates River in the north (v. 18). During the golden age of David and Solomon, Israel did indeed control most of this area (1 Kings 4:21), but normally their northern border did not extend beyond Hamath. The Promised Land per se was confined to the area between Dan and Beersheba, and this was the land divided among the twelve tribes (cf. Deut. 34:1-4). Even though Abraham was an alien in Canaan, God reiterated His promise that some day the whole land would belong to his family and it would be theirs forever (13:15; 17:8).

When Abraham purchased from the Hittites the cave and field of Machpelah in Hebron so that he could bury Sarah, the possession of the Promised Land had begun (23:17-20). By this purchase Abraham was in effect gaining title to the whole land, although it would be hundreds of years before full possession would become a reality (cf. 15:13). Most of the patriarchs were buried in the cave of Machpelah, a symbol that Canaan would eventually become the resting place of the whole nation (cf. Josh. 1:13).

Normally, covenants are ratified by solemn ceremonies, and chapter 15 contains the account of such a ceremony. Abraham was instructed to kill a heifer, a goat, and a ram, cut them in two, and arrange the halves in two rows. Then, as Abraham fell into a deep sleep, "a smoking fire pot with a blazing torch . . . passed between the pieces" (v. 17). Since fire is often a symbol of God (cf. Ex. 3:2; 13:21), the fire pot and torch no doubt represent the Lord. By passing between the pieces, God was committing Himself to the terms of the covenant with a self-maledictory oath. If He violated the covenant, He would in effect be subject to the same fate as the animals. It is significant that the Hebrew expression "make a covenant" is literally "cut a covenant," referring no doubt to the sacrifice of animals in connection with the ratification of the covenant (cf. Ex. 24:5-8).[64]

There is only one other reference to the actual passing between the pieces of an animal, however. In Jeremiah 34:18-19, the Lord condemned the men of Judah for breaking a covenant guaranteeing freedom for Hebrew slaves. Even though they cut a calf in two and "walked between the pieces," they violated their agreement and earned God's wrath in the process. In Genesis 15 only the Lord passed between the pieces, not Abraham. This was a one-sided covenant in which God unconditionally guaranteed that His promises to Abraham would be fulfilled, and because He guaranteed it, this was "an everlasting covenant."

The sign of the covenant. Almost twenty-five years after the original promise, the Lord appeared to Abraham and confirmed His covenant with him. To commemorate this occasion, both Abraham and Sarah were given new names. Up to this point, their names had been "Abram," meaning "exalted Father" (referring to God), and "Sarai," meaning "princess" or "princess-like." In anticipation of the birth of Isaac, Abram is given the name "Abraham," meaning "father of many," and Sarai becomes "Sarah," which also means "princess." In spite of the fact that Abraham and Sarah only had one son through the surrogate mother Hagar, it is now revealed that Abraham will be the "father of many nations" (17:4) and Sarah will be "the mother of nations" (17:16). This was startling news to a husband and wife aged ninety-nine and ninety.

Along with the name change, God announced to Abraham that he and his male descendants would have to be circumcised as the sign of the covenant between God and him. From this day on, every male would have the foreskin of his reproductive organ cut off or he would "be cut off from his people" (17:14). Other nations, such as Egypt, also practiced circumcision, but for them it was associated with reaching puberty. Abraham's descendants were to be circumcised when they were eight days old in order to be included in the covenant. The singling out of the male organ emphasized the need for sexual purity, but circumcision was primarily a symbol of Israel's consecration to God. The physical "cutting" was an indication of submission and commitment to the God of Abraham.

On several occasions the Bible talks about the need to "circumcise" a person's heart so that he will be humble and responsive to God's Word (cf. Lev. 26:41; Deut. 10:16). If someone's heart is circumcised, he will love the Lord

---

64. At Mari, early second millennium texts use the expression "killed a donkey" with the meaning of "made a covenant."

with all his soul (Deut. 30:6). According to the prophets, physical circumcision was not enough, for God demanded a wholehearted commitment from His people (cf. Jer. 4:4).

The responsibilities of the covenant. Although the Abrahamic Covenant is called repeatedly an "everlasting" covenant, there is a sense in which it was conditional for individual Jews.[65] As noted above, all the males had to be circumcised and thus "keep my covenant" (17:9), and chapter 18 mentions that Abraham was faithful in teaching his children and his servants "to keep the way of the Lord" so that they might receive what God promised him (v. 19). Abraham himself had to leave his father's household to journey to the Promised Land, and in 26:5 we are told that "Abraham obeyed me and kept my requirements, my commands, my decrees and my laws." Such terms sound like a description of the Sinai Covenant and imply that if Abraham had been alive when Moses received the law he would have eagerly obeyed God's commands. In Genesis 14:20 we learn that Abraham gave a tithe to Melchizedek (cf. 28:22), an indication that some of the later requirements of the law may have been revealed to Abraham.

Ironically, the most dramatic example of Abraham's obedience involved an action that ran counter to the later levitical prohibition against child sacrifice (Lev. 18:21). When God asked Abraham to sacrifice Isaac as a burnt offering, the faith of the patriarch was severely tested and the whole covenant appeared to be in jeopardy. Yet by his obedience Abraham demonstrated that he loved God more than Isaac and that he was willing to give up his precious son. When God saw Abraham's commitment, He intervened to spare Isaac's life and renew his promise to multiply his offspring (22:16-18).

The confirmation of the covenant. After the death of Abraham the Lord appeared to Isaac and Jacob and reiterated His commitment to the covenant. Usually, a restatement of the covenant promises occurred during a time of crisis in the life of a patriarch. In spite of opposition or danger, God would provide for His own, and He would never abandon the family of Abraham.

In chapter 26 Isaac faces the twin problems of a famine and a group of hostile Philistines. The solution might have been a trip to Egypt, as Abraham had done earlier. But the Lord appeared to Isaac and told him to stay in the land, where God would be with him and would multiply his descendants. All these blessings belonged to Isaac "because Abraham obeyed me" (v. 5). Later, when Isaac dug a well and the Philistines did not dispute its ownership, the Lord appeared once more and repeated His promises. Again, Isaac would be blessed "for the sake of my servant Abraham" (v. 24).

---

65. Ronald Youngblood, "The Abrahamic Covenant: Conditional or Unconditional?" in M. Inch and R. Youngblood, eds., *The Living and Active Word of God* (Winona Lake, Ind.: Eisenbrauns, 1983), pp. 31-46.

In many respects the blessing of Abraham seemed to elude his grandson Jacob, whose deceptive ways brought him into conflict with his own brother. Yet the Abrahamic Covenant was confirmed with Jacob more than with any other of the patriarchs. Even Isaac—who clearly preferred Esau—wound up mistakenly blessing Jacob, almost quoting Genesis 12:3 in the process:

> May those who curse you be cursed
> and those who bless you be blessed.
>   (27:29)

When Jacob had to flee for his life to avoid an enraged Esau, he had a dream and saw the Lord standing above a stairway leading to heaven. Even though Jacob was leaving the Promised Land and heading for Mesopotamia, God promised to be with him and to bring him back to Canaan eventually. Some twenty years later Jacob returned home and after about thirty years came back to Bethel, where God again appeared to him. By now Jacob had eleven sons, but God said that "a nation and a community of nations will come from you" (35:11). It was the same promise God had given Abraham before the birth of Isaac (17:6). Abraham's descendants had not yet become innumerable, but the process of fruitfulness had begun.

Soon a twelfth son was born, but disaster struck when the favorite son, Joseph, had apparently been torn limb from limb. But like Isaac on Mount Moriah, Joseph figuratively rose from the grave when Jacob learned that he was still alive and in fact "ruler of all Egypt" (45:26). Invited to join his beloved son, Jacob prepared to journey to Egypt. Would God approve of this departure from the Promised Land? On his way south Jacob heard the word of the Lord in a vision, and again it was a promise that Jacob's family would return to Canaan. Meanwhile, that family would become "a great nation" in Egypt (46:27). Seventy went with Jacob to Egypt (46:27), but about two million would participate in the Exodus (cf. 12:37).

Just before his death, Jacob reminded Joseph of God's promise to him at Bethel, assuring Jacob that Canaan would be his as an everlasting possession (48:3-4). With Joseph's two sons before him, Jacob proceeded to adopt them as his own, thereby giving Joseph the birthright. His two sons, Manasseh and Ephraim, would be tribes in their own name, giving Joseph a double-share in the inheritance. Appropriately, Ephraim means "twice fruitful," an indication that God had blessed Joseph in exile and that God would continue to make the descendants of Abraham fruitful in fulfillment of His covenant. In his final blessing, Jacob referred to Joseph as "a fruitful vine" (49:22), recalling the meaning of the name "Ephraim" and anticipating the fruitfulness of Jacob's descendants. The almighty God (El-Shaddai) who established His covenant with Abraham (cf. 17:1-2) would abundantly bless the descendants of Jacob and Joseph (49:25). Aware that the Promised Land was Canaan and not Egypt, Joseph made his brothers promise to carry his bones to Canaan after his death (50:25).

THE HISTORICITY OF THE PATRIARCHS

As we move from the primeval to the patriarchal period, we come to an era that is firmly within historical purview. Thanks to the work of archaeologists, the period from 2000-1600 B.C.—called the Middle Bronze Age—has yielded extensive evidence from Mesopotamia, Egypt, and Palestine. With the onslaught of higher critical views about the origin of the Pentateuch toward the end of the nineteenth century, there unfortunately arose a growing skepticism about the historicity of the patriarchs. Julius Wellhausen ruled out the possibility of any genuine historical knowledge about the patriarchs, and the form critic Hermann Gunkel relegated the stories about the patriarchs to the realm of saga or legend.[66] Major German scholars of the twentieth century such as Gerhard von Rad and Martin Noth have maintained this largely negative assessment of our knowledge of the patriarchs.

In America, however, the rise of archaeology and the study of the ancient Near East produced a more positive approach to the patriarchal period. W. F. Albright, the leading archaeologist from 1930 to 1960, wrote that there was no reason to doubt the general accuracy of the historical pictures given in Genesis.[67] One of his students, John Bright, has developed this view most fully in his classic *History of Israel*,[68] placing Abraham toward the start of the second millennium. Clay tablets from the Mesopotamian cities Mari (18th century B.C.) and Nuzi (15th century) contributed valuable information about life in this period.

During the 1970s the moderate views of the Albright school have been challenged by a group of scholars who sought to connect the patriarchs with the first millennium B.C. rather than the second. Led by T. L. Thompson[69] and John van Seters,[70] these scholars claim that others have ignored important evidence from the first millennium that correlates more fully with the patriarchal accounts. If they are right, the accounts are not likely to be historical, Mosaic authorship is of course ruled out, and the Graf-Wellhausen documentary hypothesis would gain new credence. In a critique of Thompson and van Seters, Kenneth Kitchen argues that they overemphasize first-millennium materials and conveniently ignore features that are unique to the second millennium.[71]

66. Herman Gunkel, *The Legends of Genesis* (New York: Schocken, 1984), pp. 19ff.
67. W. F. Albright, *The Biblical Period from Abraham to Ezra* (New York: Torch, 1963), p. 5.
68. Second ed., Philadelphia: Westminster, 1972, pp. 76-102.
69. T. L. Thompson, *The Historicity of the Patriarchal Narratives*, BZAW 133 (1974).
70. John van Seters, *Abraham in History and Tradition* (New Haven: Yale U., 1975).
71. Kenneth Kitchen, *The Bible in Its World* (Exeter: Paternoster, 1977), pp. 58-59.

As in the case of other important biblical figures, there are no explicit references to the patriarchs outside of the Scriptures. The question of their historicity must be studied in the light of the names, events, and culture described in the biblical text. The evidence is considerable and points clearly to an authentic second millennium setting.

Political factors. The patriarchs were sometimes in touch with kings and pharaohs, but unfortunately few of their names are given. Prior to the time of Solomon's son Rehoboam, Egyptian rulers were identified in the Bible only by the general title "Pharaoh," a practice that is equally frustrating in the book of Exodus. In Genesis 14, however, we are given the names of four kings who invade the region around Sodom and Gomorrah and carry off goods and captives. Since Abraham's nephew Lot was among the captives, Abraham became involved in his rescue and led a surprise attack against the four kings. Although none of the four can be positively identified, their names are similar to actual kings who reigned early in the second millennium. "Kedorlaomer" is an Elamite name composed of Kutir (or "Kudur") plus X, and Arioch is similar to the name Arriyuk or Arriwuk found in the Mari tablets from the eighteenth century B.C. The name Tidal (Hebrew *tid'al*) is the equivalent of Tudkhalia, the name of several Hittite kings who ruled anywhere from 1700-1200 B.C. in Asia Minor.[72] In each case it would have been difficult for a first millennium writer to introduce such authentic names into the text. Kitchen also points out that a coalition of the sort would have been possible prior to the reign of the powerful Hammurapi of Babylon about 1700 B.C. but not later.[73]

Another indication of the antiquity of this chapter is the unusual nature of the names of the people who lived near the Dead Sea. When Kedorlaomer and his allies attacked this area, they encountered the Rephaites, Zuzites, Emites and Horites. From Deuteronomy 2:10 and 20 we learn that the Rephaites and Emites used to live in the region later occupied by the Moabites and Ammonites during the time of the Exodus, and the Horites lived in Edom before the descendants of Esau defeated them (Deut. 2:12). Part of Og's kingdom of Bashan was also "known as a land of the Rephaites" (Deut. 3:13).

The freedom with which Abraham and his family moved about in the fertile crescent also ties in well with early second millennium conditions. His trip to Egypt is reminiscent of the famous painting from a tomb at Beni Hasan showing a group of thirty-seven Asiatics arriving in Egypt.[74] The roads were open, allowing armies and private citizens to travel long distances without great difficulty.

In several chapters there is mention of the Philistines and their kings, who were in uneasy contact with both Abraham and Isaac. This early reference to the

---

72. See Kitchen, *Ancient Orient*, pp. 43-44.
73. Ibid., pp. 45-46.
74. Roland de Vaux, *The Early History of Israel* (Philadelphia: Westminster, 1978), p. 226.

Philistines is somewhat surprising since they did not seem to have arrived in Palestine in large numbers until about 1200 B.C. In Genesis their center is Gerar, a city a little farther from the Mediterranean than the Pentapolis familiar to us from the book of Judges. Although they argue with the patriarchs over wives and wells (cf. 20:1-7; 26:8-11, 19-22), the Philistines of Genesis seem to be more peaceful than the contemporaries of Samson. In light of the connection between the Philistines and the island of Crete (also known as "Caphtor") it may be significant that an early invasion of the Caphtorites is mentioned in Deuteronomy 2:23.[75] If Cyrus Gordon's identification of Minoan "Linear A" as Semitic is accepted, it would help explain the Semitic aspects of Philistine culture.[76]

Proper names. The similarities between the names of the patriarchs and names found in extrabiblical sources from about 2000 B.C. stand as one of the strongest arguments for the historicity of the patriarchs. In recent years, the publication of tablets from Ebla in Syria have added an exciting corpus of names to this study. Dated at about 2300 B.C., the Ebla tablets refer to a king named Ebrum (or Ebrium), which is very close to the name of Abraham's ancestor Eber (Gen. 11:14-16).[77] Individuals called Ishmail and Ishrail also appear in the texts, names which are closely related to Ishmael and Israel. Since these individuals lived centuries before the patriarchs, they cannot be identified with the biblical figures, but their appearance indicates that names of this sort were borne by real people.

The name "Abraham" can be compared to Aburahan, found in the Egyptian Execration Texts of about 1800 B.C., and Jacob is close to the name "Yaqub-il." Other helpful parallels are Yasmakh-El (Ishmael) from the tablets found at Ugarit (13th century B.C.).[78] The name of Jacob's son Zebulun is quite similar to the Old Babylonian Zabilanu. Although Thompson argues that names that are similar to the patriarchs can also be found in first millennium sources, the few that he does find come from the late eighth and early seventh centuries.[79] There are virtually no parallels for several centuries at the start of the first millennium.[80]

Social customs. By a study of social customs it is hoped that we can "set the general historical background [of the patriarchs] in a sharper focus than would otherwise be the case."[81] Because of the longevity of particular customs, however, it is sometimes difficult to determine the chronological limits in every

75. Kitchen, *Ancient Orient*, pp. 80-81.
76. C. H. Gordon, *Antiquity* 31 (1957), pp. 124-30.
77. G. Pettinato, *The Archives of Ebla* (Garden City, N.Y.: Doubleday, 1981), pp. 69-71.
78. Kitchen, *Ancient Orient*, p. 48; *The Bible in Its World*, p. 68.
79. Thompson, *Patriarchal Narratives*, pp. 30-35.
80. Cf. La Sor et al., *Survey*, pp. 102-3.
81. M. J. Selman, "Comparative Customs and the Patriarchal Age," in *Essays on the Patriarchal Narratives*, ed. A. R. Millard and D. J. Wiseman (Winona Lake, Ind.: Eisenbrauns, 1983), p. 134.

case. Here again there are those who believe that the first millennium has been overlooked, but as in the study of personal names, most of the evidence places the culture of the patriarchs squarely in the first part of the second millennium.

According to most scholars, certain materials related to the Hurrians and Hittites have been misused, particularly some of the Hurrian materials from the city of Nuzi, a site near Kirkuk in Iraq. The wife-sister marriage developed by Speiser in connection with Genesis 12, 20, and 26[82] has now been largely discounted,[83] and the same is true regarding the reason for Rachel's theft of Laban's household gods.[84] No longer do scholars feel that possession of the gods was primarily related to gaining title to an inheritance. Similarly, the proposed connection between Abraham's purchase of the cave of Machpelah (Gen. 23) and the Hittite law code is now very doubtful. Both the date of the law code and its relevance to the distant hills of Palestine raise questions about any possible relationship.[85]

On the positive side, a careful study of Old Babylonian law codes has been more fruitful in clarifying patriarchal practices, and in some cases these materials have supported evidence from the later (15th century) Nuzi tablets. One such example concerns a man's adoption of a slave as an heir. In Genesis 15:2-3 Abraham refers to a servant named Eliezer from Damascus as the one who will be the heir to his estate. In an Old Babylonian letter from Larsa it mentions that a man who has no sons could adopt a slave as his son,[86] and apparently Abraham was considering this option. Tablets from Nuzi also refer to this custom. Although he had twelve sons, Jacob nonetheless adopted Joseph's sons Ephraim and Manasseh as his own (Gen. 48:5). The adoption of grandsons is also referred to in a Ugaritic text and in paragraph 170 of the law code of Hammurapi.[87]

When Abraham learned that his servant Eliezer would not be his heir but that he would have a son of his own (15:4), he followed another Near Eastern custom to produce that heir. Sarah had a slave girl named Hagar, and she became a surrogate mother for her mistress. Later, Rachel used the same method by giving her servant Bilhah to Jacob to produce Dan (30:2-7). This practice is paralleled by sections 144, 146, and 163 in the Hammurapi law code as well as by a text from Nuzi.[88] In such instances, the child belonged legally to the main

---

82. See Speiser, *Genesis*, AB, pp. 91-94.
83. See C. J. Mullo Weir, "The Alleged Hurrian Wife-Sister Motif in Genesis," *Transactions of the Glasgow University Oriental Society* 22 (1967-68), pp. 14-25; van Seters, *Abraham in History*, pp. 71-76.
84. M. Greenberg, "Another Look at Rachel's Theft of the Teraphim," *JBL* 81 (1962), pp. 239-48.
85. H. A. Hoffner, Jr., "Some Contributions of Hittitology to Old Testament Study," *Tyndale Bulletin* 20 (1969), pp. 33-35.
86. Selman, "Comparative Customs," p. 136.
87. I. Mendelsohn, "A Ugaritic Parallel to the Adoption of Ephraim and Manasseh," *IEJ* 9 (1959), pp. 180-83.
88. Selman, "Comparative Customs," pp. 127, 137. The Nuzi text is HSS 5 67.

wife and not to the slave girl, and normally neither the child nor the natural mother was sold or sent away. This helps explain why Abraham was so upset when God told him to send away Hagar and Ishmael permanently (Gen. 21:11-13).[89]

Since Ishmael was Abraham's oldest son, this raises the question of inheritance rights. Apparently the sons of concubines did not normally share equally with the sons of a man's wife (or wives).[90] Isaac was the only son of Sarah and inherited everything Abraham owned (25:5). Before his death, however, Abraham "gave gifts to the sons of his concubines" (25:6), and this probably included Ishmael also. The oldest son was entitled to the birthright, normally a double-share of the inheritance. When Esau sold his birthright to Jacob (25:33), he was following a custom some scholars say has a parallel in the Nuzi tablets. Others argue that the tablets in question do not deal specifically with future inheritance rights. In any case, there are several examples that describe the transference of part of an inheritance from brother to brother.[91] The birthright itself could be transferred from one son to another by the father if a serious breach of conduct occurred. Reuben forfeited the birthright by sleeping with his father's concubine Bilhah (35:22; 49:3-4).

The issue of inheritance was also involved in the complaint registered by Jacob's wives Rachel and Leah against their father Laban. Apparently Laban had not given them the portion of the bride payment that was usually transferred to the girls as a dowry. When Rachel and Leah complained that Laban "has used up what was paid for us" (32:15), the Hebrew idiom involved ('ākal kesep) is identical to the Akkadian equivalent (kaspa akālu) found five times in the Nuzi tablets.[92] The existence of such a precise parallel to the biblical wording again places the patriarchs in a second millennium rather than a first millennium context.

THE NEAR-SACRIFICE OF ISAAC

In all of the Bible there are few chapters that can compare with Genesis 22 in dramatic power and theological significance. Here is a demonstration of Abraham's love for God and commitment to Him that is overwhelming and inspiring. At the same time we are given a picture of God's profound love for mankind, because the same God who stopped Abraham from killing Isaac "did not spare his own Son, but gave him up for us all" (Rom. 8:32). There is a clear parallel between Isaac and Jesus in Hebrews 11:17, where Isaac is called Abra-

---

89. Kitchen, *The Bible in Its World*, p. 71.
90. Cf. Hammurapi law, section 170; Selman, "Comparative Customs," p. 137.
91. Selman, "Comparative Customs," p. 116; Thompson, *Patriarchal Narratives*, pp. 280-85.
92. Selman, "Comparative Customs," pp. 123, 138; Speiser, *Genesis*, AB, pp. 244-45.

ham's "one and only son" (cf. Gen. 22:2). The Greek term (*monogenēs*) is the same one applied to Christ in John 3:16.

Isaac was Abraham's unique son in that he was the only son of Sarah and was the bearer of the covenant. As we observe the pain of Abraham as he took Isaac to Mount Moriah, we are given a glimpse of the heart of God the Father as He sent His Son to the cross. This perspective is not drawn out in the gospels as fully as it is in Genesis. Within the context of the Pentateuch, the near-sacrifice of Isaac helps us understand the meaning of the animal sacrifices described mainly in Leviticus. Such sacrifices were clearly substitutionary, for the animal was accepted on behalf of the offerer "to make atonement for him" (Lev. 1:4). When Abraham released Isaac and offered in his place "a ram caught by its horns," we are given a drastic example of substitution. In the same way we think of Christ as "the Lamb of God, who takes away the sin of the world" (John 1:29). Isaac's death would not have accomplished redemption, for he was a sinful human being, remarkable as his submission to Abraham may have been. But Jesus was sinless, and His death was the only sacrifice that could truly atone for sin.

From the perspective of the covenant, Abraham was, of course, perplexed about God's command. Why would God promise to fulfill the covenant through Isaac (cf. 21:12) and then ask Abraham to put him to death? No wonder this is called a test (22:1), for God would quickly learn what was in Abraham's heart (cf. Deut. 8:2, 16). By his response Abraham would demonstrate whether or not he loved Isaac more than God. This ordeal was also a test of Abraham's faith, and we find that Abraham did cling to the truthfulness of God's earlier promises. From Hebrews 11:17 we learn that Abraham believed "that God could raise the dead, and figuratively speaking, he did receive Isaac back from death." After all, Isaac had been given life in the dead womb of Sarah, and the same Lord who had brought about his miraculous birth could raise Isaac from the dead if necessary. Was this faith behind Abraham's statement to his servants that "we will worship and then we will come back to you" (22:5)?

The place to which Abraham took Isaac was called "the region of Moriah" (v. 2). According to 2 Chronicles 3:1, Mount Moriah was the site of Solomon's Temple and was known throughout the kingdom period as the Temple mount. It was there that Solomon and his successors offered countless sacrifices, and after the Exile the Temple was rebuilt at the same location. Earlier, Abraham had conversed with Melchizedek at this very area, if Salem and Jerusalem are to be identified (cf. 14:18). Moriah lay just north of ancient Jerusalem, and it would become the center of worship for Abraham's descendants after David captured the city about 1000 B.C.

By his obedience Abraham clearly demonstrated that he feared God, as the angel acknowledged (v. 12). He trusted God implicitly and reverently submitted to His command in spite of the nature of the request. In so doing, Abraham set an example for his descendants, who were constantly taught to fear the Lord. On another important mountain—Mount Sinai—the Israelites were awestruck as God revealed Himself to them in thunder and lightning. God had come to test them so that, like Abraham, they would fear God and refrain from sinning (Ex. 20:18-20). Whatever the situation and whatever the need, "the Lord will provide" (Gen. 22:14).

Although we do not know how young Isaac was at the time of his ordeal, the issue of child sacrifice deserves some mention. Nearby nations such as the Ammonites and Phoenicians condoned child sacrifice, but kings of Israel were harshly condemned for this practice (cf. 2 Chron. 33:6). God's favor was not gained through shedding of innocent blood. In a bizarre incident recorded in 2 Kings 3:26-27, the king of Moab offered his firstborn son—the crown prince —as a sacrifice to ward off almost certain defeat. Such drastic action indicated that the king was desperate to appease his god, but the method was an abomination to the God of Israel (cf. Lev. 18:21).

As noted above, Abraham's obedience became the occasion for a restatement of the covenant promises. A chapter that began as a threat to the chosen son ended with a firm commitment to the expansion and success of the nation as a people singularly blessed by God (22:15-18).

THE ORIGIN OF THE TWELVE TRIBES

Like the number seven, the number twelve takes on significance in Genesis.[93] Abraham's brother Nahor had twelve sons (22:20-24) as did his son Ishmael (25:13-16), but the most famous occurrence of "twelve" is tied to the family of Jacob. Throughout the Old Testament we are told about the twelve tribes of Israel and their geographical allotments, and even in the New Testament the twelve disciples and the twelve gates of the new Jerusalem (Rev. 21:12) reflect the same ideal.

According to some scholars, the names of the twelve tribes refer only to groups and not individuals,[94] but the Genesis account points to a literal twelve sons. Most of them were born in Mesopotamia, and Exodus tells us that they became a large nation in Egypt. But their ultimate destiny was the land of Canaan.

Jacob's journey to Paddan Aram was occasioned by his dispute with Esau over the blessing of Isaac. Encouraged by Rebekah, Jacob had lived up to his name by deceiving his father and obtaining the coveted blessing. The result was a conflict with his brother that would continue between their descendants perpetually. When Jacob reached Haran he happily located his mother's family, but he was not prepared for the hard lessons he would learn from Rebekah's brother

93. But John J. Davis says that the number seven is the only number used symbolically in Scripture with any consistency. Cf. *Biblical Numerology* (Grand Rapids: Baker, 1968), p. 116.
94. van Seters, *Abraham in History*, p. 39.

Laban. Jacob fell deeply in love with Laban's daughter Rachel only to discover after seven years of work that he was given Leah instead. In this country, explained Laban, the oldest daughter always gets married first.

Jacob was also given his beloved Rachel, but it was Leah who had the children—Reuben, Simeon, Levi, and Judah in rapid succession. Understandably Rachel became jealous and cried out for a child. Like Sarah, she gave her servant Bilhah to Jacob to produce offspring for her, and Leah followed suit with Zilpah. Suddenly Jacob had four wives, divided into at least two factions, and down through the years the Rachel and Leah tribes competed for family leadership. Jacob made matters worse by favoring Joseph and Benjamin, arousing the jealousy of Leah's offspring. Eventually, Leah's sons tried to get rid of Joseph and sold him to traders on their way to Egypt (37:38). In later years the Joseph tribes (especially Ephraim) and Judah vied for leadership, and after Solomon's reign the kingdom was split in half.

Unlike the children of Abraham's concubines (cf. 25:6), the sons of Jacob's concubines received inheritances as full members of the family. Perhaps this was partially due to the fact that the two concubines—Zilpah and Bilhah—had been given by Laban to Leah and Rachel as part of the dowry (29:24, 29).[95] Their main function was to be servants to Jacob's wives, but when Rachel had difficulty becoming pregnant, Bilhah became a surrogate mother (30:3). Not to be outdone, Leah gave Zilpah to Jacob to produce children on her behalf (30:9). The four boys born to the servant girls—Dan, Naphtali, Gad, and Asher—counted as part of the twelve, but none of the four ever became prominent. The tribe of Dan was known best, owing to the exploits of Samson in the book of Judges.

When Rachel finally became pregnant and gave birth to Joseph, Jacob was ready to return to Canaan. But first he built up his flocks and herds after Laban agreed to give him all the newborn speckled, spotted, and streaked sheep and goats. Through God's intervention Jacob's share of the flocks grew dramatically, upsetting Laban and his sons. With the agreement of his wives, Jacob decided to return to his homeland secretly to avoid further trouble, but Laban found out about their departure and set out in pursuit. When he caught up with Jacob he complained bitterly about the way Jacob was deceiving him (31:26) and about the theft of his gods. Unknown to Jacob, Rachel had stolen Laban's household gods, and she kept them hidden in her camel's saddle while Laban searched for them. Her excuse to Laban for remaining seated was that she was having her period (31:35).

There has been much discussion about Rachel's reason for taking these idols (cf. "Social Customs" above). Apparently she wanted them for protection, for guidance (cf. Ezek. 21:21), or even to promote fertility. Her attachment

---

95. Cf. Selman, "Comparative Customs," p. 137.

to these idols illustrates the strong influence of paganism upon Laban's family. Once they reached Canaan, Jacob urged all the members of his household to get rid of their foreign gods and to worship the Lord (35:2). Several centuries later the descendants of Jacob left Egypt only to become involved in the worship of the golden calf. When Moses became aware of their idolatry he took stern measures to put an end to their apostasy (Ex. 32:4, 20).

One reason Jacob spent twenty years with Laban was the fear of having to face Esau. As that dreaded encounter drew near, Jacob prayed for God's protection and even wrestled with an angel during the night. In the midst of his spiritual and physical struggle, Jacob was given the new name of "Israel," meaning "he struggles with God" (35:28). He who had been a deceiver and had used schemes of all kinds to achieve his goals now submitted to God in this life-changing experience. Jacob became Israel and received God's blessing. After such a harrowing experience, the meeting with Esau was almost anticlimactic, but happily the two brothers were reconciled and were able to live in peace.

Peace is not the theme of chapter 34, however, when two of Jacob's sons, Simeon and Levi, orchestrate a treacherous attack against the prominent city of Shechem. Angered by the rape of their sister Dinah, Jacob's sons used deceit to get revenge on the whole city, including the leaders, Hamor and Shechem. If the Lord had not intervened, other Canaanites probably would have wiped out Jacob's small clan (cf. 34:30; 35:5). The conflict between Jacob's family and the Canaanites did not erupt in full force until the nation of Israel left Egypt and returned to conquer the Promised Land (cf. Joshua 6).

THE STRUCTURE OF THE JOSEPH NARRATIVE

The last of the *toledoth*, the "accounts" in Genesis, is the account of Jacob (37:2) containing the record of his sons' activities and particularly the story of Joseph. Found in chapters 37-50, this account is the most beautiful from a literary point of view, moving from a description of bitter jealousy between brothers to a portrayal of deep brotherly concern and reconciliation. For Jacob the story begins with the apparent death of his beloved Joseph and ends with unspeakable joy as father and son are reunited. Through it all shines the unmistakable presence of God who takes the hatred of man and uses it to save the entire family and many other lives besides (cf. 50:20). Rarely has God's providence been so evident in such an extended passage.

The Joseph narrative also provides a transition from Mesopotamia and Canaan to the land of Egypt, where the drama contained in Exodus unfolds. Though briefly visited by Abraham (12:10-20), Egypt now becomes the home for the twelve tribes where—thanks to Joseph's foresight—they can retain their religion and traditions without too much interference. Placed by Joseph in the district of Goshen in the northeastern part of Egypt, the family of Jacob lived within easy range of Canaan (47:27). But little did they know how difficult it would be to return to the Promised Land.

Although the Lord had revealed Himself in dreams earlier in Genesis (cf. 28:12), when we come to the Joseph narrative the dreams now occur in pairs, and they are symbolic in nature. Joseph himself had the two dreams indicating his superiority to his brothers—dreams that so incensed them that they decided to get rid of him (37:5-11). While languishing in an Egyptian prison, Joseph later interpreted the dreams of Pharaoh's cupbearer and baker, dreams that were similar in nature but very different in their interpretation (40:7-19). The two dreams of Pharaoh—which were also interpreted by Joseph—had essentially the same meaning (41:25-27) and of course opened the way for Joseph's rise to prominence.

The Joseph narrative is a tightly knit whole, and chapter 38 with its description of Judah seems to be intrusive. Upon closer examination, however, chapter 38 is an integral part of the development of the entire story and helps us understand why Joseph and not Judah received the birthright (1 Chron. 5:1). Judah fails miserably in this chapter, first by only half-heartedly following the practice of levirate marriage and second by sleeping with a supposed prostitute.[96] His daughter-in-law Tamar, to whom Judah refused to give his last son, took matters into her own hands by posing as a prostitute and becoming pregnant through Judah. One of her twin sons, Perez, became the ancestor of David (Ruth 4:18-22) and of Christ (Matt. 1:1-6). Initially, Judah had ordered Tamar to be burned to death (38:24) but changed his tune when he was identified as the father (v. 26).

Judah's moral weakness stands in sharp contrast to Joseph's ability to resist temptation in chapter 39. When Potiphar's wife invited him to sleep with her, Joseph refused and fled the scene. Even though he had been abandoned by his own brothers and sold into slavery, Joseph remained a faithful son of the Abrahamic Covenant by rejecting sexual immorality (cf. 39:9).

In the blessing of Jacob in chapter 49 Judah is given the right to rule the tribes, a position as full of honor as the blessing received by Joseph. What happened between chapters 38 and 49 to account for such a change in Judah's status? I believe the answer lies in Judah's courageous offer to guarantee the safety of Benjamin when Jacob finally allowed his youngest son to make the trip to Egypt. When Benjamin was caught with the silver cup in his sack, the other brothers were offered their freedom, but Judah begged the Egyptian official to release Benjamin and keep him as a slave (44:33-34). At this display of love for both Benjamin and Jacob, Joseph finally told his brothers who he was and threw his arms around them (45:1-15).

---

96. According to the Hittite law code, section 193, a father-in-law could perform the levirate duties if no brother was available. Cf. *ANET*, p. 196; O. R. Gurney, *The Hittites* (Baltimore: Penguin, 1961), p. 101.

Joseph's startling revelation was the culmination of a lengthy process wherein he tested his brothers. After they arrived in Egypt to buy grain, he set in motion a plan to find out if the brothers were as jealous of Benjamin as they had been of him and if they still cared little about their father's feelings. To do this, Joseph at first treated his brothers harshly but at the same time put their money back in their sacks. Then he gave Benjamin larger portions of food to observe the brothers' reaction (43:34).

The final exam involved the placing of Joseph's silver cup in Benjamin's sack—a plan that Joseph may have devised after hearing how his mother had hidden the household gods from Laban (31:34). The unsuspecting brothers were dumbfounded when Benjamin's sack contained the missing cup. Returning to Joseph they resigned themselves to spending the rest of their lives as slaves in Egypt—a fate that their descendants would sadly have to endure. But Joseph had the perfect solution: leave Benjamin in Egypt and return home to Canaan. If they did this, Joseph would know that their hearts had not changed much over the years. It would tell him that they still did not have much love for Benjamin and that they did not care if Jacob died in sorrow. To Joseph's great joy, however, the brothers did not take the easy way out. They had clearly repented of their earlier sin and could now share God's blessing under Joseph's care.

Given the Egyptian setting of the Joseph narrative, it is not surprising that a study of specific terms and practices can help us appreciate the historical background of the story. As in the case of the Mesopotamian materials, most of the evidence points toward a second millennium context. For example, the word *sārîs*, used to describe Potiphar in 37:36 and 39:1, is translated "eunuch" elsewhere in the Old Testament. Since Potiphar was a married man and since eunuchs were rarely found in ancient Egypt, this poses a serious problem. But Kenneth Kitchen has shown how the word *sārîs* changed its meaning from "official" or "courtier" in the second millennium to "eunuch" in the first millennium.[97] The other books in the Old Testament that have *sārîs* all come from the first millennium and use the term in its later sense. When Potiphar purchased Joseph, he paid twenty shekels of silver, the correct sum for a slave at about 1800 B.C. By the fifteenth century B.C. the price had climbed to thirty shekels, and it rose to fifty shekels in the first millennium.[98]

Joseph's meteoric rise to power placed him in a position second-in-command to Pharaoh himself, a position the Egyptians called vizier. According to Genesis 41:43 he was in charge of the whole land of Egypt, and in 45:8 Joseph is called "father to Pharaoh, lord of his entire household and ruler of all Egypt." It is also possible that the obscure term *'abrēk* (41:43), translated "make way" or "bow down," is a word that actually means "vizier." The Akkadian *abarakku*,

97. See Kitchen, *Ancient Orient*, pp. 115-66.
98. Ibid., pp. 52-53.

meaning "steward," may be related to *'abrēk*.[99] Semites were known to have achieved high positions in the Egyptian government at an early date, so Joseph's success would not have been unprecedented.[100]

When Joseph was rushed into Pharaoh's presence to interpret his dreams, the Egyptian background of the story is unmistakable. In characteristic fashion Joseph shaved off his beard (41:14), for the clean-shaven Egyptians were very different from the bearded Semites and other Asiatics. Normally shaving off one's beard was a sign of mourning for a Semite (cf. Jer. 41:5), and if anyone was compelled to shave his beard it was considered an insult (cf. 2 Sam. 10:4-5). Since Joseph had been a prisoner, however, he was not really in a position to complain, and since he was being taken to the king's court it would be absolutely necessary to be clean shaven and properly attired. In his subsequent role as a top administrator, Joseph likely kept his beard off indefinitely, and his Egyptian appearance contributed to the effectiveness of his disguise when his brothers came to buy grain. Egypt was also renowned for its fine linen, so when Joseph was put in charge of the whole country he was dressed in robes of fine linen (41:42). The mention of the signet-ring and gold chain underscore the authority of Joseph, although such symbols were known in other countries as well (cf. Esther 3:10).

In theory Egypt had always been the property of the pharaoh and the people his tenants, but as a result of Joseph's economic policies the theory became a fact.[101] During the seven years of plenty the Egyptians had to contribute 20 percent of their harvest to the government (41:34), and during the years of famine the people spent all the money they had to buy these same crops (47:15). After that they traded their livestock for food, and when the animals were gone, they sold Pharaoh their land in exchange for food (47:19-20). In effect the people became serfs to whom the land was leased, and after the famine ended a fifth of the harvest had to be returned to the Pharaoh perpetually.[102] Genesis notes that the priests did not have to sell their land and were thus able to retain their powerful position vis-à-vis the pharaoh (47:22, 26).

Because of the valuable service rendered to Egypt by Joseph, when he and his father, Jacob, died their bodies were embalmed following the usual lengthy procedure (50:2-3, 26). The mummification process was of course well-known in Egypt and marks another genuine feature of the Joseph narrative. Although Joseph "was placed in a coffin in Egypt" (50:26), his goal was to be buried in Canaan, the Promised Land where Israel as a nation would experience the fullness of God's blessing (vv. 24-25).

99. W. G. Lambert, *Babylonian Wisdom Literature* (Oxford: Clarendon, 1960), p. 259.
100. Kitchen, *The Bible in Its World*, p. 74. Roland de Vaux says that a later writer attempted to glorify Joseph by making him appear to be the vizier. Joseph's name is not included in any available list of viziers (*Early History*, pp. 297-98).
101. J. D. Douglas, ed., *New Bible Dictionary* (Grand Rapids: Eerdmans, 1962), p. 659.
102. Cf. de Vaux, *Early History*, pp. 305-6.

4

EXODUS

Like Genesis, Exodus is a powerful and dramatic book of beginnings as it depicts the descendants of Abraham becoming a well-organized nation. Exodus is a book of salvation and deliverance, relating how the Israelites gain their freedom from Egypt under the mighty hand of God. The firstborn of Egypt die as the Passover angel spares the precious sons of Israel for whom the blood of the lamb was shed. At Mount Sinai God reveals Himself to Israel and enters into a covenant with them, a covenant summarized in the Ten Commandments. There in the Sinai desert God gives to Israel the Tabernacle, a sanctuary where the people can worship the Lord who now dwells in their very midst.

TITLE

The Greek translators of the Old Testament gave the name "Exodos" to the second book of the Pentateuch. It was a superb title, since the word means "exit" or "departure" and since the book describes the departure of Israelites from Egypt after a difficult period of slavery. The word appears in the Greek Bible in Exodus 19:1. The English "Exodus" is the Latin variation of the Greek word and is found in the Vulgate, the splendid Latin translation of Jerome.

The Hebrew title is "These are the names of" taken from the first words of the book. Unlike "In the beginning" for Genesis, the Hebrew title does not fit the overall content of the book very well, but it does link Exodus with Genesis 46:8, where the names of Jacob's sons are also given. In Exodus 1:2-5 the order is slightly different, giving the sons of Leah and Rachel before the four sons of the concubines. The "seventy" who came to Egypt became an innumerable host before finally gaining their release from Egypt.

PURPOSE AND SCOPE

The book of Exodus was written to describe the difficulties of the Israelites in Egypt and the faithfulness of the God who rescued them from their bondage. Not only did the Lord deliver them from Egypt, He entered into a formal covenant with the nation at Mount Sinai and taught them how to live and how to worship. Through the giving of the Ten Commandments, God showed the Israelites how to maintain a proper relationship with Him and with one another. The instructions about the Tabernacle enabled the people to approach the Lord and to be conscious of His presence among them.

Among the promises to Abraham was the assurance that his descendants would be fruitful and multiply (cf. Gen. 35:11-12), and in the early verses of Exodus we learn that this did indeed happen in Egypt (1:7). When the covenant was instituted, however, Abraham was also told that his descendants would "be enslaved and mistreated four hundred years" in a foreign land (Gen. 15:13). That grim prediction was fulfilled in Egypt as the Israelites suffered greatly, at least during the latter part of the four hundred years. But God did not forget His covenant with Abraham and, through the mediation of Moses, delivered His people from the house of slavery.

For the Israelites, the great themes of salvation and redemption were inextricably linked with the Exodus from Egypt. God was a God who above all else rescued Israel from their horrible situation and won their freedom with His mighty hand. While accomplishing His purposes God revealed His character to the Israelites and the Egyptians when He made known to them His name "Yahweh." Appearing to Moses in the burning bush, God disclosed that He was the great "I AM" and that He would be with His people in their distress (Ex. 3:12, 14). Through the plagues and the miracle of crossing the Red Sea the Israelites came to know more fully who Yahweh really was (Ex. 6:3), and through these acts of judgment the Egyptians learned the hard way that Israel's God was "the Lord" (Ex. 7:5). He was the Lord of history, "majestic in holiness, awesome in glory, working wonders" (Ex. 15:11).[1]

When God spared the firstborn sons of the Israelites, He instituted the feast of the Passover, which became a calendar-changing event (cf. 12:2). The blood of a lamb had to be placed on the door frame of each house on the fourteenth day of the month, and the angel of the Lord "passed over" each house where the blood was visible (cf. v. 13). The death of a lamb in place of the death of the eldest son served as a dramatic illustration of substitutionary atonement (cf. also Gen. 22:13) and is used in the New Testament with reference to Christ when He is called "our Passover lamb" (1 Cor. 5:7; John 1:29). Throughout the Old Testament the Passover was the most important of the religious festivals and served as a reminder of God's mercy and deliverance. The Last Supper observed by Jesus and His disciples was a celebration of the Passover meal.

Before completing the relatively short journey to Canaan the Israelites spent a year at Mount Sinai, receiving instructions from the Lord and preparing to fight the Canaanites. This strategic interlude was designed to turn a disorga-

1. Cf. Walter Kaiser, "Exodus," in *EBC* (Grand Rapids: Zondervan, 1990), 2:292-93.

nized band of slaves into a cohesive nation, one that was deeply committed to the God of their fathers. At Mount Sinai God revealed Himself to the people and entered into a covenant with them. Called the Sinai, or Mosaic, Covenant, this agreement is also known as the Old Covenant and has given its name to the Old Testament.

Here at Mount Sinai Israel was given the key principles to godly living summed up in the Ten Commandments, and these were followed by specific guidelines for how to apply the Ten Commandments (chaps. 21-23). When Israel agreed to obey God and keep His covenants, God promised that they would be His special nation, "a kingdom of priests and a holy nation" (19:5-6). To help them achieve this lofty goal, the Lord designed a Tabernacle and appointed priests to serve there. God Himself would "dwell among them" (25:8), and when the sanctuary was completed "the glory of the Lord filled the tabernacle" (40:35). Under Moses' supervision the Tabernacle was constructed and Moses' brother Aaron became the high priest. As beautiful as it was simple, the Tabernacle enabled the Israelites to worship God and to keep Him at the center of their lives.

While Moses was on Mount Sinai receiving the Ten Commandments and the design for the Tabernacle, the rest of the nation was at the foot of the mountain getting involved in the worship of the golden calf.[2] Aaron lost control of the people and allowed them to talk him into fashioning an idol for them (Ex. 32:1-4). This was a flagrant violation of the second commandment, and Moses sharply condemned Aaron for his action. Aaron was supposed to make atonement for the people rather than lead them into sin. How could the nation fall into apostasy so soon after agreeing to the terms of the covenant in chapter 24?

In light of Israel's refusal to be a holy nation, the Lord vowed to destroy them and start all over again with Moses, making him into "a great nation" (32:10; cf. Gen. 12:2). But Moses pled with God on the basis of His promises to Abraham and the patriarchs (32:13), and total judgment was averted. Moses broke the two tablets containing the Ten Commandments as a sign that the people had broken the covenant (32:19), but the Lord gave him two new tablets when he climbed Mount Sinai again (cf. 34:1, 27-28). In spite of the judgment that befell part of the nation, God used this occasion to reveal to Moses His goodness, compassion, and mercy (cf. 33:19; 34:6).

LITERARY STRUCTURE

Like Genesis, Exodus is a mix of literary genres, including narrative, poetry, legal, and cultic materials. The book begins with a rapid survey of the expe-

---

2. In June 1990 archaeology professor Lawrence Stager of Harvard University uncovered a small calf at the site of the ancient Philistine city of Ashkelon. The tiny, well-preserved figure was about four and a half inches in length and height. Its body was made of bronze, and its legs and head were silver. The find apparently dates to about 1550 B.C. and indicates that calf-worship was common in Canaan as well as in Egypt even prior to the time of Moses.

rience of the Israelites in Egypt after the death of Joseph. Verses 1-6 provide a link to Genesis by referring to the twelve sons of Jacob, who are also listed in Genesis 46. Joseph is emphasized, indicating that the author assumes that the reader is familiar with the last fourteen chapters of Genesis. But in contrast to the favored position of Jacob's family while Joseph ruled Egypt, the Israelites found themselves reduced to slave status. Most of chapters 1-12 describe the suffering of the people and the role of Moses in gaining their freedom. This beautifully interconnected narrative tells about the birth of Moses, his expulsion from Egypt, and his return forty years later to challenge Pharaoh. When Pharaoh refused to release the Israelites, God sent the plagues to judge Egypt and demonstrate His power. The plagues seem to be arranged in three groups of three followed by the dramatic tenth plague. Many of the plagues were directed at specific deities to show their inherent weakness.

After the death of the firstborn we are given a narrative account of the Exodus, the crossing of the Red Sea, and the journey to Mount Sinai (12:31–18:27). Interspersed in the narrative are lists of regulations for the celebration of the Passover (12:43-49) and the feast of Unleavened Bread (13:3-10) as well as the consecration of the firstborn (13:2, 11-16). Chapter 15 contains a magnificent song of victory commemorating the startling defeat of the mighty Egyptians at the Red Sea. This powerful hymn contains many archaic elements, much like Genesis 49.[3] In chapters 15-17 we are also introduced to the grumbling and quarreling of the people. Their complaints become an all too familiar refrain in Exodus and later in Numbers (cf. Ex. 15:24; 16:2, 7; 17:2).

With the arrival of the nation in the Desert of Sinai, we come to the main legal section of the book, which is sometimes called "the Book of the Covenant" (24:7). Chapters 19-24 contain a list of the covenant stipulations—the Ten Commandments—and a whole series of specific laws spelling out some of the implications of the Ten Commandments. Scholars sometimes refer to the Ten Commandments as *apodictic* statements, which are given in the form of "You shall/You shall not." This type of law is rare in other ancient law codes but has parallels with the stipulations that appear in treaties. For example, the Hittite king Mursilis tells his vassal king, "Do not turn your eyes to anyone else" in an attempt to secure his firm allegiance.[4] Similarly, God told Israel, "You shall have no other gods before me" (Ex. 20:1).

A more common legal form is *casuistic* or *case* law, which is given in an "if-then" arrangement. "If you commit this crime, then you will suffer the following penalty." The material in Exodus 21:1–22:17 is largely presented in casuistic form and deals with such areas as the treatment of servants and penalties

---

3. Cf. W. F. Albright, *Yahweh and the Gods of Canaan* (Garden City, N.Y.: Doubleday, 1968), pp. 12-13.
4. The treaty between Mursilis II and Duppi-Teshub of Amurru, *ANET*, p. 204.

THE LITERARY STRUCTURE OF EXODUS

Part 1: Exodus (Historical Narrative)

The Oppression of Israel	Chap. 1
The Call of Moses	Chaps. 2-6
The Ten Plagues	Chaps. 7-11
The Exodus and Journey to Mount Sinai	Chaps. 12-18

The Passover (chap. 12)
The Feast of Unleavened Bread (13:3-10)

Part 2: Legal Section

The Book of the Covenant	Chaps. 19-24

The Ten Commandments (chap. 20)
(Covenant Stipulations)

Part 3: Worship

Instruction for Building the Tabernacle	Chaps. 25-31

Ends with command to keep the Sabbath (31:12-17)

False Worship: The Golden Calf	Chaps. 32-34
The Building of the Tabernacle	Chaps. 35-40

Begins with command to keep the Sabbath (35:1-3)

for assault and battery or for stealing or damaging personal property. Laws about sexual misconduct, the treatment of the poor, and honesty in court are also included. In chapter 24 Moses describes the covenant ratification ceremony as the people promise to obey God.

The final sixteen chapters of the book deal with the Tabernacle, except for the golden calf episode found in chapters 32-34. In chapters 25-31 God gives Moses instructions about the building of the Tabernacle and the craftsmen who would do the work. Then in chapters 35-40 Bezalel and his associates construct the Tabernacle and its furnishings. Each of these sections has a paragraph about keeping the Sabbath, first at the end of the instruction materials (31:12-17) and second at the beginning of the construction process (35:1-3). Since the Sabbath was the sign of the Mosaic Covenant (31:13), the Lord was careful to remind the people not to work on the Sabbath, not even when they were making the Tabernacle.[5]

Before Moses had a chance to come down from Mount Sinai and bring God's word to the people, the worship of the golden calf had begun. Chapters

5. Cf. Ronald Youngblood, *Exodus*, Everyman's Bible Commentary (Chicago: Moody, 1983), pp. 112-13.

32-34 thus interrupt the Tabernacle accounts to emphasize the contrast between God's holiness and man's sinfulness. A rebellious nation needed a place where offerings could be presented to make atonement for sin to purify the people. Through the construction of the Tabernacle, God provided a way for Israel to approach Him.

The Exodus from Egypt became the main illustration in the Bible of God's ability to save His people. It took a mighty God to deliver Israel "from the power of Pharaoh" (Deut. 7:8) and centuries later from the power of Babylon (Isa. 52:9; see "God as Redeemer" in chap. 1). When the infant Jesus was taken from Egypt back to Palestine, Matthew quotes Hosea 11:1, a verse that referred to the Exodus: "Out of Egypt I called my son" (Matt. 2:15). In the New Testament most allusions to the Exodus and redemption compare deliverance from slavery to deliverance from sin (cf. Rom. 3:24). Through Christ the believer has been rescued "from the dominion of darkness" just as the Israelites were freed from Pharaoh's oppressive power (Col. 1:13-14).

LIBERATION THEOLOGY

The remarkable deliverance of Israel from Egypt and its slavery has become associated in recent years with the development of liberation theology. Taking their cue from the seminal work of Gustavo Gutierrez, *A Theology of Liberation*,[6] a number of theologians have dedicated their writings to the liberation of the poor and oppressed, particularly in the countries of Latin America. Juan Segundo and José Miranda are other scholars who have written about the need for social revolution to obtain the freedom of oppressed peoples. Often capitalism is identified as the villain that perpetrates social and economic injustice, and Marxism is appealed to as a solution to the dilemma. Although most of the liberation theologians are Roman Catholics, they do not hesitate to appeal to the writings of Hegel and Marx and in some ways are trying to Christianize Marx. The goal is not atheistic Communism, but Marx's class analysis and economic views are very evident among liberation theologians. European influence on the movement has come from Jürgen Moltmann's *Theology of Hope* with its emphasis on God as the one who makes all things new.[7]

The book of Exodus has also been utilized by other groups seeking relief from oppression, most notably American blacks involved in the civil rights movement. Moses' request to Pharaoh, "Let my people go" (5:1), has become a watchword of Americans who feel that they have been discriminated against. Though such a slogan would have applied more precisely during the time of slavery, it still serves as a denunciation of all kinds of oppression. One of the contributions of liberation theology is its emphasis on social justice, and this is

---

6. Gustavo Gutierrez, *A Theology of Liberation* (Mary Knoll, N.Y.: Orbis, 1973).
7. cf. Emilio Núñez, *Liberation Theology*, trans. Paul Sywulka (Chicago: Moody, 1985), p. 197.

certainly an important theme of Exodus, as well as of the later prophets (cf. Isa. 10:1-2). Because of the suffering of the Israelites in Egypt, God urged them to show particular kindness to poor people and aliens (cf. Ex. 23:6, 9). The cruelty of Egypt's taskmasters was long remembered (Ex. 5:16), so proper treatment of servants and employees was important to the Jews. Wherever the causes of poverty can be removed, governmental leaders should be actively involved.

In their use of Exodus, liberation theologians are sometimes guilty of reading their ideas into the text. Those who suggest that the Israelites revolted against Pharaoh are overlooking the main elements of the story. Moses asked for permission to lead the people into the desert to worship God, not to install a new form of government over Egypt. When deliverance finally came, it was accomplished through the sovereign power of God rather than the stubborn resolve of the Israelites.[8] Even after their release, some of the people felt that things had been better in Egypt than out in the desert, and they longingly recalled the food they enjoyed in Egypt (cf. 16:3). Such complaining sounds a warning for those who advocate revolt in order to achieve freedom. What sort of "freedom" will the people enjoy under a new regime? Those who point an accusing finger at the oppression of capitalist governments often ignore the oppressive tactics of socialists or Communist regimes.

With their emphasis on making improvements in the social order, liberation theologians define salvation almost exclusively in political terms and ignore a person's need of salvation from sin. Sin is in fact defined as man's inhumanity to man[9] rather than as rebellion against God. Yet in Genesis 15:6 Abraham is made righteous by believing the Lord, and the same term is used in connection with the Exodus. When the Israelites saw God's great power in overthrowing the chariots of Pharaoh, they "put their trust in him and in Moses his servant" (Ex. 14:31). It was God who had saved them from Egypt, and it was He who saved them from sin. In their zeal for political reform, liberation theologians tend to overlook the need for the salvation of the individual soul. Evangelism is not important because, for them, good living conditions in the present world constitute salvation. Eternal realities fade into insignificance before the all-consuming needs of the here and now.

THE SIGNIFICANCE OF THE PLAGUES

When Abraham and Sarah traveled to Egypt to find relief from famine, Pharaoh unwittingly took Sarah into his harem only to be inflicted with "serious diseases" (Gen. 12:17). The word for "disease" (*nega‘*) is also used in Exodus 11:1 to describe the plague on the firstborn. Whereas the episode over Sarah was unpleasant for the Pharaoh and his household, it was nothing like the experience

8. Ibid., p. 190.
9. Walter Elwell, ed., *EDT* (Grand Rapids: Baker, 1984), p. 636.

of the later Pharaoh, who had to deal with the ten plagues. Never before had a nation challenged the power of God only to be overwhelmed by an incredible series of catastrophes. Pharaoh thought he was dealing with the revolt of a helpless and enslaved people; instead he wound up in conflict with God Almighty and nearly brought about the destruction of his entire nation.

THE PURPOSE OF THE PLAGUES

When Moses and Aaron appeared before Pharaoh, their goal was to secure the release of the Israelites from Egypt. God had heard the cry of His people and was going to rescue them from the land of slavery. Since Pharaoh would not listen to Moses, God performed signs and wonders to convince Pharaoh to let Israel go. These miracles are called "mighty acts of judgment" in 6:6 and 7:4, because Egypt deserved the punishing hand of God for mistreating the Israelites. After all, Joseph had brought great blessing to Egypt with his God-given foresight, but later pharaohs took advantage of the Israelites and reduced them to slavery.

At this time in history Egypt was one of the most powerful nations on earth and was proud of its heritage and religions. But by means of the ten plagues, Pharaoh and his people learned the hard way that there was no one like the God of Israel, who was supreme in heaven and earth (cf. 7:5; 9:14). The Israelites also came to know in a more profound way that Yahweh was indeed Lord (cf. 6:3, 7) and were instructed to tell their descendants what the Lord accomplished (10:2). According to Exodus 9:16 and 18:11, the plagues were a demonstration to the whole world that the Lord God of Israel was more powerful than any other God. He was the sovereign one, controller of the forces of nature and before whom "the nations are like a drop in a bucket" (Isa. 40:15).

Many commentators believe that some of the plagues were directed against specific Egyptian deities to reveal their impotence. For example, the Nile River was worshiped as the god Hopi because the overflow of the Nile irrigated all of Egypt's crops. The plague on livestock may have been a direct rebuke against the bull-gods, Apis and Mnevis, and the ram-god, Khnum. In the ninth plague, "total darkness covered all Egypt" (10:22), bringing the nation to a complete standstill. Where was Ra, the sun-god, who was revered as one of the main Egyptian deities? None of the gods was able to step in and stop the calamities announced by Moses.

THE HARDENING OF PHARAOH'S HEART

Several times in these chapters mention is made of Pharaoh hardening his heart or of God hardening Pharaoh's heart. Does this mean that Pharaoh really had no choice in the matter, that a sovereign God had decided his fate in advance? Whereas it is true that the first two references state that God "will harden" Pharaoh's heart (4:21; 7:3), the next seven mention that Pharaoh hardened his own heart (7:13, 14, 22; 8:15, 19, 32; 9:7). Not until after the sixth plague does it actually say that "the Lord hardened Pharaoh's heart" (9:12). Thus, it appears that Pharaoh had every opportunity to respond to the intense pleas to release Israel, and even his own magicians recognized in the third plague "the finger of God" (8:19). But Pharaoh remained stubborn and unyielding, and finally God confirmed that hardened condition and insured his continued obstinacy. When Paul states that God "hardens whom he wants to harden" (Rom. 9:18) and uses Pharaoh as his example, he nonetheless argues that God is just (v. 14) and that His action is not arbitrary. Yes, God is sovereign and fully in control, but that does not eliminate man's free will and the bearing of responsibility for his choices.[10] Berkouwer has noted that it is difficult to distinguish between sovereignty and arbitrariness. Since there is no authority that can call God to account, what seems to us an arbitrary decision is not really that at all.[11] God acts in accord with His purposes and plans, which are righteous and holy.

The hardening of Pharaoh's heart is paralleled by the experience of Sihon King of Heshbon, who refused to give the Israelites passage through his land (Num. 21:21-23). According to Deuteronomy 2:30 the Lord "made his spirit stubborn and his heart obstinate" in order to give Israel the victory. The verb "made stubborn" (*hiqšâ*) is used in connection with Pharaoh (cf. Ex. 7:3), though it is followed by "heart" and not "spirit." "Make obstinate" (*'immēṣ*) does not occur in the Pharaoh account but is clearly a synonym of the other terms used.

Several passages refer to the Israelites as a "stiff-necked" people (Deut. 9:13; 10:16), and Psalm 95:8 alludes to the time they hardened their hearts in the wilderness. Eventually, Israel's stubbornness would lead to the Babylonian Exile (cf. Lev. 26:41), but it is nonetheless clear that in His grace and mercy God loved Israel and chose her "above all nations" (Deut. 10:15). Neither Pharaoh nor Israel acted independently of God but were part of the sovereign plan by which God revealed His power and glory.[12]

THE PATTERN OF THE PLAGUES

Most of the plagues begin with the request of Moses and Aaron that the Israelites be allowed to go free. This is followed by a description of the plague itself and the response of Pharaoh and his officials. Sometimes Pharaoh asks Moses to pray to the Lord so that the plague will end (8:8, 29; 9:28), and in some instances he agrees at least partially to Moses' demands. In plagues one–five

10. Youngblood, *Exodus*, pp. 45-46; Victor P. Hamilton, *Handbook on the Pentateuch* (Grand Rapids: Baker, 1982), pp. 167-74.
11. G. C. Berkouwer, *Divine Election* (Grand Rapids: Eerdmans, 1960), pp. 55.
12. Ibid., p. 247.

and seven we are told that Pharaoh hardened his own heart, and in plagues six and eight–ten God hardened Pharaoh's heart.

The plagues seem to be arranged in three groups of three, followed by the climactic tenth plague. Plagues one, four, and seven—the first plague in each set—are introduced by a warning from Moses to Pharaoh in the morning. The last plague in each set—three, six, and nine—takes place without any announcement in advance.[13] Beginning with the fourth plague, the text states that the region of Goshen, where the Israelites lived, was not struck. Exemption from the effects of the plagues is also mentioned with reference to the fifth, seventh, ninth, and tenth plagues (9:4, 26; 10:23; 11:7), although it is likely that the Lord made a distinction between the Egyptians and Israelites in plagues six and eight also. With respect to the tenth plague, the Israelite firstborn were protected only if the blood of the Passover lamb was applied to the doorposts (cf. 12:13).

The destructive nature of plagues seven–nine may indicate increasing severity as God's judgments proceed. The plague of hail was the worst storm ever to strike Egypt (9:24), and according to Pharaoh's officials the locust plague left the country in ruins (10:7). All this preceded the worst disaster of all—the death of the firstborn—a final crushing blow to Pharaoh and his people.

THE PLAGUES AS NATURAL DISASTERS

In an attempt to explain the sequence of the plagues, Greta Hort has suggested that an unusually high inundation of the Nile could have been the precipitating factor.[14] Excessive rains could have brought down large amounts of red sediment from Ethiopia, turning the Nile blood red and killing some of the fish. A week later frogs, already infected with Bacillus anthracis, would have moved inland to escape the polluted Nile. The piles of dead frogs left throughout the land likely spread the cattle disease of plague five. Because of the high floodwaters, plentiful breeding grounds would have been available for the gnats and flies of plagues three and four, and they in turn could have caused the boils or skin anthrax of plague six. The hailstorm would have occurred some months later in January or February, destroying the flax and barley but not the wheat and spelt, which would have been left for the locusts.[15]

Even if this theory is correct and the order of the plagues followed along natural lines, the timing of the plagues and their intensification required supernatural control. Without God's intervention Moses and Aaron could not have foreseen the coming of these disasters with such precision. And there is no way to account for the tenth plague on naturalistic grounds. God may have used natu-

---

13. U. Cassuto, *A Commentary on the Book of Exodus* (Jerusalem: Magnes, The Hebrew U., 1967), pp. 92-93.
14. G. Hort, "The Plagues of Egypt," *ZAW* 69 (1957); pp 84-103; *ZAW* 70 (1958), pp. 48-59.
15. Cf. Kenneth Kitchen, *Ancient Orient and Old Testament* (Chicago: InterVarsity, 1966), pp. 157-58.

ral means up to that point, but the death of the firstborn sons required supernatural action.

Taken as a whole the Bible has relatively few periods in which miracles are plentiful. After the time of Moses we must wait until the ninth century B.C. and the prophetic ministries of Elijah and Elisha when once again God intervened decisively through miraculous signs. In the New Testament there are, of course, numerous miracles connected with the ministry of Christ as the last days begin (cf. Heb. 1:2). At the culmination of the last days as recorded in the book of Revelation, it is interesting to note that the judgments described are sometimes similar to the plagues of Egypt. In chapter 8 a third of the sea is turned into blood (v. 8), and a third of the sun becomes dark (v. 12). The ugly and painful sores associated with the outpouring of God's wrath (Rev. 16:2) and the falling of huge hailstones in 16:21 are also reminiscent of the plagues. Perhaps in Revelation we are to think of the deliverance of the righteous as a kind of final Exodus from the bondage of a wicked world.[16] The forces of Satan will be defeated as decisively as Pharaoh and his armies.

THE INDIVIDUAL PLAGUES

1. The plague of blood. Since the waters of the Nile were so critical to the well-being of the Egyptians, the first plague delivered a powerful message to Pharaoh. The blood-red color of the Nile may have come from the tons of red soil carried by the White Nile and Blue Nile (see above), and, combined with a type of algae called flagellates, proved to be deadly to the fish.[17] These problems with the Nile, which probably occurred in July and August, began a sequence of death and destruction that grew steadily worse in subsequent months. If Cassuto is correct in linking the wood and stone articles of 7:19 with idols, the blood that was poured over the gods would have defiled them and further insulted the deities of Egypt.[18]

2. The plague of frogs. The frog was the symbol of the Egyptian goddess Heqt, who was depicted as a woman with a frog's head. Since Heqt was a goddess of fertility, the reference to frogs swarming into bedrooms in Exodus 8:3 may be an allusion to her accustomed role, now sadly achieving quite the opposite result. When Moses asked the pharaoh to set the time for the removal of the frogs, he was demonstrating God's sovereignty over time, for the Lord responded to Moses' prayer (Ex. 8:9-13).[19]

16. *NIV Study Bible*, ed. Kenneth Barker (Grand Rapids: Zondervan, 1985), p. 1935.
17. Cf. Kaiser, "Exodus," in *EBC*, p. 350. Cf. the use of "blood" for "blood red" in Joel 2:31.
18. Cassuto, *Exodus*, p. 99.
19. Youngblood, *Exodus*, p. 54.

3. The plague of gnats. God's sovereignty was even more pronounced when Aaron struck the ground with his staff and the dust became gnats. Whereas it is likely that "dust" refers to the immense number of gnats, the wording is reminiscent of God forming man "from the dust of the ground" (Gen. 2:7). Pharaoh's magicians acknowledged the creative power of the Lord when they said, "This is the finger of God" (Ex. 8:19). According to Psalm 8:3 the heavens are the work of God's fingers, and in Exodus 31:18 the Ten Commandments are "inscribed by the finger of God." God clearly revealed His will in the Decalogue, and He was vividly demonstrating His power through the plagues. When Jesus drove out demons "by the finger of God" the forces of evil were being defeated (Luke 11:20).

4. The plague of flies. Egypt's troubles continued when vast hordes of flies covered the whole country except for the region of Goshen, where the Israelites lived (8:22). Devastation was so widespread that "the land was ruined" by the multiplying pests (8:24). These exact words, *tiššāḥēt hā'āreṣ*, are used in Genesis 6:11 to describe the corruption of the earth before the Flood. Just as God sent the Flood to judge the earth, so He was sending the plagues to punish Egypt for her evil. Faced with impending disaster, Pharaoh softened his stance somewhat and told Moses and Aaron to sacrifice in the land. But since shepherds were detestable to the Egyptians (cf. Gen. 46:34), Moses knew that sacrifices would likely be offensive to them also, so he insisted on offering sacrifices in the desert.

5. The plague on livestock. When Pharaoh once again hardened his heart, the hand of God struck the land a fifth time, this plague destroying the nation's livestock. The anthrax disease might have been contracted from the piles of dead frogs still left in the land or from the flies of plague four. Since a number of animals were associated with specific deities, this fifth plague may have dealt a powerful blow against Egypt's religion. Apis was the sacred bull of Ptah, the well-known god of crafts, and Hathor, the goddess of joy, was portrayed with the ears of a cow.[20] But no god was able to save the animals from the terrible scourge sent by the Lord.

6. The plague of boils. Included among the curses Moses warns the Israelites about in Deuteronomy 28 is a reference to "the boils of Egypt" (v. 27), a clear allusion to this sixth plague. Many feel that the boils were a kind of skin anthrax, a black abscess that turns into a pustule.[21] It was probably related to the disease that struck the livestock in the previous plague and was likely spread by infected flies. These boils were extremely painful and particularly affected the knees and legs (Deut. 28:35), making it difficult for the magicians to "stand before Moses" either literally or figuratively. When Moses tossed into the air

20. Cf. J. D. Douglas, ed., *New Bible Dictionary* (Grand Rapids: Eerdmans, 1962), p. 351.
21. Cf. Hort, "The Plagues of Egypt," pp. 101-3.

handfuls of soot from a furnace to launch the plague (9:10), his actions linked the suffering of the Egyptians to the slavery of the Israelites. The furnace—or brick kiln—was the symbol of Israel's bondage (cf. 1:14).

7. *The plague of hail.* The third trio of plagues began with a hailstorm described as the worst that Egypt had ever known (9:18, 24). Normally Egypt receives very little rainfall, especially in Upper Egypt, and since hailstorms of any kind are rare, the impact of this storm was even more powerful. Before the plague began Moses told the pharaoh that God had raised him up to show him His power (v. 16), and the storm itself was a mighty message from the Lord. Later at Mount Sinai God spoke to the Israelites through thunder and lightning (cf. Ex. 19:16) as He gave them the Ten Commandments, and this earlier storm was an important revelation for Pharaoh. For the first time Pharaoh admitted that he had sinned (v. 27), but he broke his promise to let the Israelites go free when the hail and thunder stopped. In the aftermath of the storm, the flax and barley harvests had been destroyed, and coupled with the loss of so many livestock in the previous plague, Egypt's economy suffered a crippling blow.

8. *The plague of locusts.* Pharaoh's economic woes continued with the onslaught of the locust hordes in March or April. Brought by strong east winds, the locusts came in unprecedented numbers and devoured anything green that had survived the hailstorm (cf. 10:12). The severity of the plague was indicated by the Lord's instruction that the Israelites tell their children and grandchildren about this harsh treatment (10:2). Ironically, the same phraseology is used in the book of Joel to introduce a locust plague that struck Israel centuries later.[22] In Moses' final words to Israel in Deuteronomy 28, he twice refers to swarms of locusts that will devastate the crops if the people rebel against God (vv. 38, 42).

9. *The plague of darkness.* Elsewhere in Scripture darkness is associated with distress, barrenness, and the judgment of God (cf. Isa. 8:22; Jer. 4:23). In Egypt, where the sun-god, Ra, was a prominent deity, darkness would have been a sign of his disfavor or, worse yet, his weakness—particularly when the other plagues had been sent in the name of the God of Israel. The darkness was doubtless associated with the khamsin, the strong winds that blow in from the desert each spring. The resultant sandstorm apparently matched the unparalleled proportions of the hail and locust plagues and completely blotted out the sun. Angered by yet another disaster, Pharaoh ordered Moses out of his sight and refused to see him again.

10. *The death of the firstborn.* According to Egyptian theology, Pharaoh was himself a god, but in this final plague the vulnerability of the king was clearly exposed.[23] Israel was God's "firstborn son" (Ex. 4:22), and since Pha-

---

22. Joel 1:2-3 contains several reflections of Exodus 10:2 and 6. Clearly the prophet is alluding to the eighth plague.
23. The king was considered to be the incarnate Horus, the falcon skygod. Cf. *NBD*, p. 57.

raoh refused to release Israel, Pharaoh's firstborn son would die as a conse-
quence (4:23). In the Near East the firstborn son enjoyed special privileges, including a double share of the inheritance, so the loss of the firstborn was a
tragedy that "would cripple the family legally and emotionally."[24] Because the
tenth plague claimed only Egyptian firstborn males—including animals—the destruction was clearly a miracle and not an epidemic. The death of the firstborn
produced an unprecedented volume of wailing throughout Egypt, but among the
Israelites there was calm and quietness (11:6-7; 12:30).

The Passover

The tenth and last plague brought the death of the firstborn and the long-
awaited permission for Israel to leave Egypt. To escape the plague themselves,
the Israelite households were instructed to sacrifice a lamb and smear the blood
on the doorposts of each house. The sacrifice of the Passover lamb as well as the
feast of Unleavened Bread were celebrated annually in commemoration of the
dramatic rescue of the firstborn. Shortly thereafter the whole nation was miraculously delivered at the Red Sea. So important were these events that from then
on this became the first month of the year. Known as the month of Abib (cf.
13:4) and later as Nisan, the Passover and Exodus marked the beginning of the
religious calendar.

THE PASSOVER LAMB

Unlike some of the older plagues in which the Israelites and their animals
were automatically exempt (cf. 8:22; 9:4), there were special instructions with
regard to the sparing of the firstborn sons. The key provision was the sacrifice of
a year-old lamb or goat and the application of the blood to "the sides and tops of
the doorframes of the houses" (12:7). The same night they were to eat the meat
"along with bitter herbs, and bread made without yeast" (12:8). When the Lord
"passed over" each house and saw the blood, He would not permit the destroying angel to strike down the firstborn son (v. 23).

As in the case of the ram that was sacrificed in place of Isaac (cf. Gen.
22:13), the substitutionary nature of the Passover lamb must have been quite
clear to the firstborn sons and their families. They knew that if the lamb was not
killed, the oldest son would die, a son who had a privileged position in the family. The New Testament writers refer to Christ as "our Passover lamb" (1 Cor.
5:7), "a lamb without blemish or defect" (1 Pet. 1:19; cf. Ex. 12:5), and the
apostle John noted that none of His bones was broken (John 19:36). According
to Exodus 12:46 and Numbers 9:12, the bones of the Passover lamb could not be

24. Youngblood, *Exodus*, p. 57.

broken. To make the connection between Christ's sacrifice and the Passover crystal clear, the gospels tell us that Christ died shortly after observing the Passover with His disciples (Matt. 26:18-30).

FEAST OF UNLEAVENED BREAD

Closely associated with the Passover was the feast of Unleavened Bread, which began on the next day and continued from the fifteenth to the twenty-first of the month. Since the people had to leave Egypt quickly, they did not have time to bake dough with yeast (Ex. 12:11, 39). In verse 8 the bread without yeast is eaten along with bitter herbs, a reminder of the hard labor they had been required to perform (cf. 1:14). As this feast was celebrated from year to year, parents reminded children about their bitter experiences in Egypt, and together they gave thanks for God's deliverance. Down through the years the feasts of Passover and Unleavened Bread virtually became one feast (cf. Mark 14:12).

REGULATIONS

The Bible is specific about how the Passover lamb was to be sacrificed and how it was to be eaten. For example, the meat had to be roasted, and it had to be eaten the same night (vv. 8-9). All who were ceremonially clean were required to celebrate this Passover, but those who were unclean could celebrate the feast exactly one month later (Num. 9:11, 13). Of special importance was the rule that all the males be circumcised. Circumcision was the sign of the Abrahamic Covenant and indicated commitment and submission to the God of Abraham (see "The Abrahamic Covenant" in chap. 3). If ever there was a time when the Israelites needed to renew their dedication to God, it would be at the Passover. According to Exodus 4:22 Israel was God's firstborn son, so the time of the Passover with its emphasis upon the firstborn was a marvelous occasion to think about the meaning of a covenant relationship. Just after the reference to Israel as God's firstborn, we are told that Moses had failed to circumcise his own son, an oversight that nearly proved fatal (Ex. 4:24-26).[25] Ironically, even with the emphasis on circumcision and the Passover, both were neglected during the wilderness wanderings and at other periods in Israel's history (cf. Josh. 5:5; 2 Chron. 30:1-5). According to Exodus 12:43-49, the Passover could also be celebrated by slaves and aliens who were part of the community, provided they had been circumcised. Foreigners and hired workers, who had no desire to worship the God of Israel, were specifically excluded, however.

---

25. Cf. the discussion in Cassuto, *Exodus*, p. 138.

DEATH OF THE FIRSTBORN

Although Pharaoh thought that his country could survive the hardships brought on by the first nine plagues, the tenth plague was more than even he could handle. To lose a firstborn son was a crushing blow, and this catastrophe befell every household, including that of the pharaoh. There was no doubt about the power of Israel's God this time. Remarkably the Egyptians gave the Israelites valuable gifts as they left, perhaps in recognition of the years of labor performed on their behalf. Abraham had been told that his descendants would be "enslaved and mistreated four hundred years" (Gen. 15:13), and it turned out to be 430 years. But now they were on their way back to the Promised Land to fulfill the Abrahamic Covenant.

CROSSING OF THE RED SEA

The joy of freedom came to an abrupt end, however, when the Israelites realized that Pharaoh had changed his mind and had sent out his chariots and officers to recapture them. How could they fight against this powerful enemy and avoid a new period of enslavement? To make matters worse, the Israelites were camped right next to the Red Sea and had no place to flee. But the angel of God who had protected the firstborn was still with Israel and placed the pillar of cloud between the opposing forces (Ex. 14:19). Then as Moses stretched his staff over the sea, the waters were miraculously divided and the people crossed on dry ground. When the Egyptians tried to follow, the waters returned to overwhelm them, destroying the soldiers and their chariots. Once more God triumphed over Pharaoh, and the crossing of the Red Sea became for all time the prime example of deliverance and salvation (cf. Isa. 51:10). News of Israel's rescue would also strike terror into the hearts of the Canaanites and neighboring nations (Ex. 15:15).

Scholars have long been stymied in their attempt to pinpoint the place where the Israelites crossed the Red Sea, partially because the term is more properly the "Reed Sea." The Hebrew word *sûp*, which corresponds closely to the Egyptian *tjuf* ("papyrus"), refers to the reeds along the bank of the Nile in Exodus 2:3 and to the seaweed in the Mediterranean in Jonah 2:5 [HB 2:6]. Since there are a series of lakes with abundant supplies of reeds and papyrus north of the Red Sea (the Gulf of Suez)—such as Lake Menzaleh and Lake Timsah—it is felt that one of these may have been the "Reed Sea" crossed by the Israelites.[26]

To complicate matters there was an ancient canal between these lakes that may have served as a wall of defense on the border, making the escape route more difficult. The term "Reed Sea" can, however, sometimes refer to the Gulf

26. Cf. *NBD*, pp. 1077-78.

of Suez (Num. 33:10-11) or the Gulf of Aqaba (Num. 14:25; 1 Kings 9:26), the two northern arms of what is commonly called the Red Sea. The strong west wind that deposited the locusts into the "Red [Reed] Sea" (Ex. 10:19) probably refers to the Gulf of Suez also.

Adding to the confusion is our difficulty in locating the places mentioned along the route of the Exodus. Succoth (Ex. 13:20) is identified with Tell el-Maskhutah west of the Bitter Lakes and was on "the desert road toward the Red Sea" (Ex. 13:18). The three places mentioned in Exodus 14:2 all seem to be in the vicinity of the Bitter Lakes, but none can be identified with certainty. If Baal Zephon is the same as the place later called Tahpanhes, which was located just south of Lake Menzaleh (cf. Jer. 2:16), the crossing may have occurred at the southern end of Lake Menzaleh or at nearby Lake Ballah.[27]

Barry Beitzel places the crossing at Lake Timsah just south of modern Ismailia, a location he believes was closer to where the desert road intersected the line of lakes.[28] On the other hand, since there is some evidence that the Gulf of Suez may have extended northward to the Bitter Lakes at one time, Walter Kaiser denotes this area at the northern tip of the Gulf as the most likely area of the crossing.[29] Regardless of where the exact spot may have been, there is no doubt that God's miraculous dividing of the sea was a mighty demonstration of His power and a clear indication of His love for Israel.

THE DATE OF THE EXODUS

In spite of substantial evidence from biblical and archaeological sources, there are two major competing theories about the date of the Exodus. One, known as the "early date," places the Exodus at about 1446 B.C. during the reign of Amunhotep II. The other, the so-called "late date," argues for 1290 B.C. as the date of the Exodus, when the great Rameses II was Pharaoh. A discrepancy of 150 years is a large one, especially when the problem could be easily solved if we knew when Joshua conquered Canaan, some forty years after the Exodus. Yet, even with all the archaeological work in Palestine and all of our knowledge of Egypt, there are still problems to be solved. Evangelicals have suggested both dates, so the issue is not simply a liberal versus conservative debate.

KEY BIBLICAL NUMBERS

The most important chronological note about the Exodus is found in 1 Kings 6:1, where the fourth year of Solomon (966 B.C.) is dated 480 years after Israel left Egypt. Such a precise figure seems to put the Exodus at 1446, but oth-

27. Kitchen, "The Exodus," *ZPEB*, 2:430.
28. Barry J. Beitzel, *The Moody Atlas of Bible Lands* (Chicago: Moody, 1985), p. 90.
29. Kaiser, "Exodus," in *EBC*, 2:292.

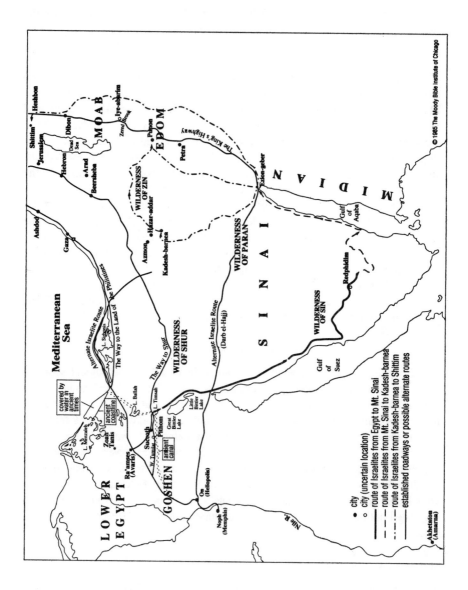

er interpretations are possible. John Bright argues that 480 is a round number composed of twelve generations of forty years each. Since the numbers "forty" and "eighty" occur with regularity in the book of Judges, perhaps "forty" equals a generation, which could refer to only twenty-five literal years.[30] Twelve times twenty-five would total only 300, correlating quite nicely with the late-date theory. Approaching the problem from a different angle, Kenneth Kitchen reasons that the 480 figure may be the sum of partly concurrent figures, giving an absolute number that is too high.[31]

Kitchen uses the same argument with reference to Judges 11:26, where Jephthah states that Israel had occupied Transjordan for 300 years.[32] Since Jephthah lived about 1100 B.C., the 300 years would refer back to c. 1400 B.C., the approximate time of the conquest according to the early-date hypothesis. Advocates of the late date must squeeze all of the book of Judges between 1250 B.C. and 1050 B.C., a difficult task even with overlapping time periods. To account for all of the judges in so short a period requires more overlapping than the book seems to allow.[33]

EGYPTIAN EVIDENCE

The name Rameses. Each of the kings of Egypt has several names, but unfortunately none of them ever appears in Genesis and Exodus. Instead, the royal title "Pharaoh"—which means "great house"—is used for each ruler. One famous name occurs twice, however, apparently in connection with Rameses II, the powerful pharaoh who ruled from 1290-1224 B.C.

In Exodus 1:11, Rameses is one of two store cities built by the Israelites, and in Genesis 47:11 we are told that Jacob and his sons settled in "the district of Rameses." From these references scholars have concluded that Rameses II was indeed the Pharaoh of the Exodus, which must have occurred early in the thirteenth century B.C. Whereas it is true that Rameses II was a prodigious builder, it is not at all certain that the city mentioned in Exodus 1:11 bore his name at first. In chapters 1 and 2 it appears that Moses had not been born until *after* Rameses was built, and yet he was eighty years old at the time of the Exodus.[34] The same problem exists with the appearance of "Rameses" in Genesis 47:11, hundreds of years before the reign of Rameses II. Apparently in both cases earlier names were updated by a later editor who used the more recent name.

30. John Bright, *A History of Israel*, 3d ed. (Philadelphia: Westminster, 1981), p. 121.
31. Kitchen, *Ancient Orient*, pp. 73-74.
32. Ibid., pp. 74-75.
33. The total number of years given is 410, far too long for the early date also. Some overlapping must have occurred, but the late date demands an excessive amount of concurrent rule.
34. Cf. Leon Wood, "Date of the Exodus," in *New Perspectives on the Old Testament*, ed. J. Barton Payne (Waco, Tex.: Word, 1970), p. 68.

Such a proleptic use also appears in Genesis 14:14, where Abraham pursued the captors of Lot as far as Dan. But the name of the city was "Laish" until the tribe of Dan captured and renamed it in the days of the judges (Judg. 18:29).[35]

Another argument against the identification of Rameses II as the pharaoh of the Exodus is the length of the reign of the king who preceded that Pharaoh. According to Exodus 2:23, Moses fled from Egypt for forty years until the pharaoh who sought his life died. Rameses' predecessor, Seti I, reigned for only twelve years, but Thutmose III, the pharaoh of the oppression according to the early date, ruled from about 1495-50 B.C. He was succeeded by Amunhotep II, who was followed to the throne by one of his younger brothers, Thutmose IV. Amunhotep's firstborn son may have perished in the tenth plague, the catastrophe which precipitated the Exodus.

The Hyksos rulers. During part of the time that the Israelites were in Egypt, a group of foreigners known as the Hyksos ("chiefs of foreign lands") ruled the country. From their capital in Tanis in the same northeastern Delta region where the Israelites lived, the semitic Hyksos ruled Egypt from about 1700-1550 B.C. Manfred Bietak believes that a colony of merchants and craftsmen from the city of Byblos north of Israel may have furnished the core of these foreign upstarts who took control of the land as the pharaohs of dynasties 15 and 16.[36] The Hyksos introduced new bronze swords and daggers, the compound bow, and especially the horse and chariot into warfare.

Since the Israelites were themselves Semites who had produced one prominent leader in Egypt, there is a great deal of interest in their relationship with the Hyksos. Did the Israelites enter Egypt during the Hyksos period or were the Israelites enslaved by the Hyksos at a later time? The answer to these questions lies partially in the identification of the Pharaoh "who did not know about Joseph" and who cruelly oppressed the Israelites (Ex. 1:8). Was this king one of the Hyksos, or was he Ahmose, the native Egyptian who drove out the hated Hyksos and founded the New Kingdom about 1550 B.C.? Those who favor a Hyksos interpretation argue that the 1550 date is too late in light of the 400 years of mistreatment predicted in Genesis 15:13. If the reference is to a Hyksos ruler of 1700 B.C. there would be at least 250 years of oppression rather than a little over a century. Second, it is asserted that fears over the growing population of the Hebrews would suit the minority Hyksos rulers better than the Egyptians, who presumably outnumbered the Israelites by a wide margin.[37] Yet the population issue could equally well point to Ahmose as the new king because by 1550 the Israelites would have had an additional century and a half to reproduce. Besides, it is more difficult to explain why the Hyksos would want to enslave their

35. Youngblood, *Exodus*, p. 14.
36. Manfred Bietak, "Problems of Middle Bronze Age Chronology: New Evidence from Egypt," *AJA* 88 (1984), p. 475.
37. Cf. Leon Wood, *A Survey of Israel's History* (Grand Rapids: Zondervan, 1970), pp. 35-37.

fellow Semites to the level indicated in Exodus 1-2. The native Egyptian dynasty that drove out the Hyksos might have used the occasion to oppress another semitic people at the same time.

Whereas the identification of the new king in Exodus 1:8 is a difficult one, there is a much greater likelihood that the pharaoh who welcomed Jacob to Egypt was not a Hyksos ruler. From the account of Joseph's rise to power we are given every indication that he was dealing with a native Egyptian dynasty. Foreigners were not allowed to eat with the Egyptians (Gen. 43:32), and all shepherds were "detestable to the Egyptians" (Gen. 46:34).[38] Since the late-date theory of the Exodus would place the arrival of the Israelites in Egypt at the beginning of the Hyksos period, this evidence places the start of the 400 years at an earlier time and harmonizes best with a 1446 Exodus.

EVIDENCE FROM JERICHO

The city of Jericho was the first stronghold captured by Joshua, and the interpretation of its remains has been the object of lively archaeological debate. John Garstang, who excavated Jericho between 1930 and 1936, thought the evidence favored the early date, but Kathleen Kenyon, who dug there from 1952 to 1958, placed the fall of Jericho in "the third quarter of the fourteenth century" and pointed out weaknesses in Garstang's conclusions.[39] Of special interest was her denial that the "double-wall" identified by Garstang with Joshua's capture came from the late Bronze period. The two walls came from a time more than 500 years before Joshua.[40] Unfortunately, the city mound suffered severe erosion after 1500 B.C., partially because Jericho was abandoned until the reign of Ahab (cf. 1 Kings 16:34).

A key point in the debate concerns the "Middle Building" above the spring, both of which date about 1350 B.C. Miss Kenyon connects it with Joshua's Jericho, but Garstang links that part of the city with the brief occupancy of King Eglon of Moab during the time of the judges (Judg. 3:13). Since Jericho at that time was apparently a small, unwalled city, the evidence seems to favor Garstang in this instance.

Garstang's main argument for the early date lay in his interpretation of the pottery found both on the mound and in the tombs. He observed that the pottery pieces and the scarabs are abundant from the time of Thutmose III (about 1500 B.C.) to Amunhotep III (about 1414-1378), but there is nothing from the reign of Akhenaton, the successor of Amunhotep. Miss Kenyon countered that scarabs

38. Gleason Archer, Jr., *A Survey of Old Testament Introduction*, rev. ed. (Chicago: Moody, 1974), p. 222.
39. Kathleen Kenyon, *Digging Up Jericho* (New York: Frederick A. Praeger, 1957), p. 262.
40. Ibid., pp. 45-46.

cannot be used for accurate dating, since they tend to be heirlooms.[41] In her opinion the pottery remains continue to about 1550 B.C., and the absence of a red-and-black bichrome ware is particularly decisive in reaching this conclusion. Known primarily from Megiddo in the north and Tell el-'Ajjul in the south, it may be questioned, however, whether this bichrome ware ever came to the hills of central Palestine or to the Jordan Valley. If not, its absence has no bearing on the date of the occupancy of Jericho. Although the pottery analysis continues to be a difficult one, Garstang's conclusions may still be the best. If he is right, the thick burned layer of ash beneath this pottery may come from Joshua's destruction of Jericho.[42]

Although Miss Kenyon's interpretation of the pottery evidence at Jericho does not support the early date of the Exodus, her overall assessment of pottery changes in Palestine is most interesting. From her study she states that a major change in Palestinian culture occurred about 1400 B.C., precisely at the time when Joshua and the Israelites would have reached Canaan if the Exodus took place about 1446 B.C.[43]

EVIDENCE FROM OTHER CITIES

Archaeologists have also been hard at work examining other sites captured by Joshua and his forces, and their excavations have uncovered a pattern of destruction primarily in the thirteenth century. Places such as Lachish, Debir, and Bethel were destroyed by fire, and the date of their demise seems to support a 1290 B.C. Exodus. But a comparison of the archaeological data and the biblical text raises several problems. In a summary of the conquest, Joshua 11:13 notes that Hazor was the only city burned by Joshua—except for Jericho and Ai as described earlier. Although Lachish was subdued in the southern campaign, the text says nothing about burning (Josh 10:32). Since a broken pot with "year four" written on it in the characteristic style of the Egyptian Pharaoh Merneptah has been found at Lachish, it is possible that the Egyptians burned Lachish.[44] This was the same Merneptah whose famous stele from about 1220 B.C. mentions that he defeated Israel in battle.[45] The invasion of the Sea Peoples about 1200 B.C. could also account for the destruction of Lachish and Debir. Many cities from Asia Minor to Egypt suffered at the hands of these migrating peoples.

Unlike Lachish and Debir, the city of Hazor does not show evidence of burning in its thirteenth century destruction level (Stratum I), and yet according to Joshua 11:13 this stronghold some nine miles north of the Sea of Galilee was

41. Ibid., p. 260.
42. Cf. Wood, "Date of the Exodus," pp. 70-73.
43. Cf. Bruce Waltke, "Palestinian Artifactual Evidence," *BSac* 129 (1972), p. 36.
44. Archer, *Survey*, p. 220.
45. Kitchen, *Ancient Orient*, pp. 59-60.

indeed burned. During the excavation, Israeli archaeologist Yigael Yadin did uncover signs of burning in Stratum III, which he attributed to one of the Egyptian pharaohs, probably Thutmose III.[46] Since this destruction would be only about fifty years before the time of Joshua according to the early-date theory, Leon Wood has suggested that the city of Stratum III may very well have been the one burned by Joshua.[47] The thirteenth-century destruction could have been connected with the victory of Deborah and Barak over another Jabin, who reigned in Hazor during the period of the judges (cf. Judg. 4:2, 24).

EVIDENCE FROM TRANSJORDAN

Ever since the surface explorations of Nelson Glueck undertaken in the late 1930s, scholars have questioned the existence of strong nations such as Edom or Moab prior to 1300 B.C. Glueck concluded that Transjordan was largely uninhabited from 1800 to 1300 B.C., so if Joshua and Moses had come prior to 1300 B.C. there would have been no enemy to oppose them.[48] But, a more recent study of sites in the central Moab plateau has shown no occupational gap there from 1500-1200 B.C.[49] From a study of other sites, J. J. Bimson has also reached the conclusion that Transjordan was in fact inhabited during the period.[50] The work of Kautz and Bimson supports the earlier views of Lancaster Harding, who found evidence of Late Bronze occupation in the territory of the Ammonites.[51]

THE AMARNA TABLETS

In 1887 a remarkable set of about 350 clay tablets was found at the Egyptian city of Tell el-Amarna. These letters from leaders of cities in Palestine and Syria were written to the pharaohs Amunhotep III and Akhenaton complaining about a group of people known as Habiru who had invaded the land. Since the two pharaohs ruled from about 1400-1360 B.C. and since the word "Habiru" is quite similar to "Hebrew," it is tempting to connect the two and to interpret the Amarna letters as external evidence of the conquest under Joshua. Under closer scrutiny, however, this view is difficult to substantiate.

First, the term Habiru, or *'Apiru* (a close equivalent), is used to describe soldiers, mercenaries, and slaves in several countries throughout the ancient Near East. From about 2000 B.C. on there are references to the Habiru (*'Apiru* in Mesopotamian, Egyptian, Ugaritic, and Hittite texts) in addition to the Amarna

46. Yigael Yadin, "Further Light on Biblical Hazor," *BA* 20 (1957), p. 44.
47. Wood, "Date of the Exodus," p. 74.
48. N. Glueck, *The Other Side of the Jordan* (New Haven: Yale U., 1940), pp. 125-34.
49. J. R. Kautz, "Tracking the Ancient Moabites," *BA* 44 (1981), pp. 27-35.
50. J. J. Bimson, "Redating the Exodus and Conquest," *Journal for the Study of the Old Testament*, Supplement Series 5 (1978), pp. 70-74.
51. Lancaster Harding, *The Antiquities of Jordan* (New York: Thomas Y. Crowell, 1959), p. 17.

materials. In most of these texts there does not seem to be any possible connection with the biblical Hebrews, and scholars generally believe "Habiru" refers to a class rather than an ethnic group.[52]

Second, the information about Habiru activities in Canaan does not line up very closely with the account given in Joshua. For example, the king of Jerusalem is named Abdi-Hepa, whereas Joshua 10:1 refers to Adoni-Zedek as the king of this important fortress. Cities such as Lachish and Gezer seem to be supporting the Habiru rather than suffering defeat at the hands of Joshua (Josh. 10:33).[53]

On the other hand, Gleason Archer has shown that some details about the Habiru fit the story of the Hebrew conquest rather well. For instance, letters to the Egyptian kings came from cities that Joshua had difficulty in capturing— places such as Jerusalem, Megiddo, Ashkelon, and Gezer. In one such letter, Abdi-Hepa of Jerusalem complained that Labayu had given Shechem to the Habiru, a piece of information that would help explain why the Israelites held a covenant renewal ceremony at Shechem (Josh. 8:30-35). A letter from the king of Megiddo refers to a leader named Yashuya, which is rather close to the Hebrew spelling of Joshua.[54] If the early date theory is correct, it is possible that the leaders of Canaan regarded the Hebrews as part of the Habiru people, though the two terms were unrelated prior to this time.

Meredith Kline has taken the position that the Habiru may be identified with the invasion of Cushan-Rishathaim recorded in Judges 3:7-11. Kline believes that this king from northern Mesopotamia may have been allied with the Hurrians of Mitanni, a powerful force in the fifteenth and fourteenth centuries.[55] Since this invasion occurred roughly about 1375 B.C. it fits within the reign of Akhenaton when complaints about the Habiru in Canaan were at their peak.

Like the other aspects of the problem of dating the Exodus and the conquest, the Habiru issue remains a difficult one. After examining the biblical, historical, and archaeological evidence, we can see that both the 1446 date and the 1290 date can be supported by impressive arguments, but at this point in the debate the case for the 1446 B.C. Exodus appears to be the stronger one.

THE NUMERICAL SIZE OF ISRAEL

Another thorny problem confronting the biblical interpreter is the staggering size of the Israelite nation as they made their way out of Egypt. According to

---

52. Roland de Vaux nonetheless argues that an ethnic interpretation may be better, "describing a group or groups of western Semites, 'Amorites' or 'Proto-Arameans' with whom the patriarchs were connected" (*The Early History of Israel* [Philadelphia: Westminster, 1978], p. 216). De Vaux has a thorough discussion of the Habiru problem on pages 105-12 and 213-16.

53. *NBD*, p. 68.

54. Archer, *Survey*, p. 276. He makes a strong case for the identification of the Hebrew and Habiru on pages 271-77.

55. M. Kline, "The Ha-Bi-Ru—Kin or Foe of Israel?—III" *WTJ* 20 (November 1957), pp. 54-61.

Exodus 12:37 "there were about six hundred thousand men on foot, besides women and children" at the time of the Exodus. This places the total population at two million at the very least. How could Moses manage such a throng and how could they survive in the desert? The number also seems to be very large in comparison with the other nations and with the armies of that era. Critical scholars have rejected the accuracy of the biblical numbers, developing a number of theories to reduce the overall population. But as clever and as well-intentioned as these theories may have been, none seem compatible with the biblical data. The books of Exodus and Numbers in particular present a consistent picture of Israel's remarkable growth and show how the nation's survival in the desert was the direct result of God's intervention.

Exodus, in fact, begins with a discussion of the amazing fruitfulness of the Israelites, who had "become much too numerous" for the Pharaoh (1:9). The king feared that in a war the Israelites might join the enemy and help overthrow Egypt, so he took measures to control the population by killing all of the Hebrew baby boys (1:10, 16). Such drastic action implies that the Israelites numbered far more than twenty or thirty thousand and that a figure of two million is not unreasonable. Since there were about seventy in Jacob's family when they first migrated to Egypt, each family would have had five or six children to reach the two million total four hundred years later.[56]

The two censuses given in Numbers correspond closely to the Exodus data. In Numbers 1:46 the number of men twenty years old or more is given as 603,550, and in 26:51, at the end of the desert wanderings, the total is 601,730. In both chapters the census is broken down into tribal units to make up the total, and in chapter 2 there are subtotals for each set of three tribes.

Because of the inherent difficulties involved in leading such a large group to the Promised Land, scholars have diligently tried to reinterpret the biblical numbers. George Mendenhall has noted that the word translated "thousand," ('*elep*) can sometimes have the meaning of "group" or "clan."[57] In Judges 6:15 Gideon links himself with the weakest "clan" in the tribe of Manasseh, and in 1 Samuel 23:23 Saul vows to track David down "among all the clans of Judah." Earlier in 1 Samuel '*elep* is rendered "unit," where it may not necessarily refer to exactly one thousand men. If six hundred "thousand" could be translated six hundred "units" and if each unit only had two hundred men, the total figure would be reduced to 120,000 men, still high but somewhat more reasonable. Yet in the census figures given in Numbers the totals are also spelled out in hundreds and tens (cf. 1:24), strongly implying that "thousand" should be taken literally. Besides, when materials were collected for the Tabernacle, half a shekel was received for each man counted in the census, and the total

---

56. Cf. Archer, *Survey*, p. 229.
57. George Mendenhall, "The Census Lists of Numbers 1 and 26," *JBL* 77 (March 1958), 52.

came to exactly 301,775 shekels, a half shekel for each of the 603,550 men (cf. 38:25-26). Clearly, the writer of Exodus and Numbers intended that these numbers be understood in their normal, literal way.

In a recent commentary on the book of Numbers, Ronald Allen has wrestled with the data and has suggested that the numbers have been intentionally exaggerated as a rhetorical device to look ahead to the day when the descendants of Israel would indeed be as innumerable as the stars. Allen cautiously suggests that the numbers have been inflated by a factor of ten, giving an actual total of 60,000 men and 250,000 to 300,000 to include women and children.[58] The discrepancy between actual and inflated numbers would be similar to the assertion in 1 Samuel 18:7 that "Saul has slain his thousands, and David his tens of thousands," an exaggeration designed to emphasize God's great blessing on Israel's first two kings. Allen acknowledges that the mathematical exactness of Exodus 38:25-26 is a formidable obstacle to his theory, but he argues that this figure was derived from the census total given in Numbers 1:46.[59] In his discussion of the number of those who died after worshiping the Baal of Peor (Num. 25:9), Allen accepts the 24,000 total at face value, partially because of the 23,000 figure contained in 1 Corinthians 10:8. This would amount to a loss of nearly ten per cent of the "actual" population of 250,000 and would make the plague that much more devastating.[60]

Even if the number of able-bodied men literally totaled 603,000, it should be noted that they did not all fight in the same battle.[61] When Moses fought the Midianites, only twelve thousand troops were sent, and Joshua used thirty thousand against Ai (cf. Num. 31:5; Josh. 8:3,12). Later, in the civil war against Benjamin, mobilization was more complete, with four hundred thousand Israelites battling twenty-six thousand men of Benjamin (Judg. 20:2,15). The size of armies varied greatly in the historical books, from hundreds of thousands of soldiers to only a few thousand (cf. 2 Chron. 13:3; 1 Kings 20:15). Attempts have been made to scale down the numbers in some of these instances also, but as Gideon learned, God could win battles with only a few hundred if necessary.

From a human perspective, feeding and clothing two million people in the desert was an impossibility, and the Scriptures make clear that supernatural provision was necessary all along the way. After three days in the desert without water, the grumbling against Moses began, but God turned bitter water to sweet at Marah and led the people to twelve springs at Elim (Ex. 15:25, 27). In the Desert of Sin God sent down manna from heaven, and these thin flakes that "tasted like wafers made with honey" were miraculously provided for the next forty years (cf. Ex. 16:31). On two occasions quail came in from the sea when

58. Ronald B. Allen, "Numbers," in *EBC*, 2:680-91.
59. Ibid., p. 690.
60. Ibid., p. 921.
61. John J. Davis, *Biblical Numerology* (Grand Rapids: Baker, 1968), p. 66.

the people craved meat (Ex. 16:13; Num. 11:31). And during those long and difficult years neither their clothes nor their sandals wore out (Deut. 29:5). Because of unbelief an entire generation perished in that desert, but the nation as a whole survived with God as their "shield and helper" (Deut. 33:29).

THE SINAI COVENANT

Three months after the Exodus, the Israelites arrived at Mount Sinai in the southeast section of the peninsula, and there God met with them in a powerful way. Following their years of slavery the people needed an opportunity to hear from God before heading for the Promised Land. God gave them specific instructions about how to live and how to worship Him. Hundreds of years earlier God had entered into a covenant relationship with Abraham, promising to make him into a great nation. Now that "great nation" needed to enter into corporate relationship with God that they might become His treasured possession. Later passages look back at the Sinai Covenant as the marriage between God and Israel, and the breaking of that covenant resulted ultimately in the "divorce" of Exile (cf. Jer. 3:8). By agreeing to obey the Lord fully, Israel did become at Mount Sinai "a kingdom of priests and a holy nation" (Ex. 19:6). They were set apart to fear God and to worship Him alone; no other nation enjoyed this special relationship with God. In 1 Peter 2:9 the apostle notes that New Testament believers have entered into these privileges as those who are chosen by God.[62]

THEOPHANY

To impress upon the nation the significance of their decision, God revealed His power and glory on Mount Sinai in an awe-inspiring display. While the people stood at the foot of the mountain, God came down to the top of Mount Sinai amid thunder and lightning, an earthquake, and billowing smoke. God's voice and the thunder seemed indistinguishable, and the people were terrified, thinking they would die. They begged Moses to do the listening for them, and promised that they in turn would listen to him (Ex. 19:19; 20:18-19). In effect they were asking Moses to be a mediator, a prophet, and by their request they were agreeing to listen closely to all of God's words through the prophet (cf. Deut. 18:15-16). This meant that Israel should have paid very close attention to the Ten Commandments and to the other laws given to them by Moses.

The fire and smoke on Mount Sinai also accompanied the presence of God at the institution of the Abrahamic Covenant (cf. Gen. 15:17) and God's appearance to Moses (Ex. 3:2). But it was the revelation at Sinai that was forever etched in the nation's memory, and in subsequent years they spoke of the Lord

---

62. "A people belonging to God": *laos eis peripoiesin* is the Greek term used in the Septuagint to translate the Hebrew *segullâ* ("treasured possession") in Ex. 19:5.

as "the One of Sinai" whenever they reflected upon His power and the way He protected His people (cf. Judg. 5:5; Ps. 68:8 [HB 68:9]).

THE TEN COMMANDMENTS

In an earlier chapter (see "The Covenants" in chap. 1) we discussed the centrality of the Ten Commandments to the Sinai Covenant. Known simply as "the Ten Words" (Ex. 34:28; Deut. 4:13; 10:4; rendered "Decalogue" from the Greek), these succinct commands summed up the requirements of the law and represent the moral law as distinguished from the civil or ceremonial law. As noted above, the Ten Commandments correspond closely to the stipulations of a treaty, another reason the Israelites should have obeyed them wholehearted-ly. "Inscribed by the finger of God" (Ex. 31:18) on two tablets of stone, the Ten Commandments were kept in the Ark of the Covenant as a sign of their im-portance. The tablets were probably duplicate copies, each containing all of the commandments. Before they could be read to the people, however, Moses broke the tablets when he saw the worship of the golden calf (32:19). Two new tablets were chiseled out and inscribed when Moses returned to the top of the mountain (34:1).

There are differences of opinion about the exact way the Ten Command-ments are divided up, but all agree that the initial commands address man's rela-tionship with God and the later commands deal with man's relationship with man. The command to keep the Sabbath is somewhat transitional, since the Sab-bath is based upon God's resting on the seventh day of creation and at the same time is closely intertwined with owner/slave or employer/employee relation-ships. The next command—"Honor your father and your mother" (20:12)—is called "the first commandment with a promise" in Ephesians 6:2.

When asked which of the commandments was the most important, Jesus quoted Deuteronomy 6:5—"Love the Lord your God with all your heart and with all your soul" (Matt. 22:37), which is a summary of the first four com-mandments. The second commandment, "Love your neighbor as yourself" (Lev. 19:18; Matt. 22:39), sums up the last six commandments.[63] From Jesus' words it is probably safe to conclude that the Ten Commandments are arranged in a descending order of importance. The first commandment prohibiting the worship of other gods is the most important, and the command against coveting would be the least significant—though still extremely important. Sadly, Israel quickly became involved in the worship of the golden calf, breaking the first two commandments (Ex. 32:4).

In the Sermon on the Mount Jesus showed the inner dimension of the law by comparing anger and hatred with murder, and lust with adultery (Matt. 5:21-22,

63. Cf. Hamilton, *Handbook*, p. 201.

27-28). Sin begins in the heart, which is "the wellspring of life," so it must be carefully guarded (Prov. 4:23). If we meditate on God's Word day and night, and if we think about things that are noble, right, and pure (Ps. 1:2, Phil. 4:7-8), we can walk in the light and avoid the works of darkness.

THE BOOK OF THE COVENANT

Taken from Exodus 24:7, this title refers in its strictest sense to 20:22–23:33, a section containing expansions and extensions of the Ten Commandments. Almost all of the commandments are referred to in one way or another, though sometimes briefly.[64] For example, the worship of God alone is the subject of 20:23 and 22:20, and idolaters must be destroyed—a strong term usually reserved for judgment on the Canaanites and Amorites (cf. Josh. 2:10). Laws about the Sabbath (the fourth commandment) are contained in 23:10-12, including mention of the sabbatical year of rest for the land. Hebrew slaves were also to be given their release "in the seventh year" (21:2). Anyone who attacks or curses his parents "must be put to death" for breaking the fifth commandment (21:15, 17), and the same was true for anyone guilty of murder (21:12, 14). If the death was accidental, however, God provided a city of refuge for the one guilty of manslaughter (21:13). Various kinds of sexual immorality are addressed in 22:16-19, and the lengthy section on theft is presented in 22:1-15. Finally, chapter 23 contains warnings against giving false testimony in court (vv. 1-9).

Throughout this section there are injunctions urging kind treatment for slaves, aliens, widows, and orphans (22:21-24); for they remembered only too well "how it feels to be aliens" from their years in Egypt (23:9). Concern for the poor in general is encouraged, for the Lord was a compassionate God (22:27). Even animals were to be treated with mercy (23:5, 12).

As noted above, several violations were punishable by death, and others were subject to "the law of retaliation," an eye for an eye and a tooth for a tooth (21:24). Repeated in Leviticus 24:20 and Deuteronomy 19:21, this law was designed to make the punishment fit the crime rather than to encourage personal revenge. And sometimes even the required penalty was modified in a humane way (21:26-27). When Jesus reacted to the "eye for eye" principle, he was showing how love could replace the desire for personal revenge (Matt. 5:38-42).

COVENANT RATIFICATION

Although the Israelites had provisionally agreed to accept the terms of the covenant in 19:8, the actual ratification ceremony is contained in chapter 24. Unlike the institution of the Abrahamic Covenant in Genesis 15, the responsibi-

64. Cf. Youngblood, *Exodus*, p. 101.

lities of the people are emphasized. Accompanied by Aaron, his two sons, and seventy elders, Moses met with the Lord after the people had twice agreed to do everything the Lord said (vv. 3, 8). In response to their affirmation Moses offered sacrifices at the foot of Mount Sinai and sprinkled part of the blood on the people as a sign that they were set apart as God's special nation. This was called "the blood of the covenant," a term that recalls the words of Christ just before He shed His own blood to institute the New Covenant (Mark 14:24).

After the sacrifices were offered, Moses and the others went partway up the mountain and participated in a meal to seal the covenant. A fellowship meal was commonly connected with the ratification of a covenant (cf. Gen. 26:30; 31:54), though the majestic surroundings of this meal were unique. Amazingly, verses 10 and 11 say that they "saw God" and lived to tell about it. Since not even Moses was allowed to see God's face (cf. Ex. 33:20), perhaps on this occasion they only saw God's feet (cf. v. 10). This was a limited revelation of God's glory but one that should have impressed upon these leaders of the people the need to keep this covenant. Moses himself was then called to the top of the mountain, now enveloped with the glory of the Lord. For forty days Moses remained in this cloud of glory and received from God instructions about the law and the construction of the Tabernacle. To the Israelites the cloud looked like a consuming fire (24:17), a symbol of the power and anger of a God who demanded obedience to the covenant (cf. Deut. 4:23-24).

A COMPARISON WITH OTHER ANCIENT LAW CODES

Students of the ancient Near East are well aware of the existence of other law codes that bear some resemblance to the biblical laws. Several are older than the Scriptures, such as the Sumerian code of Ur-Nammu (twenty-first century), the code of Bilalama of Eshnunna written in Akkadian (twentieth century), and most famous of all, the Akkadian code of King Hammurapi of Babylon (eighteenth century). Other important discoveries were the Hittite code from Asia Minor, going back to the sixteenth century, and the Middle Assyrian laws, found on clay tablets dated in the reign of King Tiglath-Pileser I (1115-1077 B.C.) but perhaps as much as three hundred years older. The longest and most important of these codes was the one attributed to Hammurapi, preserved on an eight-foot stele of black diorite and discovered in the ancient Elamite capital of Susa in 1902 from where it was carried off to the Louvre in Paris by French archaeologists.[65]

Among the hundreds of laws found in these codes are some that are quite close to verses in Exodus or Deuteronomy,[66] but almost all of them are given in casuistic rather than apodictic form. Known especially from the Ten Commandments, the apodictic style is also characteristic of the stipulations found in Near

65. *NBD*, pp. 501-2.
66. Cf. Brevard Childs, *The Book of Exodus* (Philadelphia: Westminster, 1974), pp. 462-63.

Eastern treaties. Strangely, the ancient law codes are not often referred to in the settling of lawsuits and may have had a greater role in the education of scribes and judges than in actual legal practice.[67] A comparison with the biblical laws reveals that the other codes set a higher value on property than they do on human life.[68] For instance, if a bull that had previously killed someone gores another person to death, according to Exodus 21:29 the owner of the bull "must be put to death" unless the family of the victim is willing to accept payment of a fine instead (v. 30). According to Hammurapi law 251, however, all that is required is the payment of a fine.[69] In cases of theft, the Hammurapi code demanded restitution ranging from tenfold to thirtyfold, much higher than the biblical fourfold or fivefold (Ex. 22:1).[70]

Laws about slaves abound in the various codes, dealing with such matters as punishment, the granting of freedom, and marriages with female slaves. Often a female slave was purchased as a concubine (implied in Ex. 21:7-8) and enjoyed greater privileges. The inheritance rights of children born to such marriages were carefully regulated.[71] In general, Exodus expresses great concern for the privileges of slaves and encourages humane treatment. Hebrew slaves were to be released after six years of labor (Ex. 21:2) and given gifts of food and animals in recognition of their valuable service (cf. Deut. 15:12-15).

The law of retaliation ("an eye for an eye, a tooth for a tooth") is also found in laws 197 and 200 of the Code of Hammurapi, but the nonbiblical codes include in addition punishment in the form of bodily mutilation. For example, if a slave strikes the cheek of one of the aristocracy, his ear is cut off.[72] Similarly, if a son strikes his father, his hand is cut off.[73] For some reason the Middle Assyrian laws demand bodily mutilation for a large number of crimes, even though that code is later than most of the others.

If a man injures another in a fight, both the Hammurapi code and the Hittite code specify that the guilty party must pay the fee charged by the physician.[74] According to Exodus 21:19 the aggressor "must pay the injured man for the loss of his time and see that he is completely healed." Laws 209-14 of the Hammurapi code deal with various penalties assessed for striking a woman and causing a miscarriage. These laws may have a bearing upon Exodus 21:22-25, which also deals with punishment for hitting a pregnant woman. In Exodus it is unclear

---

67. William W. Hallo and William K. Simpson, *The Ancient Near East: A History* (New York: Harcourt Brace Jovanovich, 1972), p. 176.
68. See M. Greenberg, "Some Postulates of Biblical Criminal Law," in *Yehezkel Kaufmann Jubilee Volume* (1960), p. 18.
69. Cf. Hamilton, *Handbook*, p. 218.
70. *ANET*, p. 166 (law 8).
71. Cf. ibid., p. 173 (laws 170-71).
72. Cf. ibid., p. 175 (law 205).
73. Ibid. (law 195).
74. Ibid., p. 175 (law 206) and p. 189 (law 10).

whether the woman gives birth prematurely or has a miscarriage, though the former is more likely on exegetical grounds.[75]

To discourage false testimony in court, law 1 of the Hammurapi code stated that a person who falsely accuses another of murder must himself be put to death.[76] The biblical parallel in Deuteromony 19:16-19 states that anyone who falsely accuses another of a crime must receive the punishment appropriate to that crime. Apparently capital punishment was intended, because the sentence "You must purge the evil from among you" is used elsewhere in connection with the death penalty (Deut. 13:5; 17:7; 21:21; 22:21, 24; 24:7). Lying was a serious offense and had to be eliminated from all aspects of community life (cf. Ex. 23:1-3).

THE TABERNACLE AS GOD'S DWELLING PLACE

After the giving of the law and the ratification of the covenant, God revealed to Moses the plans for the Tabernacle, God's special dwelling place among his people. Instead of remaining on Mount Sinai enshrouded in a cloud of glory, the Lord was willing to come down and fill the Tabernacle with the same cloud of glory. True, the people could not enter His presence directly, but mediated by Moses, Aaron, and the priests, Israel had amazing access to the Almighty God. God had promised to be with the people—as the name Yahweh itself suggests (Ex. 3:12)—and now He would remain with them in the camp. Like the later Temple of Solomon modeled after it, the Tabernacle was the perfect structure to teach Israel about God and how He could be approached. Although there were similarities between this sanctuary and other ancient temples, the Tabernacle was unique and designed by God Himself (25:8).

The significance of the Tabernacle can be seen in the names given to it. Along with "tabernacle," which means essentially "dwelling place," the building was first called "a sanctuary," that is, "a place of holiness," stressing the transcendence of God (25:8).[77] When the glory of the Lord filled the Tabernacle (cf. 40:34), the structure was set apart from all other sanctuaries. At night the cloud looked like fire, just as it had appeared on Mount Sinai (cf. Num. 9:16). Another name for it was the Tent of Meeting, the place where God spoke to Moses and where He met with the Israelites and received their sacrifices and offerings (29:42-43). The word "tent" indicates that the Tabernacle was a portable structure. "Whenever the cloud lifted from above the Tent, the Israelites set out" to find a new location (Num. 9:17). The entire structure was dismantled and then reassembled at the new campsite. A fourth name for the Tabernacle

---

75. The Hebrew of verse 22 literally says, "and her children come out," an expression not used elsewhere to describe miscarriage.
76. *ANET*, p. 166.
77. Youngblood, *Exodus*, pp. 114-15.

was "the Tent of the Testimony" (Num. 9:15; cf. Ex. 38:21), an indication that the Ark of the Testimony containing the two tablets of the law was kept in the Most Holy Place.

The Tabernacle proper was divided into two sections, a holy place measuring 30 feet by 15 feet and a Most Holy Place that measured 15 feet on each side. Inside the Most Holy Place was the Ark of the Testimony with its atonement cover, the most important article in the entire structure. The holy place contained a table with the bread of the Presence, the golden lampstand, and the altar of incense. Between the two sections was "the shielding curtain," which barred the way to the Most Holy Place (cf. 39:34). Around the Tabernacle was a courtyard that measured 150 feet by 75 feet and contained the bronze altar of burnt offering and the bronze laver.

The materials for the Tabernacle were contributed by the people and their leaders as freewill offerings to the Lord, and more than enough was received in this fashion (35:20, 29; 36:6-7). The bronze totaled about two-and-a-half tons and the silver about three-and-three-quarters tons. The gold—which was used mainly for the sacred furniture inside the sanctuary—amounted to a little more than a ton (cf. 38:24, 25, 29). The curtains and the priests' garments were made mainly out of linen and blue, purple, and scarlet yarn (26:1; 28:5). Coverings made of ram skins and of the hides of sea cows—the "dugong" of the Red Sea—were also placed over the Tabernacle for protection (36:19). Substantial amounts of acacia wood were used for the boards, furniture, and posts of the Tabernacle and its courtyard. Found in the Sinai peninsula and as far north as Jericho, acacia wood is as hard as oak and very valuable for building.[78] Two men were primarily responsible for building the Tabernacle: Bezalel from the tribe of Judah and Oholiab from the tribe of Dan, both highly skilled craftsmen. Significantly, Bezalel was filled with the Spirit of God (31:3; 35:31), the first reference to the filling of the Spirit in Scripture. Just as prophets and apostles were empowered to proclaim God's Word, so Bezalel was given the artistic ability to construct the Tabernacle that speaks to us about our God. Bezalel and Oholiab were carpenters, metal workers, designers, embroiderers, and stonecutters (cf. 35:32-35), and they were assisted by many other skilled workers (36:1). Following the plans God gave to Moses on Mount Sinai, these talented individuals completed the Tabernacle in less than a year.

The first part of the Tabernacle described in Exodus was the Ark of the Testimony, also known as the Ark of the Covenant (25:22; Num. 10:33). A wooden chest 3.75 feet long and 2.25 feet wide and high, the Ark was the only article in the Most Holy Place. It was overlaid with pure gold and had two cherubim made "out of hammered gold at the ends of the cover" (25:11, 18). The cherubim may have looked like the winged sphinxes carved into the armrests of some an-

---

78. Ibid., p. 114.

cient thrones, and elsewhere the cherubim are angelic creatures associated with the presence of God (Ezek. 10:2-3).[79] In 2 Samuel 6:2 God is said to be "enthroned between the cherubim that are on the ark." The Most Holy Place was the throne room of God on earth and the Ark was His footstool (cf. Ps 132:7-8). When Moses entered the Tabernacle "to speak with the Lord," God spoke to him "from between the two cherubim" (Num. 7:89). At the Ark of the Covenant, God met with man in a unique way (cf. Ex. 25:22).

The cover to which the cherubim belonged was called the "atonement cover" because that was the place where the high priest sprinkled blood once a year on the Day of Atonement (Lev. 16:14). More than any other sacrifice, the blood of the goat presented in this way symbolized the appeasement of the wrath of a holy God, who was willing to forgive the sin of the people and to meet with them.

As noted earlier, Moses was instructed to place in the Ark the "tablets of the Testimony" (Ex. 31:18), the Ten Commandments that epitomized the entire covenant (Ex. 25:16, 21). Two other items were also placed in the ark: a jar of manna (Ex. 16:33-34) and Aaron's staff that budded (Num. 17:10). Sometimes the Ark accompanied Israel's troops into battle as a sign that God would scatter the enemy before them (cf. Num. 10:33-36; 14:44).

If the Most Holy Place represented God's throne room, the holy place may be compared to a royal guest chamber where His people wait before Him as symbolized by the bread of the Presence, the light on the lampstand, and the incense ascending from the altar of incense.[80] The bread of the Presence (the "showbread") consisted of twelve loaves of bread that represented the twelve tribes of Israel. Set on a small table about three feet long and two-and-one-quarter feet high, the loaves were replaced every Sabbath day and were eaten only by the priests (Lev. 24:8-9). The bread was an offering to the Lord of the fruit of the people's labor, but at the same time it served to acknowledge God's provision of food for the nation.

On the south side of the Tabernacle across from the table stood the seventy-five-pound pure gold lampstand (or "menorah") with its central shaft and six branches. On top of the shaft and each of the branches was a saucer-like lamp with a wick fed by olive oil. The lampstand may have represented God as a light to Israel or perhaps Israel as a light to the Gentiles (Isa. 42:6), reflecting the glory of the Lord by their godly lives.[81]

Right in front of the curtain that shielded the Most Holy Place stood a small wooden altar overlaid with gold. Only three feet high and one-and-one-half feet square, this altar of incense was used twice a day by Aaron and his sons, and on

79. *NIV Study Bible*, p. 123.
80. Ibid., p. 127.
81. Ibid., p. 125; cf. Youngblood, *Exodus*, p. 120.

the Day of Atonement the horns of the altar were smeared "with the blood of the atoning sin offering" (Ex. 30:10). Unlike the altar of burnt offering in the courtyard, the altar of incense was never used for animal sacrifices. Only a specially blended fragrant incense could be burned on this altar (cf. 30:34-35), and the smoke represented the prayers that the people offered to God (cf. Ps. 141:2; Luke 1:10).

Although some interpreters have overemphasized the typological significance of the Tabernacle, the symbolism of this unique structure is nonetheless rich and meaningful. Above all the Tabernacle pictures God's desire to dwell among His people (Ex. 25:8), and when John the apostle described the incarnation of Christ, he said that "the Word . . . made his dwelling among us" or, more literally, "tabernacled among us" (John 1:14). The same verse speaks of seeing Christ's glory—not the cloud that filled the Tabernacle but the miracles He performed and His resurrection. When Christ died "the curtain of the temple was torn in two from top to bottom" (Mark 15:38), and that curtain represented the body of Christ, who through His death gave believers access to the Most Holy Place and the very presence of God (Heb. 10:19-22). Through the one sacrifice of His body, the sins of all mankind were paid for, something that the blood of bulls and goats could never do (Heb. 10:4, 12).

The olive oil that burned in the lamps on the lampstand probably symbolized the empowering work of the Holy Spirit. This is strongly implied in Zechariah's vision of the lampstand and the two olive trees in which the governor Zerubbabel was one of the olive trees and was "anointed to serve the Lord" (Zech. 4:14). In verse 6 we are told that Zerubbabel will finish rebuilding the Temple by the power of God's Spirit. The same connection between anointing oil and the empowering of the Spirit was present when David was anointed king over Israel. "From that day on the Spirit of the Lord came upon David in power" (1 Sam. 16:13).

When the cloud identified with the glory of the Lord filled the Tabernacle (Ex. 40:34), the Israelites knew that the Lord was pleased with the newly built tent and that He would indeed live among them. The same God who had displayed His power through the plagues and who had revealed Himself at Mount Sinai would now be present to guide the nation on its journey to the Promised Land. When the Lord spoke to Moses at the burning bush and commissioned him to lead the Israelites out of Egypt, He had said, "I will be with you" (Ex. 3:12). Here, at the end of the book of Exodus, Moses and all the people worshiped this one who had proved His love for them and had chosen them to be His "treasured possession" (19:5).

5

LEVITICUS

Although Leviticus contains many details about natural matters, a careful reading of the book can help us learn much about worship and holy living. The emphasis in Leviticus upon sacrifices and offerings enables us to appreciate the meaning of Christ's sacrifice on Calvary, and the description of the Day of Atonement in chapter 16 is especially important in this regard. In Leviticus we learn that sin must be dealt with and that God demands holy living. The people of God were to be different from their pagan neighbors, and the specific instructions about purity and morality have many contemporary applications.

TITLE

"Leviticus" means "relating to the Levites," a title given to this book by the translators of the Septuagint and adapted by the Latin Vulgate in the fourth century A.D. Since much of the book deals with the responsibilities of the priests, who all belonged to the tribe of Levi, the title is an appropriate one. The rest of the Levites assisted the priests in their ministry, but surprisingly they are mentioned only in 25:32-34. In some respects the book is concerned as much with laypeople as with the priests, for there are instructions about how the Israelites were to bring their offerings and how they were to celebrate the festivals (especially in chap. 23). Worship was not limited to the priests and Levites but was to be an integral part of the life of all Israel.

The Hebrew title for the book is "and he called" (*wayyiqra'*), referring to the Lord calling to Moses from the Tabernacle (1:1). This expression underscores the significance of the words that God was about to speak to Moses, but it does not reveal much about the general contents of the book.

PURPOSE AND SCOPE

Leviticus tells how a sinful people could approach a holy God and how they could live holy lives. To make atonement for their sins the Lord prescribed a series of sacrifices culminating in the offerings presented by the high priest on the

Day of Atonement. The covenant people were expected to avoid sexual immorality and to obey all of the Lord's commandments. If anyone ignored these laws and commandments, the penalties were severe (cf. 10:2; 20:1-27). In chapter 26 the nation is warned that if they break God's covenant in the Promised Land the results will be famine, disease, defeat, and eventually deportation.

When the glory of the Lord filled the Tabernacle at the end of Exodus (40:34), the Israelites were very much aware of the presence of God. God had come to live among the twelve tribes, a people who were to be "a kingdom of priests and a holy nation" (Ex. 19:6). In a world filled with unholiness Israel was taught to distinguish between the holy and the profane, the clean and the unclean. This affected the practical areas of diet, healthful habits, and sexual behavior, as well as ceremonial matters and separation from other gods. God set high standards for the nation, and, as leaders of the people, the priests were subject to even higher standards (cf. 21:7-8). The priests were responsible for the overall ministry of the Tabernacle, so any disobedience on their part brought swift punishment. The same fire that consumed the burnt offering and signaled approval of the Aaronic priesthood consumed the rebellious sons of Aaron two verses later (9:24; 10:1-2). Severe as it was, the death of Nadab and Abihu demonstrated to all the people the requirements of their holy God. Privilege and position did not give them the luxury of violating the Lord's command.

In the midst of a book filled with ritual and ceremony stands a verse cited by Christ as the second greatest commandment: "Love your neighbor as yourself" (Lev. 19:18; Matt. 22:39; Mark 12:31). Quoted more often than any other verse in the Old Testament, Paul indicates that the entire law is summed up in this single command (Gal. 5:14; cf. Rom. 13:9). If the people love the Lord with all their hearts (Deut. 6:5) and their neighbors as themselves, they will be well along the way to holy living. "Neighbor" includes the alien who "lives with you in your land" (19:33). Since the Israelites remembered what it was like to be aliens in Egypt, they must not mistreat such individuals.

To enable the people to be cleansed of their sin and to express their dedication to God, the Lord provides for them a series of sacrifices and offerings in chapters 1-7. With Aaron and his sons officiating, these sacrifices were presented "before the Lord," the one whose law had been violated but who was willing to forgive. Atonement was made for those who confessed their sin and offered an animal to die as a substitute for the sinner.

Chapters 11-15 deal with the topic of uncleanness and defilement in relation to food, skin diseases, and bodily discharges. Although uncleanness was not the same as sinfulness, it typified sin and impurity. Anyone affected by a skin disease or a bodily discharge had to be cleansed through special ceremonies. The most important cleansing ritual of all, however, which involved the high priest on the Day of Atonement, brought about the forgiveness of Israel's sin. On this one day of the year, the priest sprinkled blood on the atonement cover in the Most Holy Place because of the sin of the people (16:15). As a sign that God had removed Israel's sin, a scapegoat symbolically carried away the sin of the nation into the desert (16:21).

Now that Israel has learned about the sacrifices and offerings that can atone for sin, chapters 17-27 discuss the practical dimensions of holy living. Often referred to as "the Holiness Code," these chapters cover a variety of topics applicable both to the people and to the priests. In several instances the laws were designed to help Israel avoid the unholy customs of its pagan neighbors, who had defiled the land by their immoral practices (cf. 18:24). Chapter 17 prohibits the eating of blood or sacrificing to goat idols, and then chapter 18 spells out illicit sexual relations, particularly those involving incest. In chapter 19 there is a restatement of several of the Ten Commandments and appropriate expansion for more precise application. If God's commands or laws are violated, the penalties to be assessed are given in chapter 20. Since the priests were set apart to God in a special way, chapters 21-22 present rules they and their families had to obey meticulously.

Chapter 23 contains a summary of the religious calendar for the entire year, reviewing the exact time of each festival and what was expected of the people. This is expanded in chapter 25 to include a discussion of the sabbatical year (every seventh year) and the Year of Jubilee (every fifty years), both of which had important economic, as well as religious, implications. If the people obeyed God's laws and commands faithfully, He promised to send them peace and prosperity and to walk among them (26:1-13). But if Israel turned their backs on God and disobeyed His law, the nation would suffer every imaginable calamity and eventually be driven out of the Promised Land (26:14-46).

Chapter 27 is something of an appendix and deals with special vows made to the Lord. These gifts of persons or property were voluntary ones given to God as expressions of thanksgiving. Perhaps they are included at the end of Leviticus to keep them separate from the required sacrifices and offerings described in the opening chapters.

LITERARY STRUCTURE

At first glance Leviticus appears to be an endless list of rules and regulations put together in rather haphazard fashion, but a closer examination reveals a greater coherence. Whereas it is true that much greater attention is given to ritual in Leviticus than in the other books of the Pentateuch, the book is still "part of the great history of Israel's journey from Egypt to the promised lands."[1] Although the narrative material in Leviticus is not extensive, what we do have in chapters 8-10 and in 24:10-16 is important to the overall structure of the book.

---

1. Gordon J. Wenham, *The Book of Leviticus*, NICOT (Grand Rapids: Eerdmans, 1979), p. 50.

In one sense the laws about sacrifices are given in chapters 1-7 to help us understand the various offerings presented at the ordination of Aaron and his sons in chapters 8-9.[2] The death of Aaron's two eldest sons in chapter 10 and the death of the blasphemer in chapter 24 are stern warnings that neither the priesthood nor the laity can ignore God's laws with impunity.

THE LITERARY STRUCTURE OF LEVITICUS

Part 1: Ritual

General Procedure (1:1–6:7)

Laws About Sacrifices	Chaps. 1-7

Regulations (6:8–7:38)

Ordination of the Priests	Chaps. 8-10

Death of Aaron's two eldest sons (chap. 10)
(narrative insert)

Regulations About Cleanness	Chaps. 11-15
*The Day of Atonement	Chap. 16

Part 2: Holy Living

HINGE: Worship at the Central Sanctuary	Chap. 17
Ethical and Moral Concerns	Chaps. 18-20
Regulations and Observances	Chaps. 21-27

Annual Festivals (chap. 23)
Death of a Blasphemer (chap. 24)
(narrative insert)
Sabbatical Year and Year of Jubilee (chap. 25)
Blessings and Curses (chap. 26)

The book begins with a two-part discussion of the most important offerings. First, the general procedure for the presentation of each offering is outlined, including the respective responsibilities of the offerer and the officiating priest. The first three offerings described—the burnt offering, grain offering, and fellowship offerings—were the "sweet savor" offerings, the ones that provided "an aroma pleasing to the Lord" (1:9; 2:2; 3:5). They were followed by the sin offering and guilt offering—the two that dealt with specific sin (4:1–6:7).

Second, in 6:8–7:38 Moses gave the regulations for the various offerings, providing additional details for the priests about how the offering was to be presented and how the animal or grain was to be disposed of. "Regulations" is a

2. Ibid., pp. 49-50.

translation of the same Hebrew word for Torah (*tôrâ*), which is usually rendered "law." But since the basic meaning of the word is "instruction" or "teaching" (cf. Prov. 1:8), "the law of the burnt offering" (6:8) refers to instructions about this offering. These laws about the sacrifices and other rituals were as important as the laws that governed personal morality and social responsibility.

"Regulations" is the basic meaning of "Torah" in chapters 11-15 also. Whether the subject be rules about food (11:46), procedures for a woman after childbirth (12:7), or an examination of contaminated articles of clothing (13:59), the translation "regulations" applies quite well. Of special importance were the regulations for the cleansing of someone who had been healed of an infectious skin disease (14:2).

Although chapter 16 with its description of the Day of Atonement is the most important ritual in Leviticus, it is nonetheless set in the historical context of the death of Aaron's sons (v. 1). If Aaron presents the sacrifices in the prescribed manner, sin will be atoned for—and Aaron will not die in the process. According to verse 34, the yearly atonement ceremony was to be "a lasting ordinance" for the nation (cf. Ex. 27:21; 29:9).

The second major section of the book (chaps. 17-27) begins with a chapter that is something of a hinge linking the chapters on ritual regulations (chaps. 1-16) with those dealing with more personal matters.[3] Chapters 18-20 are a combination of apodictic and casuistic laws that sound much like Exodus 20-23. The prohibitions against slander or showing favoritism in court (19:15-16) are very similar to Exodus 23:2-3, and sorcery is condemned in both books (Ex. 22:18; Lev. 19:26). The close relationship between the Book of the Covenant in Exodus 20-23 and Leviticus 18-20 shows that the earlier emphasis on ceremony in Leviticus was not intended to replace the ethical and moral concerns of the covenant. On the contrary, the words "I am the Lord your God, who brought you out of Egypt"—which introduce the Ten Commandments in Exodus 20:2— are repeated in Leviticus 19:36.[4] These words, which have been identified with the historical prologue of the treaty/covenant, help to stamp Leviticus as a covenant document also. In this regard, perhaps the regulations about the yearly festivals in chapter 23 and the sabbatical year and Year of Jubilee in chapter 25 could be considered part of the covenant stipulations. The emphasis upon the Sabbath in chapter 23 and the seven sevens of years in chapter 25 are an expansion of the fifth commandment in the Decalogue. And as pointed out by Wenham, the blessings and curses of chapter 26 are "entirely appropriate to a covenant document."[5]

3. Ibid., p. 241.
4. Cf. Samuel Schultz, *Leviticus*, Everyman's Bible Commentary (Chicago: Moody, 1983), p. 94.
5. Wenham, *Leviticus*, p. 29.

THE MEANING OF THE SACRIFICIAL SYSTEM

To the Western mind, a study of the sacrifices and offerings appears to be a tedious chore and not very relevant to the New Testament believer. After all, if Christ's sacrifice rendered the Levitical sacrifices obsolete, why should we bother with details about the slaughter of animals and the sprinkling of blood? Perhaps the most important reason is the fact that the New Testament describes Christ's death in terms of Old Testament sacrifices, making a knowledge of the Levitical system essential to the understanding of our faith. In 1 John 1:2 we are told that Christ is "the atoning sacrifice for our sins," and Hebrews 9:22 states that "without the shedding of blood there is no forgiveness." Significant sections of Hebrews draw upon the ceremonies and rituals of Leviticus to explain the work of Christ, including a specific reference to the sin offering (Heb. 13:11-12). Without a basic knowledge of Leviticus, Hebrews will remain a closed book to the Christian.

Throughout the Old Testament are numerous references to sacrifices and offerings in the life of the nation as well as in individual lives. Although the prophets sometimes gave the impression that sacrifices were useless (cf. Isa. 1:11-14), the purpose of such preaching was to shake the people out of their lethargy. Ritual for ritual's sake was wrong (cf. 1 Sam. 15:22), but if the individual brought a sacrifice with a repentant attitude and a heart full of praise, the whole experience was an exciting moment of worship (cf. Ps. 4:5). Malachi declared that the backslidden tended to bring sick animals as sacrifices, reflecting the sinfulness of their hearts (Mal. 1:6-8).[6]

One of the basic words for "offering" (*qorbān*) is derived from the verb "to bring near."[7] When sacrifices were offered, man came near God, with the hope that the sacrifice would be accepted and sin atoned for. Reconciliation with God was the goal of the worshiper, whose sinfulness always made it difficult to approach the Almighty. Sin aroused the wrath of God, so the sacrifice was presented to appease the righteous wrath of a holy God. In several instances God's anger at the rebellion of Israel brought about a terrible plague against the people. When Korah and his followers died, Moses told Aaron to fill his censer with incense and make atonement for the rest of the people, because "wrath has come out from the Lord" (Num. 16:46). Even so, "14,700 people died from the plague" (Num. 16:49). Later in Numbers the people were guilty of idolatry and sexual immorality, and another plague broke out. This time Aaron's grandson

---

6. See Herbert Wolf, *Haggai and Malachi*, Everyman's Bible Commentary (Chicago: Moody, 1976), pp. 69-70.
7. Note the term "Corban" in Mark 7:11, when the Pharisees were presenting a gift in the wrong way.

Phinehas drove a spear through two of the offenders and "made atonement for the Israelites" (25:13). In one sense the death of a sacrificial animal was always a ransom to save the life of the offerer, who really deserved to die for his sin.[8]

GENERAL PROCEDURE

Regardless of which sacrifice was offered, normally the following pattern was observed: (1) The animal had to be a healthy specimen, free of any defect,

THE BLOOD SACRIFICES

Name	Animals	Purpose
Burnt Offering	Bull, sheep, goat, dove, or pigeon	To make atonement for sin in general; an expression of the worshiper's devotion and commitment to the Lord
Sin Offering	For priest or whole community: a bull For a leader: a male goat For ordinary citizen: a female lamb or goat, or two doves or pigeons	To make atonement for specific sins
Guilt Offering	Ram	To make atonement for specific sins where restitution was possible; 20 percent penalty
Fellowship Offerings:		
1. Thanksgiving Offering	Male or female cow, sheep, or goat (the offerer and friends could eat part of the animal)	To express thanks for a particular blessing
2. Votive Offering	Same	To express thanks for answered prayer (made in the form of a vow)
3. Freewill Offering	Same (though animal could have defect)	To express one's love for God

Order when presented in a series: sin (or guilt)—burnt—fellowship. The burnt offering and fellowship offering were usually accompanied by a grain offering and drink offering.

8. Cf. Wenham, *Leviticus*, pp. 27-28.

for God demanded the very best. Peter referred to Christ as "a lamb without blemish or defect," the sinless Son of God (1 Pet. 1:19, 22; cf. Heb. 9:14). (2) The person bringing the offering placed his hand on the head of the animal as a sign that the animal was dying in his place (1:4). The substitutionary nature of sacrifice was most clearly seen in the offering of Isaac (Gen. 22:13). (3) Then the offerer had to slaughter the animal near the altar of burnt offering in the courtyard. Without the death of the victim, the sacrifice would not be accepted. (4) The priest sprinkled some of the blood either on the altar of burnt offering or on the altar of incense inside the Holy Place. (5) Depending on the kind of sacrifice, the priest burned all or part of the animal on the altar of burnt offering. The fat, which was considered the best part of the animal, was always burned (3:16). (6) Except for the burnt offering and certain forms of the sin offering, part of the animal could be eaten by the priest or the offerer or both. This has special significance for the fellowship offerings.

THE BURNT OFFERING

The most common of all the sacrifices, the burnt offering was presented in a wide variety of situations. It is also called the "whole burnt offering," because the entire animal was consumed by the flames—except for the hide, which belonged to the priest (Lev. 7:8; Deut. 33:10). Male animals were required and—depending on the wealth of the individual involved—could be a bull, sheep, goat, or even a dove or pigeon (1:1-17; cf. Luke 2:24). The priests had to sacrifice a lamb as a burnt offering every morning and evening without fail, and the fire on the altar was never allowed to go out (Ex. 29:38-43; Lev. 6:8-13; Num. 28:3-8). Every Sabbath and New Moon and at the celebration of the annual festivals, additional burnt offerings were required (Num. 28:9–29:11). Like the fellowship offering—with which it was often combined—the burnt offering was usually accompanied by grain offerings and drink offerings (cf. Num. 15:1-5).

The burnt offering was often an expression of the worshiper's devotion and commitment to the Lord and along with the fellowship offering was presented on occasions of national importance also. When the covenant was renewed on Mount Ebal (Josh. 8:31) and at the great dedication of Solomon's Temple (1 Kings 8:64), the people sacrificed burnt offerings and fellowship offerings. At times of national catastrophe these offerings were presented to effect reconciliation with God and "to make atonement" (Judg. 20:26; 2 Sam. 24:25). Usually the sin or guilt offerings made atonement for iniquity, but even on the Day of Atonement the burnt offering followed the sin offering to make atonement for Aaron and the people (Lev. 16:24).

The burnt offering, grain offering, and fellowship offering are sometimes referred to as "an aroma pleasing to the Lord" (1:9; 2:2; 3:5). First mentioned in connection with Noah's sacrifice after the Flood, "the pleasing aroma" indicates that God is delighted with the offering (Gen. 8:21). Another translation for "pleasing" is "soothing," a term implying that sacrifices usually address the anger of God. Even though such offerings are intended to be acts of worship, the offerer was still a sinner who did not deserve to be accepted by God. Ultimately the wrath of God was fully appeased by the death of Christ, who "gave himself up for us as a fragrant offering" (Eph. 5:2). Christ's death was linked typologically to a burnt offering in the near-sacrifice of Isaac, whose place on the altar was taken by a ram that was sacrificed as a burnt offering (Gen. 22:13).

THE GRAIN OFFERING

Although the grain offering was usually presented in conjunction with burnt offerings and fellowship offerings, it is treated as a distinct offering in 2:1-16 and 6:14-23. The grain offering was made of fine flour mixed with olive oil and incense, and it could be "baked in an oven or cooked in a pan or on a griddle" (7:9). Before the offering was baked or cooked, a priest took a handful of the fine flour mixed with oil and incense and burned it "as a memorial portion on the altar" (2:2). The rest of the offering belonged to the priests and was eaten by them (v. 3).

Normally no yeast or honey could be added to the grain offering, perhaps because they cause fermentation (2:11). On the other hand, verse 13 specifies that salt should be added to all of the offerings, probably because salt prevents the spoiling of food and symbolizes the lasting nature of the covenant. In other places where salt is mentioned, the word "everlasting" is linked with the salt of the covenant (Num. 18:19; 2 Chron. 13:5). If the grain offering was presented to the Lord as an offering of firstfruits, yeast or honey were apparently acceptable (Lev. 2:12; 23:17). In those instances it was not connected with the burnt offering.

THE FELLOWSHIP OFFERING

Of all the offerings, the most joyous and most flexible was the fellowship offering. Earlier translations called this sacrifice "the peace offering," because the Hebrew word is built on the term *shalom,* which often means "peace." Shalom also denotes "wholeness" and "well-being," however, and the emphasis in this offering is primarily on the communion and fellowship of the offerer and his family with the priests and the Lord. The fellowship offering was an expression of praise to God for His goodness and for answered prayer.

There were three different kinds of fellowship offerings: (1) The thanksgiving offering was presented in response to a particular blessing (7:12-15). (2) The votive offering was brought after a time of acute distress had elicited a vow from the offerer (cf. Jonah 2:9). (3) The freewill offering was presented as an expression of gratitude and love for God without focusing on any specific blessing (7:16-18). In presenting one of the fellowship offerings, the individual could bring a male or female cow, sheep, or goat (3:1-16), and in the case of the free-will offering, even a deformed or stunted animal was acceptable (22:21-23).

The unique feature of the fellowship offering was that the offerer, along with his family and friends, was permitted to eat part of the sacrificed animal. As always, the fat belonged to the Lord and was burned on the altar, the breast and right thigh were given to the priests (7:28-34), and the rest of the meat was eaten by the offerer and his family either on the day of the sacrifice or the next day (7:15-17). This was a time of rejoicing before the Lord, feasting together and acknowledging his blessing. After Hannah had vowed to give her son to the Lord for lifelong service, she took Samuel to the sanctuary and presented a peace offering out of gratefulness for answered prayer (1 Sam. 1:24-28).

As noted above, peace offerings were presented on occasions of national importance. When the Sinai Covenant was ratified, some of the leaders met with God and presented burnt offerings and fellowship offerings (Ex. 24:5). Centuries later when Saul was crowned as the first king of Israel, the people "sacrificed fellowship offerings before the Lord, and . . . held a great celebration" (1 Sam. 11:15). King Solomon offered twenty-two thousand cattle and a hundred and twenty thousand sheep and goats as the nation gathered to dedicate the Temple he had built (1 Kings 8:63-65). Since Israelite families ate the Passover lamb together, Wenham suggests that the Passover was "a specialized type of peace offering."[9] When Christ observed the Passover at the Last Supper, He shared the bread and the cup with His disciples in a way reminiscent of the meal associated with the fellowship offering.

THE SIN OFFERING

Probably the most important sacrifice was the sin offering, which always preceded the other sacrifices and played such a key role on the Day of Atonement. If a person committed a sin—even unintentionally—he had to bring a female lamb or goat as a sin offering, or if the offerer was poor, two doves or pigeons, or two quarts of flour (5:1-13). The fat of the lamb or goat was burned on the altar and the rest of the animal was eaten in the courtyard of the Tabernacle by the officiating priest and his sons (6:24-29). If a leader of the community sinned, he had to bring a male goat as a sin offering (4:22-26).

If a priest sinned, or if the whole community was guilty of sin, a bull had to be sacrificed and its blood was taken inside the Tabernacle and sprinkled in front of the inner curtain. The fat, kidneys, and covering of the liver were burned on the altar of burnt offering, and the rest of the bull was taken outside the camp

9. Ibid., p. 82.

and burned. None of it was eaten (4:3-21). In Hebrews 13:11-12 the death of Christ "outside the city gate" is compared to the burning of the sin offering "outside the camp."

Both unintentional sins and sins of omission required sin offerings for forgiveness (cf. Lev. 5:1-4), as did lengthy periods of uncleanness. According to 12:6, a woman had to bring a sin offering several weeks after childbirth. Someone who had recovered from a serious skin disease or a bodily discharge of some kind also had to present a sin offering (cf. 14:19; 15:15). Usually, the sin offering was followed by a burnt offering.

THE GUILT OFFERING

Closely linked with the sin offering was the guilt offering, which also dealt with specific sin. Although there was some overlap between the two offerings, the guilt offering was required when restitution was possible after another person had been wronged. For example, if someone was guilty of theft or extortion, he had to return what was taken and pay a penalty of 20 percent (6:1-5). If neither the person wronged nor a close relative was still alive, the total amount due was given to the priest (Num. 5:5-10). To acknowledge his guilt before the Lord, the individual had to offer a ram as a guilt offering, which, except for the fat parts, belonged to the priest and his sons (see above).

From a study of Leviticus 6:1-7 and Numbers 5:6-7, it seems clear that not all of the sins involved were unintentional. Apparently deliberate sins could also be forgiven provided that the individual repented and confessed his sin.[10] Forgiveness for all sin ultimately came through the death of Christ, and it is significant that Isaiah 53 with its description of Christ as the Lamb on whom the iniquity of us all was laid (vv. 6-7) refers to our Lord's death as a guilt offering (v. 10). By His death Christ made full and perfect compensation for the sins of the world.

Whenever the different sacrifices were offered together, the sin or guilt offering always came first, followed by the burnt and fellowship offering (Lev. 9:22; Num. 6:16-17). This order was important theologically, for confession of sin had to precede the consecration of the worshiper to God (represented by the burnt offering). Third came the fellowship offering, which reflected the reestablishment of communion and fellowship with God.[11] Through these offerings sin could be atoned for, and a cleansed and forgiven people could enjoy the presence of their God.

---

10. Cf. Jacob Milgrom, *Cult and Conscience: The ASHAM and the Priestly Doctrine of Repentance* (Leiden: E. J. Brill, 1976), pp. 109-10.
11. *NIV Study Bible*, ed. Kenneth Barker (Grand Rapids: Zondervan, 1985), p. 150.

THE ROLE OF THE PRIESTS AND LEVITES

The smooth functioning of the sacrificial system depended on the effective ministry of a consecrated priesthood, set apart to approach God on behalf of the people. In Leviticus 8-9 Aaron and his sons are officially ordained as priests and begin this important ministry. Prior to their ordination Moses himself served as a priest and led the nation in worship. Back in Genesis the patriarchs occasionally performed a priestly role, building altars and presenting burnt offerings and drink offerings to the Lord (Gen. 22:13; 35:14). Once the Abrahamic Covenant had been established, the patriarchs wanted to maintain that relationship and keep their families pure before God (cf. Gen. 35:1-3). Similarly, when the Mosaic Covenant was being instituted, Moses built an altar at the foot of Mount Sinai and "sent young Israelite men" to present burnt offerings and fellowship offerings (Ex. 24:4-5). When the tribe of Levi rallied to Moses' side during the golden calf crisis, God set them apart to be His special ministers. Aaron and his descendants were to serve as priests on a permanent basis, and the rest of the Levites were to assist the priests in the work at the Tabernacle.

Although in one sense Israel as a whole was to be "a kingdom of priests and a holy nation" (Ex. 19:6), the family of Aaron had to maintain a level of purity and ceremonial cleanness beyond that of their fellow countrymen. They were the only ones who could enter the Holy Place, sprinkle the blood of the sacrifices, and eat the meat that was "holy" to the Lord. And the high priest was the only one who could enter the Most Holy Place on the Day of Atonement to sprinkle blood on the Ark of the Covenant.

THE HIGH PRIEST

In both Exodus and Leviticus the main focus is upon the ministry of the high priest, who was the mediator between God and the nation. Because of his sacred duties, the high priest had to maintain a higher standard of holiness than anyone else. He could not become ceremonially unclean, not even at the death of his father or mother, and the woman he married had to be a virgin (Lev. 21:11, 13). In view of the dignity and honor of his office, the high priest wore a special set of beautiful garments. One of these was the ephod, an apron-like garment made out of linen, as well as blue, purple, and scarlet yarn and strands of gold thread (Ex. 39:2-5). Fastened to the shoulder straps were two mounted onyx stones with the names of six sons of Jacob on each stone. Attached to the ephod was the "breastpiece for making decisions," a nine-inch-square cloth pouch that had twelve precious stones, also representing the twelve tribes (Ex. 28:15, 21). The breastpiece also contained the mysterious Urim and Thummim, some sort of dice or lots that were used to determine the will of God (Ex. 28:30).

Meaning "lights and perfections" or "curses and perfections," these stones were cast to give a positive or negative response to a question.[12] In this way, the will of God could be determined (Num. 27:21).

Another feature unique to the dress of the high priest was a turban to which a plate of pure gold was attached. On this sacred diadem were engraved the words "Holy to the Lord" (Ex. 39:30-31), an inscription which symbolized the ideal the nation hoped to achieve as well as the special consecration of the high priests to the Lord.[13] The holiness of the high priests was especially important on the Day of Atonement (see below).

THE OTHER PRIESTS

Although the high priest bore the primary responsibility for the religious life of the nation, he received valuable assistance from his sons. They too wore special "tunics, sashes, and headbands . . . to give them dignity and honor" as they carried out important functions along with their fathers (Ex. 28:40). Aaron's son Eleazar was in charge of the entire Tabernacle and the Levites who worked there, especially the Kohathites (Num. 3:32; 4:16). His brother Ithamar also supervised the Levites, particularly the clans of Gershon and Merari (Ex. 38:21; Num. 7:8).

In addition to their administrative functions, the priests officiated at the Tabernacle when the various sacrifices were presented. They were also responsible for determining if individuals had been healed of various diseases, and if so the priests superintended the cleansing rituals (Lev. 14:2-3; Deut. 24:8). As messengers of the Lord, priests were given the task of teaching the Israelites the decrees of the law, so that the Lord's commands would not be violated (Lev. 10:11; Mal. 2:7). When questions about the law came up in court, the priests exercised a judicial function and handed down decisions (cf. Deut. 17:8-11).

Since the wars Israel fought were sometimes entered at the mandate of the Lord and were considered "holy wars," the priests would be there accompanied by the Ark of the Covenant and other sacred furniture (cf. Num. 31:6). The priests also blew the silver trumpets to give signals in battle (Num. 10:8; Josh. 6:4-5). Their presence—along with the Ark—was a sign that God was among His people and would drive out the enemy before them (Num. 10:35).

THE LEVITES

When the firstborn sons of the Israelites were spared during the climactic tenth plague in Egypt, God declared that all the firstborn were His. But instead

12. Cf. Wenham, *Leviticus*, pp. 139-40; Ronald Youngblood, *Exodus*, Everyman's Bible Commentary (Chicago: Moody, 1983), pp. 126-27.
13. Cf. W. H. Gispen, *Exodus*, Bible Student's Commentary (Grand Rapids: Zondervan, 1982), p. 272.

of segregating the firstborn and separating them from their families, God chose the whole tribe of Levi to be His special servants (Num. 3:11-13). In this role the Levites were a "gift" to Aaron and his sons "to do the work at the Tent of Meeting" (Num. 18:6). Though the Levites could not serve as priests, they were able to assist the priests in their work and to carry the Tabernacle whenever the camp was moved. The clans of Gershon and Merari were responsible for carrying the heavier parts of the Tabernacle and its courtyard, such as the frames, posts, tents, and curtains (cf. Num. 3:25-26, 36), while the clan of Kohath carried the sacred furniture and the other articles used in the sanctuary (cf. Num. 3:31). Men between the ages of twenty-five and fifty were allowed to do this work (Num. 8:24-25).

Since the Levites were not given any inheritance in the Promised Land, the Israelites were commanded to give their tithes to the Levites. The Levites in turn were to give a tenth of those tithes to the priests as an offering to the Lord (Num. 18:21-28). Unhappily the irregular tithing of the other tribes often left the Levites with little income.

THE ORDINATION OF THE PRIESTS

Prior to assuming the heavy responsibilities of the priesthood, Aaron and his sons were ordained in an impressive seven-day ceremony. Great care was taken to cleanse and purify the priests so that they could minister on behalf of the people. After washing Aaron and his sons with water, Moses poured some anointing oil on Aaron's beard, probably a symbol of the empowerment of the Holy Spirit (cf. the end of chapter 4). Next, Moses offered a sin offering and a burnt offering in recognition of the fact that atonement must be made for the priests. After sacrificing the ram of ordination, Moses sprinkled some blood on Aaron's right ear, right thumb, and the big toe on his right foot (Lev. 8:22). This threefold application of blood symbolized the priests' need to listen closely to God's command, to do their work faithfully, and to walk in God's ways.

When the week-long ritual was completed, Aaron and his sons began their ministry. First, Aaron offered a sin offering for himself, because, like the rest of the people, he was a sinner who needed forgiveness. The book of Hebrews mentions that the priests had to offer sacrifices for their own sin every day, but Christ was the perfect High Priest who offered Himself as a sacrifice "once for all" (Heb. 7:27). After presenting the sin offering and burnt offering for himself, Aaron presented the offerings on behalf of the people. In a remarkable demonstration of God's acceptance of these sacrifices and His approval of the ministering priests, fire from heaven consumed the burnt offering on the altar (Lev. 9:24). This miracle was similar to the descent of the glory of the Lord upon the newly erected Tabernacle in Exodus 40:34, and the people responded in joyful worship.

THE DEATH OF NADAB AND ABIHU

Up to this point Aaron and his sons had obeyed God's instructions meticulously as they prepared to be priests. But for some reason, Aaron's two oldest sons, Nadab and Abihu, presented to the Lord incense that did not contain the ingredients specified in Exodus 30:30-34. By offering unauthorized incense contrary to God's command (cf. Ex. 30:9), Aaron's sons were immediately struck dead. "Fire came out from the presence of the Lord"—the very same words that had signaled God's approval of Aaron's sacrifice in Leviticus 9:24 (10:2). Two verses later it is the fire of judgment that consumes Aaron's sons. Understandably Aaron was badly crushed as it appeared that the priesthood would collapse almost before it began. What had gone wrong? Had the sons been careless, or had they been drunk? In verse 8 the Lord told Aaron "not to drink wine or other fermented drink" when ministering in the Tabernacle "or you will die." Those who approached God had to be pure in every way. Nadab and Abihu had been privileged to be on Mount Sinai when the covenant was established (cf. Ex. 24:9), and they were highly honored as the sons of Aaron, but privilege brings responsibility and the bearing of consequences.

The shocking death of Nadab and Abihu can be compared with the fate that befalls Ananias and Sapphira in Acts 5. Just after "tongues of fire" came upon the believers and the Holy Spirit filled them (Acts 2:3-4), an apparently devout couple was struck down for lying to Peter about a gift. There it was the beginning of the church; in Leviticus, it was the inauguration of the priesthood. At these two crucial periods God let it be known that He demanded holiness and that sin brought judgment and death.[14]

The Meaning of "Clean" and "Unclean"

Closely related to the concepts of "holy" and "profane" are the terms "clean" and "unclean" (Lev. 10:10). All these words are used both in a ritual and moral sense. For example, an "unclean" land is a sinful or pagan country (cf. Josh. 22:19; Amos 7:17), but a person can become "unclean" simply by attending a funeral (cf. Num. 6:7). Meat becomes "holy" by virtue of being part of a sacrificed animal, and loaves of bread that are placed on the table in the sanctuary are also "holy" (Lev. 24:9). These different uses carry over into the New Testament, where we encounter "unclean," that is, "evil," spirits and "unclean" children, that is, those who have unsaved parents (1 Cor. 7:14). The last example is especially confusing, because Paul argues that if one of the parents is a believer, the children born to that family are "holy." This does not mean that the children are automatically saved but that they will enjoy the godly

14. Cf. Schultz, *Leviticus*, pp. 47-48.

influence of one parent.[15] Drawing upon his knowledge of how holiness and uncleanness are transmitted according to the Old Testament, Paul makes a pointed application to the difficult issue of mixed marriages.

"Cleanness" has the basic meaning of "purity," as illustrated by the pure gold with which the Ark of the Covenant and the sacred table were overlaid (cf. Ex. 25:11, 24). Through the process of refining, metals were purified of their dross (cf. Mal. 3:2-3). A second meaning is "healthy," or "whole." In chapters 13-14 there are regulations for those suffering from various skin diseases who were "unclean" because of their condition. When Naaman dipped himself in the Jordan River, he was cured of his leprosy and his flesh "became clean" (2 Kings 5:14). Normally a priest examined someone who had recovered from a skin disease and, if he appeared healthy and whole, the priest pronounced him clean (Lev. 13:23, 28). Since the ultimate result of disease is death, it is not surprising that any contact with a dead body makes an individual unclean also. Uncleanness was contagious, but never more so than when death was involved.[16] By virtue of being set apart to minister in the sanctuary, priests were holy and had to maintain strict separation from the dead (21:1-2, 11). Uncleanness and holiness were not supposed to be combined in any way.[17]

Women were ritually unclean during their menstrual flow or for a number of weeks after giving birth (cf. 12:1-5), and sexual intercourse made a couple unclean until evening. Bodily discharges of any kind rendered a person unclean, and anything or anyone the person touched also became unclean (chap. 15).

In spite of the uncleanness associated with intercourse or childbirth, this does not in any way imply that sex is sinful. It is a reminder, however, that we are all sinners from the time of conception (cf. Ps. 51:5) and that sexual activity outside of marriage is sinful. Since uncleanness and holiness do not mix, this ritual requirement also ruled out any cultic prostitution in Israel. Blatant immorality and sexual perversion defiled the land of Canaan and was one reason God drove out its inhabitants (Lev. 18:24-25).

Although "unclean" and "sinful" are not synonymous, the two can be equated in a metaphorical way. When Isaiah had a vision of God in the Temple, he described himself as "a man of unclean lips" (Isa. 6:5). So overwhelmed was he by the presence of God that he was acutely aware that his words were sinful and he needed cleansing. On the national level a major source of uncleanness in Israel was idolatry. The worship of idols and images constituted sin of

15. W. Harold Mare, "1 Corinthians," in *EBC*, ed. Frank Gaebelein (Grand Rapids: Zondervan, 1976), 10:230.
16. Cf. Wolf, *Haggai and Malachi*, pp. 43-44.
17. See the excellent discussion in Wenham, *Leviticus*, pp. 19-20.

the worst kind, and repeatedly the land had to be cleansed of this evil (cf. 2 Chron. 34:3-4; Jer. 2:23).[18]

CLEAN AND UNCLEAN FOOD

In Leviticus 11 and Deuteronomy 14, Moses distinguishes between food that is clean, and hence edible, and food that is unclean, and hence detestable. Scholars have puzzled over the reasons behind these distinctions and have offered the following explanations.

1. The division into clean and unclean was arbitrary, given to the Israelites to test their obedience to God. Such an approach, though supported by some of the rabbis, has little to commend it.

2. The distinctions were designed to keep Israel separate from pagan religious practices. God chose Israel to be a special people and to be different from other nations, especially in their moral behavior (Lev. 18:24). These particularly degrading aspects of pagan worship—especially those involving the occult—that used certain animals may have been the reason for their ban in Israel. The pig was used in the worship of underworld deities and was employed in Canaanite rituals as well.[19] But other animals—such as the bull—were commonly used in Egyptian and Canaanite worship, and yet the bull was considered clean in Leviticus and could be sacrificed on the altar.

3. The distinctions were made for hygienic reasons, since the unclean animals and birds were more often carriers of disease. R. K. Harrison has noted that the vegetarian diet of the clean animals meant that they would be less likely to transmit infections than animals that ate rapidly decaying flesh in such a warm climate. The pig carried several parasitic organisms that could cause serious infection, especially trichinosis,[20] and Isaiah 66:17 compares eating the flesh of pigs with eating "rats and other abominable things." Most of the unclean birds preyed on carrion and could cause infection, and fish without scales often fed on sewage and carried dangerous bacteria.[21] For this reason, other nations in the ancient Near East also considered such food unacceptable. R. Laird Harris argues strongly that most of these laws promoted the public health and would help protect the Israelites from the diseases of Egypt (Ex. 15:26). By observing these laws, the Jews would have been largely free from parasites and worms and would have enjoyed more healthy living conditions in which to develop.[22] Although health factors can explain why some food was branded as unclean, it does not account for all of the items. And if hygiene was the main reason for

18. Cf. E. Yamauchi, *TWOT*, ed. R. Laird Harris et al. (Chicago: Moody, 1980), 1:349.
19. Cf. Isa. 65:4; Wenham, *Leviticus*, p. 167.
20. R. K. Harrison, *Introduction to the Old Testament* (Grand Rapids: Eerdmans, 1969), p. 605.
21. Ibid., p. 606.
22. R. Laird Harris, "Leviticus," in *EBC*, 2:529-30.

pronouncing food clean or unclean, why did Jesus declare all food clean in the New Testament (Mark 7:19)? Were health laws unnecessary by the first century A.D.?[23]

4. Cleanness is a matter of wholeness or normality. According to anthropologist Mary Douglas, the animals, birds, and fish that are clean are those that conform wholly to the class to which they belong.[24] Animals that have a split hoof *and* that chew the cud are clean, and those that lack one of these "normal" characteristics are unclean. Flying insects that walk on all fours exhibit confusion between the bird realm and insect realm and are thus not pure members of the class. Just as priests had to be free from any physical deformity (cf. Lev. 21:17-21), so any deviation from normality within a particular class rendered that member unclean. Douglas's view presents an interesting variation on the symbolic interpretation of the food laws, which emphasized the similarities between clean animals and righteous Israelites. But her "normality" approach seems to run counter to the creation account in Genesis 1, which labeled all of God's creatures as "good" (cf. 1:25) and hence "normal." Harris also objects to Douglas's definition of normality and observes that since most animals are unclean, it is hard to see why the clean animals should be regarded as the normal ones.[25]

In some respects there is truth in all of the above explanations, and it may not be necessary to select only one alternative as the correct one. Perhaps a combination of factors determined what was clean and unclean as God chose what was best for His people. By obeying these regulations and all of the other laws laid down in the Pentateuch, Israel could be a holy nation, enjoying the presence of a holy God.

THE DAY OF ATONEMENT

The most important day of the year was the Day of Atonement, "Yom Kippur," which came on the tenth day of the seventh month (September-October). On this day the high priest entered the Most Holy Place and sprinkled blood before the Ark of the Covenant. Since the Most Holy Place was God's throne room (see the end of chapter 4), entrance there could bring death (cf. 16:1-2). Ironically, in the one chapter that emphasizes the Holy of Holies more than any other, it is never called *qōdeš haqqodāšîm* ("the Holy of Holies"), the normal Hebrew phrase. Instead it is referred to as *haqqōdeš*, which is usually translated "the Holy Place," and indicates the area where the lampstand, the table, and the altar of incense were located (cf. Ex. 26:33). In a sense the entire sanctuary became one "Holy Place," and only Aaron was allowed anywhere in the building.

23. Wenham, *Leviticus*, p. 168.
24. Mary Douglas, *Purity and Danger*, rev. ed. (London: Routledge and Kegan Paul, 1978), p. 53.
25. Harris, "Leviticus," in *EBC*, 2:526.

Before entering the sanctuary Aaron put on a special set of linen garments, rather than the more beautiful robe and tunic he usually wore (cf. v. 4, 32). This simpler dress may have symbolized more fully the purity required on this day.

Aaron's job was to make atonement for the sin of the nation, but he could not do this until he had made atonement for himself and his household. So first he offered a bull as a sin offering for himself and his family, and taking a censer so that the smoke of fragrant incense would "conceal the atonement cover above the [ark of the] testimony," he stepped inside the Most Holy Place and sprinkled the bull's blood "on the front of the atonement cover" and "before the atonement cover" (vv. 13-14). Only then could Aaron sacrifice a goat as a sin offering for the people and take its blood and sprinkle it on the atonement cover (v. 15).

According to verse 16 Aaron's actions also made atonement for the Most Holy Place itself, and he sprinkled blood in the Tent of Meeting (probably the altar of incense in the Holy Place; Ex. 30:10) and on the altar of burnt offering in the courtyard to make atonement for them. The entire sanctuary had to be cleansed and consecrated "from the uncleanness of the Israelites" (v. 19). Both the bull's blood and the goat's blood had to be used to cleanse the altar of burnt offering, because it had been defiled by the sinfulness of the priests and the people (v. 18).[26]

Another unique feature of the Day of Atonement was the sending of a second goat into the desert to carry away the sins of Israel. This live goat—called the scapegoat—was sent to a solitary place after Aaron placed his hands on it and confessed over it all the sins of the people.[27] The symbolism of the scapegoat illustrated that through the sin offering sin had been effectively removed from the camp (cf. Ps. 103:12). Atonement had been made, and God had forgiven His people for their wickedness and rebellion (v. 21).

After the scapegoat ritual Aaron put on his regular priestly garments and presented the burnt offerings for himself and the people. In this way Aaron expressed the renewed devotion of the Israelites as those cleansed from their sin. To make the Day of Atonement meaningful to the people in general, all the Israelites had to deny or humble themselves the entire day (v. 29; cf. 23:26-32). No work of any kind was allowed (v. 31), and the self-denial undoubtedly included fasting and prayer. Each individual needed to bow low before God and to confess his sins.

---

26. Wenham, *Leviticus*, p. 232.
27. "Scapegoat" is a translation of the Hebrew *'azā'zēl*, which probably has the literal meaning of "goat of removal." In the intertestamental period, "azazel" was the name of a demon (cf. Enoch 8:1), and some interpreters believe that the goat was being sent back to the devil in the wilderness. But J. H. Hertz (*Leviticus* [London: Oxford U., 1932], p. 156) has rightly noted that Leviticus 17:7 condemns sacrifices to goat idols (or "demons"), making it unlikely that the scapegoat ritual was connected with a demon in any way.

In accord with normal procedure for sin offerings (see above), those parts of the animals not burned on the altar were taken outside the camp and burned (v. 27), a custom with which the writer of Hebrews compared Christ's death "outside the city gate" (Heb. 13:11-12). Romans 8:3 also speaks of Christ's death as a sin offering, and Hebrews notes that our Lord did not have to offer a sacrifice for His own sins first (Heb. 7:27).

Most of the New Testament comparisons between the Day of Atonement and the death of Christ emphasize the provision of access into the Most Holy Place. When Christ died, the curtain in the Temple was torn in two (Matt. 27:51), and Christ as our High Priest "entered the Most Holy Place once for all by his own blood" (Heb. 9:12). Unlike the Aaronic priests who had to enter the inner room every year, Christ entered heaven itself and lives in the presence of God (Heb. 9:7, 24). As those redeemed through Christ's blood, "we have confidence to enter the Most Holy Place" and "draw near to God" (Heb. 10:19, 22). This privilege should not be taken lightly but rather should motivate us to live holy and blameless lives as the children of a loving Father.

HOLY LIVING

Through the sacrifices and offerings, the Israelites were given the means to approach God and make atonement for sin. A holy God required repentant hearts and sacrifices that were presented in the right way. A holy God also demanded that His people live holy lives, and chapters 17-25 spell out some of the specifics involved. Three times the Israelites were told to be holy because God was holy (19:2; 20:7, 26).

One of the major hindrances to holy living was the low moral and spiritual level of the nations surrounding Israel. Repeatedly the Lord warned them not to behave like the Egyptians or the Canaanites, whose wicked customs the Lord abhorred (18:3; 20:23). Because of the sins of the Canaanites, God was evicting them from the land, and Canaan would belong to Israel (18:24; 20:24). If the Israelites followed their customs and practices, they too would be driven into exile (18:24). Sexual immorality was rampant among the nations, so Leviticus 18 warns Israel against incest, homosexuality, bestiality, and prostitution. The Canaanites were well-known for their homosexuality (cf. Gen. 19:5), and prostitution of various kinds was also common, of which the most insidious form was temple prostitution. Both men and women could work as "sacred" prostitutes by dedicating their earnings to the deity in whose temple they worked. Such a practice was detestable to the Lord (Deut. 23:17-18). The close relationship between sexual immorality and idolatry is graphically illustrated by Israel's involvement in the working of the Baal of Peor. When they were invited to attend the sacrifices, the men committed fornication with Moabite women and brought down God's wrath upon thousands (Num. 25:1, 9).

Equally detestable to the Lord was the worship of the Ammonite god Molech, which often included child sacrifice. Known also in Phoenicia north of Israel, this practice was condemned in Leviticus 18:21, and the death penalty was assessed to anyone who offered a child to Molech (20:1-5). Closely linked with child sacrifice were the sins of divination and sorcery and any consultation with mediums and spiritists (Lev. 20:6; Deut. 18:10-12). All such practices were strongly denounced as illegitimate means of contacting deity. According to Deuteromony 18:15, God raised up prophets such as Moses to make His will known to Israel. When Balaam was hired by the king of Moab to curse Israel, he expected to use sorcery and divination (cf. Num. 22:40; 24:1) to accomplish his purpose, but the Spirit of the Lord came upon him and he proceeded to bless Israel instead (Num. 24:2-9; see below).

Included in the list of unlawful sexual relations are several that were permitted in patriarchal times. Marriage to one's half-sister was prohibited in 18:98, a rule that would have kept Abraham from marrying Sarah (cf. Gen. 20:12). And Jacob's difficulties with Leah and Rachel may have been behind the prohibition against marrying two sisters (Lev. 18:18; cf. Gen. 30:1).[28] In our study of the structure of the Joseph narrative, we commented about Judah's involvement with his daughter-in-law Tamar in Genesis 38. Although such a union was permitted by the Hittites, Leviticus 18:15 bans the practice among the Israelites.

Earlier (see "Purpose and Scope") we noted the importance of the statement "love your neighbor as yourself" as a summary of the law (19:18). Showing kindness to neighbors and concern for the poor and the alien were marks of the people of God. During harvesttime the Israelites were supposed to leave the gleanings in the fields so that the poor could gather them (19:9-10), and recalling their own harsh experiences in Egypt, the people were to love aliens as themselves (v. 34).

In a sense concern for the disadvantaged also lay behind the law about sabbatical years, for every seventh year the land was to "lie unplowed" and the poor were allowed to take whatever grew (Ex. 23:11; Lev. 25:1-7). Every seven sabbaths of years—once every forty-nine years—there was to be a Year of Jubilee that brought "liberty throughout the land" (25:10). Hebrew slaves were to be released and all land reverted to its original owners. If a man had fallen upon hard times he could lease his land to another to raise money, but in the fiftieth year it returned to the family whose inheritance it was. This was a way to prevent individuals from being poor perpetually, and it also involved recognition that the land really belonged to God, not to Israel. He would give it to them in

---

28. John Murray (*Principles of Conduct* [Grand Rapids: Eerdmans, 1957], pp. 253-56) interprets verse 18 as a statement in favor of monogamy, since the word "sister" can also mean "another" woman. But in light of the many specific relationships mentioned in the chapter, including several other clear references to "sister," it is unlikely that Murray is correct.

accord with His promise to Abraham, and the people were not supposed to hoard land and "take advantage of each other" (25:17, 23; cf. Isa. 5:8).

If a man had to sell some of his property, a relative had the right to repurchase or "redeem" the land for him. If the original owner himself became prosperous, he could buy the property back before the Year of Jubilee. When God rescued Israel from Egypt, He "redeemed" them, gaining their freedom and returning them to the Promised Land (see "God as Redeemer").

To encourage the people in their spiritual lives there were several festivals scattered throughout the year, in addition to the weekly Sabbath. Leviticus 23 presents a summary of these events, which took place between the first and seventh months, or roughly from March until October. All of those festivals are referred to as "sacred assemblies" (vv. 2-4, 7, 8, 21, 24, 27, 35, 37), days of rest that were set apart to the Lord, and by observing these special seasons the Israelites were reminded of God's faithfulness and goodness.

The first and last festivals—the Passover and the feast of Tabernacles—commemorated the Exodus and the founding of the nation in the Sinai desert. Those two festivals, along with the feast of Weeks, marked the three times a year when all of the men had to appear before the Lord at the sanctuary (Ex. 23:14-17; Deut. 16:18). Called the pilgrimage feasts, these three occasions afforded an opportunity for the people to renew their allegiance to the Lord and to sense their unity as a nation. After settling in the Promised Land, it became all too easy for the tribes to go their separate ways and become distant from one another and from the Lord.

The religious calendar was closely aligned with the agricultural year and the different harvests. The feast of Passover and Unleavened Bread (see "The Passover" in chap. 4) came at the time of the barley harvest in the spring, and the feast of Weeks was celebrated during the wheat harvest in June. The seventh month (September-October) contained three festivals, the feast of Trumpets, the Day of Atonement (see above), and the feast of Tabernacles and coincided with the ripening of grapes, figs, and olives. In October or November the fall rains began, and a new agricultural year got underway. By celebrating the festivals at these harvest times the Israelites gave thanks to God for His provision of food and were protected from the influence of pagan harvest festivals with their immorality and idolatry.

The feast of Weeks (or "Harvest"; Ex. 23:16) was observed fifty days (seven weeks) after the Passover and for this reason came to be known in New Testament times as "Pentecost," the Greek word for fifty (cf. Acts 2:1). It was the only pilgrimage feast that was confined to one day, but it did commemorate the crucial wheat harvest. A firstfruits offering of new grain was presented to the Lord along with an assortment of blood sacrifices. Although it was a day of "sacred assembly" (Lev. 23:21), the feast of Weeks was also a time to "rejoice before the Lord" and to share with family members and with the poor their abundant provisions of food (Deut. 16:10-12).

The final festival of the year, the feast of Tabernacles, was also the most joyous. Called the feast of Ingathering in Exodus 23:16, it marked the end of the summer harvest and functioned somewhat like our Thanksgiving Day. For seven days, from the fifteenth to the twenty-first day of the month, the people were to live in booths made of palm fronds and leafy branches to recollect the huts and tents in which the Israelites lived during the wilderness journey. The whole family was to recall the hardships of the past and to give thanks for the abundance of Canaan, the land in which their joy could "be complete" (Deut. 16:15). According to Numbers 29:12-34, a large number of burnt offerings and one sin offering were sacrificed each day.

On the twenty-second day of the month a sacred assembly brought to an end not only the feast of Tabernacles but the whole cycle of feasts starting with the Passover. God had blessed His people both materially and spiritually, and they were never to forget all of His benefits (cf. Deut. 8:10-14).[29]

THE CHALLENGE TO OBEY

With the prospect of a life in Canaan that would be prosperous and joyful, the nation of Israel had every reason to obey God's commands. In Leviticus 26:1-13 the Lord summarizes the happy results that such obedience would bring, but in verses 14-39 He warns them about the consequences of rebellion against Him. Such a list of blessings and curses was often found at the end of legal texts, and as in Leviticus 26 the curses usually outnumbered the blessings.[30] Ancient Near Eastern treaties also contained blessings and curses, but in reverse order. The biblical order indicates that, even though the Sinai Covenant and especially its renewal in Deuteronomy are closely connected with the treaty form, the legal nature of the text remains important. At the end of the Book of the Covenant in Exodus 23:20-33 there is also a list of blessings and implied curses to encourage the people to respond positively to the giving of the law.

Leviticus 26 begins with a warning against idolatry and a plea to keep the "sabbaths and have reverence for my sanctuary" (vv 1-2). Since Israel was God's people and He walked among them (v. 12), God promised that obedience would bring the blessings of rain and abundant crops, of victory over enemies and a secure peace. Wild animals would not ravage the land, and all would be able to lie down without fear (v. 6). In accord with the Abrahamic Covenant, God would increase their numbers greatly (v.9; cf. Gen. 22:17).

On the other hand, if the people chose to disobey, the Lord would bring disease and drought, with failing crops, diminishing flocks and herds, and a

29. Cf. Wenham, *Leviticus*, pp. 305-6.
30. Cf. the Hammurapi Law Code, *ANET*, pp. 178-80.

dwindling population (vv. 16, 19-22). Israel's armies would be defeated in battle, and cities would be besieged, bringing plagues, famine, and even cannibalism (vv. 25-29). Eventually the cities would be captured, and the people who survived would be scattered among the nations while the land lay in ruins. Three times the text states that God will punish Israel "seven times over" for her sins (vv. 18-21, 28). In line with its usage elsewhere, the number seven apparently stresses the completeness of the judgments, a meaning supported by the extensive list of catastrophes in this chapter.[31]

"Seven" also figures prominently in the discussion of the sabbatical years in verses 34 and 35. "When the Israelites go into exile, the land will rest and enjoy its sabbaths" (v. 34). This is a prophecy that the instructions given about sabbatical years in chapter 25 will not be followed, and according to 2 Chronicles 36:21 the seventy-year Babylonian Captivity did in fact allow the land to catch up on "its Sabbath rests." This means that between 1400 and 586 B.C. more than half of the sabbatical years were missed.

In verse 25 Israel's sins are described as "the breaking of the covenant," and in spite of the fact that Leviticus spends many chapters talking about various sacrifices, offerings will not be sufficient to atone for the nation's sins (v. 31). The people must repent of their sin and rebellion, and if they do so, God promised to "remember the covenant" He made with their ancestors and bring the captives back to Israel (vv. 42, 44). This grim prediction of the nation's destiny is expanded in Deuteromony 28-30, as Moses urges the people to ever be vigilant and to keep sin from ruining their future. It was a theme taken up by many of the prophets also, but unfortunately their warnings went unheeded.

31. Cf. Ps. 79:12 and John J. Davis, *Biblical Numerology* (Grand Rapids: Baker, 1968), p. 119.

6

NUMBERS

After a year at Mount Sinai receiving instruction about life in the Promised Land, the Israelites headed north toward their ultimate destination. Possessors of a legal code and a system of worship superior to any other nation, Israel seemed certain to enter Canaan in triumph. Along the way, however, lack of faith stalled the people an incredible thirty-eight years, and an entire generation died wandering in the wilderness. Instead of behaving like God's chosen people, the Israelites murmured and complained and endured God's judgment on several occasions. Yet at the end of the forty years in the Sinai desert, God proved faithful to His promise and led Israel to the edge of the Promised Land.

TITLE

The fourth book of the Pentateuch is called "Numbers" because of the censuses contained in chapters 1 and 26. A translation of the Septuagint's *Arithmoi*, "Numbers" is an accurate title in light of all the lists and figures given in the book. In addition to the census figures for the twelve tribes and the Levites, the book contains a detailed list of the tribal offerings at the dedication of the Tabernacle in chapter 7. Totals are also given for the weekly and monthly sacrifices and for the number of arrivals offered in the yearly festivals (chaps. 28-29). In two of the most discouraging chapters of the book we are told of the death of 14,700 and 24,000 Israelites as plagues broke out because of sin (16:49; 25:9). Toward the end of the book there is a detailed list of the plunder taken from the Midianites (31:32-47) and a description of the number and size of the Levitical cities in chapter 35.

The Hebrew title, taken from the first verse, is "in the desert" (*bammid-bār*), and this too is a fitting description of the book in light of the thirty-eight years during which the Israelites wandered about in the Sinai desert. For all of those who were twenty or older when the nation left Mount Sinai, the desert became a burial site as well.

PURPOSE AND SCOPE

After almost a year at Mount Sinai, Israel was ready for the journey to the Promised Land, and Numbers tells how the tribes were organized for this march. Because of the negative report of the spies and the unbelief of the people, God condemned the nation to wander in the desert for forty years. The judgment that fell upon the people time and time again demonstrated that God demanded strict adherence to the terms of the covenant. Yet at the end of the forty years the Lord Himself proved faithful to the covenant by giving the Israelites victories in Transjordan. Before the new generation entered Canaan, however, they were given additional instructions about political and religious matters in the Promised Land.

In Exodus and Leviticus, Israel had been given detailed instructions about the moral, civil, and ceremonial laws that they were to follow. Equipped with the Book of the Covenant, the Tabernacle, and a priesthood to minister on their behalf, the nation was now ready for life in the Promised Land. Before beginning their journey, however, the individual tribes were counted and organized, and each was assigned a position in the order of march and in the encampment around the Tabernacle. Although the Levites were not counted among the twelve tribes, they were responsible for carrying the Tabernacle and all its furnishings (Num. 1:50).

"All the men twenty years old or more" were counted with a view "to serve in the army" (1:20), whereas all the Levites "from thirty to fifty years of age" were assembled "to serve in the work in the Tent of meeting" (4:3). Interestingly, the same Hebrew word (ṣābā') appears in both verses, indicating that the Levites' work in the service of the Lord was just as important as the other tribes' service in the army. The role of the Levites is spelled out in chapters 3 and 4, and in chapter 8 they are set apart to their ministry in an impressive ceremony. Although members of other tribes could not join the Levites and assist in their work, anyone had the option of taking a Nazirite vow and dedicating himself or herself to the Lord (chap. 6). Usually this involved a limited time period, but individuals such as Samson and Samuel were lifelong Nazirites.

The Israelites began their journey northward when "the cloud lifted from above the tabernacle" (10:11), and in a span of only a few weeks they should have reached the Promised Land. But along the way "the people complained about their hardships" (11:1), about their diet of manna (11:4-6), and about Moses' wife (12:1). Strangely Miriam and Aaron were among those who spoke against Moses. These complaints were a portent of greater problems to come, because when spies were sent from Kadesh-Barnea to explore the Promised Land, the majority were convinced that Canaan could not be captured (13:28-29). In spite of the protests of Caleb and Joshua, the Israelites refused to believe they could conquer the Promised Land, in effect rebelling against the Lord. Angered by their response, God threatened to destroy the whole nation and start all over again with Moses (14:12), but after Moses' impassioned plea the Lord relented. Yet He did punish the nation by sentencing them to forty years of wandering in the desert, where the entire adult population would die (14:32-34).

Eventually the nation returned to Kadesh (20:1), but little is known about the long years of travel. From the names recorded in Numbers 33 we know something about the journey, but many of the places are impossible to locate. According to Joshua 5:7, the boys born in the desert were not circumcised, an indication that the Passover was not observed and that covenant responsibilities were generally neglected. Moses also faced a rebellion led by the Levite named Korah and by two men from the tribe of Reuben, Dathan and Abiram. Apparently Korah was jealous of Moses' religious prominence, and the two men from Reuben (Jacob's oldest son) were looking for political power. After a warning of impending judgment, the ground split apart and swallowed up the leaders, and another 250 men were struck down by fire from the Lord (16:31-35). To confirm God's choice of Moses and Aaron, a staff with Aaron's name on it "budded, blossomed and produced almonds" (17:8) and was kept near or in the Ark of the Covenant along with the two tablets of the law and a jar of manna (v. 10; cf. Ex. 16:34; 25:16; Heb. 9:4).

As the years of wandering came to an end, both Miriam and Aaron died (Num. 20:1, 28), and Moses received the sad news that he would not be able to enter the Promised Land either. Exasperated at the complaining of the people, Moses failed to honor the Lord when he struck the rock to bring forth water. His anger and lack of trust in God cost him the opportunity to participate in the conquest of Canaan (20:12-13). Yet Moses would play the leading role in the capture of Transjordan and even caught a glimpse of victory in Canaan when the Israelites destroyed the southern city of Arad (21:1-3). Neither Edom nor Moab would allow Israel to travel through their territory, so the people were forced to take a circuitous route as they made their way around the Dead Sea. During the journey there was a new outburst of complaining punished by a plague of venomous snakes. When Moses interceded for the people, God told him to put a bronze snake on a pole, and those who were bitten could look at it and live (20:4-9). The snake on a pole became a symbol of the salvation accomplished in the hearts of those who look in faith to the one who hung on a cross (John 3:14-15).

After circumventing Edom and Moab, the Israelites defeated Sihon king of the Amorites and Og king of Bashan, victories that gave them effective control of Transjordan (21:21-35). Then they set up camp in the plains of Moab opposite Jericho. Alarmed at the size and power of Israel, Balak king of Moab hired the seer Balaam to come and curse the Israelites; but although he tried to comply, Balaam delivered a series of oracles that proved to be a blessing rather than a curse (23:7–24:24). Yet Balaam did manage to bring a curse on Israel by advising the king of Moab to involve the Israelites in idolatry and immorality, and the resultant judgment brought death to twenty-four thousand (25:1-9; cf. 31:16).

In spite of the terrible catastrophe, the nation would be allowed to enter the Promised Land, and chapters 26-36 anticipate conditions in Canaan. There are rules regulating inheritance rights for women in chapters 27 and 36, rules about vows in chapter 30, and about the conduct of war in chapter 31. The boundaries of Canaan are outlined in chapter 34, followed by a discussion about the towns for the Levites. Six of these towns were to be designated as cities of refuge, where those who killed someone accidentally could find safety. Three were to be on each side of the Jordan River because the tribes of Reuben, Gad, and half of Manasseh asked for and received their inheritance in Transjordan (chap. 32). Before agreeing to their request, Moses made these tribes promise that they would send troops west of the Jordan to help the nation conquer Canaan (32:20-32).

LITERARY STRUCTURE

Like the other books in the Pentateuch, Numbers contains a variety of literary genres and is not restricted to lists and ritual procedures. It is true, however, that the census lists in chapters 1 and 26 form a kind of inclusio, giving population totals at the beginning and end of the forty-year wilderness experience. The totals are remarkably similar, though the tribe of Simeon suffered a loss of thirty-seven thousand men, probably reflecting the decimation of that tribe as a result of the worship of the Baal of Peor in chapter 25. That calamity on the plains of Moab forms a second inclusio with the earlier rebellion at Kadesh-Barnea recorded in chapter 13. Like the census of chapter 1, the tragic episode of unbelief in connection with the report of the spies came early in the forty-year period. Neither generation—the adults who perished in the desert nor their children camped near the Jordan—deserved to enter the Promised Land. But in His grace God allowed the new generation to enter Canaan and see the Abrahamic Covenant fulfilled.

Unhappily, disobedience was not confined to chapters 13-14 and 25, for another major rebellion is described in chapter 16. Hamilton has noted that after the first two episodes there are chapters that talk of God's provision of cleansing in the future (chaps. 15, 19).[1] The ceremony involving the ashes of a red heifer and the water of cleansing is unique to Numbers. In his *Introduction to the Old Testament as Scripture*, Brevard Childs argues that purification is a unifying theme of Numbers. Much of the book deals with the distinctions between the holy and the profane.[2]

---

1. Victor P. Hamilton, *Handbook on the Pentateuch* (Grand Rapids: Baker, 1982), p. 347.
2. Published in Philadelphia by Fortress (1979). See p. 199.

LITERARY STRUCTURE OF NUMBERS

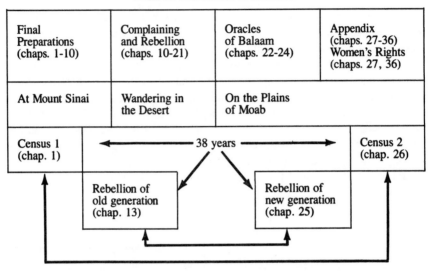

Geography plays an important role in Numbers. In the first ten chapters the Israelites are still at Mount Sinai preparing for their journey to Canaan. From 10:11–21:35 the nation is on the move, spending thirty-eight wasted years in the Sinai desert before turning north once more and heading for the Promised Land. They reach the plains of Moab along the Jordan in 22:1, and the rest of the book has its setting there. Most of the narrative material is contained in the middle section, often in conjunction with the people's complaints and rebellion. In chapter 33 there is a detailed listing of the campsites used by the Israelites from the Exodus until they reached the plains of Moab. The places are mentioned in rapid succession, with only a few comments about important events.

The various lists in Numbers are usually arranged according to the twelve tribes and given in the same formula. In the census contained in chapter 1 the paragraphs are identical, except for the name of the tribe and the final total. The later census (chap. 26) included the names of the different clans in each tribe, but again the paragraphs are arranged in the same way. The repetition is even more extensive in chapter 7, which records the gifts of the twelve tribal leaders at the dedication of the Tabernacle. Each day a different leader brought his offering, but the five-verse description for each offering is the same throughout a very long chapter. As noted above, the tribe of Levi is treated separately from the other tribes, with careful attention to the three clans and their different functions. At the end of the book the measurements of a Levitical city are given and a full description of the role of the six cities of refuge (chap. 35).

Poetry may seem out of place in a book filled with lists and totals, but several remarkable poetic passages do occur in Numbers. Chapter 6 ends with the three-verse priestly blessing that Aaron and his sons were to pronounce upon the Israelites, bestowing upon them the Lord's grace and peace (6:24-26). Whenever the people broke camp, the Ark of the Covenant led the way as a symbol of God's presence with them. On such occasions Moses said, "Rise up, O Lord! May your enemies be scattered; may your foes flee before you" (10:35). Moses realized that the Lord's favor and blessing were more important than the strength of Israel's armies.

Warfare also provided the background for three poems in chapter 21, one of which was cited from "the Book of the Wars of the Lord" (v. 14). The longest of the three (vv. 27-30) was apparently an Amorite song commemorating the earlier victory of Sihon over the Moabites. In subsequent years the Israelites would sing about their victory over Sihon and Og as they celebrated God's goodness to them (Pss. 135:11; 136:19-20).

The best-known poetry in Numbers is the seven oracles spoken by Balaam after he saw the Israelites poised on the edge of the Promised Land. These magnificent poems talk about Israel's future glory and coming Messiah (especially 24:17), leaving no doubt that God has blessed them. The first four oracles are from eight to eleven poetic verses in length and are introduced by narrative material involving, in particular, Balak king of Moab (chaps. 23-24). The last six verses of chapter 24 contain the final three oracles, only a verse or two in length and briefly introduced (24:20-25).[3]

In a sense the concluding eleven chapters of the book constitute an appendix, dealing with issues that would affect life in the Promised Land. Inheritance matters form an important part of this discussion, and the claims of Zelophehad's daughters are handled both at the beginning (chap. 27) and end (chap. 36) of this section. Like the Levites—who also had no direct inheritance in Canaan (cf. 26:62; 35:2)—women were to be treated kindly and fairly.

THE ORGANIZATION OF THE TRIBES

When the Israelites arrived at Mount Sinai they were a disorganized group of fugitives who had just been freed from slavery. When they left Mount Sinai a year later, they were the possessors of a legal code and a worship manual and a solid cadre of leaders.

THE TWELVE TRIBES

Ever since the birth of Jacob's last son, Benjamin, the Israelites were known by their twelve units. When the tribe of Levi was separated from the oth-

---

3. Cf. *NIV Study Bible*, ed. Kenneth Barker (Grand Rapids: Zondervan, 1985), p. 224.

ers for special duty at the Tabernacle, their place was taken by a division of the family of Joseph into two tribes—Ephraim and Manasseh. By receiving a double share of the inheritance (two tribes instead of one), Joseph was thus given the birthright, an honor befitting his noble accomplishments (cf. 1 Chron. 5:1-2). In the two censuses, Ephraim and Manasseh are identified as the sons of Joseph (Num. 1:32; 26:28), but their order is reversed. Both chapters group the tribes by threes according to their arrangement around the Tabernacle. The sons of Leah are mentioned first, followed by Rachel's sons, then those of the concubines.

On four different occasions we are given the names of the twelve leaders of the tribes, both in connection with the censuses and with the dedication offerings for the Tabernacle (cf. 1:5-15; 7:12-83). These men assisted Moses and Aaron in compiling census figures and in the general administration of the tribes (1:4). Since four of the tribes played a leading role in each of the groups (Judah, Reuben, Ephraim, Dan), it is likely that the heads of these tribes carried additional responsibility. Although not counted among the others, the tribe of Levi was also divided into three groups, and the leaders of each of these clans are named (3:24, 30, 35). Eleazar son of Aaron was "the chief leader of the Levites" (3:32).

ARRANGEMENT OF THE TRIBES

As a symbol of the central place to be given to the Lord in the life and worship of the nation, the Tabernacle was located in the middle of the camp. God was pleased to dwell among them, and the people were to be aware of His presence at all times. To the east of the Tabernacle at the position of greatest honor were the living quarters of Moses and Aaron and their families (3:38). The Levites were to set up camp on the other three sides as a buffer between the Tabernacle and the other tribes (1:53). The rest of the Israelites had to keep their distance from the sacred tent or face death.

As noted above, the twelve tribes were arranged in four groups around the Tabernacle (see chart). On the east lay the camp of Judah, which also contained the divisions of Issachar and Zebulun, fellow sons of Leah (2:3-8). To the south were the three divisions of Reuben, including Simeon and Gad. Gad was a son of Leah's servant girl Zilpah and occupied the position that Levi would have filled (cf. Gen. 30:11). The other three sons of the servant girls were situated to the north, led by the divisions of Dan (Num. 2:25- 31). Meanwhile, the Rachel tribes (Ephraim, Manasseh, and Benjamin) camped to the west of the Tabernacle.[4] By this arrangement the maximum homogeneity of the tribes was achieved, a factor designed to reduce friction as the difficult journey began.

4. The position of the twelve tribes around the Tabernacle parallels to some extent the location of the twelve gates around Ezekiel's holy city, named after the twelve tribes. There are three gates on a side, though the groupings do not match Numbers (Ezek. 48:30-35). Also compare the twelve gates of the New Jerusalem in Rev. 21:12-13.

NORTH

EAST

Army of Judah (1)
Division of Judah
Division of Issachar
Division of Zebulun
(Leah)

Army of Dan (6)
Division of Dan   (Bilhah: Rachel)
Division of Asher (Zilph: Leah)
Division of Naphtali (Bilhah)

(2) Merari

Moses
and
Aaron

TABERNACLE

(2) Gershon

(4) Kohath

Army of Reuben (3)
Division of Reuben (Leah)
Division of Simeon (Leah)
Division of Gad   (Zilpah)

SOUTH

Army of Ephraim (5)
Division of Ephraim
Division of Manasseh
Division of Benjamin
(Rachel)

WEST

ORGANIZATION OF TRIBES
AND ORDER OF MARCH

The numbers refer to the order of
march according to Num. 10:14-25

THE ORDER OF MARCH

Guided by trumpet blasts sounded by the priests, the tribes set out on their journey in a prescribed order. The divisions of the camp of Judah led the way, a position that matched the prominent role this tribe was destined to play. Jacob had predicted that a ruler would come from Judah (Gen. 49:10), and although the reign of David was still centuries away, the tribe of Judah often took the lead in Israel (cf. Judg. 1:2). Caleb ranked with Joshua as one of the few men of faith who believed God's word in that generation (13:6, 30).

After Judah came the Levitical clans of Gershon and Merari, who carried the heavier parts of the Tabernacle (10:17). By surrounding the Tabernacle with thousands of men, the Israelites prevented any enemy from attacking and seizing the silver, gold, and valuable curtains. The sacred furniture was carried by the Kohathites, who followed the camp of Reuben. According to 10:21, the men of Kohath came a little later in the order of march so that the Tabernacle could be set up before they arrived at the next campsite. The most sacred article of all— the Ark of the Covenant—was probably carried at the head of the entire procession as a symbol of God's presence with His people (cf. 10:33-36). At the end of the line of march came the armies of Ephraim and Dan, poised to protect against rear-guard action.

It is of interest to note that the same order was followed when the tribes presented their offerings at the dedication of the altar. The leader of Judah brought his gift first, and the head of the tribe of Naphtali came last (7:12, 78). From a military standpoint, the fourfold division of the tribes has a parallel in the campaign of Rameses II against the Hittites. Four separate Egyptian armies marched north to Kadesh on the Orontes River, and after the first army had suffered heavy losses, the troops that followed helped to rescue their fellow soldiers.[5]

REBELLION AT KADESH BARNEA

The Kadesh that was pivotal for the Israelites was the southern city of Kadesh Barnea, about forty miles south of Beersheba. Only a two-week journey from Mount Sinai, Kadesh was intended to be a brief pause on the way to the Promised Land.

REPORT OF THE SPIES

At the request of the people, Moses selected twelve men to spy out Canaan and bring back a full report (cf. Deut. 1:22). The men chosen were not the leaders of the tribes but presumably younger men who could endure the rigors of this

---

5. Yohanan Aharoni and Michael Avi-Yonah, *The Macmillan Bible Atlas*, rev. ed. (New York: Macmillan, 1977), p. 38.

mission. Among them were representatives of the most influential tribes: Hoshea son of Nun—whom Moses renamed Joshua (13:16)—from Ephraim, and Caleb son of Jephunneh from Judah. Joshua had been Moses' aide for some time (cf. Ex. 24:13) and probably led the expedition. The men traveled about 250 miles north to Lebo Hamath, the northern limit of the Promised Land, and took forty days to explore the land (Num. 13:21, 25). When they returned they spoke in glowing terms of the fruitfulness of the country God had given to them, but they also observed the fortified cities and the tall, powerful warriors who lived there. According to the majority of the spies it would be impossible to capture Canaan and drive out its inhabitants. Joshua and Caleb presented a much different minority report, arguing that with God's help they could conquer the land (14:8-9).

From a human perspective it was true that cities surrounded by high walls were difficult to capture. To the spies the walls appeared to extend "up to the sky" (cf. Deut. 1:28), and normally fortified cities had to be besieged, starving out the inhabitants over a period of months or even years.[6] Siege weapons could help, but the Israelites had neither the weapons nor the time to take the land by this means. The description of the tall warriors in Canaan was also an accurate one. Centuries later the Philistine giant Goliath terrorized Saul and his troops, and everyone cowered before the nine-foot warrior. The Anakites of Hebron were likewise tall and strong, and renowned for their military prowess (cf. Deut. 2:10).

But Joshua and Caleb believed in the power of God, and they had witnessed the defeat of Pharaoh and his chariots at the Red Sea. If God could destroy that army, he could enable Israel to defeat Jericho. From Joshua 6 we know that God honored their faith by leveling the walls of Jericho without a siege. At the age of eighty-five Caleb was able to drive the Anakites out of Hebron and take over the city. Later, about 1020 B.C., the teenager David dared to believe that God would give Goliath into his hands, and with a sling and a stone felled the mighty Philistine.

REBELLION OF THE PEOPLE

Unfortunately most of the Israelites did not have the faith of a Joshua, Caleb, or David, and the majority report sounded convincing to them. As they thought about the problems they would face trying to capture the Promised Land, they became discouraged and turned against Moses and Aaron. Their hopes of gaining a homeland disintegrated, and they talked of returning to Egypt and perhaps salvaging a few more years for their wives and children (14:1-4).

6. The city of Samaria withstood a three-year siege before succumbing (cf. 2 Kings 17:5), and Jerusalem lasted eighteen months before the Babylonians could breach the walls in 586 B.C. (cf. 2 Kings 25:1-4).

When Joshua and Caleb saw what was happening, they repeated their claim that it was possible to capture Canaan. The Lord was with them, and none of the people of Canaan could stand before Israel's God. In spite of their impassioned plea, however, the Israelites refused to believe them, and in effect they rebelled against God (14:9). Even though God had rescued them from Egypt and revealed Himself to them at Mount Sinai, the people were filled with doubt about God's ability to give them Canaan and fulfill the Abrahamic Covenant. Like Pharaoh, they were hardening their hearts and ignoring God's clear command (cf. Ps. 95:7-8), and their unbelief cost them an opportunity to enter the land of rest (cf. Heb. 3:16-18).

PUNISHMENT DECREED

In response to Israel's unbelief the Lord spoke to Moses and announced that He would destroy the nation and start all over again with Moses. This was the second time that God had threatened to obliterate His people, and for the second time Moses begged Him to relent. As he had done in the golden calf episode (cf. Ex. 32:11-13), Moses reminded the Lord that the Egyptians would hear about Israel's demise and that His reputation would be tarnished. Since the Lord was slow to get angry and abounded in love, He could again forgive His people, though He would not "leave the guilty unpunished" (Num. 14:18; cf. Ex. 34:6-7).

In His mercy and grace God granted Moses' request and forgave His rebellious people. But because they treated Him with contempt and had already complained several times about their lack of water and food since the Exodus, the Lord decreed that that generation would perish in the desert (Num. 14:22-23). Not one of those twenty years old or more would ever reach Canaan except for Joshua and Caleb, who had not wavered in their commitment to the Lord. For forty years—one year for each day the spies spent in Canaan—the Israelites would wander in the desert, until the whole generation died out (14:34). The ten spies who had presented the negative report were struck down immediately and died of a plague (v. 37) as judgment for the greater responsibility they bore in influencing the entire nation.

During the forty years the rest of the nation suffered for rebelling along with the spies, and their children also suffered for the unfaithfulness of their parents (vv. 33, 34). The second commandment refers to "punishing the children for the sin of the fathers to the third and fourth generation" (Ex. 20:5), a verse quoted by Moses in his intercessory prayer (Num. 14:18). Ironically, the children, whom the people thought would be taken as plunder in Canaan (v. 3), were the very ones who would conquer the Promised Land. God would "bring them in to enjoy the land" that their parents would never see (v. 31).

Deeply disturbed by the severity of the punishment meted out, the people admitted that they had sinned and decided to attack Canaan after all. But it was already too late, and neither Moses nor the Lord went with the people. Without God's blessing, the Israelites were soundly defeated by the Amalekites and Canaanites living in the southern part of the hill country. Although the land was destined to be theirs as the children of Abraham, they could not occupy it for almost forty more years.

FORTY YEARS IN THE WILDERNESS

Between Numbers 15:1 and 20:1 the Scriptures give a brief description of life in the desert before the Israelites returned to Kadesh Barnea. These chapters cover approximately thirty-eight years, which must have been filled with considerable complaining and discouragement. The adults had nothing to look forward to except death, and the younger generation was wasting its best years moving aimlessly from campsite to campsite. As might be expected, there was major opposition to Moses and Aaron, and at the end of this period even Moses offended the Lord and was forbidden to enter the Promised Land. But entrance into Canaan remained the goal of the nation and is mentioned as early as 15:2.

THE REBELLION OF KORAH, DATHAN, AND ABIRAM

In an effort to overthrow Moses and Aaron there was a well-organized revolt led by individuals from the tribes of Levi and Reuben. The ringleader of the group was a Levite named Korah, who belonged to the favored clan of Kohath, whose members carried the sacred furniture of the Tabernacle (cf. Num. 7:9). But Korah was not a son of Aaron, so he could not officiate at any of the sacrifices offered at the sanctuary, and apparently he was jealous of the powerful position of both Moses and Aaron. Why did they set themselves above the other Israelites? Korah was supported by Dathan and Abiram, from the tribe of Reuben, who was Jacob's firstborn son. Normally the firstborn son was the leader of the family, so they thought their tribe was being slighted. In verses 12-14 Datham and Abiram accuse Moses of failing to lead the Israelites into the Promised Land. He had taken them from Egypt, "a land flowing with milk and honey," and had brought them into a desert to die. Earlier the people had referred in their complaints to the variety of food available in Egypt (Num. 11:5), but like Dathan and Abiram they had forgotten about the hard taskmasters and the slavery.

To settle the dispute, Moses had Korah and his 250 followers put fire and incense in censers and present them to the Lord. When the men approached the Tent of Meeting the Lord appeared and told Moses and Aaron that he would "put an end" to the entire assembly. As he had done earlier (cf. 14:12), Moses cried out to the Lord and begged him to spare the people. After the Israelites moved a safe distance away from the tents of the leaders, the ground split apart and swallowed up Korah, Dathan, Abiram, and their households. Not all Korah's sons died, however, an indication that they had not joined the rebellion (cf. 26:11; Ps. 49, heading). The 250 men who offered incense were struck down by fire from the Lord, just like the two sons of Aaron in Leviticus 10:2 (Num. 16:35).

Upset by the death of their countrymen, the rest of the Israelites "grumbled against Moses and Aaron" and accused them of killing the Lord's people (v. 41). Once again the Lord became angry and threatened to wipe out all of them. Quickly Moses told Aaron to take incense and fire and make atonement for the people before a plague consumed all of them. Nonetheless the plague claimed 14,700 lives as the judgment of God fell (v. 49).

Lest the people challenge the prerogatives of the Aaronic priests again, Moses had representatives of the twelve tribes bring a staff into the Tabernacle. The next day only Aaron's staff had budded and blossomed and even produced almonds, and Moses put that rod inside the Ark of the Covenant as a sign that God had chosen Aaron and his family to be the priests (Num. 17:10; Heb. 9:4).

THE DISOBEDIENCE OF MOSES AND AARON

At the end of the years of wandering the Israelites returned to Kadesh Barnea, where Miriam died and was buried (20:1). By now almost all of the older generation had died and their children were preparing to enter the Promised Land. But the surviving Israelites closely resembled their parents in that they complained about the lack of water and food and wished that they had died in the desert (Num. 20:2-5). They longed for figs, grapes, and pomegranates, the food they would have enjoyed in Canaan had their parents not rebelled (cf. Num. 13:23), but their own opposition to Moses and Aaron put in jeopardy the prospect of reaching Canaan.

As in chapters 14 and 16 the glory of the Lord again appeared, and the Lord told Moses to speak to a rock and it would pour out its life-giving water (Num. 20:8). When Moses and Aaron had gathered the assembly, Moses proceeded to disobey the Lord by striking the rock twice with his staff. Apparently his frustration with forty years of leading a rebellious nation got the better of him, and this new round of complaining angered Moses greatly. The younger generation was repeating the mistakes of their elders in spite of God's intervention time and time again. As a result of Moses' rash actions, the Lord told him that he would not enter the Promised Land. Both Moses and Aaron "did not trust in me enough to honor me as holy" there at the waters of Meribah, so neither of them would ever see Canaan (v. 12). Elsewhere Moses' actions are described as "breaking faith" with God and failing to uphold His holiness (Deut. 32:51). By his angry words and impetuous actions Moses had not shown the proper respect for God's presence.[7] Later Moses prayed that the Lord would relent and permit him to see Canaan, but his request was refused (Deut. 3:23-26).

When the Israelites left Kadesh and came to Mount Hor, God told Moses to ascend the mountain with Aaron and his son Eleazar. After placing Aaron's sacred garments on Eleazar to identify him as the new high priest, Moses bid farewell to his beloved brother. Although he was old and had lived a full and fruitful life, Aaron died because he and Moses had rebelled against the Lord's command at Meribah (20:24).

MILITARY VICTORIES ON THE WAY TO CANAAN

As the nation journeyed toward Canaan, the dawning of a new age was marked by several important victories. The first was a reversal of the battle almost forty years earlier that had ended in a crushing defeat at the hands of the Amalekites and Canaanites (14:45). This time the king of Arad from southern Canaan attacked the Israelites, and in response to prayer, the Lord gave Israel the victory. Several cities were totally destroyed according to the policy applicable to Canaan in general (Num. 21:1-3; Deut. 7:2). No captives, livestock, or valuables were to be taken as plunder, for everyone and everything was under God's judgment.

In order to reach the eastern shore of the Jordan River opposite Jericho the Israelites had to travel around the countries of Edom and Moab. Neither king gave Israel permission to cross his territory, and the Lord did not allow Moses to attack these descendants of Esau and Lot (Num. 20:18; Deut. 2:5, 9). When the Israelites approached the land of the Amorites north of Moab and the Arnon River, King Sihon marched out to confront them. Cities such as Heshbon fell to the Israelites, and they captured all of the land in Transjordan between the Arnon and the Jabbok rivers. Traveling farther north, Moses also defeated Og, king of Bashan, and took control of Gilead and the area around the Sea of Galilee (Num. 21:33-35). These victories greatly facilitated the conquest of Canaan by eliminating enemies east of the Jordan, and the people were encouraged by these convincing triumphs. By defeating Og, who was one of the giant Rephaites (Deut. 3:11), Israel knew it could also conquer the tall and powerful warriors west of the Jordan who had so intimidated the spies a generation earlier (cf. Num. 13:28, 33). When two men were sent by Joshua to spy out Jericho, they learned through Rahab that the victories over Sihon and Og had indeed demoralized the people of Canaan (Josh. 2:10-11).

7. *NIV Study Bible*, p. 219.

THE WILDERNESS THEME IN SCRIPTURE

The experiences of the Israelites in the wilderness are referred to elsewhere in Scripture as a grim warning about the consequences of rebellion and disobedience. In a passage quoted at length in Hebrews, the psalmist urged the Israelites not to harden their hearts like their forefathers and miss the opportunity of entering God's rest (Ps. 95:7-11). The "rest" to which the Israelites looked forward was to be found in the land of Canaan, which God promised would be their "resting place" after the years of slavery in Egypt and the difficulties of the wilderness (Ex. 33:14; Deut. 12:9). Under the leadership of Joshua the people finally did enter that "rest" and enjoyed significant stretches of peace and prosperity in the Promised Land (Deut. 25:19; Josh. 21:44).

The writer of Hebrews draws an analogy between Israel's experience and the life of a believer, who likewise must deal with difficulties and temptations and obey the call to be faithful. Just as Israel had been redeemed from Egypt and gloriously freed, so the believer has been redeemed by the blood of Christ and has been freed from sin's bondage. As the recipient of God's gracious kindness, the believer should echo the words of the Israelites, who promised at Mount Sinai to "do everything the Lord has said" (Ex. 19:8). Yet Israel's failure to honor that commitment demonstrated just how easy it is to forget one's sincere vows. In Hebrews we are urged to learn from Israel's mistakes and to maintain an attitude of trust and belief. If we refuse to believe His promises and instead harden our hearts, we are in danger of missing God's rest and forfeiting His blessing.

The believer's "rest" is called a "Sabbath-rest" and is compared with the seventh day of creation when God rested from His own work (Heb. 4:9). Although the exact sense of this "Sabbath-rest" is unclear in Hebrews,[8] we do know that the Israelites were often guilty of breaking the Sabbath, a kind of rebellion analogous to their often defiant attitude in the wilderness. Like the Israelites, we too are quick to ignore God's guidance and to grumble and complain, thereby stunting our growth in grace and laying ourselves open to the disciplining hand of God.[9] Israel's behavior brought death to a whole generation and may have made the conquest of the Promised Land much more difficult. Unbelief and rebellion will always help the enemy of our souls and bring disgrace to the cause of Christ. God does not want His children to stumble around in the wilderness but to be a light to the nations and to bring blessings to all people (cf. Gen. 12:3).

8. For several possible interpretations, cf. Robert H. Gundry, *A Survey of the New Testament*, rev. ed. (Grand Rapids: Zondervan, 1981), p. 318.
9. R. K. Harrison, *Numbers*, WEC (Chicago: Moody, 1990), pp. 27-28.

The Enigmatic Role of Balaam

After conquering most of Transjordan, the Israelites set up camp in the plains of Moab opposite Jericho. Their proximity to the territory of Moab just to the south prompted Balak king of Moab to take action against them, for he feared that his country would be the next to fall (22:2-3). Supported by the leaders of Midian, Balak sent messengers to Balaam son of Beor, asking him to come from his home near the Euphrates River and put a curse on Israel. His reputation as a diviner and prophet made it likely that he could devise a way to harm Israel, and a generous fee was offered to encourage a prompt response (22:7, 17). Moab had suffered humiliation at the hands of the Amorites and was hoping to avoid subjection to the powerful Israelites.

BALAAM AS PROPHET

In light of the references to divination and sorcery (22:7; 24:1) and Balaam's close association with Moab and Midian, the pagan nature of his ministry seems well established. Yet the remarkable content of his prophecies and the Lord's interaction with him make it sound as if he was—or had been—a prophet of Yahweh. When the elders of Moab and Midian came to ask for his help, Balaam said that "the Lord has refused to let me go with you" (22:13). Five verses later Balaam refers to "the Lord my God" as if he were a genuine worshiper of Yahweh (v. 18). In his oracles he twice says that he "hears the words of God" (24:4,11), and in 24:2 "the Spirit of God came upon him" as he delivered his oracle. Balaam also refers to God as "Most High" and "the Almighty," names known by Abraham in Genesis (24:4, 16),[10] and the last two lines in 24:9 about the differing fates of those who bless or curse Israel almost sound like a quotation taken from the Abrahamic Covenant (Gen. 12:3). The content of Balaam's oracles is remarkable, even including what may be a messianic prophecy in 24:17.

Nevertheless most interpreters view Balaam as a pagan diviner who was used by God in spite of being ranked with the false prophets.[11] Balaam is compared with the Mesopotamian *baru* priests, who were very much involved with animal divination. When Balaam received pieces of sacrificed cattle and sheep (22:40), he would have examined in particular the livers of these animals in order to predict the future. Divination may also have been the reason for the sacri-

---

10. Cf. Gen. 14:19-20 for "Elyon" and 17:1 for El Shaddai, "God Almighty."
11. See especially Ronald B. Allen, "The Theology of the Balaam Oracles," in *Tradition & Testament: Essays in Honor of Charles Lee Feinberg*, ed. John S. Feinberg and Paul D. Feinberg (Chicago: Moody, 1981), pp. 79-119; "The Theology of the Balaam Oracles: A Pagan Diviner and the Word of God" (diss., Dallas Theological Seminary, 1973). Also cf. Walter C. Kaiser, Jr., in *TWOT* (Chicago: Moody, 1980), 1:112; G. Ernest Wright, *Biblical Archeology* (Philadelphia: Westminster, 1963), p. 73.

fices of bulls and rams in 23:1-2. In 24:1 we are told that Balaam "did not resort to sorcery" since the Lord was putting the words in his mouth each time anyway. Balaam realized that in spite of his personal preferences he had no choice but to deliver the oracle God gave to him. This was made clear when the angel of the Lord confronted him with a drawn sword on his way to Moab. On that occasion the renowned "seer" could not see the angel blocking his path, but his donkey was well aware of the danger—and even instructed her master (22:21-35).[12]

One interesting way of explaining Balaam's knowledge of Israel and the Lord is the possibility that he may have come originally from Edomite or Ammonite stock. In Genesis 36:32 there is mention of a king of Edom named Bela son of Beor, which is very close to "Balaam son of Beor."[13] If Balaam had connections with Edom, we could understand the hostility he would be expected to have toward Israel and why Balak might have known about him. The Ammonite hypothesis is based on a textual variant in Numbers 22:5, where several Hebrew manuscripts and ancient versions read "in the land of the Ammonites" rather than "in his native land."[14] Ammon, like Edom, was a neighbor of Moab.

In an Aramaic prophetic text recently discovered at Deir 'Alla in Jordan archaeologists have uncovered further words attributed to "Balaam son of Beor." The text speaks of Balaam as a seer, and he is once again cast in the role of one who pronounced curses upon others. Since this material was found in a sanctuary or shrine of some kind, it is an interesting confirmation of the reputation Balaam possessed.[15]

If Balaam had at one time been a true prophet of the Lord, we could compare the coming of the Spirit upon him with the work of the Spirit upon King Saul after he had been rejected as king. When Saul was pursuing David at Ramah, the Spirit of God came upon him and he began to prophesy (1 Sam. 19:23). Saul had no intention of prophesying but was helpless to do anything else. In the same way Balaam spoke words of blessing, which neither he nor King Balak wanted to have expressed.

BALAAM'S PROPHECIES

After all the effort and expense of securing Balaam's services, King Balak could hardly believe his ears when Balaam began to speak. Instead of cursing

---

12. Allen, "The Theology of the Balaam Oracles," p. 97.
13. In Hebrew "Bela" has one less consonant than "Balaam": *Bela'* vs. *Bil'am*. Albright ("The Oracles of Balaam," *JBL* 63 [1944], p. 232) connects *Bil'am* with the Amorite name *Yabil'ammu*, "the (divine) uncle brings."
14. The difference in Hebrew is *benê 'ammô* vs. *benê 'ammôn*.
15. Cf. J. Hoftijzer and G. van der Kooij, *Aramaic Texts from Deir 'Alla* (Leiden: Brill, 1976), pp. 173-92, 268-82; J. Hoftijzer, "Prophet Balaam in a Sixth Century Aramaic Inscription," *BA* 39 (1976), pp. 11-17; Harrison, *Numbers*, p. 293.

Israel, Balaam proceeded to bless them repeatedly. As he looked at the Israelites from various vantage points, he observed that they were numerous and powerful, free from misfortune and misery. For the first time in the Pentateuch God is called Israel's King, and He was the one who rescued them from Egypt (23:4-5). Though once held captive by the mighty Pharaohs, Israel is now ready to "rise like a lioness" and devour the prey (23:24). The themes of the Exodus and of Israel's lion-like strength are repeated in the third oracle (24:8-9). This time Balaam speaks of Israel's human king, who "will be greater than Agag" (v. 7). An Amalekite king named Agag was defeated in battle by Israel's first king, Saul, though an earlier Agag may have ruled Amalek in the days of Moses (cf. Ex. 17:8-13; 1 Sam. 15:8).[16] Amalek's ruin is also noted in 24:20, perhaps a reference to their subsequent defeat at the hands of David (cf. 1 Sam. 30:17-18; 2 Sam. 8:12).

In the climactic fourth oracle Balaam utters what many believe may be a messianic prophecy: "A star will come out of Jacob; a scepter will rise out of Israel" (24:17). "Star" is a metaphor for a king in Isaiah 14:12, and "scepter" is found in another important pronouncement of blessing, Genesis 49:10 (see "Salvation" and "The Messiah" in chapter 1). Identified as "a ruler" in verse 19, this prophecy probably begins with David and anticipates the Messiah.[17] Israel's king will not only "crush the foreheads of Moab," but Edom will also be conquered (v. 18). As he heard Balaam's pronouncements, Balak's worst fears were realized, and he knew what was in store for Moab and its neighbors. The curse he hoped for had been turned into a torrent of blessing (cf. Deut. 23:5; Neh. 13:2); the promises made to Abraham were about to be fulfilled in this great nation poised to conquer Canaan and eventually all of the surrounding countries.

BALAAM'S DEADLY ADVICE

After listening to a description of Israel's glorious future in the oracles of Balaam, we are ill prepared for the catastrophe that strikes the Israelites in chapter 25. Instead of growing strong and enjoying the blessing of God, the chosen people are overcome by sin, and thousands perish in a deadly plague. From Numbers 31:16 we learn that Balaam did find a way to curse Israel after all by advising the Moabite women to invite the Israelites to worship Baal with them and get them involved in immorality. By attending the sacrifices and bowing before the gods of Moab, the Israelites were guilty of idolatry, and since the worship of Baal often included fertility rites, the people were soon entrapped in

---

16. Cf. *NIV Study Bible*, p. 226; Gordon J. Wenham, *Numbers*, TOTC (Downers Grove, Ill.: Inter-Varsity, 1981), p. 178.

17. Wenham, *Numbers*, pp. 178-79.

sexual immorality. Like those other sad occasions in which Israel rebelled, God sent a plague to punish His people, and twenty-four thousand died.

In order to stop the plague, drastic action was taken by Phinehas, the son of the new high priest Eleazar and grandson of Aaron. When Phinehas saw an Israelite taking a Midianite woman into his tent right in front of Moses and the assembled people, he drove a spear through both of them, an execution that reflected God's own anger with the sinners and "made atonement for the Israelites" (25:13).[18] As a result of his courageous action, Phinehas and his descendants were given "a covenant of a lasting priesthood" (v. 12). The Israelite who was executed was a leader of the tribe of Simeon, and apparently many of those who died in the plague belonged to that tribe. In the census of chapter 26, the totals for Simeon are substantially lower than those given in chapter 1 (cf. 26:14 and 1:23).

BALAAM'S DEATH AND LEGACY

The effectiveness of Balaam's advice probably earned him the handsome reward Balak had promised him. But he did not get to enjoy it very long because of his presence among the Midianites, who were the objects of God's vengeance. Because of the key role played in the seduction of Israel by Cozbi, the daughter of a Midianite leader, God ordered Moses to attack the Midianites in his final military action. According to Numbers 31:8 the Israelites killed the five kings of Midian and Balaam son of Beor. The man who had prophesied Israel's ascendancy and military victories became himself a victim in battle. By his clever advice he had brought a curse on Israel, but he in turn was cursed as well (cf. 24:9).

In the New Testament Balaam is compared with false prophets and false teachers who loved "the wages of wickedness" (2 Pet. 2:15). They were godless men who turned "the grace of God into a license for immorality" and "rushed for profit into Balaam's error" (Jude 4, 11). In Revelation the teaching of Balaam is linked with the heretical sect of the Nicolaitans, who apparently were involved with idolatry and immorality while pretending to be part of the church in Pergamum (Rev. 2:6, 14-15). Each of these passages paints a portrait of Balaam as a dangerous and deceptive leader with impure motives.

PREPARATION FOR THE PROMISED LAND

In spite of the calamity that befell the nation there on the plains of Moab, God in His grace was going to bring the Israelites into Canaan. Before they crossed the Jordan to begin the conquest, the Lord gave Moses additional in-

---

18. Ibid., p. 188.

structions about various problems the people would face. Of special importance were issues dealing with tribal allotment and family inheritance.

THE INHERITANCE RIGHTS OF WOMEN

In the census recorded in chapter 26 there is special mention of the five daughters of Zelophehad son of Hepher (v. 33). Since Zelophehad did not have any sons, the daughters asked Moses if they could inherit the property that normally would have gone to the sons. After bringing their case before the Lord, Moses decided in favor of the five daughters and established a law regulating the transfer of an inheritance. If a man had no sons or daughters his property was given to his brothers and then to his father's brothers (27:8-10). Later the leaders of the clan of Gilead from the tribe of Manasseh raised a question about the potential marriages of Zelophehad's daughters to men from other tribes. If that happened the land would be "added to that of the tribe they marry into" (Num. 36:3). To prevent this occurrence, Moses decreed that the girls must marry "within the tribal clan of their father" (v. 6), and they complied by marrying "their cousins on their father's side" (v. 11). A classic example of the importance of a family inheritance can be seen in Naboth's refusal to sell his property to King Ahab in Jezreel (1 Kings 21:2-3). When Jezebel confiscated the property to satisfy her husband, it spelled doom for the dynasty of Ahab (1 Kings 21:19).

JOSHUA'S COMMISSIONING

During the entire forty-year period in the desert Joshua had been Moses' general and top assistant, so it is not surprising that he was selected to be the man to lead Israel into the Promised Land. Moses had known from the beginning that Joshua would be his replacement, because in a battle against the Amalekites shortly after the Exodus, God had told Moses to make sure that Joshua knew that Amalek was to be destroyed (Ex. 17:14). As part of his training, Joshua had climbed Mount Sinai with Moses when Moses met with God (Ex. 24:13). When the two returned after forty days, Joshua watched as Moses dealt with the crisis sparked by the worship of the golden calf. An even greater crisis arose after the spies announced that Canaan could not be conquered, but Joshua along with Caleb had the faith to believe that God would give Israel victory (cf. Num. 14:6-9). Over the years Joshua had been a reliable and capable aide, full of faith in the Lord and an experienced military leader. Anyone who attempted to follow Moses as leader would have a difficult job at best, but with the help of Eleazar the high priest and with the support of the people, Joshua was equal to the task.

In response to the Lord's command Moses laid his hand on Joshua and gave him some of his authority (Num. 27:18-20). While the whole assembly looked on, Moses had Joshua stand before Eleazar and commissioned him as the new leader (27:22-23). From Deuteronomy 3:25 we learn that Moses prayed for an opportunity to cross the Jordan and see Canaan, but God refused his request and pointed to Joshua as the one who would bring the Israelites into the Promised Land (Deut. 3:28).

THE BATTLE AGAINST MIDIAN

After Midianite women had become involved in the seduction of Israel in connection with the worship of the Baal of Peor, God told Moses to treat the Midianites as enemies (Num. 25:17). As one of his final actions Moses mobilized the Israelites and led them in a holy war against Midian. Since God had given the order for this war, Phinehas the priest played a major role in the battle. He had been the one who courageously executed two of the major offenders in the Peor fiasco (Num. 25:8), so it was fitting that he accompany the troops. Phinehas took with him "articles from the sanctuary," presumably including the Ark of the Covenant as the primary symbol of God's presence (31:6).[19] A thousand men from each of the tribes were called to the battle to show that the entire nation was united "to carry out the Lord's vengeance" on Midian (31:3).

In the ensuing battle the Israelites defeated the Midianites and killed all the troops, including the five kings of Midian. They captured the women and children and took the herds and flocks as plunder (31:7-9). Normally in wars against enemies outside of Canaan, this was to be the accepted procedure, and captive women could be taken as wives (cf. Deut. 20:14; 21:10-14). But because the Midianite women had led the Israelites into apostasy and immorality earlier, Moses ordered them to be killed. All of the males were likewise executed, and only the girls who were virgins were spared. The amount of plunder taken was immense, and Moses divided it equally between the soldiers and the rest of the community. From the soldiers' share, one out of every five hundred persons and animals was given to the priests "as the Lord's part" in this holy war (31:28-29). From the community's half, one out of every fifty was turned over to the Levites. This careful division of the plunder set a pattern of fairness to be followed in Canaan also. All of the people received a share of the spoils, including the priests and Levites as the Lord's special representatives. Although some of the battles in Canaan entailed the total destruction of people and animals (cf. Josh. 6:21), large quantities of plunder were accumulated and needed to be shared with all the Israelites—not just the warriors (cf. Josh 22:8).

TRIBAL INHERITANCE IN TRANSJORDAN

Ever since God had told Abraham that He would give his descendants the land of Canaan (Gen. 12:7), the Israelites had looked forward to permanent

19. Cf. Martin Noth, *Numbers*, OTL (Philadelphia: Westminster, 1968), p. 229.

possession of this cherished territory. So it must have come as somewhat of a shock to Moses when the tribes of Reuben and Gad asked if they could have their inheritances east of the Jordan (Num. 32:4-6). The area captured from Sihon and Og contained excellent grazing land, suitable for the large herds and flocks of these tribes. But why were the people of Reuben and Gad eager to stop short of the national goal?

Moses was upset at their request and accused the two tribes of repeating the sin of their parents, whose rebellion at Kadesh Barnea brought about the forty years of wandering in the desert (32:8-13). He was afraid that when the other tribes heard about the desire of their brothers, they might become discouraged and return to the desert. But the leaders of Reuben and Gad assured Moses that they were not trying to divide the nation and promised that they would send troops across the Jordan to help conquer the land of Canaan. Only after the conquest of the Promised Land would they return to their families in Transjordan and settle down (32:16-19). Their answer satisfied Moses, who agreed to assign the inheritances of these two tribes—along with the half-tribe of Manasseh—to the former land of the Amorites east of the Jordan. As a result of this decision, the other nine and a half tribes had more land to divide among themselves in Canaan, but it became more difficult for the twelve tribes to function as a unified nation. During the days of the judges, civil war broke out between tribes east and west of the Jordan, with substantial loss of life (cf. Judg. 12:4-6). The two and a half tribes also were vulnerable to attack from the Ammonites, Moabites, and later the Arameans of Damascus.

Strictly speaking, Transjordan was not part of the "holy land," and on one occasion Joshua referred to it as "defiled" (literally "unclean") land. The Lord's land was "where the Lord's tabernacle stands," the earthly dwelling place of the Almighty (Josh. 22:19). Moses longed to cross the Jordan and enter Canaan, which really constituted the Promised Land. Yet at the same time God told Moses to select three cities as cities of refuge on each side of the Jordan (Num. 35:14). These six towns were places to which anyone who had accidentally killed someone could flee and find protection from the avenger of blood (35:15). The six were among the forty-eight towns given to the tribe of Levi as their inheritance. Since the Levites had no tribal territory per se, they were assigned cities and pasture lands among all the other tribes. This included a number of cities from the tribes east of the Jordan (cf. Josh. 21:27, 36-39). The presence of Levites on both sides of the river seems to support the legitimacy of the claim that Transjordan rightfully belonged to the Israelites.[20]

Nonetheless the eastern tribes did feel a sense of estrangement from their brothers, an attitude demonstrated by an incident after the conquest of Canaan.

---

20. Note the force of Jephthah's argument when he states that God gave to Israel the territory of the Amorites in Transjordan (Judg. 11:21-23).

On their way back home, the troops from Reuben and Gad built a memorial altar in Canaan close to the Jordan River (Josh. 22:10). They built the altar as a witness that they worshiped the Lord and that they participated in the conquest. If the western tribes ever said that the eastern tribes had "no share in the Lord," the altar stood as a memorial to the unity of the nation and to the faith that bound them together (Josh. 22:25-27).

The lessons learned by all of the tribes in the book of Numbers were difficult ones to be sure. Their well-organized march to Canaan had turned into forty years of aimless wandering marked by persistent rebellion. But now the new generation waited at the edge of the Promised Land, buoyed by the great victories over Sihon and Og and assured by God's blessing. They were filled with hope and courage as a new leader, Joshua, was ready to replace Moses. Before his death, however, Moses presented a series of final exhortations to the nation, urging the tribes to follow the Lord wholeheartedly as they entered the land flowing with milk and honey.

7

DEUTERONOMY

Moses was one of the greatest leaders who ever lived, and in Deuteronomy we are given his final words to the nation of Israel. In a series of speeches Moses challenged the new generation to obey the terms of the Sinai Covenant and to follow the Lord wholeheartedly. If they truly loved the Lord, such obedience would not be tedious, but a response growing out of a deep commitment. Moses urged Joshua and the people to be strong and courageous and to take possession of the Promised Land. Undergirded by "the everlasting arms" of "the eternal God" (Deut. 33:27), Israel could experience the fullness of God's blessing as they served the Lord in their new homeland.

TITLE

The final book of the Pentateuch gains its name from the Greek *deuterono-mion touto* of Deuteronomy 17:18, which means "this second law giving." Actually the Hebrew expression means more accurately "a copy of this law," but the popular use of "second law" does link the book with the Sinai Covenant of Exodus, with which Deuteronomy is closely associated. Along with the repetition of the Ten Commandments in chapter 5, Deuteronomy contains many laws that are similar to those found in Exodus, especially in the Book of the Covenant (Ex. 21-23).[1] It was certainly Moses' desire to remind the nation of its responsibility to keep the precepts of the law and to abide by the terms of the Sinai Covenant.

As is sometimes the case, the Hebrew title, "These are the words," is taken from the first verse of the book. Since this title is rather vague, however, the book is occasionally referred to as *mišneh hattôrâ*, "a copy of the law" (cf. 17:18), or simply *mišneh*. The phrase "this Book of the Law" occurs in 28:61; 29:21; 30:10; and 31:26, and "this law" is also frequently used.[2]

1. Cf. J. A. Thompson, *Deuteronomy*, TOTC (Downers Grove, Ill.: InterVarsity, 1975), p. 27.
2. Louis Goldberg, *Deuteronomy*, Bible Study Commentary (Grand Rapids: Zondervan, 1986), p. 11.

Deuteronomy is quoted some eighty times in the New Testament and is cited in all books except for John, Colossians, 1 Thessalonians, 2 Timothy, and 1 and 2 Peter.[3] Of these, the most famous are the Shema in 6:4-5 and the verses quoted by Jesus during His temptation (6:13, 16; 8:3).

PURPOSE AND SCOPE

In his last words to Israel, Moses effectively led the nation to renew the Sinai Covenant as he reflected upon the forty years in the desert. The book was designed to remind the Israelites of God's faithfulness and to encourage them to love the Lord with all their hearts. Since the nation was finally ready to enter Canaan, Moses dealt with a number of issues he had not previously addressed, including instructions for future kings (17:14-20). This was important because throughout Deuteronomy God was preeminently Israel's king, the suzerain who demanded the allegiance of the whole nation (cf. 33:5).[4] If the people obeyed the Lord and His commandments, they would be richly blessed (28:1-14); if they chose to rebel, they would experience calamity after calamity and be driven out of the land (28:15-68).

The fifth book of Moses is different from the other four in somewhat the same manner as the book of John is different from the three synoptic gospels. Both Deuteronomy and John contain significant amounts of new material and give us important discourses of Moses and Jesus (cf. John 13-17) at the end of their lives. The two books emphasize the need to love God and to serve Him faithfully.

After four decades in the desert, Moses was eager to challenge the younger generation to follow God with their whole hearts. Now that their parents had died during the desert wanderings, Moses renewed the covenant made at Mount Sinai and sought both to encourage and to warn those who would actually take possession of the Promised Land. A great opportunity lay before them, but there were also dangers that could drive the nation far from God. They needed the same commitment that had been voiced by their parents at Mount Sinai along with a much better record of obedience. In light of what had happened so recently on the plains of Moab (cf. Num. 25:1-9), the new generation seemed equally susceptible to rebellion against God.

As Moses addressed the Israelites in these final messages, he reflected upon many of the experiences they had shared in the desert. In the first four chapters Moses described the key events that took place during the forty years, starting with the mission of the spies and the rebellion at Kadesh Barnea. Skipping quickly over the years of wandering, he described the Lord's command to by-

3. Thompson, *Deuteronomy*, p. 11.
4. P. C. Craigie, *Commentary on the Book of Deuteronomy*, NICOT (Grand Rapids: Eerdmans, 1976), p. 65.

pass the lands of Edom, Moab, and Ammon as they made their way northward. All of those nations were relatives of Israel, and God had given them their land even as He had given Israel Canaan (Deut. 2:5, 9, 19). But the Israelites were allowed to attack the Amorites, and in 2:24-3:11 Moses gives a somewhat fuller account of the victories over Sihon and Og than the one found in Numbers 21. After the conquest of Transjordan, Moses assigned the land to the tribes of Reuben and Gad and the half-tribe of Manasseh (3:12-20). These victories were a great encouragement to the Israelites, and Moses challenged them to continue on in triumph to Canaan. Moses stressed that if the people remembered the goodness of God who redeemed them from Egypt and if they obeyed the laws and decrees revealed to them on Mount Sinai, they would indeed "live long in the land" the Lord was giving them (4:40). But should they choose to rebel against the Lord and worship idols, they would be destroyed and driven out of Canaan (4:26-27).

To renew the Sinai Covenant with the new generation, Moses repeats the entire Ten Commandments in chapter 5, for they contain the key stipulations of the covenant (see "The Ten Commandments" in chapter 4). Those who heard these commands at Mount Sinai were quick to ignore them, worshiping the golden calf and bringing upon themselves the wrath of God (Deut. 9:7-9). But God had chosen Israel as His special people and would faithfully keep "his covenant of love to a thousand generations" (7:9; 10:12). In light of His gracious provision for Israel, why did the nation hesitate to love God with all their hearts? If they truly loved Him, they would fear Him and "serve him only" and faithfully keep His commandments (6:5, 13; 10:12; 11:1). With all its rules and regulations, the Sinai Covenant was nonetheless based on love, and Israel's obedience should have issued out of their love for God.[5] During the last forty years they had been given food and drink in a miraculous way and had been protected from "venomous snakes and scorpions" (8:15). In spite of all their difficulties, their clothes did not wear out and their feet did not swell, providing additional reasons that they should have been eager to obey the Lord out of grateful hearts (8:4).

Once they reached Canaan, the Israelites would be faced with new challenges that would prove to be a stern test to their faith. To help them survive in a hostile setting, Moses articulated specific decrees and laws that in some cases were modifications of the laws given in Exodus, Leviticus, and Numbers. For example, although offerings still had to be presented at the central sanctuary, "at the place the Lord will choose," the people could slaughter animals and eat meat in any of the towns where they lived (12:14-15). Every third year the Israelites were to store their tithes in their hometowns to provide for the Levites and

5. Samuel J. Schultz, *The Gospel of Moses* (New York: Harper & Row, 1974), p. 6.

other needy people (14:28-29; 26:12). This represented a change from earlier instruction about tithing given in Numbers 18:21-28.

Since Canaan was a land filled with many forms of pagan worship, Moses warned the people about diviners, sorcerers, mediums, and spiritists (18:9-11). In contrast to such detestable practices, Moses urged Israel to listen closely to prophets whom God would raise up. Those who spoke in the Lord's name would declare the message God wanted His people to hear (18:15-19). But if false prophets arose and spoke presumptuously, they were to be put to death (18:20). Anyone who claimed to be a prophet and at the same time encouraged idolatry was guilty of rebellion against the Lord and deserved to die (cf. 13:1-5).

In Jacob's blessing upon the twelve tribes, he predicted that "the scepter will not depart from Judah," an indication that a king would ultimately come from Judah (Gen. 49:10). Moses likewise anticipated the appointment of a king and set down guidelines for his rule. The future monarch must pay close heed to the law of Moses, and he "must not acquire great numbers of horses," "accumulate large amounts of silver and gold," or marry many wives (Deut. 17:16-17). Otherwise his heart would stray from the Lord, and he would trust in his own resources and alliances (v. 17). In spite of this warning, King Solomon was especially guilty of extensive acquisitions in all three areas, to the ultimate detriment of his kingdom (cf. 1 Kings 11:1-6).

The practice of polygamy lay behind Moses' decree that the right of the firstborn belonged to the "actual firstborn" rather than the son of his favorite wife.[6] To minimize the evil effects of divorce, Moses outlawed the remarriage of a divorced woman to her first husband if she had married a second man (24:1-4). If a man died before his wife had a son, the man's brother was responsible to marry the widow, and the first son "shall carry on the name of the dead brother" (Deut. 25:5-10). This custom—known as levirate or "brother-in-law" marriage—is best illustrated in the marriage of Ruth and Boaz (Ruth 4:5).[7]

Following the long recital of decrees and laws contained in chapters 12-26, Moses tried to motivate the people as he reviewed the blessings and the curses that lay in store for them. When they reached the Promised Land, the tribes were instructed to travel to the important city of Shechem, and there renew the covenant on Mount Gerizim and Mount Ebal. Sealing their vows with an oath, the Israelites promised to obey the terms of the covenant and to serve the Lord (cf. 29:12). If they were faithful to the Lord, the nation would be richly blessed, enjoying victory over their enemies and a growing population. Their flocks and herds would increase dramatically, and their crops would be abundant (28:1-14).

---

6. Cf. Barry J. Beitzel, "The Right of the Firstborn in the Old Testament (Deut. 21:15-17)," in *A Tribute to Gleason Archer*, ed. W. C. Kaiser, Jr., and R. F. Youngblood (Chicago: Moody, 1986), pp. 179-90.
7. Although Boaz was not a brother-in-law, he was a close relative, and as a "kinsman-redeemer" he also bought the land that had belonged to Naomi's husband (Ruth 4:3; cf. Lev. 25:25).

If they disobeyed, however, the reverse would be true, and 28:16-19 is exactly opposite to 28:3-6. Rebellion would bring defeat in battle, drought, and disease, and swarms of locusts would devastate the crops (v. 42). Eventually foreign armies would besiege Israel's cities, break down the walls, and take the people captive, scattering the Israelites "from one end of the earth to the other" (v. 64). The curse section was a lengthy one—from verse 15 to verse 68—but it did not deter the people from stubborn disobedience. Like Leviticus 26, Deuteronomy 28 turned out to be a prophecy of the horrible punishment Israel would ultimately receive.

In chapters 31-34 Moses gives his final words to the nation, this time in poetic form. The song of Moses in chapter 32 reminded the Israelites of God's faithfulness and their sinfulness and describes the judgment in store for them. Whenever the people sang it, they testified to the greatness of their God, whose "works are perfect" and "who does no wrong" (v. 4).[8] Before he died Moses blessed the tribes, just as Jacob had done in Genesis 49. Whereas Joseph again receives lengthy praise (33:13-17), the blessing of Judah is very brief (v. 7), and Simeon is completely omitted. Simeon's brother Levi is treated in a positive fashion, owing to the courageous action of that tribe during the golden calf crisis (33:8-11; cf. Ex. 32:26-29).

When Moses climbed Mount Nebo, where he died and was buried by the Lord Himself, Joshua succeeded him as the nation's leader. Commissioned by Moses and "filled with the spirit of wisdom," Joshua was well-prepared to assume his new role (34:9). No one could compare with Moses, "whom the Lord knew face to face," (34:10), but strengthened by the Lord, Joshua had been assured that he would bring Israel into the Promised Land (31:23).[9]

LITERARY STRUCTURE

More has been written about the literary structure of Deuteronomy than about any of the previous four books, partially because of the intriguing similarities between Deuteronomy and ancient Near Eastern treaties. As noted in chapter one, the outline of Deuteronomy follows the major features of a treaty, particularly Hittite treaties of the late second millennium B.C.:[10]

---

8. Note the impact of this chapter on the prophetic books (see chap. 1, especially "The Names of God").
9. Cf. "The Significance of Moses" in chap. 1 and "Preparation for the Promised Land" in chapter 6.
10. Cf. Kenneth Kitchen, *The Bible in Its World* (Exeter: Paternoster, 1977), p. 80.

A COMPARISON OF DEUTERONOMY AND HITTITE TREATIES

Deuteronomy	Normal Hittite Order
Historical Prologue (chaps. 1-4)	Historical Prologue
Stipulations (chaps. 5-26)	Stipulations
Blessings (chaps. 27-30)	Witnesses
Curses	Curses
Witnesses (chaps. 31-34)	Blessings

In Deuteronomy the "witnesses" section follows the curses and blessings, and the order of the curses and blessings is reversed. By placing the blessings before the curses and by including a much larger number of curses than blessings, Deuteronomy follows the pattern of early second millennium law codes. Kenneth Kitchen has noted that the Hammurapi law code contains only two blessing clauses before a series of forty curses.[11] Since Deuteronomy is so closely connected to both law and covenant, it is not surprising that in some respects it follows legal patterns.

THE LITERARY STRUCTURE OF DEUTERONOMY

Title/Preamble	1:1-5
Historical Prologue	1:6–4:43
Stipulations	4:44–26:19
Blessings, Curses	27-30
Witnesses	31-34

PREAMBLE

Hittite suzerain-vassal treaties began with a preamble identifying the Hittite king as the one initiating the agreement. In Deuteronomy 1:1 we are told that Moses was the one who addressed Israel, not as the suzerain himself but as one who represented the Lord, the God of the covenant.

HISTORICAL PROLOGUE

After the preamble Hittite treaties contained a historical prologue that reviewed the political interaction between the two countries. Generally the suzerain referred to ways in which he or his predecessors had helped the vassal nation, hoping that these kindnesses would encourage the vassal to show allegiance to the Hittite king.[12] In Deuteronomy 1-4 Moses recalls what God did for Israel in the Exodus from Egypt and during the perilous years in the wilderness (cf. 2:24–3:11; 4:33-34).

---

11. Kenneth Kitchen, *Ancient Orient and Old Testament* (Chicago: InterVarsity, 1966), pp. 97-98 n. 41; cf. *ANET* pp. 178-80.
12. Meredith Kline, *Treaty of the Great King* (Grand Rapids: Eerdmans, 1963), p. 52.

The historical prologue was probably the most distinctive feature of second-millennium treaties and helps in the effort to place the writing of Deuteronomy in the time of Moses.[13] But Weinfeld argues that the seventh-century B.C. Assyrian treaties of Esarhaddon provide a closer parallel to Deuteronomy, partly because of the lengthy curse section found in both texts. Weinfeld admits that the Assyrian treaties do not have a historical prologue, but he points out that a number of first-millennium treaties are damaged at the beginning where the historical prologue would have been placed.[14]

STIPULATIONS

The longest section in Deuteronomy—corresponding to the stipulations of the treaty form—is divided into two parts. Chapters 5-11 are of a more general nature whereas chapters 12-26 contain specific laws and regulations covering a wide range of topics. Since Deuteronomy is basically a renewal of the covenant made at Mount Sinai, it is not surprising that chapter 5 repeats the Ten Commandments from Exodus 20 with only slight variations. In the fourth commandment keeping the Sabbath is required because God had rescued Israel from slavery in Egypt, whereas in Exodus 20:11 the people are to rest on the Sabbath because God rested on the seventh day during the creation week. Both were excellent reasons, but the Exodus was a reminder that in Canaan the Israelites needed to treat their servants and the poor and the needy with kindness (cf. 15:15; 16:12; 24:18, 22).

When a Hittite king renewed a treaty with a vassal state—usually after a change of monarch—he would bring the stipulations up to date, and this may explain some of the changes in the specific laws found in chapters 12-26 (see "Purpose and Scope" above). The new generation faced special problems as they anticipated life in the land of Canaan. A major change had to do with the location and manner of their worship, and the first and last chapters in this section both deal with the subject of presenting tithes and offerings (12:4-14; 26:1-15). Apart from this example of "inclusio," it is difficult to uncover the organization of these chapters, but Stephen A. Kaufman has proposed that the material follows the order of the Ten Commandments in chapter 5.

In an elaborate study Kaufman argues that by means of organizational patterns and a logic not easily discernable by the Western mind these chapters do indeed parallel the Ten Commandments.[15] Some chapters line up better than others, with chapter 12 corresponding quite nicely to the first two commandments

13. Cf. Kitchen, *Ancient Orient*, p. 95; also see chapter 2 in this volume.
14. M. Weinfeld, *Deuteronomy and the Deuteronomic School* (Oxford: Clarendon, 1972), p. 67; also cf. J. A. Thompson, *The Ancient Near Eastern Treaties and the Old Testament* (London: Tyndale, 1964), pp. 14-15.
15. Stephen A. Kaufman, "The Structure of the Deuteronomic Law," *Maarav* 1-2 (1978-79), pp. 105-58.

and chapter 15-16 dealing with sabbatical materials. But the assertion that "honor your father and mother" corresponds to the regulations about judges, kings, and prophets (all lumped together under the category of "authority") begins to stretch our credulity. The section on false witnesses in 19:15-21 occurs unexpectedly with the sixth commandment rather than the ninth.[16] Kaufman must work so hard to make his theory fit that serious questions are raised about the whole endeavor.

Besides, in other places when the Ten Commandments are expanded and developed—such as the Book of the Covenant in Exodus 21-23 or in Leviticus 19—the order of the commandments is not rigidly followed. Leviticus 19, for example, begins by urging respect for one's parents and observance of the Sabbath, both in verse 3. Then it precludes the worship of idols in verse 4 and much later in the chapter returns once more to the Sabbath issue (v. 30).[17] There seems to be a flexibility in handling the Commandments that should caution us not to expect too much order in Deuteronomy 12-26. Nevertheless, Kaufman is to be commended for his prodigious effort to uncover the structure of this section. His article contains many helpful insights.[18]

When a treaty was concluded there was usually a formal oath of obedience taken by the vassal and attested by the gods.[19] Evidence of such an oath can be seen in Deuteronomy 26:17, which states that the Israelites "have declared this day that the Lord is [their] God." On Mount Sinai the previous generation had declared that they would "do everything the Lord has said" (Ex. 19:8).

BLESSINGS AND CURSES

To impress upon the nation the seriousness of the covenant, chapters 27-30 contain an important series of blessings and curses. In chapter 27 Moses gives instructions for the renewal ceremony to be held at Shechem—a ceremony referred to more briefly in 11:26-32. The main body of stipulations (chapters 12-26) comes between these two references to the covenant renewal ceremony.[20] Although there are far more curses than blessings in chapter 28, the fact that there are any blessings at all points again to a second millennium date for Deuteronomy. In first millennium treaty documents there are numerous curses but no blessings.[21] Additional blessings are found in chapter 33, the record of Moses' final words to the twelve tribes.

16. Ibid., pp. 113-14.
17. Cf. Gordon J. Wenham, *The Book of Leviticus* (Grand Rapids: Eerdmans, 1979), p. 264.
18. Kaufman's effort is comparable to the work of scholars who are trying to determine the connections between seemingly unrelated proverbs in Proverbs 10-22. Recent studies show that there is greater order in the arrangement than had previously been thought.
19. Kitchen, *Ancient Orient*, p. 94; cf. *ANET*, p. 203.
20. Craigie, *Deuteronomy*, p. 327.
21. Kitchen, *Ancient Orient*, p. 96.

WITNESSES

Most ancient treaties contained an imposing list of gods who were witnesses to the formation of the agreement. Deities from the pantheons of both nations were included, with the hope that respect for these gods would inspire the vassal nation to adopt a stance of obedience to the terms of the treaty. Since the Israelites worshiped only one God, a different kind of "witness" was required. The Song of Moses, given in the form of a covenant lawsuit (see chapter 1), is called a witness for the Lord against the Israelites (31:19). The "Book of the Law" was another witness (31:26), and every seven years at the feast of Tabernacles the law containing the terms of the covenant was to be read to the people (31:10-11). Occasionally Hittite treaties refer to the public reading of the document as a reminder of the stipulations incumbent upon the vassal nation.[22] To make sure that a treaty document was not lost, both parties to the agreement kept a copy in a temple in their respective countries. When Moses wrote "this law" he gave it to the priests for safe-keeping in the Tabernacle (31:9; cf. "The Tabernacle" in chapter 4).

Included in the list of witnesses in some of the Hittite treaties were "heaven and earth" or "the gods of heaven and the gods of the earth."[23] As a way of calling on all of creation to join the Lord as a witness to the covenant, Moses summoned "heaven and earth" three different times as witnesses against Israel (30:19; 31:28; 32:1). Centuries later the prophets also called on heaven and earth to testify that the people had rebelled against God and deserved to be punished (cf. Isa. 1:2; Jer. 2:12).

DEUTERONOMY AS EXHORTATION

Deuteronomy is not only an account of the renewal of the covenant, it is also a record of the addresses of Moses to the nation.[24] Throughout the book Moses spoke to the Israelites in a series of messages that are often sermonic in style. Even where he dealt with specific laws, Moses exhorted and encouraged the nation to obey the Lord fully (cf. 15:1-6). This sort of preaching about the law is sometimes referred to as "parenesis."[25] Occasionally Moses brought together events that were widely separated chronologically (cf. 1:34-37), and in other places he included insights that were parenthetical in nature (cf. 5:5). Time after time he challenged the Israelites to follow the Lord and experience great blessing. In spite of all their failures in the desert, what God was asking them to do was within their reach and not at all too difficult (30:11-14; cf. Rom. 10:6-7).

22. Cf. *ANET*, p. 205; M. Kline, *The Structure of Biblical Authority* (Grand Rapids: Eerdmans, 1972), pp. 121-23; Kitchen, *Ancient Orient*, p. 97.
23. Cf. *ANET*, pp. 205-6.
24. Cf. Craigie, *Deuteronomy*, p. 89.
25. Cf. Thompson, *Deuteronomy*, pp. 13, 24-25.

THE CENTRALITY OF THE "SHEMA"

During the last several decades a great deal of attention has been given to the "credos" of 6:20-24 and 26:5-9 identified by Gerhard von Rad in 1938 (see "Tradition Criticism" in chapter 2). But another passage has emerged as a bona fide creedal statement, and that is the "Shema" of Deuteronomy 6:4-9. Named after the Hebrew word for "Hear" in verse 4, the Shema has been called the fundamental dogma of the Old Testament and was identified by Christ as the most important of all the commandments (Mark 12:29-30).

> Hear, O Israel: The Lord our God, the Lord is one. Love the Lord your God with all your heart and with all your soul and with all your strength. (6:4-5)

In each of the places where this passage is quoted in the gospels, Christ also mentions the second greatest commandment: "Love your neighbor as yourself," taken from Leviticus 19:18 (see "Purpose and Scope" in chapter 5). Two of the three gospels add "mind" to "heart," "soul," and "strength" (Mark 12:30; Luke 10:27), and Matthew 22:37 has "mind" in place of "strength." The basic teaching is that the Israelites were to love God with their whole being, including the intellect, emotions, and will. In eight other passages the people were told to love, serve, or obey the Lord with all their heart and soul, for that kind of devotion would enable them to avoid the perils and pitfalls that lay ahead in Canaan (cf. 4:29; 10:12; 11:13; 13:3; 26:16; 30:2, 6, 10).

There was only one individual in the Old Testament of whom it was said that he turned to the Lord "with all his heart and with all his soul and with all his strength," and that was King Josiah (cf. 2 Kings 23:25). In 621 B.C. Josiah conducted a thorough reform in Judah, ridding the land of the high places, idols, mediums, and spiritists that had drawn the nation away from God (2 Kings 23:19, 24). Like Jehoshaphat and Hezekiah before him, Josiah was serious about obeying the Mosaic law and was highly honored for his faithfulness. Moses' contemporaries, Joshua and Caleb, also "followed the Lord wholeheartedly" and were the only two adults to survive the desert and enter the Promised Land (Num. 32:11-12).

Those who were fully committed to the Lord demonstrated by their attitude and actions that "the Lord is one" (Deut. 6:4). In a world that acknowledged the existence of many gods Israel was supposed "to have no other gods before me" (Ex. 20:3; Deut. 5:7). This first of the Ten Commandments was a clear statement of the uniqueness of Israel's God. Whereas the nations might worship other gods with great dedication, the Israelites had received abundant evidence that "there is no god besides me" (4:35; 32:39). Yahweh was the Creator of heaven and earth and had redeemed Israel from bondage (see 32:6 and "The

Theology of the Pentateuch" in chapter 1). At the Red Sea, Pharaoh and his army learned the hard way that Yahweh was God (Ex. 14:18), and King Balak of Moab could not thwart the purposes of the God of Israel (Num. 23:21-23). Nonetheless Moses warned the people that the Canaanites served many gods who could become a temptation in the future. Unless the Israelites avoided inter-marriage with the residents of Canaan, they would soon worship their gods and experience the Lord's anger (cf. 6:14; 7:4).

To underscore the importance of 6:4-5 and other similar exhortations, Moses urged the people to use every means to teach these commandments to their children. Whether at home or walking along the road, parents were encouraged to talk to their children constantly about God's requirements. Eventually the Jews took verses 8-9 literally, writing the passage on strips of parchment that were put into small leather boxes called phylacteries. Every morning before praying, Jewish men tied the phylacteries to their left arms and their foreheads.[26] It also became common practice to attach small containers with Scripture verses to the door frames of houses (v. 9). The passages that were normally placed in those boxes were Exodus 13:1-16; Deuteronomy 6:4-9; and 11:13-21.[27] Over the years this custom deteriorated into a legalistic exercise, and by New Testament times the Pharisees and teachers of the law wore their phylacteries to impress the populace (Matt. 23:5).

When Jesus was tempted by Satan for forty days in the desert of Judea, two out of the three verses He used to refute the devil were taken from Deuteronomy 6—and the other was 8:3. In response to Satan's urging that He throw Himself down from the highest point of the Temple, Jesus quoted 6:16—"Do not put the Lord your God to the test" (Matt. 4:7). When Satan offered Him all the king-doms of this world if Jesus would bow down before him, the Lord responded, "Worship the Lord your God, and serve him only" (Matt. 4:10; cf. Deut. 6:13). By resisting these temptations, Jesus succeeded where Israel as a nation had failed in its own wilderness ordeal. His use of these verses from chapter 6 indi-rectly emphasized the importance of the Shema in verses 4-9 and implied that anyone who loved the Lord wholeheartedly and was thoroughly familiar with His commands could foil the plans of Satan.

Toward the end of the general section of the stipulations, part of the Shema is repeated in a slightly expanded fashion. Verses 18-20 of chapter 11 are very similar to 6:6-9 and emphasize the need for parents to know the Lord's com-mands to teach Him to their children. By linking the command to fix God's words in their hearts and minds with the injunction to tie them as symbols on their hands and foreheads (v. 18), Moses was probably indicating that the latter should be taken metaphorically and not literally. The Israelites were not required

26. Goldberg, *Deuteronomy*, p. 66.
27. Ibid.

to write the Lord's commands on the door frames of their houses, but their minds were to be so saturated with God's laws and decrees that all conversation and activity was to be dominated by them. If this were true, Israel would occupy Canaan for many, many years to come, enjoying the blessing of God (11:21).

THE COVENANT CURSES:
PARADIGM FOR THE PROPHETS

Almost as well known as the Shema are chapters 28 and 29 with their extensive catalog of the covenant curses. Like Leviticus 26, Deuteronomy 28 begins with about a dozen verses of blessing, but the curses that follow are even more numerous than those in Leviticus. Along with additional warnings in chapters 19 and 30, these curses form a kind of climax to the whole Pentateuch, urging the Israelites to respond to God in obedience and escape the severe judgment that would otherwise lie ahead.

A strong indication of the importance of these chapters is the emphasis placed upon them in the prophetic books. In both the major and minor prophets there are repeated allusions to specific words and concepts contained in Deuteronomy 28-29. The judgment announced by the prophets is linked directly with the curses described by Moses, leaving no doubt that Israel's troubles were caused by her disobedience. The nation broke the terms of the Mosaic Covenant and thereby incurred the wrath of God and the fulfillment of the curses.

DROUGHT AND CROP FAILURE

Just as Israel's obedience would bring abundant rains and healthy crops (28:8, 12), so her disobedience would be followed by sparse rain and meager crops. According to 28:23 "the sky over your head will be bronze, the ground beneath you iron."[28] Without rain "the ground is cracked," and "the farmers are dismayed," for the crops will be sure to fail (Jer. 14:4). Hosea lamented over the stalk that had no bend (8:7), and Haggai groaned because of the drought "on the grain, the new wind, [and] the oil" (Hag. 1:11; cf. Deut. 28:38-40). In a graphic description of a meager harvest, Isaiah spoke of a ten-acre vineyard that would produce only six gallons of wine and of six bushels of seed that would produce less than a bushel of grain (5:10). Even if the people should manage to grow crops, swarms of locusts would devour them (Deut. 28:38, 42). The prophet Joel compared the Day of the Lord to a dreadful locust plague that ravaged the land (1:4).

---

28. In the Vassal Treaties of Esarhaddon (lines 526-30), there are references to a copper sky that allows no rain and to soil that becomes iron. Cf. *ANET*, 3d ed. with Supplement (1969), p. 539.

DISEASE AND BLINDNESS

During their lengthy tenure in Egypt the Israelites were acquainted with a number of "horrible diseases" (Deut. 7:15), and the plagues with which God afflicted the Egyptians were of unparalleled intensity. If the Israelites rebelled against God in the future, Moses warned that they would be afflicted with "the boils of Egypt and with tumors, festering sores and the itch" (Deut. 28:27). They would also be plagued "with wasting disease, with fever and inflammation," illnesses no doubt aggravated by drought and famine (28:22). In Isaiah 1 —a chapter that follows the pattern of a covenant lawsuit[29]—the prophet spoke about the nation's "wounds and welts and open sores" (v. 6). Jeremiah also lamented the pitiful condition of the people and looked for "balm in Gilead" and for a physician who could bring healing (Jer. 8:22). Both Amos and Jeremiah spoke of famine and of the plagues that God sent to punish Israel (Jer. 24:10; Amos 4:10).

Included among the various diseases are "blindness and confusion of mind" (Deut. 28:28), and Isaiah was keenly aware that in the eighth century the nation was spiritually blind and deaf. Their inability to see and understand is also mentioned in Isaiah 29:9; 42:19; 43:8; and 59:10. During the Exile the prophet Ezekiel tried to minister to a rebellious people who had eyes and ears but could not see or hear (Ezek. 12:2).

INVASION AND CAPTIVITY

Although the Israelites were about to conquer the Promised Land and drive out the current residents, Moses warned that disobedience would ultimately lead to expulsion for Israel also. Foreign armies would invade Canaan and defeat the Israelites in battle (Deut. 28:25). "Like an eagle swooping down," a nation from far away would ravage the land and lay siege to the cities, bringing untold suffering (Deut. 28:49, 51-52). Because of the cutting off of food supplies, parents would be forced to eat their own children in an attempt to survive (28:53-57). But eventually the cities would be captured, and those still alive would be deported to foreign lands. Uprooted from the Promised Land, the Israelites would be scattered among the nations to live in constant dread or to serve as slaves (28:37, 63-68).

Moses' solemn words must have been recalled periodically when foreign invaders oppressed the Israelites during the time of the judges (e.g., Judg. 6:1-6), but it was the later prophets who repeated the curses of Deuteronomy in their

---

29. Herbert M. Wolf, *Interpreting Isaiah* (Grand Rapids: Zondervan, 1985), p. 73; see "The Impact of the Pentateuch on the Prophetic Books" in chapter 1 of this volume.

preaching. During the eighth century B.C. Amos predicted that the prosperous Israelites would be sent into exile (5:27; 6:7), and several decades later Isaiah foresaw the invasion of a powerful army that would devastate the land (5:26-30; 7:20-25). The Assyrians did in fact take the Northern Kingdom into exile in 721 B.C., but the Southern Kingdom of Judah failed to learn from this catastrophe. About a century later the prophet Jeremiah drew heavily from Deuteronomy 28 as he described the invasion of a nation "whose language you do not know," this time a reference to the armies of Babylon (Deut. 28:49; Jer. 5:15). A key theme in Jeremiah is the uprooting of Judah and the exile of the nation (cf. 1:10; 31:28), and toward the end of his prophecy, Jeremiah recounted the grim details of the capture of Jerusalem (Jer. 39, 52). In the book of Lamentations he refers to the cannibalism that took place during the siege of the chosen city of David (4:10).

DISGRACE

At Mount Sinai Israel had been singled out as God's "treasured possession" among the nations (Ex. 19:5), but her status would be changed drastically as all these calamities befell her. When God inflicted punishment on her, Israel would become "a thing of horror and an object of scorn and ridicule" in all the nations where she would be scattered (Deut. 28:37). Israel had gained her freedom from the slavery of Egypt, and her new country was to be a land of liberty (cf. Lev. 25:10), but Jeremiah declared that Israel would be given " 'freedom' to fall by the sword, plague and famine" as her apostasy deepened (Jer. 34:17). By breaking the covenant with God, Israel would bring disgrace upon the name of the Lord wherever her people went. Jeremiah repeatedly referred to the shame and ridicule to which Israel would be subjected (cf. 15:4; 24:9; 25:9; 26:6; 29:18; 42:18; 44:12), and Isaiah and Ezekiel similarly spoke of the reproach and scorn that lay ahead for the disobedient nation (Isa. 43:28; Ezek. 5:14-15).

CURSE REVERSALS:
THE PROMISE OF BLESSING

Ever since the early chapters of Genesis the Pentateuch has been a mixture of blessings and curses. In the Garden of Eden God cursed the serpent who had deceived Eve, and He cursed the ground that Adam would struggle to till (3:14, 17). When Cain killed Abel he was put under a curse and condemned to be a restless wanderer on the earth (4:11-12). Generations later the sin of mankind had escalated to the point that God had to send a flood and destroy the earth. When the waters had finally subsided God promised never again to "curse the ground because of man," and He pronounced a blessing on Noah and his sons who were to repopulate the earth (8:21; 9:1). Before the end of Genesis 9, however, Noah's son Ham dishonored his father, and a curse was placed on Ham's son Canaan, who would be "the lowest of slaves . . . to his brothers" (9:25).

The people who were destined to subdue the Canaanites were the descendants of Abraham, a man God called out of Mesopotamia and promised to bless in an extraordinary way. From the opening description of the Abrahamic Covenant in Genesis 12:1-3 to the words of Moses the servant of the Lord in Deuteronomy 33, the nation of Israel was lavishly endowed with God's blessing. Even the man Israel—who as Jacob the deceiver hardly deserved God's favor—experienced God's blessing in a mighty way, and at the end of his life he peered into the future and pronounced a blessing on each of his twelve sons (Gen. 49). In spite of oppression in Egypt the descendants of Jacob multiplied greatly, and after the Exodus the seer Balaam reluctantly admitted that he could not curse "those whom God has not cursed" and proceeded to bless Israel in a remarkable series of oracles (Num. 23:8; 24:5-9; see "The Enigmatic Role of Balaam" in chap. 6).

The only way that Israel could fail was if she violated the terms of the covenant God made with her on Mount Sinai. In both Leviticus 26 and Deuteronomy 28 the curses for disobedience are spelled out, and they became a tragic prophecy of the calamities that would befall the nation. But even after the curse took effect and Israel suffered disaster after disaster, God promised that He would graciously restore His people. When the people confessed their sins and returned to the Lord with all their hearts, He would rescue them from foreign lands and bring them back to Canaan (Lev. 26:40-45; Deut. 30:1-10).

This hope of restoration likewise became a prominent theme in the books of the same prophets who recorded the fulfillment of the covenant curses.[30] Like Deuteronomy 28:38, Joel predicted a devastating locust plague in Joel 1:4, but he also looked forward to the day when "the mountains will drip new wine, and the hills will flow with milk" (Joel 3:18). Jeremiah anticipated a time when the Israelites would again rejoice over "the grain, the new wine and the oil" (Jer. 31:12), and Isaiah announced that God would make Israel's deserts "like Eden, her wastelands like the garden of God" (Isa. 51:3). With similar exuberance Amos spoke of the day "when the reaper will be overtaken by the plowman and the planter by the one treading grapes" (Amos 9:13).

According to Deuteronomy 28:28 the disobedient nation would be afflicted with blindness, but in a passage that described the transformation of the nation, Isaiah predicted that the eyes of the blind would one day see (29:18). In Isaiah 35:4-5 the healing of the blind and the deaf is associated with the messianic age (cf. Matt. 11:5). When Christ ministered on earth He brought about both physi-

---

30. For a more complete discussion of curse reversal in the prophets see Herbert Wolf, "The Transcendent Nature of Covenant Curse Reversals," in *Israel's Apostasy and Restoration*, ed. Avraham Gileadi (Grand Rapids: Baker, 1988) pp. 319-25.

cal and spiritual healing, and through His death He reversed the ultimate curse that lay upon mankind because of sin. By hanging on the cross He was under God's curse, for this was true of "anyone who is hung on a tree" (Deut. 21:23).

The prophets also spoke of the day when the Exile would be over and the people of Israel would be regathered from all the lands to which they had been banished (Jer. 32:37). Once again the streets would be full of children, and city borders would have to be extended to hold the growing population (cf. Isa. 54:1-2). Instead of suffering at the hands of an invading army (Deut. 28:49), Israel will enjoy the assistance of other nations. Foreigners will be attracted to Israel and to her God and will stream to Mount Zion to learn about the ways of the Lord (cf. Isa. 2:2-4; 55:5). Israel will be a light to the nations, and her physical and spiritual restoration will bring blessing to the whole world.

In his final blessing pronounced on the twelve tribes, Moses—the greatest of the prophets—likewise engaged in some curse reversal. When Jacob had spoken of the tribe of Levi, he condemned the rash action of Levi in the destruction of Shechem (Gen. 49:5-7). But at Mount Sinai the tribe of Levi had rallied to Moses' side during the crisis precipitated by the worship of the golden calf (Ex. 32:28-29). As a result of their courage and obedience, God set apart the tribe of Levi, and Moses acknowledged that those who offered sacrifices and taught the law to Israel would be descendants of Levi (Deut. 33:10). They had loved the Lord wholeheartedly and thereby fulfilled the most basic principle of the law (Deut. 6:5).

In the last verse of chapter 33—the final words of Moses—the great lawgiver ascribes blessing to the nation as a whole:

> Blessed are you, O Israel! Who is like you, a people saved by the Lord? (v. 29)

Although he had seen the people at their worst, Moses had also seen their God face to face, and because of the greatness of the Lord, Moses knew that ultimately blessing would come upon the chosen people and through them upon the whole world.

BIBLIOGRAPHY

REFERENCES ON THE PENTATEUCH

GENERAL REFERENCES ON THE PENTATEUCH

Aharoni, Y. *The Land of the Bible*. Philadelphia: Westminster, 1967.

Albright, William F. *From the Stone Age to Christianity*. Baltimore: Johns Hopkins U., 1946.

Allis, Oswald T. *God Spoke to Moses*. Philadelphia: Presb. & Ref., 1951.

————. *The Five Books of Moses*. Philadelphia: Presb. & Ref., 1953.

Anderson, J. Kerby, and Harold G. Coffin. *Fossils in Focus*. Grand Rapids: Zondervan, 1977.

Archer, Gleason L., Jr. *A Survey of Old Testament Introduction*. Rev. ed. Chicago: Moody, 1974.

Bailey, Lloyd R. *The Pentateuch: Interpreting Biblical Texts*. Nashville: Abingdon, 1981.

Baker, W. C. *Reliving Genesis and Exodus*. Valley Forge, Pa.: Judson, 1978.

Barton, George A. *Archaeology and the Bible*. 7th ed. Philadelphia: American Sunday School Union, 1944.

Beegle, Dewey M. *Moses, the Servant of Yahweh*. Grand Rapids: Eerdmans, 1972.

Bermant, Chaim, and Michael Weitzman. *Ebla: A Revolution in Archaeology*. New York: New York Times, 1979.

Blenkinsopp, J. *Pentateuch*. Edited by L. Bright. London: Sheed and Ward, 1971.

Bright, John. *A History of Israel*. Philadelphia: Westminster, 1972.

Brueggemann W., and H. W. Wolff. *The Vitality of Old Testament Tradition*. Atlanta: John Knox, 1975.

Brueggemann, W. "Kingship and Chaos (A Study in Tenth Century Theology)." *CBQ* 33 (1971): 317-32.

Cassuto, U. "The Beginning of Historiography Among the Israelites." *Biblical and Oriental Studies* 1 (1973): 7-18, 71-78.

Cazelles, H. "Theological Bulletins on the Pentateuch." *BibTB* 2 (1977): 3-24.

Childs, Brevard. *Introduction to the Old Testament as Scripture.* Philadelphia: Fortress, 1979.

Clifford, Richard J. "Cosmogonies in the Ugaritic Texts and in the Bible." *Or* 53 (1984): 183-201.

Clines, David J. A. "The Theme of the Pentateuch." JSOTSup 10. Sheffield: 1978.

Custance, Arthur C. *Science and Faith.* Doorway Papers 8. Grand Rapids: Zondervan, 1978.

Davidson, Francis, Stibbs, and Kevan, eds. *The New Bible Commentary.* Grand Rapids: Eerdmans, 1962.

DeYoung, Donald B., and John C. Whitcomb. "The Origin of the Universe." *GTJ* 1 (1980): 149-61.

Erdman, C. R. *The Pentateuch.* Old Tappan, N.J.: Revell, 1968.

Fensham, F. Charles. "Transgression and Penalty in the Book of the Covenant" *JNSL* 5 (1977): 23-41.

Finegan, Jack. *Light from the Ancient Past.* 2d ed. Princeton: Princeton U., 1959.

Foster, W. R. "The Meaning of Biblical History." *GTJ* 4 (1963): 3-8.

Freedman, David Noel. "Who Asks (or Tells) God to Repent?" *BRev* 1 (1985): 56-59.

Gettys, J. M. *Survey of the Pentateuch.* Atlanta: John Knox, 1962.

Good, Robert M. "The Just War in Ancient Israel." *JBL* 104 (1985): 385-400.

Gordon, Cyrus R. "Biblical Customs and the Nuzu Tablets." *BA* 3(1) (Feb. 1940).

Gordon, Cyrus H. *Ancient Near East.* New York: Norton, 1965.

Hamilton, Victor P. *Handbook on the Pentateuch.* Grand Rapids: Baker, 1982.

Harris, R. Laird; Gleason Archer; and Bruce Waltke. *Theological Wordbook of the Old Testament.* Chicago: Moody, 1981.

————. "An Alternative to Evolution." *Presbyterian* 5 (1979): 99-109.

Harrison, R. K. *An Introduction to the Old Testament.* Grand Rapids: Eerdmans, 1969.

Hasel, Gerhard F. *The Remnant: The History and Theology of the Remnant Idea from Genesis to Isaiah.* 3d ed. Berrien Springs, Mich.: Andrews U., 1980.

Hayden, R. E. "Hammurapi." *ISBEnc* 2 (1982): 604-8.

Kaiser, Walter C., Jr. *Toward Old Testament Ethics*. Grand Rapids: Zondervan, 1983.

Kaufmann, Yehezkel. *The Religion of Israel*. Translated by Moshe Greenberg. Chicago: U. of Chicago, 1960.

Keil, C. F., and F. Delitzch. *Biblical Commentary on the Old Testament: The Pentateuch*. Grand Rapids: Eerdmans, 1949.

Kitchen, Kenneth A. *Ancient Orient and Old Testament*. Chicago: InterVarsity, 1966.

————. *The Bible in Its World*. Downers Grove, Ill.: InterVarsity, 1977.

Klein, Ralph W. "The Message of the Pentateuch." *Die Botschaft* (1981): 57-66.

Kline, Meredith G. *The Treaty of the Great King*. Grand Rapids: Eerdmans, 1963.

Kurichianil, J. "Prayer in the Life and Ministry of Moses." *ITS* 23 (1986): 229-47.

Livingston, G. Herbert. *The Pentateuch in Its Cultural Environment*. Grand Rapids: Baker, 1974.

Long, B. O. "Prophetic Call Traditions and Reports of Visions." *ZAW* 84 (1972): 494-500.

Lucas, E. C. "Covenant, Treaty, and Prophecy." *Them* 8 (1982): 19-23.

Marks, John H. *The Pentateuch*. Nashville: Abingdon, 1983.

Martens, E. A. *God's Design: A Focus on Old Testament Theology*. Grand Rapids: Baker, 1981.

McCarthy, Dennis J. "An Installation Genre?" *JBL* 90 (1971): 31-41.

————. *Treaty and Covenant: A Study in Form in the Ancient Oriental Documents and in the Old Testament*. Rome: Pontifical Biblical Institute, 1978.

McConville, J. G. "The Pentateuch Today." *Them* 8 (1982): 5-11.

McCurley, Foster R. *Ancient Myths and Biblical Faith: Scriptural Transformations*. Philadelphia: Fortress, 1983.

McNamara, M. *The New Testament and the Palestinian Targum to the Pentateuch*. Rome: Pontifical Biblical Institute, 1966.

Milgrom, Jacob. "Of Hems and Tassels." *BARev* 9 (1983): 61-65.

Miller, Patrick D., Jr. "Enthroned on the Praises of Israel: The Praise of God in Old Testament Theology." *Int* 39 (1985): 5-19.

Murray, John. *Principles of Conduct*. Grand Rapids: Eerdmans, 1957.

————. *Redemption—Accomplished and Applied*. Grand Rapids: Eerdmans, 1957.

Nelson, J. Robert. *Science and Our Troubled Conscience*. Philadelphia: Fortress, 1980.

Newell, William R. *Studies in the Pentateuch*. Grand Rapids: Kregel, 1983.

Oswalt, John N. "A Myth Is a Myth Is a Myth: Toward a Working Definition." *Spectrum* (1982): 135-45.

Parunak, H. Van Dyke. "Transitional Techniques in the Bible." *JBL* 102 (1983): 525-48.

Paterson, David L. "A Thrice Told Tale: Genre, Theme and Motif." *BR* 18 (1973): 30-43.

Pfeiffer, Charles F. *Old Testament History*. Grand Rapids: Baker, 1973.

————. *The Book of Genesis–Leviticus*. Grand Rapids: Baker, 1957-58.

Phillips, Anthony. "Another Look at Adultery." *JSOT* 20 (1981): 3-25.

Plaut, Gunther W. *The Torah: A Modern Commentary*. New York: Union of American Congregations, 1974.

Pratt, Richard L. "Pictures, Windows and Mirrors in Old Testament Exegesis." *WTJ* 45 (1983): 156-67.

Pritchard, James B. *Ancient Near Eastern Texts Relating to the Old Testament*. Princeton: Princeton U., 1950.

Purvis, J. D. *The Samaritan Pentateuch and the Origin of the Samaritan Sect*. Washington, D.C.: Howard U., 1968.

Ramm, Bernard. *The Christian View of Science and Scripture*. Grand Rapids: Eerdmans, 1954.

Rand, H. "Figure-Vases in Ancient Egypt and Hebrew Midwives." *IEJ* 20 (1970): 209-21.

Rashi. *Commentaries on the Pentateuch*. New York: Norton, 1970.

Robinson, G. "The Prohibition of Strange Fire in Ancient Israel. A New Look at the Case of Gathering Wood or Kindling Fire on the Sabbath." *VT* 28 (1978): 301-17.

Rosenberry, J. "Meanings, Morals, and Mysteries: Literary Approaches to Torah." *Response* 26 (1975): 67-94.

Schultz, Samuel J. *The Gospel of Moses*. Chicago: Moody, 1979.

Snaith, Norman H. *The Distinctive Ideas of the Old Testament*. Philadelphia: Westminster, 1946.

Soggin, J. Alberto. *Introduction to the Old Testament*. Translated by John Bowden. Philadelphia: Westminster, 1976.

Stannard, Russel. *Science and the Renewal of Belief*. London: SCM, 1982.

Stek, J. H. "Salvation, Justice and Liberation in the Old Testament." *CalvTJ* 13 (1978): 133-65.

Suelzer, A. *The Pentateuch*. New York: Herder and Herder, 1964.

Thomas, D. Winton. *Documents from Old Testament Times*. London: Nelson, 1958.

Thurman, L. Duane. *How to Think About Evolution and Other Bible-Science Controversies*. Downers Grove, Ill.: InterVarsity, 1978.

Torrance, Thomas F. *Christian Theology and Scientific Culture*. New York: Oxford U., 1981.

————. *Reality and Evangelical Theology*. Philadelphia: Westminster, 1982.

Ukleja, P. Michael. "Homosexuality and the Old Testament." *BSac* 140 (1983): 259-66.

Unger, Merrill F. *Archeology and the Old Testament*. Grand Rapids: Zondervan, 1954.

Van Der Woude, A. S., ed. *The World of the Old Testament*. Bible Handbook, vol 2. Translated by Sierd Woudstra. Grand Rapids: Eerdmans, 1989.

Vaux, Roland de. *Ancient Israel, Its Life and Institutions*. New York: McGraw, 1961.

————. *The Early History of Israel*. Translated by David Smith. Philadelphia: Westminster, 1973.

Walton, John H. *Chronological Charts of the Old Testament*. Grand Rapids: Zondervan, 1978.

Weinburg, N. *The Essential Torah*. New York: Block, 1974.

Whybray, R. N. *The Making of the Pentateuch: A Metrological Study*. JSOTSup, no. 53. Sheffield: JSOT, 1987.

Wiseman, D. J. "Is It Peace?—Covenant and Diplomacy." *VT* 32 (1982): 311-26.

Wiseman, Donald J., and Edwin Yamauchi. *Archaeology and the Bible: An Introductory Study*. Grand Rapids: Zondervan, 1979.

Wood, Leon J. *A Survey of Israel's History*. Grand Rapids: Zondervan, 1970.

Wormhoudt, A. *The Five Books as Literature*. Gladesville, Australia: Shakespeare Head, 1961.

Wright, G. Ernest. *Biblical Archaeology*. Philadelphia: Westminster, 1957.

Young, Edward, J. *An Introduction to the Old Testament*. Grand Rapids: Eerdmans, 1949.

Zeitlin, S. *Studies in the Early History of Judaism*. 2 vols. New York: Ktav, 1974.

CRITICISM ON THE PENTATEUCH

Andersen, F. I. *The Hebrew Verbless Clauses in the Pentateuch*. Nashville: Abingdon, 1970.

Armerding, Carl E. *The Old Testament and Criticism*. Grand Rapids: Eerdmans, 1983.

Brandon, S. G. F. *Religion in Ancient History*. New York: Scribner's, 1969.

Brueggemann, W. "The Kerygma of the Priestly Writers." *ZAW* 84 (1972): 397-414.

Carpenter, Eugene E. "Pentateuch." *ISBE* 3. Grand Rapids: Eerdmans, 1986: 740-53.

Cassuto, U. *The Documentary Hypothesis and the Composition of the Pentateuch*. Edited and translated by I. Abragams. Jerusalem: Magnes, 1972.

Ellis, P. F. *The Yahwist: The Bible's First Theologian*. Notre Dame: Fides, 1968.

Fox, M. V. "The Sign of the Covenant: Circumcision in the Light of Priestly Etiologies." *RB* 81 (1974): 557-96.

Gerbrandt, Gerald E. *Kingship According to the Deuteronomic History* (SBL). Decatur, Ga.: Scholar's, 1986.

Green, William H. *The Higher Criticism of the Pentateuch*. Grand Rapids: Baker, 1978.

Groningen, G. Van. "An Apologetic Approach to Mosaic Authorship." *VoxR* 11 (1978): 9-21.

Gunkel, Hermann. *The Legends of Genesis: The Biblical Saga and History*. New York: Schocken, 1984.

Johnstone, W. "The Mythologizing of History in the Old Testament." *ScotJT* 24 (1971): 201-17.

Kaiser, Walter C., Jr. *Classical Evangelical Essays in Old Testament Interpretation*. Grand Rapids: Baker, 1973.

Kaufmann, S. "The Structure of Deuteronomic Law." *Maarav* 1 (1979): 105-58.

Kikawada, Isaac M. "Some Proposals for the Definition of Rhetorical Criticism." *Semitics* 5 (1977): 67-91.

Kikawada, Isaac M., Arthur Quinn. *Before Abraham Was: A Provocative Challenge to the Documentary Hypothesis*. Nashville: Abingdon, 1985.

Labuschagne, C. J. "Additional Remarks on the Pattern of the Divine Speech Formulas in the Pentateuch." *VT* 34 (1984): 91-95.

La Verdicre, E. A. "The Elohist 'E'." *BiTod* 55 (1971): 427-33.

Lee, J. A. *A Lexical Study of the Septuagint Version of the Pentateuch.* Decatur, Ga.: Scholar's, 1983.

Leverson, Jon D. "Who Inserted the Books of the Torah?" *HTR* 68 (1975): 203-33.

McCarthy, D. J. *Berit and Covenant in Deuteronomistic History.* Leiden: Brill, 1972.

McEvenue, S. "Word and Fulfillment: A Stylistic Feature of the Priestly Writer." *Semitics* 1 (1970): 104-10.

McEvenue, S. E. *The Narrative Style of the Priestly Writer.* Rome: Pontifical Biblical Institute, 1971.

Milgrom, J. "The Priestly Doctrine of Repentance." *RB* 82 (1975): 186-205.

Montgomery, R. M. *An Introduction to Source Analysis of the Pentateuch.* New York: Abingdon, 1971.

Nelson, Richard D. *The Double Redaction of the Deuteronomistic History.* JSOTSup, no. 18. England: JSOT., 1982.

Noth, M. *A History of Pentateuchal Tradition.* Translated by B. W. Anderson. Englewood Cliffs, N.J.: Prentice Hall, 1972.

Orlinsky, H. M., ed. *Notes on the New Translations of the Torah.* Philadelphia: Jewish Pubn., 1969.

Patrick, Dale. "The Covenant Code Source." *VT* 27 (1977): 145-57.

Peckham, Brian. *The Composition of the Deuteronomic History.* Harvard Semitic Museum Monographs. Decatur, Ga.: Scholar's, 1985.

Petersen, D. L. "Covenant Ritual: A Traditio-Historical Perspective." *BibRes* 22 (1977): 7-18.

Polzin, Robert M. "Martin Noth's *A History of Pentateuchal Traditions.*" *BASOR* 221 (1976): 113-20.

_____. *Moses and the Deuteronomist: A Literary Study of the Deuteronomic History.* New York: Harper, 1981.

Rendtorff, R. "Traditio-Historical Method and the Documentary Hypothesis." *PrWcJesSt* 5 (1969): 5-11.

Rendtorff, Rolf. "The Future of Pentateuchal Criticism." *Henoch* 6 (1984): 1-14.

Segel, Moses Hirsch. *The Pentateuch, Its Composition and Contents and Other Biblical Studies.* Jerusalem: Magnes, 1968.

Silver, A. H. *Moses and the Original Torah.* New York: Macmillan, 1961.

Soggin, J. A. *Ancient Israelite Poetry and Ancient 'Codes' of Law and the Sources 'J' and 'E' of the Pentateuch.* VTSup. Leiden: Brill, 1975.

Thompson, R. J. *Moses and the Law in a Century of Criticism Since Graf.* VTSup. 3 vols. Leiden: Brill, 1970.

Tigay, J. H. "An Empirical Basis for the Documentary Hypothesis." *JBL* 94 (1975): 329-42.

Tucker, Gene M. *Form Criticism of the Old Testament.* Philadelphia: Fortress, 1971.

Van Seters, John. "Recent Studies on the Pentateuch: A Crisis in Method." JAOS 99 (1979): 663-72.

————. *Abraham in History and Tradition.* New Haven: Yale U., 1975.

Vink, J. G. "The Date and Origin of the Priestly Code." *OTS* 15.

von Rad, Gerhard. *The Problem of the Hexateuch and Other Essays.* New York: McGraw, 1966.

Wenham, Gordon. "The Perplexing Pentateuch." *VE* 17 (1987): 7-21.

Wijngaards, J. N. M. *The Dramatization of Salvific History in the Deuteronomic School.* Leiden: Brill, 1969.

Zevin, E. *The Birth of the Torah.* New York: Appleton, 1962.

REFERENCES ON GENESIS

BOOKS ON GENESIS

Aalders, G. Charles. *The Book of Genesis.* 2 vols. Bible Student's Commentary. Grand Rapids: Zondervan, 1981.

Anderson, Berhard W. *Creation in the Old Testament.* Philadelphia: Fortress, 1984.

Anworth, T. *Creation, Evolution and the Christian.* London: Evangelical, 1970.

Asimov, I. *Words in Genesis.* Boston: Houghton, 1962.

Banner, Jacob. *The First Book of the Bible.* Translated by E. I. and W. Jacob. New York: Ktav, 1974.

Barnhouse, D. G. *Genesis: A Devotional Exposition.* Grand Rapids: Zondervan, 1973.

Blenkinsopp, J. *From Adam to Abraham.* London: Longman and Todd, 1965.

Blumenthal, Warren B. *The Creator and Man.* Lanham, Md.: U. of America, 1980.

Boice, James M. *Genesis: An Expositional Commentary, Volume 2.* Grand Rapids: Zondervan, 1985.

Bonhoeffer, D. *Creation and Fall.* Translated by J. C. Fletcher. New York: Macmillan, 1965.

Bosley, H. A. *Sermons on Genesis.* Nashville: Abingdon, 1964.

Brean, H. N., ed. *The Date and Purpose of Genesis Three*. Philadelphia: Temple, 1974.

Brueggemann, Walter. *Genesis*. Interpretation: Bible Commentary for Teaching and Preaching. Atlanta: John Knox, 1982.

Cameron, Nigel, M.D. *Evolution and the Authority of the Bible*. Exeter: Paternoster, 1983.

Candlish, R. S. *Studies in Genesis*. Grand Rapids: Kregel, 1979.

Cassuto, Umberto. *A Commentary on the Book of Genesis*. 2 vols. Jerusalem: Magnes, 1961.

Clements, R. E. *Abraham and David*. Naperville, Ill.: Allenson, 1967.

Coats, George W. *Genesis, With an Introduction to Narrative Literature*. Grand Rapids: Eerdmans, 1983.

Cochrane, Charles G. *The Gospel According to Genesis: A Guide to Understanding Genesis 1-11*. Grand Rapids: Eerdmans, 1984.

Custance, Arthur C. *Genesis and Early Man*. Grand Rapids: Zondervan, 1975.

———. *Noah's Three Sons: Human History in Three Dimensions*. Doorway Papers 1. Grand Rapids: Zondervan, 1975.

Davidson, Robert. *Genesis 1-11*. Cambridge NEB Commentary. New York: Cambridge, 1973.

Davies, J. D. *Beginning Now. A Christian Exploration of the First Three Chapters of Genesis*. Philadelphia: Fortress, 1971.

Davis, John J. *Paradise to Prison: Studies in Genesis*. Grand Rapids: Baker, 1975.

Delitzsch, Franz. *A New Commentary on Genesis*. 1887. Reprint. Minneapolis: Klock & Klock, 1978.

Dillow, Joseph C. *The Waters Above: Earth's Pre-Flood Vapor Canopy*. Chicago: Moody, 1981.

Doukhan, J. B. *The Genesis Creation Story: Its Literary Structure*. Berrian Springs, Mich.: Andrews U., 1982.

Dye, D. L. *Faith and the Physical World*. Grand Rapids: Eerdmans, 1966.

Elliott, R. H. *The Message of Genesis*. Nashville: Broadman, 1961.

Esses, J. *Jesus in Genesis*. Plainfield, N.J.: Logos International, 1974.

Evans, J. M. *Paradise Lost and the Genesis Tradition*. New York: Oxford, 1968.

Filby, F. A. *Creation*. Old Tappan, N.J.: Revell, 1964.

———. *The Flood Reconsidered*. London: Pickering, 1970.

Fokkelman, J. P. *Narrative Art in Genesis: Specimens of Stylistic and Structural Analysis.* Translated by Puck Visser-Hagedoom. Amsterdam: Van Gorcum, 1975.

Frair, Wayne, and Percival Davis. *A Case for Creation.* Chicago: Moody, 1983.

Freitheim, T. E. *Creation, Fall and Flood.* Minneapolis: Augsburg, 1969.

Gage, Warren Austin. *The Gospel of Genesis. Studies in Protology and Eschatology.* Winona Lake, Ind.: Carpenter, 1984.

Gibson, John C. L. *Genesis, Chapters 1-11.* The Daily Study Bible, vol. 1. Philadelphia: Westminster, 1981.

———. *Genesis, Chapters 12-50.* The Daily Study Bible, vol. 2. Philadelphia: Westminster, 1982.

Gispen, W. H. *Genesis I.* Commentary on the Old Testament. Kampon: Kok, 1974.

———. *Genesis II.* Commentary on the Old Testament. Kampon: Kok, 1979.

Graves, Robert, and Raphael Petai. *Hebrew Myths, The Book of Genesis.* Garden City, N.Y.: Doubleday, 1964.

Green, W. H. *The Unity of the Book of Genesis.* Grand Rapids: Baker, 1979 (1895).

Gutzke, M. G. *Plain Talk on Genesis.* Grand Rapids: Zondervan, 1975.

Hanson, R. S. *The Serpent Was Wiser: A New Look at Genesis 1-11.* Minneapolis: Augsburg, 1972.

Hargreaves, J. *A Guide to the Book of Genesis.* London: SPCK, 1969.

Harris, R. Laird. *Man, God's Eternal Creation.* Chicago: Moody, 1971.

Heidel, Alexander. *The Babylonian Genesis.* Chicago: U. of Chicago, 1942.

———. *The Gilgamesh Epic and Old Testament Parallels.* 2d ed. Chicago: U. of Chicago, 1949.

———. *Noah and Utna Pishtim: Monotheism and Moses.* Edited by R. J. Christian. Lexington, Mass.: Heath, 1969.

Jackson, Thomas A. "Creation Stories of the Ancient Near East." *BibIll* (1986): 20-25.

Heinze, T. F. *The Creation vs. Evolution.* Grand Rapids: Baker, 1970.

Herbert, A. S. *Genesis 12-50.* London: Student, 1962.

Holt, J. M. *The Patriarchs of Israel.* Nashville: Vanderbilt, 1964.

Houston, James. *I Believe in the Creator.* Grand Rapids: Eerdmans, 1980.

Hunt, I. *The World of the Patriarchs.* Old Tappan, N.J.: Prentice Hall, 1967.

Kidner, Derek. *Genesis.* London: InterVarsity, 1967.

Klotz, J. W. *Genesis and Evolution.* St. Louis: Concordia, 1970.

Knight, G. A. F. *Theology in (Metaphorical, Homiletical) Pictures: A Commentary on Genesis, Chapters One to Eleven.* Edinburgh: Handsel, 1981.

Kravitz, W. *Genesis: A New Interpretation of the First Three Chapters.* New York: Philosophical Library, 1967.

Lead, E. *Genesis as Myth and Other Essays.* London: Jonathan Cage, 1970.

Leibowitz, N. *Studies in the Book of Genesis.* Translated by A. Newman. Jerusalem: World Zionist Organization, 1972.

Lewis, J. P. *A Study of the Interpretation of Noah and the Flood in Jewish and Christian Literature.* Leiden: Brill, 1968.

Liebler, C. C. *In the Beginning.* New York: Vantage, 1972.

Lowenthal, E. I. *The Joseph Narrative in Genesis.* New York: Ktav, 1973.

Maatman, R. W. *The Bible, Natural Science and Evolution.* Grand Rapids: Reformed Fellowship, 1970.

McCarthy, D. J. *Treaty and Covenant.* Rome: Pontifical Biblical Institute, 1978.

McComiskey, Thomas Edward. *The Covenants of Promise: A Theology of the Old Testament Covenants.* Grand Rapids: Baker, 1985.

Mendenhall, G. E. *The Tenth Generation.* Baltimore: Johns Hopkins U., 1973.

Meyer, F. B. *Abraham.* London: Marshall, Morgan and Scott, 1978.

Millard, A. R., and D. J. Wiseman, eds. *Essays on the Patriarchal Narratives.* Winona Lake, Ind.: Eisenbrauns, 1983.

Miller, Patrick D. *Genesis 1-11: Studies in Structure and Theme.* JSOTSup 8. Sheffield.

Moltmann, Jurgen. *The Future of Creation. Essays on the Theology of Creation.* London: SCM, 1979.

Morgenstern, J. *The Book of Genesis.* 2d ed. New York: Schocken, 1965.

Morris, Henry M. *Biblical Cosmology and Modern Science.* Nutley, N.J.: Craig, 1970.

————. *The Genesis Record.* Grand Rapids: Baker, 1976.

Morris, Henry M., and Gary E. Parker. *What Is Creation Science?* San Diego: Creation Life, 1982.

Moses ben Nahman, Gerondi. *A Commentary on Genesis Chapters 1-6.* Leiden: Brill, 1960.

Murray, R. L. *From the Beginning.* Nashville: Broadman, 1964.

Newman, Robert C., and Herman J. Eckelman. *Genesis One and the Origin of the Earth.* Grand Rapids: Baker, 1981.

Overman, R. H. *Evolution and the Christian Doctrine of Creation: A Whiteheadean Interpretation.* Philadelphia: Westminster, 1967.

Patten, D. W. *The Biblical Flood and the Ice Epoch: A Study in Scientific History.* Grand Rapids: Baker, 1966.

_____. *The Noachian Flood and Mountain Uplifts: A Symposium on Creation.* Grand Rapids: Baker, 1969.

_____., ed. *A Symposium on Creation II.* Grand Rapids: Baker, 1970.

_____. *A Symposium on Creation V.* Creation Research Society. Grand Rapids: Baker, 1975.

Pearce, E. K. V. *Who Was Adam?* Exeter, England: Paternoster, 1967.

Phillips, John. *Exploring Genesis.* Chicago: Moody, 1980.

Pun, Pattle P. T. *Evolution: Nature and Scripture in Conflict?* Grand Rapids: Zondervan, 1982.

Rad, Gerhard von. *Genesis: A Commentary.* Translated by J. H. Marks. Philadelphia: Westminster, 1973.

Radday, Yehuda T. *An Analytical Linguistic Key-Word-in-Context Concordance to the Book of Genesis: Computer Bible 18.* Wooster, Ohio: Biblical Research Associates, 1979.

Radday, Yehuda T., and Haim Shore. *Genesis: An Authorship Study in Computer-assisted Statistical Linguistics.* Rome: Pontifical Biblical Institute, 1985.

Ramm, Bernard. *The Christian View of Science and Scripture.* Grand Rapids: Eerdmans, 1954.

Redford, D. B. *A Study of the Biblical Story of Joseph.* VTSup. London: Brill, 1970.

Renchens, H. *Israel's Concept of the Beginning.* New York: Herder and Herder, 1964.

Rendsburg, Gary A. *The Redaction of Genesis.* Winona Lake, Ind.: Eisenbrauns, 1986.

Reno, C. A. *Evolution on Trial.* Chicago: Moody, 1970.

Ross, Allen P. *Creation and Blessing: A Guide to the Study and Exposition of Genesis.* Grand Rapids: Baker, 1988.

Rust, E. C. *Science and Faith, Towards a Theological Understanding of Nature.* New York: Oxford, 1967.

Sailhamer, John H. "Genesis." In *EBC*, vol. 1. Edited by Frank E. Gaebelein. Grand Rapids: Zondervan, 1990.

Sarna, Nahum M. *Understanding Genesis: The Heritage of Biblical Israel.* New York: Schocken, 1970.

Schaeffer, Francis A. *Genesis in Space and Time.* Downers Grove, Ill.: InterVarsity, 1972.

Skinner, John. *A Critical and Exegetical Commentary on Genesis*. Edited by Samuel R. Driver et al. UK: T and T Clark, 1930.

Snaith, N. H. *Notes on the Hebrew Text of Genesis*. London: Epworth, 1965.

Speiser, E. A. *Genesis*. AB, vol. 1. Edited by William F. Albright and D. N. Freedman. New York: Doubleday, 1964.

Spier, J. H. *The Creation*. New York: Doubleday, 1970.

Stevens, Sherrill G. *Layman's Bible Book Commentary: Genesis*. Nashville: Broadman, 1978.

Stigers, Harold G. *A Commentary on Genesis*. Grand Rapids: Zondervan, 1976.

Thielicke, H. *How the World Began*. Philadelphia: Fortress, 1961.

Thompson, C. *A Geologist Looks at Genesis*. New York: Vantage, 1976.

Travis, M. M. *The Divine Drama*. Cranbury, N.J.: Barnes, 1967.

Vawter, B. *A Path Through Genesis*. London: Sheed and Ward, 1973.

―――――. *On Genesis: A New Reading*. Garden City, N.Y.: Doubleday, 1977.

Vos, Howard F. *Beginnings in the Old Testament*. Chicago: Moody, 1975.

―――――. *Genesis*. Chicago: Moody, 1982.

Waskow, A. I. *God Wrestling*. New York: Schocken, 1978.

Wenham, Gordon J. *Genesis 1-15*. WBC. Waco, Tex.: Word, 1987.

Westermann, Claus. *Beginning and End in the Bible*. Translated by K. Crim. Philadelphia: Fortress, 1972.

―――――. *Genesis*. Grand Rapids: Eerdmans, 1987.

―――――. *The Promises to the Fathers: Studies on the Patriarchal Narratives*. Translated by D. Green. Philadelphia: Fortress, 1980.

Whitcomb, John C., and Henry M. Morris. *The Genesis Flood*. Grand Rapids: Baker, 1961.

White, D. M. *Holy Ground*. Grand Rapids: Baker, 1962.

Wilder-Smith, A. E. *Man's Origin, Man's Destiny*. Wheaton, Ill.: Harold Shaw, 1968.

Willis, John T. *Genesis*. Living Word Commentary on the Old Testament. Austin, Tex.: Sweet, 1979.

Wiseman, P. J. *Ancient Records and the Structure of Genesis: A Case for Literary Unity*. Nashville: Nelson, 1985.

―――――. *Clues to Creation in Genesis*. London: Marshall, Morgan and Scott, 1977.

Young Davis A. *Christianity and the Age of the Earth*. Grand Rapids: Zondervan, 1982.

―――――. *Creation and the Flood: An Alternative to Flood Geology and Theistic Evolution*. Grand Rapids: Baker, 1977.

Young, E. J. *Studies in Genesis One*. Philadelphia: Presb. & Ref., 1965.

Youngblood, Ronald. *Faith of Our Fathers*. Glendale, Calif.: Regal, 1976.

————, ed. *The Genesis Debate*. Grand Rapids: Baker, 1986.

————. *How It All Began*. Ventura, Calif.: Regal, 1980.

Zimmerman, P., ed. *Rock Strata and the Bible Record*. St. Louis: Concordia, 1970.

PERIODICALS ON GENESIS 1-11

Alexander, P. S. "The Targumin and Early Exegesis of 'Sons of God' in Genesis 6." *JJS* 23 (1972): 60-71.

Allaway, R. H. "Fall or Fall-Short?" *ExpTim* 97 (1986): 108-10.

Anderson, Bernhard W. "From Analysis to Synthesis: The Interpretation of Genesis 1-11." *JBL* 97 (1978): 23-29.

————. "Unity and Diversity in God's Creation, A Study of the Babel Story." *CurTM* 5 (1978): 69-81.

Bailey, J. A. "Initiation and the Primal Woman in Gilgamesh and Genesis 2-3." *JBL* 89 (1970): 137-50.

Barre, Lloyd M. "The Poetic Structure of Genesis 9:5." *ZAW* 96 (1984): 101-4.

Basset, F. W. "Noah's Nakedness and the Curse of Canaan, a Case of Incest?" *VT* 21 (1971): 232-37.

Birney, L. "An Exegetical Study of Genesis 6:1-4." *JETS* 13 (1970): 43-52.

Bishop, Ronald E. "The Protevangelium." *BibIll* 14 (1987): 28-29.

Blum, E. R. "'Shall you not surely die?'" *Them* 4 (1978): 58-61.

Bromiley, G. W. "Evolution." ISBEnc 2 (1982): 212-15.

Brueggemann, W. "Of the Same Flesh and Bone." *CBQ* 32 (1970): 532-42.

Bryan, David T. "A Reevaluation of Genesis 4 and 5 in Light of Recent Studies in Genealogical Fluidity." *ZAW* 99 (1987): 180-88.

Bube, Richard H. "Creation (A): How Should Genesis Be Interpreted?" *JASA* 32 (1980): 34-39.

————. "Creation (B): Understanding Creation and Evolution." *JASA* 32 (1980): 174-78.

Burtness, J. M. "What Does It Mean to 'Have Dominion over the Earth'?" *Dialog* 10 (1971): 221-26.

Carvin, Walter P. "Creation and Scientific Explanation." *ScotJT* 36 (1983): 289-307.

Clark, W. M. "The Flood and the Structure of the Pre-Patriarchal History." *ZAW* 83 (1971): 174-211.

————. "The Righteousness of Noah." *VT* 21 (1971): 261-80.

Clines, D. J. A. "Noah, Flood, 1: Theology of the Flood." *Faith and Thought* 100 (1972): 128-42.

————. "The Significance of the 'Sons of God' in the Context of the Primeval History." *JSOT* 13 (1979): 33-46.

————. "The Tree of Knowledge and the Law of Yahweh." *VT* 24 (1974): 8-14.

Cohn, Robert L. "Narrative Structure and Canonical Perspective in Genesis." *JSOT* 25 (1983): 3-16.

Dahlberg, Bruce T. "On Recognizing the Unity of Genesis." *Theology Digest* 24 (1976): 360-67.

Davies, Philip R., and David M. Davies. "Pentateuchal Patterns: An Examination of C. J. Labuschagne's Theory." *VT* 32 (1982): 268-96.

Davis, Steve. "Stories of the Fall in the Ancient Near East." *BibIll* 13 (1986): 36-40.

Dumbrell, W. J. "Genesis 1-3, Ecology, and the Dominion of Man." *CR* 21 (1985): 16-26.

Fisher, L. R. "An Ugaritic Ritual and Genesis 1:1-5." *Ugaritica* 6 (1969): 197-205.

Frymer-Kensky, Tikva. "The Atrahasis Epic and Its Significance for Our Understanding of Genesis 1-9." *BA* 40 (1977): 147-55.

Fujitushe. "Theology of Hope in Genesis 1-11." *BiTod* 80 (1975): 519-27.

Goodman, M. L. "Non-Literal Interpretations of the Genesis Creation." *GTJ* 14 (1973): 15-38.

Gordon, Cyrus H. "Ebla and Genesis 11." *Spectrum* (1982): 125-34.

Granot, M. "For Dust Thou Art." *BethM* 17 (1972): 310-19.

Hannah, John D. "Bibliotheca Sacra and Darwinism." *GTJ* (1983): 37-58.

Harrison, R. K. "Genesis." IBSEnc 2 (1982): 431-33.

Hartman, T. C. "Some Thoughts on the Sumerian King List and Genesis 5 and llb." *JBL* 91 (1972): 25-32.

Hasel, Gerhard F. "Genesis 5 and 11: Chronogenealogies in the Biblical History of Beginnings." *Origins* 7 (1980): 46, 48.

————. "Recent Translations of Genesis 1:1, a Critical Look." *BiTrans* 22 (1971): 154-68.

————. "The Genealogies of Genesis 5 and Their Alleged Babylonian Background." *AUSS* 16 (1978): 361-74.

————. "The Meaning of 'Lights' in Genesis 1:1f." *Andrews University Semitic Studies* 13 (1975): 58-66.

————. "The Significance of the Cosmology in Genesis in Relation to Ancient Near East Parallels." *Andrews University Semitic Studies* 10 (1972): 1-20.

Heckelman, Joseph. " 'Excess': The Hidden Root of Evil." *DD* 12 (1984): 237-45.

Hendel, Ronald S. "When the Sons of God Consorted with the Daughters of Men." *BRev* 3 (1987): 8-13, 37.

Hesse, Eric W., and Isaac M. Kikawada. "Jonah and Genesis 1-11." *AJBI* 10 (1984): 3-19.

Howe, Frederic R. "The Age of the Earth: An Appraisal of Some Current Evangelical Positions, Part 1." *BSac* 142 (1985): 23-37.

————. "The Age of the Earth: An Appraisal of Some Current Evangelical Positions, Part 2." *BSac* 142 (1985): 114-29.

Hummel, Horace D. "The Image of God." *ConcordJ* 10 (1984): 83-93.

Joines, Karen Rudolph. "The Serpent in Gen. 3." *ZAW* 87 (1975): 1:11.

Kikawada, Isaac M. "Genesis on Three Levels (Creation and Babel Form an Inclusio to Adam-Cain-Noah)." *AJBI* 7 (1981): 3-15.

Kline, Meredith G. "Primal Parousia." WTJ 40 (1977): 245-80.

Landes, George M. "Creation and Liberation." *USQR* 33 (1979): 79-89.

Lewis, A. H. "The Localization of the Garden of Eden." *BETS* 11 (1968): 169-75.

Luke, K. " 'The Nephilim Were on the Earth.' " *BibBh* 9 (1983): 279-301.

McCarthy, Dennis J. " 'Creation' Motifs in Ancient Hebrew Poetry." *CBQ* 29 (1967): 393-406.

Millard, A. R. "The Etymology of Eden." *VT* 34 (1984): 103-6.

Miller, J. M. "The Descendants of Cain: Notes on Genesis 4." *ZAW* 86 (1974): 164-74.

Milne, D. J. W. "Genesis 3 in the Letter to the Romans." *RTR* 39 (1980): 10-18.

Moberly, R. W. L. "Did the Serpent Get It Right?" *JTS* 39 (1988): 1-27.

Nardoff, Bruce D. "A Man to Work the Soil: A New Interpretation of Genesis 2-3." *JSOT* 5 (1978): 2-14.

Navone, J. "The Myth and the Dream of Paradise." SR 5 (1975): 152-61.

Newman, Aryeh. "Genesis 2:2, An Exercise in Interpretive Competence and Performance." *BiTrans* 27 (1976): 101-4.

Newman, Robert C. "The Ancient Exegesis of Genesis 6:2, 4." *GTJ* 5 (1984): 13-36.

Nicol, George B. "The Threat and the Promise." *ExpTim* 94 (1982): 136-39.

Nielsen, Edward. "Creation and the Fall of Man." *HUCA* 43 (1972): 1-22.

Orlinsky, Harry M. "The Plain Meaning of Genesis 1:1-3." *BA* 46 (1983): 207-9.

Patte, D., and J. Parker. "A Structural Exegesis of Genesis 2 and 3." *Semeia* 18 (1980): 55-75.

Porter, B., and U. Rapport. "Poetic Structure in Genesis 9:7." *VT* 21 (1971): 363-68.

Rice, G. "Cosmological Ideas and Religious Truth in Genesis 1." *JRT* 23 (1966): 15-30.

————. "The Curse That Never Was." *JRT* 29 (1972): 5-27.

Rieman, P. A. "Am I My Brother's Keeper?" *Int* 24 (1970): 482-91.

Robinson, Robert B. "Literary Functions of the Genealogies of Genesis." *CBQ* 48 (1986): 595-608.

Ross, Allen P. "The Curse of Canaan." *BSac* 137 (1980): 223-40.

————. "The Table of Nations in Genesis 10—Its Structure." *BSac* 137 (1980): 340-53.

Ruger, Hans Peter. "On Some Versions of Gen. 3:15, Ancient and Modern." *BiTrans* 27 (1976): 105-10.

Sailhamer, John. "Exegetical Notes: Genesis 1:1–2:4a." *TJ* 5 (1984): 73-82.

Sasson, Jack M. "Word-Play in Gensis 6:8-9." *CBQ* 37 (1975): 165-66.

Sawyer, J. F. A. "The Meaning of 'The Image of God' in Genesis 1-11." *JTS* 25 (1974): 418-26.

Scullion, J. J. "New Thinking on Creation and Sin in Genesis 1-11." *AusBR* 22 (1974): 1-10.

Selman, Martin J. "Comparative Methods and the Patriarchal Narratives." *Them* 3 (1977): 9-16.

Soggin, J. A. "God as Creator in the First Chapter of Genesis." *BibOrPont* 29 (1975): 88-111, 120-29.

Thompson, P. E. S. "The Yahwist Creation Story." *VT* 21 (1971): 197-208.

Trible, P. "Eve and Adam: Genesis 2-3 Reread." *ANQ* 14 (1972): 251-58.

Trudinger, L. Paul. "Not Yet Made or Newly Made, A Note on Genesis 2:5." *EvQ* 47 (1975): 67-69.

Tucker, G. M. "The Creation and the Fall: A Reconsideration." *LexTQ* 13 (1978): 113-24.

Van Gemeren, Willem A. "The Sons in Genesis 6:14." *WTJ* 43 (1980): 320-48.

Walsh, Jerome T. "Genesis 2:4b–3:24, a Synchronic Approach." *JBL* 96 (1977): 161-77.

Walton, John. "The Antediluvian Section of the Sumerian King List and Genesis 5." *BR* 44 (1981): 207.

Weeks, Noel. "The Hermeneutical Problems of Genesis 1-11." *Them* 4 (1978): 12-19.

Weinberg, Werner. "Language Consciousness in the O.T." *ZAW* 92 (1980): 185-204.

Weinfeld, M. "Genesis 7:11; 8:1-2 Against the Background of the Ancient Near Eastern Tradition." *WO* 9 (1978): 224-48.

Wenham, Gordon J. "The Coherence of the Flood Narrative." *VT* 28 (1978): 336-48.

Wickham, L. R. "The Sons of God and the Daughters of Men: Genesis 6:2 in Early Christian Exegesis." *ITS* 19 (1974): 134-47.

Wilfong, Marsha M. "Genesis 2:18-24." *Int* 42 (1988): 58-63.

Williams, A. J. "The Relationship of Genesis 3:20 to the Serpent." *ZAW* 89 (1977): 357-74.

————. "Genesis 3:15, a Protevangelium?" *CBQ* 36 (1974): 361-65.

————. "The Breath of His Nostrils: Gen. 2:7*b*." *CBQ* 36 (1974): 237-40.

Woudstra, Marten H. "Recent Translations of Genesis 3:15." *CalvTJ* 6 (1971): 194-203.

————. "The Story of the Garden of Eden in Recent Study." *VoxR* 34 (1980): 22-31.

Wyatt, Nicolas. "Interpreting the Creation and Fall Story in Genesis 2-3." *ZAW* 93 (1981): 10-21.

Zemek, George J., Jr. "Aiming the Mind: A Key to Godly Living." *GTJ* 5 (1984): 205-27.

PERIODICALS ON GENESIS 12-50

Alexander, T. Desmond. "Genesis 22 and the Covenant of Circumcision." *JSOT* 25 (1983): 17-22.

Barr, James. "*Erizo* and *Ereido* in the LXX: A Note Principally on Genesis 39:6." *JSS* 19 (1974): 198-215.

Battenfield, J. R. "A Consideration of the Identity of the Pharaoh of Genesis 47." *JETS* 15 (1972): 77-85.

Breitbart, Sidney. "The Akedah—A Test of God." *DD* 15 (1986/87): 19-28.

Brodie, L. T. "Jacob's Travail (Jer. 30:1-13) and Jacob's Struggle (Genesis 32:22-32)." *JSOT* 19 (1981): 31-60.

Brueggemann, Walter. "'Impossibility' and Epistemology in the Faith Tradition of Abraham and Sarah." *ZAW* 94 (1984): 615-34.

Burrows, M. "Levirate Marriage in Israel." *JBL* 59 (1940): 23-33.

————. "The Ancient Oriental Background of Hebrew Levirate Marriage." *BASOR* 77 (1940): 2-15.

————. "Abraham's Sacrifice of Faith: A Form-Critical Study of Genesis 22." *Int* 27 (1973): 389-400.

————. "The Joseph Story and Ancient Wisdom: a Reappraisal." *CBQ* 35 (1973): 285-97.

————. "Widows Rights: A Crux in the Structure of Genesis 38." *CBQ* 34 (1972): 461-66.

————. "From Canaan to Egypt. Structural and Theological Context for the Joseph Story." *CBQ* Monograph Series 4. Washington: Catholic Biblical Association of America, 1976.

Diamond, J. A. "The Deception of Jacob: A New Perspective on an Ancient Solution to the Problem." *VT* 34 (1984): 211-13.

Dilling, D. R. "The Atonement and Human Sacrifice." *GTJ* 5 (1975): 23-43.

Emerton, J. A. "Some Problems in Genesis 38." *VT* 25 (1975): 338-61.

————. "The Riddle of Genesis 14." *VT* 21 (1971): 403-39.

Eslinger, Lyle M. "Hosea 12, 5*a* and Genesis 32, 29: a Study in Inner Biblical Exegesis." *JSOT* 18 (1980): 91-99.

Exum, Cheryl J. "The Mothers of Israel: The Patriarchal Narratives from a Feminist Perspective." *BRev* 2 (1986): 60-67.

Feldman, Emanuel. "Joseph and the Biblical Echo." *DD* 13 (1985): 161-66.

Fishbane, M. "Compositon of the Jacob Cycle." *JJS* 26 (1975): 15-38.

Frankema, R. "Some Remarks on the Semitic Background of Chapters 29-31 of the Book of Genesis." *OTS* 26 (1972): 53-64.

Friedman, Richard Elliot. "Deception for Deception." *BRev* 2 (1986): 22-31, 68.

Gaston, L. "Abraham and the Righteousness of God." *HBT* 2 (1980): 39-69.

Gevirtz, Stanley. "Abram's 318." *IEJ* 19 (1969): 110-13.

————. "The Reprimand of Reuben (Gen. 49:3-4)." *JNES* 30 (1971): 87-98.

————. "Of Patriarchs and Puns: Joseph at the Fountain, Jacob at the Ford." *HUCA* 46 (1975): 33-54.

Goldin, Judah. "The Youngest Son, or Where Does Genesis 38 Belong?" *JBL* 96 (1977): 27-44.

Hallo, William W. "As the Seal upon Thy Heart." *BRev* 1 (1985): 20-27.

Hasel, G. F. "The Meaning of the Animal Rite in Genesis 15." *JSOT* 19 (1981): 61-78.

Heckelman, Joseph A. "Was Father Isaac a Co-Conspirator?" *DD* 13 (1985): 225-34.

Helyer, Larry R. "The Separation of Abram and Lot: Its Significance in the Patriarchal Narratives." *JSOT* 26 (1983): 77-88.

Houtman, C. "Jacob at Mahanaim." *VT* 28 (1976): 37-44.

———. "What Did Jacob See in His Vision at Bethel?" *VT* 27 (1976): 337-51.

Jacobson, Howard. "A Legal Note on Potiphar's Wife." *HTR* 69 (1976): 177.

Jagendorf, Zvi. "'In the morning, behold, it was Leah': Genesis and the Reversal of Sexual Knowledge." *Proof* 4 (1984): 187-92.

Moran, W. L. "Genesis 49:10 and Its Use in Ezekiel 21:32." *Bib* 39 (1958): 405-25.

Morrison, Martha A. "The Jacob and Laban Narrative in Light of Near Eastern Sources." *BA* 46 (1983): 155-64.

Muilenburg, J. "A Study in Hebrew Rhetoric: Repetition and Style." *VT* 1 (1953): 97-111.

Neff, R. W. "The Annunciation in the Birth Narrative of Ishmael." *BibRes* 17 (1972): 51-60.

———. "The Birth and Election of Isaac in the Priestly Tradition." *BibRes* 15 (1970): 5-18.

Niditch, Susan. "The Wronged Woman Righted: an Analysis of Genesis 38." *HTR* 72 (1979): 143-49.

Oden, Robert A. "Jacob as Father, Husband, and Nephew; Kinship Studies in the Patriarchal Narratives." *JBL* 102 (1983): 189-205.

Peck, J. "Note on Genesis 37:2 and Joseph's Character." *ExpTim* 82 (1970): 342.

Peck, William J. "Murder, Timing, and the Ram in the Sacrifice of Isaac." *ATR* 58 (1976): 23-43.

Rapaport, Y. "The Time Has Come to Return the Biblical Flood Story to Its Former Glory." *Beth Mikra* 29 (1983/84): 208-14.

Rendsburg, Gary A. "Notes on Genesis XXXV." *VT* 34 (1984): 361-66.

———. "Double Polysemy in Genesis 49:6 and Job 3:6." *CBQ* 44 (1982): 48-51.

Robertson, O. Palmer. "Genesis 15,6: New Covenant Expositions of an Old Covenant Text." *WTJ* 42 (1980): 259-89.

Robinson, G. "The Idea of Rest in the Old Testament and the Search for the Basic Character of Sabbath." *ZAW* 92 (1980): 32-42.

Rogers, C. L. "The Covenant with Abraham and Its Historical Setting." *BSac* 127 (1970): 241-46.

Ross, Allen P. "Jacob at the Jabbok, Israel at Peniel." *BSac* 142 (1985): 338-54.

―――. "Jacob's Vision: The Founding of Bethel." *BSac* 142 (1985): 224-37.

Rotenberry, P. "Blessing in the Old Testament: A Study of Genesis 12:3." *ResQ* 2 (1958): 32-36.

Roth, W. M. W. "The Wooing of Rebekah: A Traditional Critical Study of Genesis 24." *CBQ* 34 (1972): 177-87.

Shanks, Hershel. "Illuminations: Abraham Cut Off from His Past and Future by the Awkward Divine Command: 'Go You!'" *BRev* 3 (1987): 8-9.

Sutherland, Dion. "The Organization of the Abraham Promise Narratives." *ZAW* 95 (1983): 337-43.

Thompson, Thomas L. "The Background to the Patriarchs: A Reply to W. Dever and Malcolm Clark." *JSOT* 9 (1978): 2-43.

―――. "A New Attempt to Date the Patriarchal Narratives." *JAOS* 98 (1978): 76-84.

Wehmeire, G. "The Theme 'Blessing for the Nations' in the Promise to the Patriarchs and in Prophetical Literature." *BangTFor* 6 (1974): 1-13.

Wenham, G. J. "The Symbolism of the Animal Rite in Genesis 15." *JSOT* 22 (1982): 134-37.

West, Stuart A. "Judah and Tamar—A Scriptural Enigma." *DD* 12 (1984): 246-52.

―――. "The Nuzi Tablets: Reflections on the Patriarchal Narratives." *DD* 8 (1980s): 12-20.

Westbrook, R. "Purchase of the Cave of Machpelah." *Israel Law Review* 6 (1971): 29-38.

Wright, G. R. H. "Joseph's Grave and the Tree by the Omphalos at Shechem." *VT* 22 (1972): 476-86.

―――. "The Positioning of Genesis 38." *ZAW* 94 (1982): 523-29.

Yamauchi, E. M. "Cultic Prostitution." *AOAT* 22 (1973).

Yarchin, William. "Imperative and Promise in Genesis 12:1-3." *SBT* 10 (1980): 164-78.

Young, D. W. "A Ghost Word in the Testament of Jacob (Genesis 49:5)?" *JBL* 100 (1981): 335-42.

Ziderman, I. Irving. "Rebecca's Encounter with Abraham's Servant." *DD* 14 (1985/86): 124-25.

Zimmerli, W. "Abraham." *JNSL* 6 (1978): 49-60.

Zimmerman, C. L. "The Chronology and Birth of Jacob's Children by Leah and Her Handmaid." *GTJ* 13 (1972): 3-12.

REFERENCES ON EXODUS

BOOKS ON EXODUS

Andreasen, Niels-Erik A. *Rest and Redemption*. Berrien Springs, Mich.: Andrews U., 1978.

Auerbach, E. *Moses*. Detroit: Wayne State U., 1975.

Barclay, W. *The Ten Commandments for Today*. New York: Harper, 1974.

————. *The Old Law and the New Law*. Philadelphia: Westminster, 1972.

Beyerlin, W. *Origins and History of the Oldest Sinaitic Traditions*. Oxford: Blackwell, 1965.

Bimson, John J. *Redating the Exodus and Conquest*. JSOTsup 5. Sheffield: JSOT, 1978.

Boecker, H. J. *Law and the Administration of Justice in the Old Testament and Ancient East*. Minneapolis: Augsburg, 1980.

Bork, P. F. *The World of Moses*. Nashville: Southern Publishing Assoc., 1978.

Cassuto, U. *A Commentary on the Book of Exodus*. Jerusalem: Magnes, 1961.

Childs, B. S. *The Book of Exodus: A Critical Theological Commentary*. Philadelphia: Westminster, 1974.

Clements, R. E. *God's Chosen People*. London: Student, 1968.

————. *Exodus*. Cambridge: Cambridge U., 1962.

Coats, G. W. *Rebellion in the Wilderness*. New York: Abingdon, 1968.

Cole, R. A. *Exodus: An Introduction and Commentary*. Downers Grove, Ill.: InterVarsity, 1973.

Cornwall, E. J. *Let Us Draw Near*. Plainfield, N.J.: Logos International, 1977.

Criswell, W. A. *The Gospel According to Moses*. Grand Rapids: Zondervan, 1960.

Dalglish, E. T. *The Great Deliverance: A Concise Exposition of the Book of Exodus*. Nashville: Broadman, 1977.

Daube, D. *The Exodus Pattern in the Bible*. London: Faber and Faber, 1963.

Davies, G. H. *Exodus*. London: Student, 1967.

Davies, G. I. *The Way of the Wilderness: A Geographical Study of Wilderness Itineraries*. New York: Cambridge U., 1979.

Davis, John J. *Moses and the Gods of Egypt: Studies in the Book of Exodus*. Grand Rapids: Baker, 1971.

Driver, S. R. *The Book of Exodus*. Cambridge: Cambridge U., 1911.

Dumbrell, William S. "The Respect of Unconditionality in the Sinaitic Covenant." In *Israel's Apostasy and Restoration*, pp. 141-55. Edited by Avraham Gileadi. Grand Rapids: Baker, 1988.

Durham, John I. *Exodus*. WBC. Waco, Tex.: Word, 1987.

Ellison, H. L. *Exodus*. Daily Study Bible. Philadelphia: Westminster, 1982.

Finegan, J. *Let My People Go*. New York: Harper, 1963.

Gispen, W. H. *Exodus*. Translated by Ed van der Maas. Grand Rapids: Baker, 1982.

Goldin, J. *The Song at the Sea*. London: Vale, 1971.

Goldman, S. *The Ten Commandments*. Chicago: U. of Chicago, 1956.

Greelay, A. M. *The Sinai Myth: A New Interpretation of the Ten Commandments*. Garden City, N.J.: Doubleday, 1972.

Harrelson, W. *The Ten Commandments and Human Rights*. Philadelphia: Fortress, 1980.

Huey, F. B., Jr. *Exodus: A Study Guide Commentary*. Grand Rapids: Zondervan, 1977.

Hyatt, J. P. *Commmentary on Exodus*. The New Century Bible Commentary. Edited by Ronald E. Clements. Grand Rapids: Eerdmans, 1980.

Jordan, James B. *The Law of the Covenant: An Exposition of Exodus 21-23*. Tyler, Tex.: Institute for Christian Economics, 1984.

Kaiser, Walter C., Jr. "Exodus." In *EBC*, vol. 2. Grand Rapids: Zondervan, 1990.

Kester, M. D. *The Peshitta of Exodus*. Winona Lake, Ind.: Van Gorcum, 1971.

Kiene, P. F. *The Tabernacle of God in the Wilderness of Sinai*. Grand Rapids: Zondervan, 1977.

Kitchen, Kenneth A. *Pharaoh Triumphant: The Life and Times of Rameses II, King of Egypt*. Warminster, England: Aris & Phillips (1982).

Knight, George A. F. *I Am; This Is My Name*. Grand Rapids: Eerdmans, 1983.

_____. *Theology as Narration. A Commentary on the Book of Exodus*. Grand Rapids: Eerdmans, 1976.

Lockman, J. M. *Signposts to Freedom*. Minneapolis: Augsburg, 1982.

Marty, M. E. *The Hidden Discipline*. St. Louis: Concordia, 1962.

Meyer, Lester. *The Message of Exodus: A Theological Commentary*. Minneapolis: Augsburg, 1983.

Moberly, R. W. *At the Mountain of God: Story and Theology in Exodus 32-34*. JSOT Monograph Ser., no. 22. England: JSOT, 1983.

Motyer, J. A. *The Revelation of the Divine Name*. London: Tyndale, 1959.

Myer, F. B. *Devotional Commentary on Exodus*. New York: Kregel, 1978.

Napier, B. D. *The Book of Exodus*. Atlanta: John Knox, 1963.

Nicholson, E. W. *Exodus and Sinai in History and Tradition*. Atlanta: Blackwell, 1973.

Noth, Martin. *Exodus, a Commentary*. Translated by J. S. Bowder. Philadelphia: Westminster, 1962.

Paul, S. M. *Studies in the Book of the Covenant in the Light of Cuneiform and Biblical Law*. Leiden: Brill, 1970.

Pink, Arthur W. *Gleanings in Exodus*. Chicago: Moody, 1964.

Plastaras, J. *The God of Exodus*. Milwaukee: Bruce, 1966.

Ramm, B. *His Way Out*. Glendale, Calif.: Gospel Light, 1974.

Rhymer, J. *The Beginnings of a People*. Dayton, Ohio: Pflaum/Standard, 1967.

Sanderson, Judith E. *An Exodus Scroll from Qumran: 4QpaleoExodus and the Samaritan Tradition*. Harvard Semitic Studies. Decatur, Ga.: Scholar's, 1986.

Sarna, N. M. *Exploring Exodus*. New York: Schocken, 1986.

Slusser, D. M. *At the Foot of the Mountain*. Philadelphia: Westminster, 1961.

Thompson, R. J. *Moses and the Law in a Century of Criticism Since Graf*. Leiden: Brill, 1970.

Wallace, R. S. *The Ten Commandments*. Grand Rapids: Eerdmans, 1965.

Waltke, Bruce K. "The Phenomenon of Conditionality Within Unconditional Covenants." In *Israel's Apostasy and Restoration*. Edited by Avraham Gileadi. Grand Rapids: Baker, 1988.

Warburton, W. *The Divine Legation of Moses Demonstrated*. New York: Garland, 1978.

Wilson, Ian. *Exodus: The True Story*. New York: Harper, 1986.

Wood, L. T. "Date of the Exodus." In *New Perspectives on the Old Testament*, pp. 66-87. Edited by J. B. Payne. Waco, Tex.: Word, 1970.

Workman, E. J. *The Book of the Law*. Hicksville, N.Y.: Exposition, 1966.

Woudstra, M. H. "The Tabernacle in Biblical-Theological Perspective." In *New Perspectives on the Old Testament*, pp. 88-103. Waco, Tex.: Word, 1970.

Wright, Christopher J. H. *An Eye for an Eye: The Place of Old Testament Ethics Today*. Downers Grove, Ill.: InterVarsity, 1983.

Youngblood, Ronald F. *Exodus*. Everyman's Bible Commentary. Chicago: Moody, 1983.

PERIODICALS ON EXODUS

Albright, William F. "From the Patriarchs to Moses Part II: Moses Out of Egypt." *BA* 36 (1973): 48-76.

Aling, Charles F. "The Biblical City of Ramses." *JETS* 25 (1982): 129-38.

Archer, G. L. "Old Testament History and Recent Archaeology: From Moses to David." *BSac* 127 (1970): 99-115.

Arden, H. "In Search of Moses." *National Geographic* 149/1 (1976): 2-37.

Auffret, Pierre. "The Literary Structure of Exodus 6:2-8." *JSOT* 27 (1983): 46-54.

Bailey, Lloyd R. "The Golden Calf." *HUCA* 42 (1971): 97-115.

————. "Exodus 22:21-27." *Int* 32 (1978): 286-90.

Batto, Bernhard F. "Red Sea or Reed Sea?" *BAR* 10 (1984): 56-63.

Beale, G. K. "An Exegetical and Theological Consideration of the Hardening of Pharaoh's Heart in Exodus 4-14 and Romans 9." *TJ* 5/2 (1984).

Beitzel, B. J. "Exodus 3:14 and the Divine Name: A Case of Biblical Paronomasia." *TJ* 1/1 (1980).

Beuken, W. A. M. "Exodus 16.5, 23. A Rule Regarding the Keeping of the Sabbath?" *JSOT* 32 (1985): 3-14.

Brichto, Herbert Chanon. "The Case of the SOTA and a Reconsideration of Biblical Law." *HUCA* 46 (1975): 55-70.

Bright, J. "The Apodictic Prohibition: Some Observations." *JBL* 92 (1973): 185-204.

Brownlee, W. H. "The Ineffable Name of God." *BASOR* 226 (1977): 39-46.

Brueggemann, W. "The Crisis and Promise of Presence in Israel." *HBT* 1 (1979): 47-86.

Butterworth, M. "The Revelation of the Divine Name?" *IndJT* 24 (1975): 45-52.

Campbell, E. F., Jr. "Moses and the Foundations of Israel." *Int* 29 (1975): 141-54.

Carmichael, C. M. "A Singular Method of Codification of Law in the Mishpatim." *ZAW* 84 (1972): 19-25.

Chirichigno, Greg. "A Theological Investigation of Motivation in O. T. Law." *JETS* 24 (1981): 303-14.

————. "The Narrative Structure of Exodus 19-24." *Bib* 68 (1987): 457-79.

Cohen A. B., and D. N. Freedman. "The Dual Accentuation of the Ten Commandments." *MasST* 1 (1974): 7-20.

Craigie, P. C. "Yahweh Is a Man of War." *ScotJT* 22 (1969): 183-88.

Cross, F. M., and D. N. Freedman. "The Song of Miriam." *JNES* 14 (1955): 240-47.

Davis, Dale R. "Rebellion, Presence, and Covenant; a Study in Exodus 32-34." *WTJ* 44 (1982): 71-87.

Dion, P. F. "The 'fear not' Formula and Holy War." *CBQ* 32 (1970): 565-70.

Doron, Pinchas. "The Motif of the Exodus in the Old Testament." *ScrB* 13 (1982): 5-8.

Drumbrell, W. "Exodus 4:24-26, A Textual Re-Examination." *HTR* 65 (1972): 285-90.

Dyer, Charles H. "The Date of the Exodus Reexamined." *BSac* 140 (1983): 225-43.

Eakin, F. E., Jr. "The Plagues and the Crossing of the Sea." *RevExp* 74 (1977): 473-82.

Faur, J. "The Biblical Idea of Idolatry." *JQR* 69 (1978): 1-15.

Ferris, Paul Wayne, Jr. "The Manna Narrative of Exodus 16:1-10." *JETS* 18 (1975): 191-99.

Freedman, D. N. "The Burning Bush." *Bib* 50 (1969): 245-46.

Gianotti, Charles R. "The Meaning of the Divine Name YHWH." *BSac* 142 (1985): 38-51.

Goldberg, Michael. "Exodus 1:13-14." *Int* 37 (1983): 398-91.

Good, E. M. "Exodus 15:2" *VT* 20 (1970): 358.

Gordon, C. H. "He Is Who He Is." *Berytuss* 23 (1974): 27.

Gunn, David M. "The 'hardening of Pharaoh's heart'; Plot, Character and Theology in Exodus 1-14." In *Art and Meaning*, pp. 72-96. Edited by D. Clines. Winona Lake, Ind.: Eisenbrauns, 1982.

Gutmann, J. "The History of the Ark." *ZAW* 83 (1971): 22-30.

Haran, M. "The Passover Sacrifice." *VTS* 23 (1972): 86-116.

Harrison, R. K. "Exodus." *ISBEnc* 2 (1982): 222-30.

Honeycutt, R. L., Jr. "Aaron, the Priesthood, and the Golden Calf." *RevExp* 74 (1977): 523-35.

House, H. Wayne. "Miscarriage or Premature Birth? Additional Thoughts on Exodus 21, 22-25." *WTJ* 41 (1978): 108-123.

Hunt, Harry B. "An Annotated Bibliography on Exodus." *SwJT* 20 (1977): 89-94.

Jackson, B. S. "The Goring Ox Again." *JJurPapyr* 18 (1974): 55-94.

————. "The Problem of Exodus 21:22-25." *VT* 23 (1973): 273-304.

Janzen, J. G. "What's in a Name? 'Yahweh' in Exodus 3 and the Wider Biblical Context." *Int* 33 (1979): 227-39.

Karlberg, Mark W. "Reformed Interpretation of the Mosaic Covenant." *WTJ* 43 (1980): 1-57.

Kearney, Peter J. "Creation and Liturgy: The P Redaction of Exodus 25-40." *ZAW* 89 (1977): 375-86.

Kidner, D. "The Origins of Israel." *TSF Bulletin* 57 (1970): 3-12.

Kitchen, K. A. "Labour Conditions in the Egypt of Exodus." *BurH* 20 (1984): 43-49.

———. "From the Brickfields of Egypt." *TB* 27 (1976): 137-47.

Klein, E. M. "Exodus 15:2." *JJS* 26 (1975): 61-67.

Kline, M. G. *"Lex Talionis* and the Human Fetus." *JETS* 20 (1977): 193-201.

Kuyper, L. J. "Hardness of Heart According to the Biblical Perspective." *ScotJT* 27 (1974): 459-74.

Lawton, Robert S. J. "Irony in Exodus." *ZAW* 97 (1985): 414.

Lemche, N. P. "The Hebrew Slave Comments on the Slave Law: Exodus 21:2-11." *VT* 25 (1975): 124-44.

Lewis, Joe O. "The Ark and the Tent." *REX* 74 (1977): 537-46.

Loewenstamm, Samuel E. "The Making and Destruction of the Golden Calf: A Rejoinder." *Bib* 56 (1975): 330-43.

———. "The Making and the Destruction of the Golden Calf." *Bib* 48 (1967): 481-90.

———. "Exodus 21:22-25." *VT* 27 (1977): 352-60.

Magonet, Jonathan. "The Rhetoric of God: Exodus 6:2-8." *JSOT* 27 (1983): 56-67.

Martens, E. A. "Tackling Old Testament Theology." *JETS* 20 (1977): 123-32.

Mattingly, Gerald L. "The Exodus Conquest and the Archeology of Transjordan." *GTJ* 4 (1983): 245-62.

Mayonet, J. "The Bush That Never Burnt." *HeyJ* 16 (1975): 304-11.

McCarthy, Dennis J. "Exodus 3:14: History, Philosophy and Theology." *CBQ* 40 (1978): 311-22.

McKay, J. W. "Exodus 23:1-5, 6-8: A Decalogue for the Administration of Justice in the City Gate." *VT* 21 (1971): 311-76.

Moster, Julius B. "Thus They Stripped the Egyptians." *DD* 16 (1987/88): 41-44.

Nicholson, E. W. "The Interpretation of Exodus 24:9-11." *VT* 24 (1974): 77-97.

————. "The Antiquity of the Tradition in Exodus 24:9-11." *VT* 25 (1975): 69-79.

————. "The Covenant Ritual in Exodus XXIV:3-8." *VT* 32 (1982): 74-86.

————. "The Origin of the Tradition in Exodus 24:9-11." *VT* 26 (1976): 275-83.

————. "The Decalogue as the Direct Address of God." *VT* 27 (1977): 422-33.

Nielson, Eduard. "Moses and the Law." *VT* 32 (1982): 87-98.

Oswalt, J. "The Golden Calves and the Egyptian Conception of Deity." *EvQ* 45 (1973): 13-20.

Patrick, D. "Casuistic Law Governing Primary Rights and Duties." *JBL* 92 (1973): 180-87.

Perdue, L. G. "The Making and Destruction of the Golden Calf: A Reply." *Bib* 54 (1973): 237-46.

Phillips, Anthony. "A Fresh Look at the Sinai Pericope." *VT* 34 (1984): 39-52, 282-94.

————. "The Place of Law in Contemporary Society." *ExpTim* 93 (1981): 108-12.

Proffitt, T. D., III. "Moses and Anthropology: A New View of the Exodus." *JETS* 27 (1984): 19-25.

Ramm, B. "The Theology of the Book of Exodus: A Reflection on Exodus 12:12." *Southwestern Journal of Theology* 20 (1977): 59-68.

Rea, John. "The Time of the Oppression and the Exodus." *BETS* 3 (1960): 58-69.

Riggs, J. R. "The Length of Israel's Sojourn in Egypt." *GTJ* 12 (1971): 18-35.

Rodriguez, Angel Manuel. "Sanctuary Theology in the Book of Exodus." *AUSS* 24 (1986): 127-45.

Sarna, Nahum M. "Exploring Exodus: The Oppression." *BA* 49 (1986): 68-80.

Sasson, J. M. "The Worship of the Golden Calf." *AltORAT* 22 (1973): 153-54.

Spencer, Michael. "Redemption in Exodus." *Emmanuel* 90 (1984): 496-503.

Stek, John H. "What Happened to the Chariot Wheels of Exodus 14:25?" *JBL* 105 (1986): 293-94.

Tate, Marvin. "The Legal Traditions of the Book of Exodus." *REX* 74 (1977): 483-505.

Tigay, J. H. "'Heavy of Mouth' and 'Heavy of Tongue': On Moses' Speech Difficulty." *BASOR* 231 (1978): 57-67.

Toit, S. du. "Aspects of the Second Commandment." *OTWerkSuidA* 12 (1969; ed. 1971): 101-10.

Vriezen, T. C. "The Exegesis of Exodus 24:9-11." *OTS* 12 (1972): 100-133.

Waldman, Nahum. "A Comparative Note on Exodus 15:14-16." *JQR* 66 (1976): 189-92.

Weinfeld, M. "The Origin of the Apodictic Law: An Overlooked Source." *VT* 23 (1973): 63-75.

Wenham, G. J. "Legal Forms in the Book of the Covenant." *TB* 22 (1971): 95-102.

Wicke, Donald W. "The Literary Structure of Exodus 1:2–2:10." *JSOT* 24 (1982): 99-107.

Wilson, R. R. "The Hardening of Pharaoh's Heart." *CBQ* 41 (1979): 18-36.

Wright, C. J. H. "The Israelite Household and the Decalogue: the Social Background and Significance of Some Commandments." *TB* 30 (1979): 101-24.

Zeligs, D. F. "Moses and Pharaoh: A Psychoanalytic Study of Their Encounter." *American Image* 30 (1973): 192-220.

Zevit, Ziony. "The Priestly Redaction and Interpretation of the Plague Narrative in Exodus." *JQR* 66 (1976): 193-211.

REFERENCES ON LEVITICUS

BOOKS ON LEVITICUS

Bonar, A. A. *A Commentary on Leviticus.* 5th ed. 1861. Reprint. Edinburgh: Banner of Truth, 1966.

De Welt, D. *Leviticus.* Joplin, Mo.: College, 1975.

Douglas, Mary. *Purity and Danger: An Analysis of the Concepts of Pollution and Taboo.* Rev. ed. London: Routledge & Kegan Paul, 1978.

Eerdman, C. R. *The Book of Leviticus.* New York: Revell, 1951.

Gray, G. B. *Sacrifice in the Old Testament: Its Theory and Practice.* 1925. Reprint. New York: Ktav, 1970.

Harris, R. Laird. "Leviticus." In *EBC,* vol. 2. Grand Rapids: Zondervan, 1990.

Harrison, R. K. *Leviticus: An Introduction and Commentary.* TOTC. Downers Grove, Ill.: InterVarsity, 1980.

Hoffner, Harry A., Jr. "Incest, Sodomy and Bestiality in the Ancient Near East." In *Orient and Occident. Essays Presented to Cyrus H. Gordon on the Occasion of His Sixty-Fifth Birthday,* pp. 81-90. Edited by H. A. Hoffner, Jr. Neukirchen-Vluyn: Neukirchener Verlag, 1973.

Jukes, A. J. *The Law of the Offerings.* London: Pickering, 1965.

Kinlaw, Dennis. "Leviticus." *Beacon Bible Commentary.* Kansas City, Mo.: Beacon Hill, 1969.

Knight, George A. *Leviticus.* Daily Study Bible. Philadelphia: Westminster, 1981.

Levine, B. A. *In the Presence of the Lord: A Study of Cult and Some Cultic Terms in Ancient Israel.* Leiden: Brill, 1974.

Lyonnet, S., and L. Sabourin. *Sin, Redemption and Sacrifice.* Rome: Pontifical Biblical Institute, 1970.

Mays, J. L. *The Book of Leviticus and the Book of Numbers.* Atlanta: John Knox, 1963.

Micklem, N. *Leviticus.* IB. Edited by G. A. Buttrick. New York: Abingdon, 1953.

Milgrom, J. *Cult and Conscience; the Asham and the Priestly Doctrine of Repentance.* Leiden: Brill, 1976.

Murray, John. *Principles of Conduct.* Grand Rapids: Eerdmans, 1957.

Neusner, J. *The Idea of Purity in Ancient Judaism.* Leiden: Brill, 1973.

Noordtzij, A. *Leviticus.* Bible Student's Commentary. Grand Rapids: Zondervan, 1982.

Noth, Martin. *Leviticus.* Philadelphia: Westminster, 1965.

Porter, J. R. *Leviticus.* Cambridge NEB. New York: Cambridge, 1976.

Schultz, Samuel J. *Leviticus.* Everyman's Bible Commentary. Chicago: Moody, 1983.

Snaith, N. H. *Leviticus and Numbers.* Nashville: Nelson, 1967.

Wenham, G. J. *The Book of Leviticus.* NICOT. Grand Rapids: Eerdmans, 1979.

PERIODICALS ON LEVITICUS

Ashbel, D. "The Goat Sent to Azazel" (Hebrew). *Beth Mikra* 11 (1965): 89-102.

Bigger, S. "The Family Laws of Leviticus 18 in Their Setting." *JBL* 98 (1979): 187-203.

Brichto, H. C. "On Slaughter and Sacrifice, Blood and Atonement." *HUCA* 47 (1976): 19-56.

Brueggemann, W. "The Kerygma of the Priestly Writers." *ZAW* 84 (1972): 397-413.

Davies, Douglas. "An Interpretation of Sacrifice in Leviticus." *ZAW* 89 (1977): 387-99.

Feinberg, C. L. "The Scapegoat of Lev. 16." *BSac* 115 (1958): 320-33.

Freedman, D. N. "Variant Readings in the Leviticus Scroll from Qumran Cave 11." *CBQ* 36 (1974): 524-34.

Garner, Gordon. "Earliest Bible Text Discovery." *BurH* 22 (1986): 51-52.

Gispen, W. H. "The Distinction Between Clean and Unclean." *OTS* 5 (1948): 190-96.

Hamilton, Victor P. "Recent Studies in Leviticus and Their Contribution to a Further Understanding of Wesleyan Theology." *Spectrum* (1982): 146-56.

Haran, M. "The Complex of Ritual Acts Performed Inside the Tabernacle." ScrHier 8 (1961): 272-302.

Hoenig, S. B. "Sabbatical Years and the Year of Jubilee." *JQR* 59 (1969): 222-36.

Hulse, E. V. "The Nature of Biblical 'Leprosy' and the Use of Alternative Medical Terms in Modern Translations of the Bible." *PEQ* 107 (1975): 87-105.

Johnson, Luke T. "The Use of Leviticus 19 in the Letter of James." *JBL* 101 (1982): 391-401.

Kaiser, W. C., Jr. "Leviticus 18:5 and Paul: Do This and You Shall Live." *JETS* 14 (1971): 19-28.

Laughlin, J. C. H. "The 'Strange Fire' of Nadab and Abihu." *JBL* 95 (1976): 559-65.

McCarthy, D. J. "The Symbolism of Blood and Sacrifice." *JBL* 88 (1969): 166-76.

McKeating, H. "Sanctions Against Adultery in Ancient Israelite Society, with Some Reflections on Methodology in the Study of Old Testament Ethics." *JSOT* 11 (1979): 52-72.

Milgrom, J. "The Biblical Diet Laws as an Ethical System." *Int* 17 (1963): 288-301.

———. "A Prolegomenon to Lev. 17:11." *JBL* 90 (1971): 149-56.

———. "The Missing Thief in Leviticus 5:20ff." *RIDA* 22 (1975): 71-85.

———. "The Priestly Doctrine of Repentance." *RB* 82 (1975): 186-205.

———. "The Concept of ma'al in the Bible and the Ancient Near East." *JAOS* 96 (1976): 236-47.

———. "The Betrothed Slave Girl, Leviticus 19:20-24." *ZAW* 89 (1977): 43-44.

Mittwoch, H. "Story of the Blasphemer Seen in Wider Context." *VT* 15 (1965): 386-89.

Moran, W. L. "The Literary Connection Between Lev. 11:13-19 and Deut. 14:12-18." *CBQ* 28 (1966): 271-77.

Rainey, Anson F. "The Order of Sacrifice in O.T. Ritual Texts." *Bib* 51 (1970): 485-98.

Robinson, G. "The Prohibition of Strange Fire in Ancient Israel." *VT* 28 (1978): 301-17.

Rowley, H. H. "The Meaning of Sacrifice in the Old Testament." *BJRL* 33 (Sept. 1950): 95-100.

Selvidge, Maria J. "Mark 5:25-34 and Leviticus 15:19-20: A Reaction to Restrictive Purity Regulations." *JBL* 103 (1984): 619-23.

Snaith, N. H. "Sin-offering or Guilt Offering?" *VT* 15 (1965): 73-80.

Strand, Kenneth A. "An Overlooked Old Testament Background to Revelation 11:1 (Leviticus 16)." *AUSS* 22 (1984): 317-25.

Weingreen, J. "The Case of the Blasphemer (Lev. 24:10ff.)." *VT* 22 (1972): 118-23.

Wenham, Gordon J. "The Theology of Unclean Food." *EvQ* 53 (1981): 6-15.

————. "Why Does Sexual Intercourse Defile?" *ZAW* 95 (1983): 432-34.

Westbrook, R. "Redemption of Land." *ILR* 63 (1977): 367-75.

Wilkinson, John. "Leprosy and Leviticus: The Problem of Description and Identification." *SJT* 30 (1977): 153-69.

————. "Leprosy and Leviticus: A Problem of Semantics and Translation." *SJT* 31 (1978): 153-66.

REFERENCES ON NUMBERS

BOOKS ON NUMBERS

Allen, Ronald B. "Numbers." In *EBC*, vol. 2. Grand Rapids: Zondervan, 1990.

————. "The Theology of the Balaam Oracles." In *Tradition and Testament: Essays in Honor of Charles Lee Feinberg*. Edited by John S. Feinberg and Paul D. Feinberg. Chicago: Moody, 1981.

Budd, Philip J. *Numbers*. WBC. Waco, Tex.: Word, 1984.

Coats, George W. *Moses vs. Amalek*. Leiden: Brill, 1975.

————. *Rebellion in the Wilderness. The Murmuring Motif in the Wilderness Tradition of the Old Testament*. Nashville: Abingdon, 1968.

Fisch, S. *The Book of Numbers*. New York: Judaica, 1971.

Gray, George Buchanan. *A Critical and Exegetical Commentary on Numbers*. ICC. Edinburgh: T & T Clark, 1903.

Harrison, R. K. *Numbers*. WEC. Chicago: Moody, 1990.

Hirsch, Samson Raphael. *Numbers.* The Pentateuch Translated and Explained, vol. 4. Translated by Isaac Levy. London: Isaac Levy, 1964.

Huey, F. B., Jr. *Numbers.* Bible Study Commentary. Grand Rapids: Zondervan, 1981.

Jones, K. E. *The Book of Numbers.* Grand Rapids: Baker, 1972.

Maarsingh, B. *Numbers.* Edited by A. S. Van der Woude and translated by John Vriend. Grand Rapids: Eerdmans, 1987.

Moriarty, Frederick L. "Numbers." In *The Jerome Biblical Commentary.* Edited by Raymond E. Brown. Englewood Cliffs, N.J.: Prentice Hall, 1968.

Noordtzij, A. *Numbers.* Bible Student's Commentary. Translated by Ed van der Maas. Grand Rapids: Zondervan, 1983.

Noth, Martin. *Numbers.* OTL. Philadelphia: Westminster, 1968.

Owens, John Joseph. "Numbers." In *The Broadman Bible Commentary.* Edited by Clifton J. Allen. Nashville: Broadman, 1970.

Riggans, Walter. *Numbers.* Daily Study Bible. Philadelphia: Westminster, 1983.

Smick, Elmer B. "Numbers." In *The Wycliffe Bible Commentary.* Edited by C. F. Pfeiffer and E. F. Harrison. Chicago: Moody, 1962.

_____. "A Study of the Structure of the Third Balaam Oracle." In *The Law and the Prophets*, pp. 242-52. Edited by John H. Skilton. Nutley, N.J.: Presb. & Ref., 1974.

Snaith, Norman H. *Leviticus and Numbers.* The Century Bible. Nashville: Nelson, 1967.

Sturdy, John. *Numbers.* Cambridge: Cambridge U., 1976.

Wenham, Gordon J. *Numbers.* TOTC. Leicester, England: Intervarsity, 1981.

PERIODICALS ON NUMBERS

Asher, Norman. "Moses and the Spies." *DD* 12 (1984): 196-99.

Bartlett, J. R. "Historical Reference of Numbers XXI:27-30." *PEQ* 101 (1969): 94-100.

_____. "Sihon and Og of the Amorites." *VT* 20 (1970): 257-77.

_____. "The Conquest of Sihon's Kingdom: A Literary Re-examination." *JBL* 97 (1978): 347-51.

Brichto, H. C. "The Case of the *Sota* and a Reconsideration of Biblical Law." *HUCA* 46 (1975): 55-70.

Butler, T. C. "An Anti-Moses Tradition." *JSOT* 12 (1979): 9-15.

Christenson, D. L. "Numbers 21:14-15 and the Book of the Wars of Yahweh." *CBQ* 36 (1974): 359-60.

Coats, George W. "Wilderness Itinerary." *CBQ* 34 (1972): 135-52.

————. "Balaam: Sinner or Saint?" *BibRes* 18 (1973): 21-29.

————. "Conquest Traditions in the Wilderness Theme." *JBL* 95 (1976): 179-90.

————. "Humility and Honor: A Moses Legend in Numbers 12. In *Art and Meaning*, pp. 97-107. Edited by D. Clines. Winona Lake, Ind.: Eisenbrauns, 1982.

Fishbane, M. A. "Accusations of Adultery: A Study of Law and Scribal Practice in Numbers 5:11-31." *HUCA* 45 (1974): 25-45.

Gilead, Chaim. "Song of Parables (Num. 21:27-30)." *Beth Mikra* 23 (1977/78): 12-17.

Hanson, H. E. "Num. XVI, 30 and the Meaning of *Bara'*." *VT* 22 (1972): 353-59.

Hoftijzer, J. "Prophet Balaam in a 6th Century Aramaic Inscription." *BA* 39 (1976): 11-17.

Kselman, J. S. "Notes on Numbers 12:6-8." *VT* 26 (1976): 500-505.

Laughlin, John C. H. "The 'Strange Fire' of Nadab and Abihu." *JBL* 95 (1976): 559-65.

Leiman, S. Z. "The Inverted *Nuns* at Numbers 10:35-36 and the Book of Eldad and Medad." *JBL* 93 (1974): 348-55.

Levine, B. A. "Critical Note: More on the Inverted *Nuns* of Numbers 10:35-36." *JBL* 95 (1976): 122-24.

Margoliot, M. "The Transgression of Moses and Aaron—Numbers 20:10-13." *JQR* 74 (1983): 196-228.

McEvenus, S. E. "A Source-Critical Problem in Num. 14:26-38." *Bib* 50 (1969): 453-65.

Mendenhall, G. E. "The Census Lists of Numbers 1 and 26." *JBL* 77 (1958): 52-66.

Milgrom, Jacob. "Priestly Terminology and the Political and Social Structure of Pre-Monarchic Israel." *JQR* 69 (1978): 65-81.

————. "The Paradox of the Red Cow (Num. 19)." *VT* 31 (1981): 62-72.

————. "Of Hems and Tassels: Rank, Authority and Holiness Were Expressed in Antiquity by Fringes on Garments." *BAR* (Winter 1983): 63-55.

Miller, P. "The Blessing of God." *Int* 29 (1975): 240-51.

Quadrah, A. "The Relief of the Spies from Carthage." *IEJ* 24 (1974): 210-14.

Rainey, A. "The Order of Sacrifices in Old Testament Ritual Texts." *Bib* 51 (1970): 485-98.

Reif, S. C. "What Enraged Phinehas? A Study of Numbers 25:8." *JBL* 90 (1971): 200-206.

Robinson, G. "The Prohibition of Strange Fire in Ancient Israel: A New Look at the Case of Gathering Wood and Kindling Fire on the Sabbath." *VT* 28 (1978): 301-17.

Sakenfeld, K. B. "The Problem of Divine Forgiveness in Numbers 14." *CBQ* 37 (1975): 317-30.

Sasson, J. M. "Numbers 5 and the 'Waters of Judgment.'" *BZ* 16 (1972): 249-51.

―――――. "A Genealogical 'Convention' in Biblical Chronography?" *ZAW* 90 (1978): 171-85.

Snaith, N. H. "A Note on Numbers 18:9." *VT* 23 (1973): 373-75.

Tosato, A. "The Literary Structure of the First Two Poems of Balaam." *VT* 29 (1979): 98-106.

Wenham, J. W. "Large Numbers in the Old Testament." *TB* 18 (1967): 19-53.

REFERENCES ON DEUTERONOMY

BOOKS ON DEUTERONOMY

Beitzel, Barry J. "The Right of the Firstborn (*pî šnayim*) in the Old Testament (Deut. 21:15-17)." In *A Tribute to Gleason Archer*, pp. 179-91. Edited by Walter C. Kaiser, Jr., and Ronald F. Youngblood. Chicago: Moody, 1986.

Bellefontaine, E. "The Curses of Deuteronomy 27: Their Relationship to the Prohibitives." In *No Famine in the Land. Studies in Honor of John L. McKenzie.* Missoula, Mont.: Scholar's, 1975.

Blair, E. P. *The Book of Deuteronomy and the Book of Joshua.* Atlanta: John Knox, 1964.

Brueggemann, W., and H. W. Wolff. *The Vitality of Deuteronomic Traditions.* Atlanta: John Knox, 1975.

Carmichael, C. M. *The Laws of Deuteronomy.* Ithaca, N.Y.: Cornell U., 1974.

Clements, R. E. *God's Chosen People: A Theological Interpretation of the Book of Deuteronomy.* Valley Forge: Judson, 1969.

Craigie, Peter. *Deuteronomy.* NICOT. Grand Rapids: Eerdmans, 1976.

Cunliffe-Jones, H. *Deuteronomy.* Torch Bible Paperbacks. London: SCM, 1951.

Francisco, C. T. *The Book of Deuteronomy.* Grand Rapids: Baker, 1964.

Goldberg, Louis. *Deuteronomy.* Bible Study Commentary. Grand Rapids: Zondervan, 1986.

Kitchen, Kenneth. "Ancient Orient, 'Deuteronomism,' and the Old Testament." In *New Perspectives on the Old Testament.* Edited by J. Barton Payne. Waco: Word, 1970.

Kline, Meredith G. *The Treaty of the Great King.* Grand Rapids: Eerdmans, 1963.

Mayes, A. D. *Deuteronomy.* NCB. Grand Rapids: Eerdmans, 1981.

McConville, J. G. *Law and Theology in Deuteronomy.* JSOTSup Series 33. England: JSOT, 1985.

McPolin, J. *God Loves His People. A Guide to Deuteronomy.* Dublin: Veritas, 1970.

Moran, W. L. "Deuteronomy." In *A New Catholic Commentary on Holy Scripture.* Camden, N.J.: Nelson, 1969.

Nicholson, E. W. *Deuteronomy and Tradition.* Philadelphia: Fortress, 1967.

Payne, David F. *Deuteronomy.* Daily Study Bible. Philadelphia: Westminster, 1985.

Phillips, A. *Deuteronomy.* New York: Cambridge, 1974.

von Rad, Gerhard. *Deuteronomy: A Commentary.* Translated by Dorothea Barton. Philadelphia: Westminster, 1966.

————. *Studies in Deuteronomy.* Studies in Biblical Theology, No. 9. London: SCM, 1953.

Ridderbos, J. *Deuteronomy.* Bible Student's Commentary. Grand Rapids: Zondervan, 1984.

Schneider, B. N. *Deuteronomy: A Favored Book of Jesus.* Grand Rapids: Baker, 1970.

Schultz, Samuel J. *Deuteronomy.* Everyman's Bible Commentary. Chicago: Moody, 1971.

Thompson, J. A. *Deuteronomy: An Introduction and Commentary.* TOTC. Downers Grove, Ill.: InterVarsity, 1978.

Weinfeld, M. *Deuteronomy and the Deuteronomic School.* Oxford: Clarendon, 1972.

Wevers, J. W. *Text History of the Greek Deuteronomy.* Goettingen: Vanderhoeck and Ruprecht, 1978.

Wright, G. Ernest. "The Lawsuit of God: A Form-Critical Study of Deuteronomy 32." In *Israel's Prophetic Heritage, Essays in Honor of James Muilenberg.* Edited by Barnard W. Anderson and Walter Harrelson (New York: Harper & Row, 1962), pp. 26-67.

PERIODICALS ON DEUTERONOMY

Abba, Raymond. "Priests and Levites in Deuteronomy." *VT* 27 (1977): 257-67.

Baker, John Austin. "Deuteronomy and World Problems." *JSOT* 29 (1984): 3-17.

Bee, R. E. "A Study of Deuteronomy Based on Statistical Properties of the Text." *VT* 29 (1979): 1-22.

Bellefontaine, E. "Deuteronomy 21:18-21: Reviewing the Case of the Rebellious Son." *JSOT* 13 (1979): 13-31.

Braulik, Georg. "Law as Gospel: Justification and Pardon According to the Deuteronomic Torah." *Int* 38 (1984): 5-14.

Brueggemann, W. "The Kerygma of the Deuteronomistic Historian. Gospel for Exiles." *Int* 22 (1968): 387-402.

Carmichael, Calum M. "A Time for War and a Time for Peace." *JJS* 25 (1974): 50-64.

————. "A Common Element in Five Supposedly Disparate Laws." *VT* 29 (1979): 129-42.

————. "Uncovering a Major Source of Mosaic Law; the Evidence of Deuteronomy 21:15–22:5." *JBL* 101 (1982): 505-20.

Cazelles, H. "Passages in the Singular Within Discourse in the Plural of Dt. 1-4." *CBQ* 24 (1967): 207-19.

Christensen, Duane L. "Prose and Poetry in the Bible. The Narrative Poetics of Deuteronomy 1, 9-18." *ZAW* 97 (1985): 179-89.

Coats, George W. "Legendary Motifs in the Moses Death Report." *CBQ* 39 (1977): 34-44.

Craigie, P. C. "Deuteronomy and Ugaritic Studies." *TB* 28 (1977): 155-69.

Daube, D. "One from Among Your Brethren Shall You Set King over You." *JBL* 90 (1971): 480-81.

Derrett, J. D. "2 Cor 6:14: A Midrash on Dt. 22:10." *Bib* 59 (1978): 231-50.

Dion, Paul E. "Deuteronomy and the Gentile World: A Study in Biblical Theology." *Toronto Journal of Theology* 1 (1985): 200-21.

Doron, Pinchas. "Motive Clauses in the Laws of Deuteronomy: Their Forms, Functions and Contents." *HAR* 2 (1978): 61-77.

Frankena, R. "The Vassal Treaties of Esarhaddon and the Dating of Deuteronomy." *OTS* 14 (1965): 122-54.

Fratheim, T. E. "The Ark in Deuteronomy." *CBQ* 30 (1968): 1-14.

Gammie, J. G. "The Theology of Retribution in the Book of Deuteronomy." *CBQ* 32 (1970): 1-12.

Haran, Menahem. "Book-Scrolls in Israel in Pre-Exilic Times." *JJS* 33 (1982): 161-73.

Hobbs, T. R. "Jeremiah 3:1 and Deuteronomy 24:1-4." *ZAW* 86 (1974): 23-29.

Janzen, J. Gerald. "On the Most Important Word in the Shema." *VT* 37 (1987): 280-300.

Kaiser, W. C., Jr. "Current Crisis in Exegesis and the Apostolic Use of Deuteronomy 25:4 in 1 Cor. 9:8-10." *JETS* 21 (1978): 3-18.

Kaufman, S. "The Structure of the Deuteronomic Law." *Maarav* 1 (1979): 105-58.

Kearney, P. J. "The Role of the Gibeonites in the Deuteronomic History." *CBQ* 35 (1973): 1-19.

Lemche, N. P. "The Manumission of Slaves—The Fallow Year—The Sabbatical Year—The Jobel Year." *VT* 26 (1976): 38-59.

Lundbom, Jack R. "The Lawbook of the Josianic Reform." *CBQ* 38 (1976): 293-302.

McBride, S. D. "The Yoke of the Kingdom: An Exposition of Deuteronomy 6:4-5." *Int* 27 (1973): 273-306.

McKay, J. W. "Man's Love for God in Deuteronomy and the Father/Teacher/Son/Pupil Relationship." *VT* 22 (1972): 428-35.

Milgrom, J. "Profane Slaughter and a Formulaic Key to the Composition of Deuteronomy." *HUCA* 47 (1976): 1-17.

Millard, A. "A Wandering Aramean." *JNES* 49 (1980): 153-55.

Miller, P. "'Moses My Servant': The Deuteronomic Portrait of Moses." *Int* 41 (1987): 245-55.

Moran, W. L. "Conclusion of the Decalogue, Ex. 20:17—Dt. 5:21." *CBQ* 29 (1967): 543-54.

Schley, Donald G., Jr. "Yahweh Will Cause You to Return to Egypt in Ships." *VT* 35 (1985): 369-72.

Schultz, Samuel J. "Did Moses Write Deuteronomy?" *Christianity Today* 19 (1975): 1094-96.

Shrager, Miriam Y. "A Unique Biblical Law." *DD* 15 (1986): 190-94.

Skehan, P. W. "The Structure of the Song of Moses in Deuteronomy." *CBQ* 33 (1971): 67-77.

Tucker, Gene W. "Deuteronomy 18:15-22." *Int* 41 (1987): 292-97.

Vries, S. J. de. "The Development of the Deuteronomic Promulgation Formula." *Bib* 55 (1974): 301-16.

Walsh, M. F. "Shema Yisrael: Reflections on Deuteronomy 6:4-9." *BT* 90 (April 1977): 1220-25.

Watson, P. "A Note on the 'Double Portion' of Dt. 21:17 and 2 Ki. 2:9." *ResQ* 8 (1965): 70-75.

Weinfeld, M. "On Demythologization and Secularization in Deuteronomy." *IEJ* 23 (1973): 230-33.

Wenham, Gordon J. "Deuteronomy and the Central Sanctuary." *TB* 22 (1971): 103-18.

_____. "The Restoration of Marriage Reconsidered." *JJS* 30 (1979): 36-40.

Wenham, Gordon J., and J. G. McConville. "Drafting Techniques in Some Deuteronomic Laws." *VT* 30 (1980): 248-52.

_____. "The Date of Deuteronomy: Linch-Pin of Old Testament Criticism." *Them* 10 (1985): 15-20.

Wevers, J. W. "The Earliest Witness to the LXX Deuteronomy." *CBQ* 39 (1977): 240-44.

Williams, W. H. "A Look Within the Deuteronomic History." *SJT* 25 (1972): 337-45.

Willis, J. T. "Man Does Not Live by Bread Alone (Dt. 8:3 and Mt. 4:4)." *ResQ* 16 (1973): 141-49.

Willoughby, Bruce E. "A Heartfelt Love: An Exegesis of Deuteronomy 6:4-19." *ResQ* 20 (1977): 73-87.

Wittstruck, Thorne. "The So-Called Antianthropormorphism in the Greek Text of Deuteronomy." *CBQ* 38 (1976): 29-34.

Zakovitch, Y. "Some Remnants of Ancient Laws in the Deuteronomic Code." *ILR* 9 (1974): 346-51.

Zevit, Ziony. "The EGLA Ritual of Deuteronomy 27:1-9." *JBL* 95 (1976): 377-90.

INDEX OF SUBJECTS AND PERSONS

INDEX OF AUTHORS

INDEX OF SCRIPTURES

OLD TESTAMENT

NEW TESTAMENT